M000219234

LUIS NAVIA, born in H⸻ ⸻ ⸻ ⸻ ⸻
as a cocaine trafficker f⸻ ⸻ ⸻ ⸻
cartels until he was arreste⸻ ⸻ ⸻ ⸻ ⸻
Journey in 2000. He was released in 2005 and began a new career
in construction. Today he also runs his own consulting business
for private clients and liaises with the United States Government in
matters related to antinarcotics law enforcement.

JESSE FINK, born in London in 1973, worked for two decades as a
journalist, editor and columnist but is best known as the author of the
memoir *Laid Bare* and two internationally bestselling biographies, *Bon:
The Last Highway* and *The Youngs: The Brothers Who Built AC/DC*.
Fink's books collectively have been translated into 12 languages and
released in over 20 countries. *Pure Narco* is his fifth book.

'If Howard Marks was the king of the cannabis smuggle, Luis Navia is the Howard Marks of the cocaine trade. Both men were well-educated individuals who found they had a forte for the organisation and shipment of drugs.

'I was on the other side of the fence in law enforcement, fighting the global fight against these smugglers, but *Pure Narco* demonstrates the "war on drugs" is not always black and white. Luis comes across as a guy you could have a beer with and actually like and respect. This is in no small part due to author Jesse Fink, who you can tell got totally along with his central character. Fink gives a balanced portrayal of his subject and allows you to see the warts.

'What *Pure Narco* brought back to me was the sheer violence of the era. I was based in Miami in the late 1980s/early '90s as a drugs liaison officer for the British Government and was working with cops who were veterans of the "Wild West" of South Florida. Pablo Escobar was on the rampage. After a bomb went off or there was a shooting in Colombia, our guys down in Bogotá would get calls from London to check they were alive. How Luis survived to tell this story is beyond belief.

'Operation Journey was my life for over two years and it was a truly world-class international case. So I was glad to be part of Luis's downfall and give him his personal road to Damascus. But until this book I really never fully realised how much our lives were intertwined. Luis's story proves fact is stranger than fiction. *Pure Narco* is a great read.'
Graham Honey, HMCE Senior Investigation Officer (Retired)

'USCS Commissioner Raymond Kelly described Operation Journey, the global law-enforcement action taken against Luis Navia and the Colombian cocaine organisation Los Mellizos, as a "powerful new blue-print for fighting the international drug trade".

'The cartel trafficked eye-watering quantities of cocaine and were well organised with a worldwide reach. Law enforcement had to be better (and luckier) than them to take them down.

'*Pure Narco* offers a rare insight into the drug traffickers' world and law enforcement's efforts to arrest them and seize the drugs.'
Graham Titmuss, HMCE Investigation Officer (Retired)

'I first met Luis Navia in Miami in 2002. He was cooperating with authorities and had some significant information to share with the United Kingdom. I remember leaving the prison after two days of visits and thinking what an amazing character he was. The discussions with

Luis changed my perspective on top-level drug trafficking and traffickers; it was a moment of enlightenment.

'Much is written and appears on screen about the drugs business but so often it misses the mark. That's not the case with this insightful book: *Pure Narco* hits the spot and tells it as it was. Law-enforcement officers have a saying that all top traffickers end up dead or in prison. Very few survive to tell the tale. Typical of the man, Luis is a survivor and tells his own tale in great depth and clarity. This is how it was. But Luis also needed a sympathetic ear to get the best out of his unique story and Jesse Fink has done that by writing the very best account of a remarkable life in cocaine trafficking.

'Contrary to what we read in news reports and see on TV, trafficking is a highly complex business. It's not just based on violence, corruption, greed and all the other stereotypes. Every big cocaine shipment happens because of the fixer, the broker, the emissary. Luis Navia was all of these. The reality is the biggest deals or shipments happen because of key individuals with the people and business skills to make things happen. Luis is one of those people. He brought people together, he solved problems, he found a way to get things done.

'What makes Luis's story so unique was his ability to transcend the politics between rival groups (cartels). His strength of personality, charm and business brain made him a valued business associate on so many major shipments. Typically, Luis made and lost a fortune: which is so often the case at the top level of international cocaine trafficking. *Pure Narco* explains how that's possible and why the business is both richly rewarding while being a precarious and perilous existence. It also explains how the big deals were conceived, planned and delivered. The mechanics of the deals are set out here, as Luis explains the key stages required for a successful shipment and deal. No other book on drug trafficking provides this level of detail.

'I knew back in the 1990s that the work we were doing was groundbreaking, and that it was an era that would be looked back upon by historians. *Pure Narco* is a great book and an important part of social history. I loved every page. Having this account from Luis Navia will be part of his legacy. If you have an interest in and want to understand how international drug trafficking really works, you must read *Pure Narco*.'
Barry Clarke, HMCE Investigation Officer (Retired)

'As a former police officer and homicide investigator in the Houston Police Department, I saw another side of drug trafficking, as I investigated murders that resulted from drug-trafficking deals gone bad to kidnappings for ransom on drug debts. I subsequently made the jump to federal law enforcement as a Special Agent with USCS, now United States Homeland Security Investigations (HSI).

'In Houston, as part of a large-scale drug smuggling investigation, I was assigned as the case agent for the prosecution of the captain and crew of the M/V *Cannes* and brought them to trial and sentencing for a shipment of cocaine that totalled four tons. We knew then that the criminal organisation behind it was large in terms of the amount of cocaine shipped worldwide – we just didn't know how large. The *Cannes* would in turn lead us to Luis Navia, one of the biggest drug traffickers ever known – but never heard of.

'Jesse Fink's in-depth, entertaining and informative account of Luis's life during the height of the cocaine trade in the United States in the 1980s and '90s is like a speck in the eyes of a race-car driver moving at 200 miles an hour, albeit a large speck. *Pure Narco* reveals how a seemingly regular "businessman" can in reality be a successful drug trafficker.'
Vicente Garcia, HSI Assistant Special Agent in Charge (Retired)

'As a former detective who investigated a number of Colombian *narcos*, I can say that Jesse Fink has done a fantastic job of bringing the violent world of the drug cartels to light through Luis Navia. Luis is one hell of a character. For all the stuff he has lived through, he should be at least 200 years old. Luis is like the proverbial cat who has nine lives. What a life!'
Roberto Diaz (pseudonym), Metro-Dade Police Department Detective (Retired)

BOOKS BY JESSE FINK

15 Days in June (2007)
Laid Bare (2012)
The Youngs (2013)
Bon (2017)
Pure Narco (2020)

PURE NARCO

ONE MAN'S TRUE STORY OF 25 YEARS INSIDE THE COLOMBIAN AND MEXICAN CARTELS

JESSE FINK AND LUIS NAVIA

JOHN BLAKE

First published in the UK by Blink Publishing
An imprint of Bonnier Books UK
80-81 Wimpole Street, London, W1G 9RE
Owned by Bonnier Books
Sveavägen 56, Stockholm, Sweden

www.facebook.com/johnblakebooks
twitter.com/jblakebooks

First published in paperback in 2020

Paperback ISBN: 978 1 78946 336 1
eBook ISBN: 978 1 78946 351 4
Audio Digital Download ISBN: 978 1 78946 322 4

British Library Cataloguing-in-Publication Data:

A catalogue record for this book is available from the British Library.

Design by www.envydesign.co.uk

Printed and bound in Great Britain by Clays Ltd, Elcograf S.p.A

1 3 5 7 9 10 8 6 4 2

John Blake Publishing is an imprint of Bonnier Books UK
www.bonnierbooks.co.uk

narco
(nɑːkəʊ)
noun
Word forms: plural -cos
informal
a drug smuggler

Collins English Dictionary

'You North Americans are very lucky. You are fighting the most important fight of all – you live in the belly of the beast'

Ernesto 'Che' Guevara

Luis Navia
To my family, for their unconditional love and support; to all those people who didn't shoot me; and to Bob and Eric: I was fortunate enough to fall into their hands

Jesse Fink
To all the victims of cocaine, the cartels and the 'war on drugs'; to my family, for tolerating my book-writing adventures; and to Greg Stock: I'll get you the $500 I owe you ASAP

'OPERATION JOURNEY' DISMANTLES COLOMBIAN ORGANIZATION
THAT SHIPPED COCAINE TO 12 NATIONS
NEARLY 25 TONS OF COCAINE SEIZED

WASHINGTON, D.C. -- The Drug Enforcement Administration,
the U.S. Customs Service, and the Joint Interagency Task
Force-East (JIATF-East) today announced the conclusion
of 'Operation Journey', a two-year, multi-national
initiative against a Colombian drug transportation
organization that used commercial vessels to haul
multi-ton loads of cocaine to 12 countries, most of
them in Europe and North America.

The investigation, which involved authorities from
12 nations and three continents, has resulted in the
arrest of 43 individuals, including the alleged leader
of the maritime drug transportation organization,
Ivan De La Vega, and several of his subordinates. A
Colombian citizen, De La Vega was arrested in Maracaibo,
Venezuela, on Aug. 16, and turned over to U.S. custody.
He faces federal drug charges in Ft. Lauderdale, Fla.

Since its inception, Operation Journey has resulted
in the seizure of 22,489 kilograms of cocaine or nearly
25 tons of cocaine. On the streets of Europe, this
cocaine could generate roughly $1 billion at the retail
level. The location of these seizures ranged from
the Netherlands to Venezuela. The operation has also
resulted in the seizure of commercial shipping vessels,
go-fast boats, and communications equipment.

The operation began as separate investigations by the
DEA Country Office in Athens, Greece, the Customs Special
Agent-in-Charge office in Houston, together with major
input from European law enforcement agencies and JIATF-
East. Over time, numerous domestic and international
agencies joined the operation. Eventually, all merged
their cases into a single probe. Prosecutors from
the Narcotic and Dangerous Drug Section of the U.S.
Justice Department's Criminal Division were brought in
to provide key legal guidance. The Justice Department
coordinated with Customs, the DEA, and officials from
other nations to develop the prosecution strategy to
dismantle this organization.

Foreign authorities played critical roles in Operation Journey, making numerous arrests and several large seizures. The operation would not have been possible without the efforts of law enforcement agencies from Albania, Belgium, Colombia, France, Greece, Italy, the Netherlands, Panama, Spain, Great Britain, and Venezuela.

The organization targeted by Operation Journey served as a one-stop shipping service for Colombian cartels interested in moving cocaine via maritime vessels to U.S. and European markets. Based in Colombia and Venezuela, the organization used a fleet of 8-to-10 commercial freighters capable of hauling huge loads of cocaine anywhere in the world. Some of these ships were owned by shipping firms in Greece and other nations, while others were owned by this Colombian organization.

U.S. agents were able to document the movement of at least 68 tons of cocaine by this organization over a three-year period. At the retail level, this amount of cocaine could generate roughly $3 billion in Europe. Several of these cocaine shipments were intercepted. Most had occurred before agents learned about them. Operation Journey culminated during the past two weeks with enforcement actions in Venezuela and Europe. As a result of a collaborative international effort, Venezuelan authorities raided the command-and-control structure of the organization, using roughly 200 anti-drug officers, as well as an array of helicopters, airplanes, and boats.

During the initial raid, Venezuelan authorities arrested Ivan De La Vega and Luis Antonio Navia. De La Vega was arrested pursuant to a provisional arrest warrant prepared by U.S. federal agents in Houston. Navia is a Cuban national with U.S. residence status. He is a U.S. Customs fugitive wanted on prior federal drug charges. Both were turned over to U.S. authorities. On August 19, U.S. agents flew the pair to the Southern District of Florida, where they face federal drug charges.

Source (abridged from the original): DEA

Contents

Contents

Northern South America and the Caribbean Sea

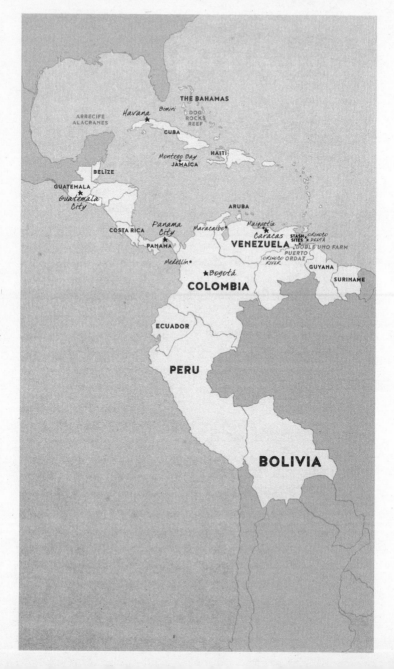

Colombia

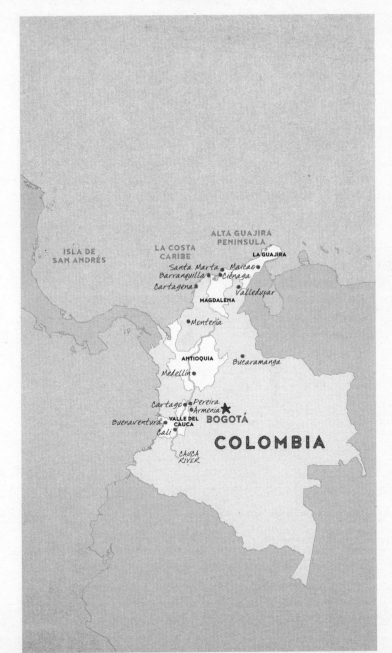

Mexico

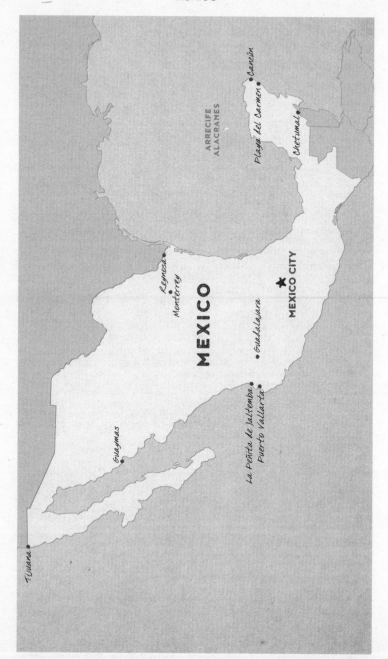

Florida (with Miami inset)

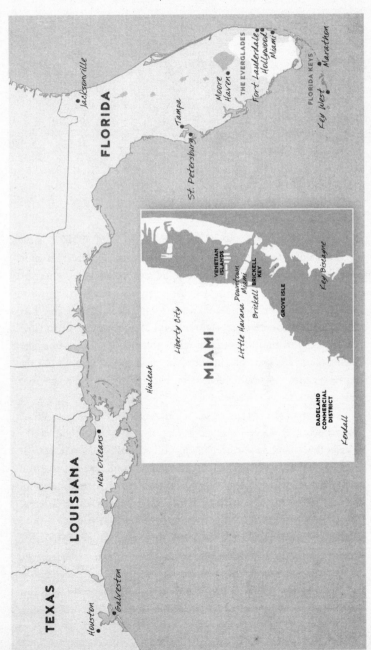

FOREWORD

The Trip

WHAT A LONG STRANGE TRIP IT'S BEEN, released in 1977, is the title of Grateful Dead's second compilation album. It's a good description of Luis Navia's life and could also have been an alternate title to this book.

Jesse Fink's account of Luis's life – his trip – as a major drug trafficker provides an entertaining and informative glimpse into the treacherous and too-often deadly realm of a cocaine smuggler during the 1980s and '90s. In parts, for good reason, it reads like the debriefing of a cooperating defendant, backed up with references that reflect Jesse's skills as a researcher.[1]

As a narcotics investigator in the early '80s for the Durham Police Department in North Carolina, I was at the opposite end of the distribution chain: undercover, buying grams and eight balls of powder cocaine. Towards the end of the '80s, Luis's and others' successful smuggling efforts were evidenced on the streets of America with an increase in the quantity and quality of cocaine, along with a decrease in its price. Near the end of my tenure with the Durham PD, one of our investigations resulted in the seizure of three kilos of cocaine that entered the United States through the Florida Keys. I now wonder if the unidentified fingerprints found on the wrappers might have been Luis's.

Anyway, my personal 'trip' continued with a four-year tour as a special agent with the United States Customs Service (USCS), beginning in 1987 on the Texas–Mexico border. At that time marijuana and small quantities of black tar heroin were the primary drugs seized at the border. Having perfected the art of smuggling, it came to no one's surprise that the Colombians utilised the Mexicans to introduce their contraband into the US. It all started with a few kilos added to loads of marijuana. After reading *Pure Narco*, I now wonder if some of the cocaine we seized in Laredo also had Luis's fingerprints on it.

Like a motivated drug trafficker, a good narcotics agent is always looking to get closer to the source. So I jumped over to the Drug Enforcement Administration (DEA) in 1991 and subsequently transferred down to Colombia. Stationed on the coast in Barranquilla, the majority of the office's investigations involved maritime smuggling. The names of the Colombians Luis worked with were part of our daily vocabulary. They were our targets.

In August 2000, I was asked to go to Venezuela and assist with an investigation run by one of the other agents in the office. Heading to Caracas from Colombia, I had limited knowledge of the case and when I arrived felt I was placed on a 'need to know' status. Again, after reading this book I have a better understanding as to why: only the traffickers benefit from interagency squabbles and infighting.

This time, however, we were able to identify the fingerprint. In doing so, it led to the arrest of USCS Special Agent Robert Harley's fugitive, Luis Antonio Navia, and the intersection of my life with Luis's own. There is no need for me to comment on my initial meeting in Maracaibo with Luis; Jesse illustrates it quite well with Luis's own words. But, as Jesse points out, Luis's story is not over.

A contemporary of Luis's, who came over to 'Team America' – what we call it when a drug trafficker turns government informant – once told me no one retires from this business. They either end up in federal prison for the rest of their life or dead.

Luis is one of the lucky ones. My wish for him is that he finishes his trip well and finds true redemption.

DEA Special Agent (Retired) Eric Kolbinsky, St. Petersburg (FL)

INTRODUCTION

Life on a Coin Toss

ADJECTIVES SUCH AS 'SINGULAR' and 'extraordinary' tend to be over-used by biographers to describe the lives of the people they're writing about, not to mention the publicists who are paid to promote their books. Actors, musicians, politicians, sportspeople, reality-TV stars: so many public figures are relentlessly hyped in the press or on social media when beyond their fleeting celebrity there's nothing really singular or extraordinary about these people's lives at all.

This, however, cannot be said for Luis Antonio Navia. For a man who is neither a public figure, nor a celebrity, nor an influencer, indeed someone you've never heard of (and I had never heard of him until I started writing what would become *Pure Narco*), he truly has led a singular and extraordinary life. If the old truism holds that everyone has a book in them, Luis has at least two or three, if not more.

Not only was this privileged son of Cuban high society one of America's most successful cocaine traffickers for nearly 25 years, but he was also a hunted international fugitive before his 16 August 2000 arrest in Maracaibo, Venezuela, in one of the biggest multinational law-enforcement takedowns of all time, Operation Journey. At its conclusion it was hailed as the biggest-ever coke bust in Venezuelan history.

Luis was convicted of serious narcotics offences, went to federal prison, got out early after cooperating with authorities, loaned his knowledge and the insights he gained from a quarter century of smuggling for the world's deadliest cartels to help the United States Government fight the so-called 'war on drugs', and today, as a reformed civilian, runs a construction business in Miami, Florida.

This is a man who knows just about everything there is to know about cocaine and just about everyone who has ever worked making it, transporting it and selling it. It's why to this day American feds and law-enforcement agencies from Great Britain and mainland Europe still come to Luis for leads or background when working important cases. It's also why Colombian cartel figures currently in jail come to him for help: as a paid private consultant, he can help build the weight of their testimonies when they cooperate in return for reduced sentences.

When a man survives so long at the top in such a bloody but lucrative business without resorting to violence or intimidation yet can still find the time to pack school lunches for his kids, a degree of *braggadocio* or egotism is perhaps to be expected. Especially when murderous drug lords such as the late Pablo Escobar and the incarcerated Joaquín Guzmán aka 'El Chapo' have become wildly popular anti-heroes to millions of people around the world. (We truly live in strange times when such amoral killers become idols. Tom Wainwright, author of the book *Narconomics*, coined a term for this phenomenon: 'reputational laundering'. It's true and damning.)

This, however, was not my experience of Luis in the two-and-a-half years I spent working on this book. I got to know him very well and cannot recall a moment when he was anything other than modest about his exploits and self-effacing. He never attempted to talk up his past when he so easily could have. Nor did he try to convince me he was anything other than a former criminal with an abiding love for making money who got busted in just about the most spectacular way possible. For those two reasons alone he is commendable.

Most remarkably, though, few *narcotraficantes* (*narcos* for short) can say they've managed to successfully juggle a normal family life while transporting billions of dollars of blow and are not only alive but walking the streets today to tell their story.[2] Even fewer go from selling grams to college students at Georgetown University in Washington, DC to operating a fleet of container ships to deliver tons to the mafia in Europe. It's the stuff of criminal fantasy but for Luis every bit of it was true.

In 2020, Luis turned 65. He referred to himself many times as 'Mr Magoo' or 'Inspector Clouseau', a comic innocent in a world of true bad guys and the polar opposite to Jon Roberts, the alleged 'cocaine cowboy' who made out in the Evan Wright book *American Desperado* and the Billy Corben documentary *Cocaine Cowboys* that he was so evil, so violent, he was two steps removed from Genghis Khan.

While preparing to write this book I began reading *American Desperado* but gave up on it a third of the way through; after the part about skinning the Việt Cộng soldier alive, it just didn't strike me as truthful.[3] The late Roberts, who died in 2011, came across as a sociopath, highly unlikeable, lacking insight and, worst of all, a shameless liar. It didn't ring true to Luis, either, who knew and worked with many of the same people Roberts did.

'Jon Roberts was a fucking psycho. He was just an asshole with a gun. I've been around a lot of killers, people who were real killers, *assassins*. If you owed them money, they assassinated you. No torturing, no bullshit, they assassinated you. Don't think what they do is the act of a coward. It's the act of a person that's determined and will carry out his determination. Nobody enjoyed skinning nobody alive. Believe me, it's a bunch of bullshit.'

At least as I saw it, Luis came across as neither criminal nor violent – rather, confoundingly normal and, for the majority of the time, even-tempered. He wasn't what I had expected for a man who had been a big-time narco. But I wasn't totally naïve: he was flawed too. There was more to his story than he let on. There was darkness behind the comedy. His affability and charm, however, made it very easy to miss.

*

In late 2017 we met through a mutual friend in Miami who doesn't want to be identified for fear of harm coming to her or her family. For months this woman urged the two of us to connect. She told me Luis had been approached by a writer for *Harper's Magazine* in the US for a profile piece but, rather than agree to tell his whole story to the press, he preferred doing his own book. He needed someone to write it. So we began emailing each other, with our anonymous female friend CCed in each conversation.

In those first few emails, Luis was cagey and seemed reluctant to share anything useful, which was perhaps understandable given that we came from different backgrounds, had opposing ideas about the importance of money, didn't know each other and were living on opposite sides of the world. I'd just spent four years writing a biography of AC/DC singer Bon Scott. Cocaine trafficking really was not in my wheelhouse, as an American might say, though I'd spent a lot of time talking to recovered drug addicts for my book on Bon. I was ready to walk away and turn my attention to something else. But soon Luis and I were speaking on the phone almost every day. Our conversations would go for hours. After that, our anonymous female friend left us to our own devices.

It's worth pointing this out right from the start: Luis is a funny man. I immediately felt engaged by his sense of humour, street lingo and crazy stories that were worthy of a Quentin Tarantino film. Had he not been a narco he would have been a great stand-up comedian and probably died of a cocaine overdose a long time ago, such is the intensity with which he has led his life. How much he padded out his stories only he can really know, though he assured me everything happened the way he told it.

For such a larger-than-life personality, though, he maintains a very private existence. He doesn't have a landline where he lives, doesn't get mail at home and doesn't have his real address on any form of official identification. His driver's licence has an address for a massage parlour in Miami.

'I cannot put my head on a pillow at night and know that my address is on a driver's licence or I get mail; I *can't*. That will never leave my body or my spirit, that lifestyle of incognito. I still keep to my old ways. I don't bring anybody home. *Nobody*.'

When one time he got an AT&T bill with his real name on it, he 'fucking freaked out' and phoned the telecommunications company to tell them, 'I've just been kidnapped in Colombia!' He requested they change it to a 'nice Jewish name' as he was still getting kidnapping threats and wanted to keep as low a profile as possible. AT&T complied 'right away'.[4]

Luis was also a complex character because while he could be genuinely endearing and lovable, a sort of diminutive, cuddly Cuban-American version of John Travolta's Chili Palmer from *Get Shorty*, some of his behaviour was not always so heartwarming, which he would justify through a well-practised line in moral relativism or equivalence. Whatever the cartels did was no worse than the US Government. Alcohol is a greater killer than cocaine but you never hear about that. And so on. Sometimes I readily bought his excuses and could see the logic of his thinking; but many more times I did not.

I never forgot he was someone who willingly consorted with (and by extension arguably abetted) some of the most violent criminals, some effectively serial killers, ever to walk the face of the earth. He liked to joke that being shot or decapitated were natural deaths 'because it's natural to the business you're in'. He's also the only person I know who can count as close personal friends half a dozen people who have appeared on the Specially Designated Nationals and Blocked Persons List, the register of terrorists and drug traffickers whose assets are frozen, among other punitive measures, by the Office of Foreign Assets Control of the United States Department of the Treasury (USDT). He even gets a mention in the Paradise Papers, second only to the Panama Papers as the biggest leak of offshore investment documents in history.[5]

So he was no angel. He'd run with some bad people. His cognitive dissonance was strong. Our anonymous female friend joked, 'Luis is like Tony Montana if he hadn't died and got caught and had started a construction business in Miami. *Scarface* as senior citizen.'

The comparison was funny but not entirely accurate: Luis was educated and had never so much as purchased a gun let alone massacred a group of Colombian assassins with Montana's 'little friend': a Colt AR-15 machine gun with attached M203 grenade launcher. But I saw her point. Any man who's spent most of his adult life in and around the cartels and its 24/7 adrenalin rush is going to have a tough time readapting to the torpor of normal society.

I hate to admit it, perhaps it was a reflection on my comparatively uneventful life, but this mix of good and evil, lightness and depravity is the very thing that made Luis an inordinately charismatic interviewee. He could be wholly unsympathetic at times because he remained so steadfastly unapologetic about his 25 years of crime, but he was the coolest person I'd ever met. He'd *lived*.

As he memorably described it, 'Gangsters want to live a great three years than just a mediocre 30. If I die, I *die*. Go out with a bang. What's life? We go on to the next one.'

Luis's life was like the adventure I'd never had: a tale of pure escapism that could sit comfortably alongside an old shopworn VHS cassette of *Romancing the Stone*. The fact of the matter is I got completely sucked in.

*

So, you might be thinking, who the hell is this guy, why is he of any consequence and why should you care about him enough to pick up this book? Like *The Wolf of Wall Street* by Jordan Belfort, when you strip it down to its core, *Pure Narco* is a story of one man's unrepentant, unapologetic greed.

Money was a driving obsession for Luis in an industry – cocaine – where it was so easy to come by that the value of it almost became meaningless. This is perhaps the reason why when he had money he dealt with it so wastefully. As long as there was another load of coke to transport, he could always make more money in 24 hours than most people would make in ten years.

Yet I believe Luis for all his ex-gangster bluster does wrestle with genuine regret and remorse for his criminal past, even if he might pretend otherwise behind the almost impenetrable shield of what I see as innate Miami *cubano* machismo, but what he regards as street-learned Colombian toughness. He is not one to make such personal admissions. Belfort, on the other hand, who ripped off so many innocent people, has never struck me as particularly guilt ridden – just an opportunistic narcissist who got lucky when Leonardo DiCaprio and Martin Scorsese decided to make a movie of his book.

As a drug-trafficking story Luis's is certainly unique: his is a tale so wild you simply couldn't make it up. As he puts it poetically in his distinctive wiseguy patois, it was like 'a fucking tornado around a fucking drain'. But it's more than that. Luis's life was also one of wasted opportunities, and there's a human message running through all of the pages that follow: appreciate what you have, right now, take advantage of the opportunities you are given and don't fuck it up.

Pure Narco is not your typical true-crime story.

*

With his receding silver hair, ample middle-aged girth, button-down shirts, neat chinos and clean sneakers, Luis looks just like any unremarkable, inoffensive Latino middle manager you might see in a South Korean SUV on an American highway going about his daily commute to his boring office job in a technology park or industrial estate. He is not the machine gun–wielding narco cliché as depicted in films or television. The only thing that gives away his freewheeling past is a penchant for elegant eyewear (a beautiful pair of clear-framed Oliver Peoples sunglasses with neck strap rarely leaves his face; he won't pose for photos without them) and an abiding love of 1970s rock.

He did have an opportunity to go straight in the early 1980s when he briefly owned/leased 22,000 acres of sugarcane and a rice mill in Florida, later a macadamia farm in Costa Rica, and again in the late 1990s when he dreamed of 'cornering the market' in Central American and Mexican coffee, but he left cash crops and all vestiges of respectability behind. Instead he fell under the spell of cocaine and became the unlikeliest of drug traffickers.

Luis was born into considerable wealth and privilege in 1950s Cuba, not the other way around like most narcos who are born into a hardscrabble life of crushing poverty in Colombia or Mexico. He arrived in 1960s Miami as a pampered kid and went to the best schools and universities in Florida and Washington, DC, where he began his drug career selling grams to fellow students. He never *had* to become a criminal; he chose his path. His introduction to the cartels in the late 1970s came not through family ties or ethnic background but by not-so-innocently meeting Bia Gálvez, a beautiful but mysterious red-haired Aruban woman at his 23rd birthday party. Then, like something out of *Body Heat*, he ran off with Bia into the hot Florida night.

The next 22 years contained enough adventures for 22 lifetimes and he got through most of it with almost complete anonymity.

Luis could have got out early, gone straight and stayed that way, but the cartels came to like him and he came to like them – and when you do a job so well, the mob eventually wants a piece of the action too.

'I always worked for the Colombian and Mexican cartels doing transport; but the Lucchese group [the mafia] in Florida was one of my clients. I worked with so many groups and nobody else did that. When I look back on how many groups I worked with, it's incredible.'

He also claims to have worked with, known intimately or had memorable encounters with some of the heavyweight players in the cocaine business of the 1970s, '80s and '90s: the aforementioned Pablo 'El Patrón' Escobar, Luis 'Miki' Ramírez, Fernando 'El Negro' Galeano, Iván 'El Enano' Urdinola, Luis Hernando 'Rasguño' Gómez, Fernando 'Marulo' Marulanda, Hernán 'Papito' Prada Cortés, the Mejía Múnera brothers, Alcides 'El Metro' Ramón Magaña of the Juárez Cartel, Cuban crime overlord Alberto Sicilia Falcón, Jamaican kingpin Leebert 'The Indian' Ramcharan, and many more.

Outside of Escobar, Galeano and Sicilia Falcón, names straight out of the Netflix series *Narcos* and *Narcos: Mexico*, most of these people and other narcos mentioned in this book are probably unfamiliar to readers. But to law-enforcement agents working in the frontline of the war on drugs and those brave journalists in Colombia and Mexico reporting on that never-ending war, they represent the crème de la crème of international drug-trafficking royalty. Luis was the Zelig of cocaine. He was independent, adaptable and non-violent. Simply put, some of the world's baddest people felt *safe* working with him.

'I didn't pose a threat to anybody and I never, *ever* failed them on a trip. I also had the common intelligence not to steal, be faithful, say the truth and do my best. Saying that, the truth and doing your best isn't going to cut it, either. "Hey, I did my best but we didn't make it" possibly goes by once, and it depends who you're working for.

'Definitely I survived because I was non-violent. Non-violence is a very powerful weapon. It's like that Gandhi shit. Non-violence can beat violence. It just takes a long time. But the main thing is good business. The people I worked with were all great personalities: rare, powerful people with fascinating trajectories. They didn't get to where they got to by being dumb. They were very smart and very different to me yet they found me interesting and they all told me I was crazier than they were.

'When I look back, I cannot classify myself as normal. The morality part and all the touching moments, I don't know. I'm not too much of a moral . . . you know, *spiritual* kind of guy. People get so carried away with "good" and "bad". Some people are just wired differently. People will do anything for money and they'll do more to make more, and they'll do whatever they need to do to protect their money. It's that easy. It doesn't take a genius to figure that one out.'

If I have any personal criticism of Luis maybe it's that he's just not remorseful enough, having done what he did and having seen what he saw. As a high-level transporter for the Colombian and Mexican cartels, he cannot completely divorce himself morally from the crimes those groups were involved in, both direct through selling a product that has addicted millions and indirect through their violence. Any which way he cuts it (and he does try and likely forever will), his time as a drug trafficker wasn't victimless; he was still complicit in the drug industry's heavy toll. For him to pretend otherwise would be utterly tone deaf to its casualties and victims. This book is not an endorsement of drug trafficking or the narco lifestyle.

But this is a point that needs to be rammed home: none of us had Luis's life. His values were shaped by his own experiences and he is a product of his family upbringing, personal circumstances and the times. He wasn't born *into* crime, though a life in it spent much of the time on the run has irrevocably altered the way he sees the world and directed his passage through it as an adult male.

Having spent the better part of three years talking to him daily, I also believe that for a former criminal he has a surprising degree of insight to recognise his character shortcomings. (I certainly witnessed him develop a deeper self-awareness as we worked on the book.) He makes up for these shortcomings with a winning personality and his strong loyalty to old friends who are incarcerated or have fallen on hard times. This same personality – humorous, reckless, impulsive and completely unconventional – is what helped him survive in such a volatile and dangerous profession for so long, allowed him to work with so many different cartels, and is ultimately what makes his story redemptive.

*

During his 25 years as a narco, Luis Antonio Navia was never a 'Colombian shipping magnate', a 'major investor', or a 'member' of Pablo Escobar's notorious Medellín Cartel, among other things that have been printed in newspaper stories or broadcast on television about his life in the drug trade. But he was responsible for the trafficking of '200 tons, easy' of cocaine,[6] worth about $10 billion on today's market prices in Europe. Some inside American law enforcement have put the number much higher – 300 tons – and that doesn't include the 25 tons in the Venezuelan jungle he was planning to shift to Europe when he got busted by the authorities for the first and last time.

Incredibly and perhaps unjustly for a crime that carried the maximum penalty of life imprisonment, he only served five years in jail of a 108-month or nine-year sentence (already reduced from an original 11 years) and was not named as an 'organiser, manager or leader in the offence', in the words of his sentencing documents, which would have got him a stiffer sentence; only for 'management responsibility over the ship which represented the property belonging to the organisation'. He was held accountable in a court of law for 9375.5 kilos, just over ten tons.

Luis never went into the United States Federal Witness Protection Program (Witness Security Program or WITSEC) and wasn't offered it. He claims anything he did say to the US Government was done with the knowledge, if not the blessing, of his criminal associates in Colombia. He accepted responsibility for his errant ways, avoided trial by pleading guilty, and did his time.[7]

He did not reoffend when he left jail, apart from a minor traffic violation in 2013. He was ordered to pay a monetary penalty of $100 for crimes that would have normally required him to pay anywhere from $17,500 to $8 million in restitution.

'One of the figures they came back with figured that I owed

$56 million in taxes, undeclared income, restitution and all that shit. It was ridiculous. My attorney, Ruben Oliva, did a great job. You don't want to do restitution. Even if you get $500,000, *man*, that's a pain in the ass to deal with. That's a big weight on you going forward. Every pay cheque they take something. So Ruben got me no restitution, a $100 fine and that was it.'

No longer a drug trafficker, fugitive or prisoner, he's free to tell his story.

*

Typically during those early months of 2018 in Sydney, Australia, I'd wake up to birdsong, a cup of coffee and a WhatsApp call from Luis, who had a habit of changing his profile photo regularly – usually a gleaming white Miami high-rise building, but other times Kim Jong-un (during the first USA–North Korea summit in Singapore) or John Belushi's character Jake Blues from *The Blues Brothers* (somewhat macabre, given Belushi was killed by a 'speedball', a mixture of cocaine and heroin).

On occasion, though, we'd get to speak on the phone only when he had a few spare minutes at his construction job. He'd been doing it full-time ever since he got out of jail and in recent times had been combining it with consulting work for the US Government. His days were full, sometimes having to drive 160 kilometres a day. Frequently we'd text, Luis usually doing so from his car between schlepping on worksites around Miami.

'Fifty per cent of my text messages to you, Jesse, are made while I'm driving. Which is a lot more dangerous than the activity I was involved in for 25 years.' Wisely, he ended up recording messages instead: 'My risk of dying while dictating is less than texting.'

There were times when he was too tired to remember much at all. He was, by his own admission, not very good with recalling exact dates from the late 1970s and early '80s, when he was off his face so much of the time on cocaine. Because of this and his tangential, non-linear way of thinking – often he'd say whatever came into his head, go on an extended riff about something inconsequential then forget what he'd originally been talking about – I had some trouble constructing timelines for parts of the book.

He flirted with pulling out altogether when he got worried the content would adversely affect his construction business or he was getting grief from 'the love of my life', Isabelle Meneses, an Ecuadorian-born, naturalised American.[8] They'd been dating since his release from prison but she would not meet me or even speak to me, such was her unbending opposition to bringing up Luis's past for this book.

Luis and I would quite often get heated with each other and frequently disagreed on various matters, not least the title (he was worried that any association with the word narco in such a prominent way would forever stain his reputation; my view was he should have thought about that much earlier, like 1979), but in all the time we worked on the book we never had a blow-up that wasn't reconcilable. That, to his credit, was a mark of the man: even if he went too far and lost his cool he'd be quick to apologise.

At the time we started work on this project, *Narcos* and its follow-up, *Narcos: Mexico*, were flavour of the month and to me Luis's story seemed like another TV series waiting to happen. He loved to talk of his dealings in Hollywood. There were a couple of aborted scripts lying about, a 'treatment'. Some industry movers and shakers – agents, directors, studio heads, investors – were apparently interested in Luis, but we needed something substantial to tie all his anecdotes together. When I initially proposed meeting him in Colombia, he was reluctant. I could sense a line had been crossed for him because of his cooperation with the US Government. There was no going back.

'It's not too good as far as safety is concerned. I do go back to Colombia but I keep a certain low profile. I don't announce my arrivals [*laughs*].'

In the end, it took a year and a half to get contracts signed and to book my plane ticket to Miami via Dallas–Fort Worth to meet Luis in person. He greeted me at the airport luggage carousel, we hugged, and within minutes of getting in his car he told me he was resigned to the fact his life could be snuffed out at any minute from an assassin's bullet. He didn't fear death but accepted what was coming to him. As someone who'd never so much as copped a speeding ticket, it was an unsettling feeling being in the car with Luis, knowing I too could be collateral damage in any prospective freeway machine-gun ambush, *Scarface* style.

Before arriving in Miami I told Luis about my daily jogs in Sydney and he complained he never got to do anything for his body, because he was too busy dealing with city compliance inspectors and construction workers. (There maybe was some truth in that, but I'd often call Luis when he was out to dinner and having a royal time with friends, or opening a bottle of whisky or vodka at home in Miami. The tinkle of ice cubes has a very distinct sound down a phone line.) He expressed a desire to start yoga and said he was in great fettle but needed to lose a few pounds around the middle. The last time he had worked out was when he was in prison, where he did it 'every day, religiously. I did a lot of pull-ups, a lot of dips. I'm very wide-shouldered. I've got a lot of muscle up here. I gotta start at least walking.'[9]

For all its mafia entanglements, though, the construction business is still a walk in the park compared to the drug trade.

'I think I did it backwards. I retired at 25, now I started to work at 50. It's crazy, man. Back in the day if you would've told me that I would be spending most of my time in metal-fabrication shops or in Hialeah [a working-class city of Miami-Dade County with a high concentration of Hispanics], I would've told you you were nuts. I deal with people on a "Fuck you, you sonofabitch, you piece of shit, you motherfucker, you dumbass" basis every day. I do not go to an office and deal with nice professional people at all. You know, I'm happy I got out of the [cocaine] business, but if you're well hooked up, it's a *hell* of a business. The thing is to know when to get out. Get out in time. Deal with it with a level head and have an exit plan. Make $10 million, invest in real estate and get the fuck out.'

*

Luis was very proud of his daughter, Juliana, 26, who was in law school and working in a law firm, and his son, Santi, 23, a budding artist and architecture student who helped his father out on job sites. They'd grown up while he was on the run in Colombia, Mexico, Panama, Jamaica and Greece and didn't know of their father's double life until he was out of jail and they were in their teens. Both are completely removed from the narco world but fully support Luis in writing his life story.

'I was a normal father and a very loving dad. We had family dinners, went to restaurants, celebrated Thanksgiving and Christmas. We were a normal family. The only difference was that I was in the drug business. My daughter used to see me walk out of the house every day in a coat and tie. It wasn't that wild shit you see on TV when they rush the kids out of the apartment because people are coming to kill them. It's a very different reality than you see all the time on TV. I watch these TV shows and think, "What fucking *world* do they live in?" You can move thousands of kilos of cocaine for the major cartels and still be a normal human being.'

That said, the body count of friends and others he'd known while moving cocaine was very high and they died in horrible ways – beheadings, torture, clubbings, shootings, plane crashes. Luis's time as a drug trafficker was far from drama free. Yet through all of the chaos around him, amid all the dangers and threats to his life, just like Mr Magoo, he had managed to stay alive.[10] Somewhat surprisingly, he wasn't sentimental about his fallen comrades.

'They all did something to deserve that. They knew what they were doing; it was their destiny. For me to survive with all the different wild and crazy shit that happened, my planets were aligned 24/7 for 25 years.'

*

I grew to like Luis very much and now consider him less the subject of this book and more a close friend. We shared many private stories and came to confide in one another over simple life matters: relationships, money, families, our purpose being on this earth. What started out as a simple writing exercise ended up affecting the way I thought about my own life, as well as the choices I'd made. Was I right to have stuck to such a straight path when I had so little financially to show for it? Why hadn't I made $100 million by my mid-40s when Luis had? It elicited many moments of introspection and reflection.

Sometimes, for a laugh, Luis would send me unsolicited videos of twerking Brazilian women or, disturbingly, bloody aftermath scenes from narco shootouts in Colombia and Mexico: heads blown off, bodies torn apart by bullets. ('I get these random videos from people, even law enforcement, that are not too nice.') Other times he would send me hilarious, philosophical voice recordings in the middle of the night while he was drunk or stoned, covering topics from the Incas to Powerball to our shared love of early '70s Elton John to The Holy Bible to the Fifth Amendment.

'You don't come through with what you promise, then you *die*. It's like the mafia story; it's biblical! It *is* the Bible! Death's the first thing about the Bible: that people will kill people. The other thing about the Bible is betrayal. People will betray people. The Bible's kinda cruel. The Bible's pretty much what the real world is about. You read the Bible, you read about everything. *Goddamit*, Adam and Eve. There's Adam, there's Eve, the apple and the snake. Thank God fucking Adam and Eve weren't Chinese, 'cause if they had have been Chinese they would have eaten the fucking snake.'[11]

Often when on the phone with Luis I'd hear Bob Marley & the Wailers, Al Green or salsa music playing in the background. Other times he'd send me videos of him drumming (he'd played since his teens and got in a lot of practice in prison), the Australian band INXS or clips from Oliver Stone's *Natural Born Killers*. The Javier Bardem scenes in the Coen Brothers' *No Country for Old Men* elicited some lengthy commentary.

Scene #1: 'This is so much bullshit. This guy's an idiot. An assassin would never want to leave another body behind. It's just more evidence and more huntdown material.'

Scene #2: 'That's another bullshit scene that breaks every rule of Smuggling 101. You get to a place, you find some dope, if there's somebody alive, you gotta kill 'em. Either you don't kill 'em and you don't steal the dope. Or you steal the dope and you kill 'em. You *never* go back to a crime scene. This sonofabitch comes *back* to a crime scene!'

I was getting one-on-one lessons in narco life. After one depressing discussion about the violence of Colombian paramilitaries, Luis joked I should 'do some mushrooms, man, go out and smoke some weed, hug a tree and then think about what I told you. Australians come from the best blood there is: outlaw blood. Twenty-five years, brother. It's got to have some side effects. I don't have that many wrinkles, so the side effects are all inside; it's all mental [*laughs*].'

I opened up old atlases to find places Luis told me about that I'd never heard of. He'd lived a fast, glamorous life in some exotic locations: Miami, Bogotá, San Andrés, Cancún, Montego Bay, Panama City, Athens. I read all the books and articles there were to read and watched all the films and documentaries there were to watch: countless Spanish names, mind-numbing statistics, endless arguments for and against the war on drugs.

In many ways the interpersonal dynamic I enjoyed with Luis was like being a detective in an interview room grilling a criminal mastermind: clues and leads would keep coming the harder I pressed. Often it felt like I was getting a debriefing of a conspiracy; but at other times I was a priest hearing confession; or a shrink diagnosing a patient. Mostly, though, I was just Luis's confidant; albeit one part of a very odd couple. For that reason I feel qualified in the pages that follow to make occasional judgements of Luis's harebrained actions, selective evasiveness or self-suiting revisionism. He is not above reproach and I think he'd be the first to admit it.

But rarely would 24 hours go by when Luis didn't give me a huge belly laugh. His humour is what helped him survive in the drug business and it was this same humour that was critical to us getting the job done and keeping our sanity during the research and interviews. Even when I hated him for the way he kept sabotaging himself with his drinking and unhealthy habits, I came to care about the man. That's what we do with our friends.

*

Pure Narco is an inside look at the drug trade from an American who talks like a smuggler, who knows the lingo, all the inner workings, all the personalities involved. A friend of Luis's, a Colombian drug trafficker who was captured in 1999's Operation Millennium (*Operación Milenio*), a DEA takedown in Colombia and Mexico that netted one of the heads of the Medellín Cartel, Fabio Ochoa Vásquez, remarked during the writing of this book that 'it's a miracle Luis is alive.

He was one of the few guys that worked with everybody, every fucking cartel in the book, was not even Colombian, and is *alive*. All it would have taken for him to be killed is one guy thinking he was a DEA agent or who didn't like him. Just out of spite or revenge they could spread a rumour he was a DEA agent. Back then they'd kill you on rumours.'[12]

Another friend of his, a high-powered Miami lawyer who represents some of the most powerful narcos in the world today, says Luis is unusual among ex–cocaine traffickers for the strength of his simultaneous relationships with law enforcement and with veterans of the drug world. He jokes Luis is a moving target: 'Whenever I'm with him I wear an extra heavy coat.'

Beyond being a biography, this book should be a deterrent for anyone considering a career in drug trafficking. It brought up some bad memories for Luis and at times it shocked me. But whenever I wavered at the risks involved, I reminded myself that *Pure Narco* was a tale worth telling. There were the mob connections (American, British, Albanian, Spanish, Italian, Russian), the stories of the glamorous women (invariably 'knockouts' or 'headturners'), the drugs, the money, the violent deaths, the ever-present spectre of Pablo Escobar during his rise as a narco – all-important action and 'colour' in a business that for the majority of the time can be utterly tedious.

'There's not a lot of action in moving dope,' says Luis, playing down the glamorisation of the drug trade. 'The plane picks up and drops off and you don't even *see* the dope.'

Yet there were difficulties for me as a writer. The benchmark for any true-crime tale is undoubtedly Nicholas Pileggi's superb 1985 book *Wiseguy*, later turned into the Martin Scorsese film *GoodFellas* with a script by Pileggi and Scorsese. The reality is it's almost a thankless task to follow.

Not that I would ever compare this book to *Wiseguy*, but Pileggi had somewhat of an authorial advantage in having grown up in an Italian-American Brooklyn neighbourhood like his subject, the late Lucchese family mobster Henry Hill, and then worked for decades as a crime reporter of the American mafia. He could infuse a lifetime's personal perspective, authority and firsthand colour to the stories Hill was telling him as a federally protected witness.

I grew up on the other side of the world to Luis, in a different era, and the South American cocaine milieu was totally foreign to me, so I was never there to experience what he had seen with his own eyes. We could only meet in Miami, owing to safety reasons, work and family commitments, and travel restrictions. It thus became a time-intensive research job. Much of the background work for *Pure Narco* involved poring over documents in Spanish and Greek, languages I don't speak. What secondary sources were available more often than not contained contradictory or inaccurate information, so verification was time consuming and not everything could be verified.

Who exactly was involved in Operation Journey was difficult to determine, even to some of the agents who were there on the ground on a 'need to know' basis in Europe and South America. A Freedom of Information request to obtain Luis's case file by one of the agents involved proved fruitless after months of haggling, most of it heavily redacted with black strikethrough lines like a classified FBI memo – a complete waste of time. In the end, reconstructing the week of Luis's attempted escape and capture took two years' work on its own. There were also things I had to leave out or obscure for the sake of his and his family's personal security.

Other times I was totally perplexed by whom exactly Luis was talking about: seemingly every second drug thug in Colombia is called 'El Mono' (Blondie), 'El Gordo' (The Fat One) or 'El Negro' (Blackie).[13] There were people he mentioned of which no photograph or documentary record seemed to exist at all, but he and others assured me that they were very real and had lived or were still living to this day. It was an elaborate jigsaw puzzle with some very dark pieces. So I have described people and events as best I can, despite working within those limitations.

But even when I thought Luis was winding me up on something or stretching the truth, things would check out if there was information at hand. There is simply no possible way a man could make all of this up, provide such a wealth of names, numbers and details that can be corroborated, and then fool the world's leading law-enforcement agencies for over a decade. If he is ever proven to be a fantasist, he is the greatest fantasist who ever lived.

At times I must admit I had my concerns Luis could well be an unreliable narrator, because the stories were simply so *out there*. So where there are any disputes over what took place, I have faithfully recorded both sides or voiced my own suspicions and Luis's reaction. Ultimately, though, this is his story; it wasn't incumbent upon me or necessary to get every available account of what happened from the people Luis knew over the course of his life. I'd need over 2000 pages to do that and, in any case, for very good reasons not everyone from his past wants to talk to a writer. Here, the most important accounts are told faithfully: those of Luis, his family, his former wife, and the agents who worked to bring him down.

Drawing out Luis's inner demons, the real meat of the story, was going to test me as an interviewer too. His was a sad tale as much as it was 'colourful'. He was much more than a mugshot – all narcos are – yet we rarely, if ever, get to see the human behind the criminal. I'd had what I considered a reasonable moral compass all my life. Luis had really only found his after 25 years of getting away with what he could. He knows that and will readily admit to it. But getting him to face up to hard truths about what he was involved in (as well as his personal complicity) was not always easy.

As his nephew Andrés Blanco puts it thoughtfully: 'Luis tends to romanticise this period of his life. It's like a defence mechanism; like at this point in your life how can you look back and feel it was all for nothing? So he looks back on it in a very romantic sense and doesn't always see the ugly side of things and what other people had to suffer and endure as a result of his decisions that, at the end of the day, caused quite a bit of suffering to people close to him. This book is his way of processing it all; it's ultimately positive.'

*

The men and women of the British and American agencies who brought Luis to justice, chief among them active USCS (later United States Immigration and Customs Enforcement or ICE) Special Agent Robert Harley and retired DEA Special Agent Eric Kolbinsky, are the real heroes of this story.[14] They'd not only saved his life by putting him in jail but they made him confront some parts of his character he'd spent the better part of his life ignoring.

Even Luis acknowledges that Harley, who lives in St. Petersburg, on Florida's Gulf Coast, 'gave me my freedom. A lot of people get out of the business and they can never adjust; very few adjust comfortably without regrets or being sour about it all. I've been able to find happiness and adjust; let's just leave it at that.'

Responds Harley: 'I gave him his freedom? Ah, not true [*laughs*]. Luis and I have had a nearly 30-year-long, odd "relationship". He's a real character; has been since high school. I think his life is a great story about choices, their consequences, and a chance at redemption not squandered. It will read like fiction.'

Luis's ex-wife Patricia Manterola, who endured so much while her husband was on the run yet kept their young family together and alive, also deserves the highest praise. When Luis says Patricia 'went through hell and back', he's really not exaggerating. After rebuilding her life following Luis's imprisonment and becoming a mortgage broker, her de facto partner Ignacio Bargueño died at the age of 50.[15] She has subsequently remarried.

Patricia met Luis when she was still a teenager and spent her 20s travelling between Colombia, Mexico and Central America with a lover who was a fugitive from the United States Marshals Service (USMS). She was only 30 when Luis was locked away in an American federal prison.

Strikingly youthful for a woman in her early 50s, with a vivacious personality, great figure, straight blonde-highlighted hair to her shoulders, a megawatt smile and the eyes of a Russian Blue cat, Patricia is a beautiful woman. A Colombian national and permanent resident of the United States, she speaks elegantly accented English, much like the Spanish actress Penélope Cruz. Her home is in Brickell, a waterside neighbourhood in Miami that has become an elite playground for Latin American and European multimillionaires, its streets clogged with Maseratis and Mercedes-AMGs. Hearing English spoken in her neighbourhood these days is rare.

'When I remember that part of my life it's like someone else lived through that, not me,' she says. 'But the good thing is it always leaves me with a smile on my face. *Everybody* liked Luis. They always found him funny. He speaks very bad Spanish [*laughs*]. Well, *now* he speaks better. Back then he would make some kind of mistake and everybody would laugh. He was fun. Everything looked like an adventure in the beginning. I was a kid. *Imagine*. I had braces. I didn't realise what I was getting into.'

*

In 2000, not long after the DEA had dismantled the Medellín and Cali cartels (operations dramatised in the first three seasons of *Narcos*), the United States Department of Justice (DOJ), the DEA (part of the DOJ), the USCS, the Joint Interagency Task Force-East (JIATF-East) and law-enforcement agencies in Great Britain, Venezuela, Colombia, the Netherlands, Greece, Italy, Albania, Panama, Belgium, Spain and France combined forces for the conclusion of Operation Journey, an elaborate two-year takedown that targeted the narco empire of Los Mellizos ('The Twins'), a Colombian cartel named after identical twin brothers Víctor Manuel Mejía Múnera and Miguel Ángel Mejía Múnera.

The Mejía Múneras were big-time traffickers and identified as such by the DEA as early as 1995. They were so powerful DEA administrator Thomas A. Constantine stated in congressional testimony that the brothers had 'links to both the North Valley and Cali syndicates' and 'will attempt to fill the void created by the arrest of the [Cali Cartel's] Rodríguez Orejuela brothers'. Madrid newspaper *La Razón* even went so far as to name them as the biggest drug trafficking 'clan' since the bloody reign of the Medellín Cartel, a state-sized drug syndicate that under the guile and tyranny of Pablo Escobar would go on to control 80 per cent of the global cocaine trade.

The mission to destroy The Twins' cartel involved 12 nations, 14 agencies, over 200 agents, boats, helicopters and sophisticated surveillance equipment, and resulted in 43 arrests. The publication of this book marks the 20th anniversary of this momentous event. So in the DEA's storied history of takedowns, Operation Journey is one of the most significant.

It had its origins in British and Spanish maritime law-enforcement operations in 1996, started out being called Operation Jezebel by Brits stationed in Colombia; *Operación Transatlántico* by the Colombians themselves; overlapped the DEA's earlier Operation Millennium, Her Majesty's Customs and Excise's (HMCE's) 11-year mega-dragnet Operation Extend, the Greeks' Operation Odessa and the US Coast Guard's (USCG's) Operation New Frontier; and in Venezuela, the location of Luis's ultimate capture, was christened *Operación Orinoco* or Orinoco 2000 after the famous river, brown like a milky coffee, that runs for 2000 kilometres from the Sierra Parima in the state of Amazonas, close to the border with Brazil, to Delta Amacuro on the Atlantic Ocean.[16]

But, as former DEA agent Eric Kolbinsky wrote in the foreword, even after its various offshoots coalesced under a single name, 'inter-agency squabbles and infighting' nearly put paid to its successful resolution. One thing I learned from writing *Pure Narco* is just how difficult it must be to mount an international antinarcotics operation when factoring in not just the serious potential for leaks but the dysfunctional politics and rivalries involved.

Operation Journey, however, proved a gamebreaker for all sorts of reasons and received saturation press coverage around the world. *The Washington Post* said it had a 'Hollywood-like conclusion' while Britain's *Sunday Telegraph* also thought it fit for the big screen, ending 'in a speedboat chase complete with volleys of bullets similar to the opening sequence of the latest Bond film'.[17]

Senior investigation officer (Gold Command) Graham Honey, who led the British effort for HMCE, says 'the half-dozen of us who were really close to that case, we look back on it as the pinnacle of a career; you will never get a case like that now. I don't think any law-enforcement organisation since that time has ever, *ever* worked a case like that where you've had the number of agencies involved, the amount of drugs being moved and *how* they were being moved. The amounts of cocaine [the cartel] was moving on those jobs was unbelievable. I don't think there's anything of that scale happening now. That was unprecedented.'

*

To give some perspective on the significance of the cocaine seizure of which Luis was involved in 2000, the following year, 2001, it was announced that 13 tons of cocaine had been intercepted on a fishing boat 1500 miles south of San Diego in the 'largest cocaine seizure in US maritime history'. The cocaine impounded in Operation Journey was *double*. The cocaine moved by ships that were being monitored by Operation Journey was *five* times that amount, and much more again was transported without ever being detected.

Luis, the man who initiated and arranged an important part of Los Mellizos' smuggling operations to Europe on a fleet of oceangoing bulk carriers, what USCS Commissioner Raymond Kelly called a 'drug armada', was the point man for the Colombian and Mexican cartels if they wanted to shift a serious amount of coke.

And no wonder it was being moved to Europe. At the time a kilo of cocaine that would cost $1700 in Colombia would fetch $50,000 in Europe, double the price it would get in the US. Do the math: 68 tons at $50,000 a 'key'.[18] That's $45 million a ton or over $3 billion for the lot. A $48,300 profit margin on a single key. The Mellizos' share of that European market was 'massive', says Luis. 'They were the top suppliers of the European market, without a fucking doubt.'

The famous 1984 raids on the huge cocaine-processing complex Tranquilandia ('Quiet Village') in the jungles of Caquetá, southern Colombia, only recovered 15 tons, which were destroyed.[19] In 2007 the United States Coast Guard (USCG) impounded 20 tons from a Panamanian cargo ship. The same year, a jointly conducted Mexican federal police and marines operation in Manzanillo claimed to have confiscated a then world-record 26 tons. Twenty-one tons were seized in California in 1989, 26.5 tons in South Florida in 2016, and almost 20 tons in Philadelphia in 2019. The largest single cocaine bust in recent Colombian history was 12 tons in 2017, but in 2019 the Colombian Government announced 94.2 metric tons (103.8 tons) had been seized in various operations over a 105-day period, mostly on the open sea.[20]

But these are just numbers; there will *always* be bigger busts. And in any case whatever is caught is only a small fraction of what actually gets through. So-called 'narco subs', crudely built semi-submersible submarines or 'low-profile vessels', now account for up to 40 per cent of drugs arriving in the United States, but only five per cent of those drugs are being intercepted.

However, when Commissioner Kelly stood before the cameras in a Washington, DC press conference to announce Luis had been arrested along with Los Mellizos' 'communications chief' Iván de la Vega Cabás in Maracaibo, Venezuela, and flown to the United States in handcuffs, he made very plain it was an enormous triumph for the authorities.[21] The timing was also deliberate, the press conference held just days before President Bill Clinton made a state visit to Cartagena to meet Colombia's president, Andrés Pastrana Arango, to cement the two countries' alliance in the war on drugs with $1.3 billion as seed money for Pastrana's anti-drug 'Plan Colombia'.

'This investigation was unique for the incredible volume of cocaine it kept off the streets of America and Europe,' said Kelly. 'This case also demonstrates what can be achieved when nations of the world work together against a common enemy. Operation Journey should serve as a model for international law-enforcement cooperation.'

When Luis describes it, though, he plays it down: 'It was like three minutes of the four-hour story. But it's what brought me down.'

*

In *Wiseguy*, Nicholas Pileggi described Henry Hill as a 'mechanic' in the American mafia and in effect that's also what Luis was in the cocaine business. He was an expert in the machinery of the drug trade and knew what went where and who did what. The difference is Hill effectively started at the bottom. Luis, by his own admission, got a Wonka Golden Ticket to the highest levels of the Colombian cartels.

Pressed on what exactly he did for these criminal groups, he says 'logistics' but the bottom line was he made them money; he was an 'earner'. However, in the structure of those same cartels for which he earned that money, he was a transporter, a delivery expert: traditionally an important position outsourced to non-Colombian nationals. Transporters were prized for their connections to lucrative markets, especially Europe, because from the early 1980s onwards US law authorities were well and truly on to the cartels and smuggling coke to North America was becoming much more difficult, dangerous and violent. Europe remains where the big money is because of the high prices people are prepared to pay for a kilo of cocaine.

'From the day I set foot in Colombia to the day I was arrested in Venezuela, I was working *all the time*. I don't have one per cent of the money I should have with the amount of "merchandise" I moved. Billions went through my hands.'

Luis believes had he not wasted so much of his life drinking and drugging, he'd have $100 million stashed away. He could have made much more if he'd actually owned the cocaine but only ever took a percentage for the transport.

'It's crazy. I don't even know where all the fucking money went, compared to what we moved. What I made with my right hand I spent with my left. I had a lot of good connections. It's *all* about connections. I was totally consumed by what I was doing and constantly thinking of the mission at hand, making sure the load will make it and have no problems and then, after that, immediately concentrating on the next load: a never-ending saga of load after load. If I lost a load, I was good for seven good ones. Because of my averages I was a very prized "batter", let's say. If we played seven times, seven times I'd hit home runs. But every once in a while I'd strike out. I had a great record as a transporter.

'I've always thought smugglers were the true essence of the cocaine business, not pushers or distributors. Smuggling is the most important part of the business because it's the part that brings in the revenue. If your loads don't make it and there is no product for the distributors to sell, then the business goes bankrupt. I always did my homework. People like me were of great value because we were the ones that put the product where the money was. The smuggle is also the toughest part of the business. There's no cutting corners.'

*

Luis worked for 'huge' cartel figures in Colombia and Mexico and 'never for a middleman', which offered him a degree of immunity and protection. No would-be kidnapper would dare try to shake down Luis when they knew the fearsome reputations of the bosses or *capos* (drug lords) behind him.

'The reason I survived was everybody knew I was not my own boss; I was always working for someone who was very feared *behind* me, and that's why people never stole merchandise from me.'

In a global drug market increasingly controlled by Mexican cartels, Europe somehow remains the domain of Colombians.

'The US had a proactive government that would fucking go chase people all over the world. I was an independent guy who had my own routes and I went to different sources of supply and I made money for them and for myself. Was I part of the Medellín Cartel? No. I worked *with* the Medellín Cartel, I worked *with* the Northern Valley Cartel, I worked *for* people from the Coast Cartel.[22] That protection saved me big time. I was a drug smuggler. I had connections to Belize, The Bahamas, Jamaica, Guatemala, Mexico, Europe, so that was all very valuable.'

And with each load Luis was involved in delivering, the thrill just ratcheted up with every 'first'. The first grams he sold at Georgetown University. The first 100 keys sent to Los Angeles.[23] The first airdrops aboard his own plane in The Bahamas. The first landings in Mexico. The first fastboats to Belize. The first freighter job. As the numbers kept getting higher – 100, 500, 1000, 2000, 3000, 4000, 5000 keys – so did the endorphin hit.

It was also harder for him to get out.

*

Luis frequently refers to himself as the 'last independent smuggler' but the sheer scale of his drug trafficking (cocaine in the *hundreds* of tons) arguably makes him the biggest homegrown cocaine smuggler in American history: more than 'The Man Who Made It Snow', the late Max Mermelstein, who went into witness protection after testifying against the Medellín Cartel; more than George Jung, played by Johnny Depp in *Blow*, who went to jail for 20 years; and more than Barry Seal, the murdered pilot and confidential informant (CI) made famous by the Tom Cruise film *American Made*. Pablo Escobar made sure Seal was killed in 1986 for betraying him.

'I lasted 25 years. I took up residence in Colombia. I was one of *them*. I married a Colombian. I stayed there. Those other guys would go down to Colombia and couldn't wait to get out.[24] I enjoyed the country. I *loved* Colombia. By far I am more Colombian than Cuban. In my heart of hearts I am Colombian. The guys from Medellín were really fucking cool. Very cultured. It was amazing to be around these people.

'But the other thing about people from Medellín is they are tough, astute and calculating. That's one thing I saw in Colombians that I never saw in Cubans. Their word was their bond but they'd kill you and they'd think nothing of it. I grew up thinking killing was the worst; then you realise humans are all a bunch of cockroaches and half of them deserve to be whacked anyway for all the shit they do.

'Either you're gonna do things right or you're not, but if you don't do things right then don't come crying to anybody if they fucking whacked you. You deserved it. You had no business going into somebody else's business and stealing from 'em. I'm not a big proponent of humans. They're not in my highest category. I'll cry more over the death of a fucking polar bear or a Bengal tiger than I will a fucking crooked human.

'Just because you're a human doesn't give you a right to life or anything, you know. What makes you special? Because you can *talk*? Some people it's better that they don't even talk. I realise how fucked up humans are and that's why I don't have the highest regard for human life. If you get whacked, you get whacked. You should definitely not go into this business and be deceitful to anybody. Especially when you know this motherfucker will whack you. Then you're just psycho, suicidal and stupid. Then it's an insult to this person's intelligence and, worse, an insult to his position as a cartel boss.'

When I asked Luis how he morally dealt with violence knowing it was part of his line of work, he was refreshingly upfront even if the import of what he was saying was slightly disturbing. Describing the brutal murder of a friend, a broker called Juan Diego, he simply says, 'He got tortured – *bad* – by Mexicans. He got killed in an unfriendly way.'

Luis's world is a netherworld where the execution of a human being is judged by degrees of kindness or friendliness, as if any murder could ever be justified.

'I'm *against* torture, Jesse. I'm *against* psychopaths. But if someone needs to get whacked, whack his ass. That was his doing. In his heart of hearts he knows what he did to suffer that fate. He must have done something wrong. I have no moral problems with that. To this day, you tell me you're a hitman, I'm like, "Hey, that's your job. That's *perfect*, man. Be good at it. This world needs everything." I had no control of yea or nay. I was never a jury or a judge. Violence wasn't my thing. I always knew I didn't stand a chance in that world as a bad guy. I never owned a gun. Killing was beyond my pay grade. I would never be an assassin. I don't like that being my business model.

'Some people think it's easy: you kill somebody, you make $100,000. But you've got to *love* what you do. I would never love killing. Killing was not born in my *soul*. What was born in my soul was making money. Maybe that's where I'm fucked up. Making money. Maybe I should have been more like a Buddhist and meditated, so my soul unites with my brain and soothes it a bit and teaches my brain a little bit of knowledge about living. Living is not only about money.'

Was he ever affected emotionally by the cartels' violence?

'I never was. In that sense, Isabelle tells me I'm amoral. I've got to be truthful with you, right?'

*

What you're about to read is a true-crime tale of a period that was largely bypassed in *Narcos* and occupies a zone relatively unexplored in drug-related non-fiction: the time between the demise of the Colombian cartels and the rise of the Mexican cartels. The utterly ruthless Mexicans operate sophisticated distribution networks through gangs in the United States and can move more cocaine through tunnels under the US–Mexico border than the Colombians could ever manage by airdropping in The Bahamas. They also move cash back into Mexico the same way. As Luis says, 'Nobody knows it came in, nobody knows it came out.'

The Colombian era seems almost romantic in comparison.

'The Colombians are always seen as foreigners and they're always getting fucked. They always want to fuck the third-world guy. There's a lot of big-money people in the United States who have made billions off the Colombian mafia and they've retired in time and they've cleaned their money and they're here in the US and they've built buildings and everything. But they gotta blame *somebody*. So they're always blaming the third-world countries; they're the source of the problem. They're the producers.

'The root of the problem is *here*, not there. The corruption is *here*. There's such a culture of non-education in America. There have been a lot of anti-drug educational programs but they haven't worked. The country uses all its money on its military budget and is so cheap, so cruel and so unjust to its own citizens that it doesn't even give them universal health care. Let alone all the money that is spent on the DEA budget on a war that has proven to be totally dysfunctional.'

Remnants of the mighty Medellín and Cali cartels still exist, along with the smaller cartels and gangs the Colombians call BACRIM (*bandas criminales* or criminal bands), but they are more likely to cooperate with each other than fight. Those cartels that remain are working with the few guerrillas still holding out in the jungle, and Mexicans and Venezuelans are shifting most of the product.[25] At time of writing, before COVID-19 or coronavirus completely shut down international travel, the United States Department of State (DOS) was advising travellers not to go to Venezuela at all, due to 'crime, civil unrest, poor health infrastructure, kidnapping, and arbitrary arrest and detention of US citizens'. In Mexico law and order has completely broken down in some areas due to the power of the cartels.

'Some cartel guys are still in Medellín. Some of them are living in Europe. Some of them are dead or in jail. Everything has *evolved*. Now you just don't have Medellín–Cali. It's all over the place. Everybody works with everybody.'

*

Today 30 per cent of the cocaine traffic to Europe, a continent that accounts for 30 per cent of the global cocaine market, goes through West Africa. The story of cocaine smuggling in the 2020s is less about Colombians in Miami than Nigerians in São Paulo. It's a global industry.

International criminal syndicates have learned from the mistakes of decades past. As part of multifarious money-laundering schemes, drug barons in Latin America are no longer putting profits into the vaults of Miami banks, exchange houses or trading companies, but into gold mines deep in the Amazon rainforest, laundering money by using front companies to sell 'dirty' gold to refineries and pocketing 'clean' cash in return.

Or they pack hundreds of millions of dollars on ships to China, where money-laundering laws are lax ('they don't believe in money laundering – money is money') and, according to Luis, 'The Chinese with the Mexican money buy like a billion of whatever – dishwashers, sewing machines, lamps, picture frames, bedsheets, kitchenware, everything you see at Walmart – and, that's it, it goes into the world market and it gets laundered.'

Illegal drugs are a $320 billion a year industry and there are 18 million users of cocaine worldwide. Over 300 million people have tried cocaine at least once in their lives. The United States, Spain, Australia and the United Kingdom are the world's biggest cocaine buyers, while tiny Albania is the biggest user of coke per capita.[26] Colombia, the land of Pablo Escobar, still produces 70 per cent of the world's cocaine, where it fetches $2200 a kilo. That same kilo sells for $53,000 to $55,000 in Europe.

The United States continues to spend $40 billion each year on the war on drugs, while its citizens spend $150 billion buying them. Mexicans have taken over the methamphetamine racket from bikers, state-based legalisation and high-quality hydroponics have effectively killed off marijuana smuggling, and opioids such as fentanyl and heroin wreak havoc in small-town America.[27] Cocaine, legally a narcotic but medically a stimulant, remains defiantly popular and accounts for the most spending on any single drug in the United States, even if overall consumption is falling in favour of marijuana and meth. In South America, coca-leaf production is at historically high levels. The biggest users of cocaine are still young people. The allure of cocaine remains as strong as ever.

*

Pure Narco is the first book I have written in official collaboration with someone else. I wanted Luis's unique, engaging voice to come through but with the right amount of background where necessary. Endnoting was essential. I have given ample space for that voice and the quotes you will read are delivered just as he said them.

Over the three weeks I spent with him in Miami in November 2019, Luis and I met almost every day for a Cuban sandwich and coffee at Latin Café 2000 on the corner of NE 25th and Biscayne Boulevard. We got to know each other extremely well, I met all his friends, workmates and family, and we found some commonality despite our disparate backgrounds, criminal histories and core beliefs.

This is above all Luis's story but it is also a chronicle of an era as well as an honest insight into Latin American narco culture. It is a tale about money, what it means to be 'rich', and knowing when enough is enough. My role was not only to record, research and write that story but shepherd into print and give historical context to what hitherto had been a collection of hazy memories and funny anecdotes told by Luis to fellow inmates in the prison yard or over long dinners with friends in Miami, Key West and Tampa.

By necessity it required some compression and rearranging of people and events into a more straightforward narrative, especially in the mid-1980s and late '90s, because there were simply so many side stories and so much to tell. In the end, pulling all these strands together was a process I was to enjoy immensely, even though Luis made it very plain to me throughout that we were both potentially putting ourselves at risk by writing this book. Dredging up 'old battle scars', as he put it, is a dangerous game.

'I got into this fucking nasty business and it didn't change me totally but it left a scar. My collateral damage is heavy. There's no life-insurance coverage in book contracts. Don't think I don't worry. Publicity sometimes can be a double-edged sword. The book could do me more harm than good. Nobody knows jack shit about me and my business. Nobody's done due diligence on me. They believe I'm just Luis Navia, the construction guy.

'I'm putting everything on the line for this. "*This fucking asshole.* I mean, this guy must have been the biggest jerk-off in history. He was in the drug business for 25 years, moved 200 tons, and now he has to dig holes." Man, that's fucked up. I'll probably leave Miami; I don't want to stay living here anyway. I'll probably change my name, move to Mexico. Become "Luis Navarro". *Boom.* Why not? I already got my kids grown up. Why do I need to be Luis Navia?'

The same night we did our first interview, he called me very late. He'd been talking to another drug trafficker friend about the journey he was about to take as an author. Coming from an unrepentant narco, what he was about to say was quite an admission.

'Smugglers are adrenalin junkies that love the rush and the thrill and they go to exotic lands to do it; to get the true thrill of this whole thing, the thrill of the *smuggle*. Getting a high off logistical feats that you put together if you use your brain. That's what it is. Pushers and distributors are just people who receive what the smugglers bring in and switch suitcases full of cash. They're just waiting to get busted. We didn't kill nobody. We were building up an enterprise; a business enterprise. We thought we were outlaws. I could walk into a restaurant and there could be ten people there with more money than I had, but I was an outlaw, like a walking deity. That was a bigger trip.

'Yet we were so mistaken because the government doesn't consider you an outlaw. Outlaws are when there are no laws. The government considers what you are doing as a continuing criminal enterprise. We were just goddamn criminals. And if we didn't kill nobody, we were associated with people that did. So when a DEA agent comes along and snaps some handcuffs on you, there you go: the big outlaw with $60 million in the bank just got arrested by the guy who makes $45,000 a year.[28]

'I was a drug trafficker in the true sense of the word: a pure narco. I stayed true to the drug business, not the killing business, not the paramilitary business, not the kidnapping business. I wasn't a part-time killer or part-time kidnapper or part-time sonofabitch. I always kept a family. Your family is so important. Even if it's just the three of you and you've got to share a hot dog, you're tight. In general, I've been a good person and cared for others, but the truth is I was involved with some nasty people. My focus was on the smuggling, although in the end it's all got a blemish of nastiness no matter what part of the overall business you're involved in.

'I had already made five, six million dollars when I owned sugar land in Florida and should have got the fuck out of the dope business, but I never got out. And that was my mistake. We were so mistaken, we thought, "Yeah, we're cool," this *adrenalin*, but you can get just the same rush by doing other things. Those people in Silicon Valley with their computers and shit, tell me they're not on a fucking high. Really, in the end it messed up my life. I mean, I'm alive, and that's great and I have some great stories but really, where's it all at? It's a miracle my family didn't get hurt more. But you can't just live life on a coin toss. And I was flipping a coin every day of my life.'

Jesse Fink, Sydney, Australia

PURE
NARCO

PROLOGUE

Do the Right Thing

9pm, Caracas, Venezuela
Saturday, 12 August 2000

THE UNRAVELLING OF LUIS ANTONIO NAVIA'S 25-year career as a narco, 12 years on the run from the law and five years as an international fugitive started when he walked out of the front doors of the Tamanaco InterContinental to his waiting taxi.

The eight-floor, 528-room concrete hotel, built in the 1950s, hadn't aged well but offered guests some respite from the sprawling *barrios* of the Venezuelan capital, nestled among an oasis of trees, tennis courts and manicured lawns just off the Autopista Prados del Este, a main highway, and right in the shadow of the green hills of the Cordillera de la Costa.

It was a quiet, tropical night in the 'City of Eternal Spring', wet but still hot, and as Luis took a moment to drag on a short Belmont cigarette, the most popular brand in the Bolivarian Republic, there was no sign of what was about to hit him.[29] For the moment, his ride – and his impending fate – could wait.

Within less than a week the 45-year-old Cuban-American would be captured by the Bolivarian National Guard of Venezuela, threatened with being cut up with a scalpel, detained at a military base, dispatched in a convoy of seven black Chevrolet Suburbans to the airport where Luis had once kept a Cessna 441 Conquest II for

3

his bicontinental drug-smuggling operations, and sent to Florida on a USCS Lockheed P-3 Orion to face the full force of stateside justice.

The plane had been configured like the cargo hold of a C-130 Hercules, with jump seats on the sides. It had been a quick 'in and out' for the US authorities with full permission from the Venezuelan Government. Luis, handcuffed, took his seat near a window for the three-hour ride. The DEA and USCS agents on board offered him water, coffee, Oreos, chocolate-chip cookies and potato chips.

As the aircraft hummed at 30,000 feet on its flight path over the Caribbean Sea, a feeling of calm came over him; a sort of tranquillity, like the weight of the world had finally been taken off his shoulders. The Carlos the Jackal of the drug world had been caught. His days as an international drug smuggler were over.

An agent seated next to Luis, sensing his uncharacteristic quietness, turned to him at one point and tapped him on the shoulder: 'Luis, you'll be alright. Just do the right thing and you will be alright.'

He was filmed when he arrived after midnight at Fort Lauderdale–Hollywood International Airport, accompanied by four agents and greeted on the tarmac by two others in navy raid jackets, one emblazoned with 'US Customs Police', the other 'DEA'. The footage would later be used in a combined DEA/USCS/JIATF-East press conference in Washington, DC in front of the world's assembled media to announce the takedown of 'one of the largest drug transportation groups ever targeted by law enforcement'.

Handcuffed but neat as always, Luis returned home to the United States dressed in a white shirt, khaki slacks and brown Sperry Top-Sider shoes. His 48-year-old, dark-skinned Colombian accomplice, Iván de la Vega Cabás, was more casual: he wore a white and navy striped polo shirt, a navy cap, navy shorts and leather sandals. His hands were tied with PlastiCuffs. Both men were nonchalantly chewing gum, like they were in the pro shop signing their scorecards after 18 holes of golf, not about to spend years in prison. The two drug traffickers seemed awfully relaxed about what awaited them, including a 90-day stretch in solitary confinement – for good reason.

The Americans had saved their lives.

PART 1
TAKEDOWN

1

El Senador

WHEN LUIS FIRST ARRIVED IN Venezuela from Italy that June, he'd entered on a fake Mexican passport under a fake name, 'Luis Antonio Novoa Alfandari', with a fake birthdate. He was pretending to be a Mexican businessman with interests in latex rubber gloves and coffee, and it was the perfect cover.[30] It was just one of many alter egos he used in his line of work. On the street, he was sometimes called 'Julio Novoa'. In South American cocaine circles, he was variously called 'El Senador' (The Senator), for his sharp dress sense, and 'The Greek', for the shipping company he now worked for in the port of Piraeus, Athens: Callisti Maritime.[31]

Located a few blocks from the water in an attractive three-storey building at 61–65 Filonos Street, Callisti was the European front for what was then the deadliest drug cartel in Colombia, Los Mellizos, named after Miguel and Víctor Mejía Múnera. Born in 1959, The Twins were Cali brothers who had worked their way up from humble beginnings as *cuida cargas* (men who control or guard loads of cocaine for the owners) on fastboats in the Pacific Coast port of Buenaventura to becoming the biggest cocaine kingpins in Colombia, with complete control of the cocaine trade in the departments of Sucre and Bolívar, and the Venezuelan state of Delta Amacuro.[32]

Only a few high-ranking people in the cartel knew Luis's real name, one of them a Mellizo himself, Víctor Mejía Múnera, another Los Mellizos *contador* or accountant Félix Antonio Chitiva Carrasquilla aka 'La Mica', who'd once moved merchandise for Pablo Escobar.[33] However, the Mejía Múnera brothers and Chitiva didn't know Luis was actually *working* for the organisation – the news of his involvement on this latest smuggling operation never got to them. He much preferred it that way and 'always kept someone in the middle' and 'was not directly involved', avoiding wherever possible face-to-face meetings with the leadership of the cartels for whom he rendered his services. In effect, he was a shadow, a ghost.[34]

In South America, Luis always had at least $20,000 in cash at his hotel and made a point of walking around with $3000 to $5000 in his pocket, 'enough to make a run'. He spent many hours at the pool getting a deep brown tan, hanging out in the bar and restaurant, and making love back in his suite to his 21-year-old, red-haired Panamanian girlfriend, Michelle Arias.[35] If ever he were in mortal danger, Luis would get on the phone to Michelle and say the codeword 'Antonio', his middle name.

They'd met drinking whisky in the upstairs lounge of the Davidoff cigar store in the World Trade Center office building in Panama City, Panama, where Michelle worked as a manager. Together the two lovers had travelled to Santo Domingo in the Dominican Republic, Madrid, Athens, Milan, and finally Venezuela. Luis, then a resident of Panama, was separated at the time from his wife and the mother of his children, Patricia Manterola, and an attempt at reconciliation hadn't panned out the way he'd hoped. Luis hadn't been the most faithful husband during his short marriage. Patricia had simply had enough of his shameless philandering, heavy drinking and 'gypsy' ways and rightly walked out.

Luis was no Antonio Banderas or Jordi Mollà. He didn't look like your stereotypical ponytailed Hispanic cocaine trafficker from Hollywood movies. He was short, just 168 centimetres tall, somewhat jowly, with salt-and-pepper-coloured hair and beard, a slightly bulbous nose, and an ample stomach courtesy of his taste for booze, good food and disdain for exercise.[36] He was constantly on edge and uncomfortable, completely stressed out from his separation from Patricia, and had developed a growing dependency on anti-anxiety medication and antidepressants.

Though Luis tried to think about his unusual predicament at the most 'three times a year', life on the run was tough on his nerves. He'd left the United States in a hurry in 1988 to preempt an indictment – a formal charging document approved by a grand jury – he thought was about to come out of Arizona. Luis had been smuggling coke on his own plane, a Panamanian-registered Merlin twin-engine turboprop, from Colombia to the resort town of Puerto Vallarta outside Guadalajara, Mexico, and then to Tucson. A white American narco in Tucson, known only to Luis as 'The Doc', his point man to the Mexican cartels, had been caught and Luis feared The Doc was about to rat him out. So he immediately fled to the coffee city of Pereira, Colombia, and continued his flourishing drug business in South America.

On 3 March 1995, he was formally indicted in the Southern District of Florida, again for drug trafficking ('conspiracy to possess cocaine with intent to distribute'), this time for a string of smuggles in the Florida Keys that Luis claims, with some justification, he did not lead. But it didn't change the fact he'd been named and outed as a cocaine smuggler. The jig was up.

Five months later, it was official: Luis was a US Government fugitive.

*

In truth, though, being forced into exile had been more than tolerable; in fact, it had been a breeze. Luis was a Latin American living in Latin America who had easily transitioned to the nuances and rhythms of life south of the border. He spoke Spanish, had enough money to buy whatever he wanted whenever he felt like it, and had a Colombian wife, Colombian daughter and Mexican son.

His only real misfortune was a 35-year-old USCS special agent, Robert Harley, who'd brought the original indictment against him out of Key West, Florida, and was doggedly working to hunt him down while clearing out hundreds of other cases in his day job.

Harley had long been burning the candle at both ends, working in a long-term undercover operation with the Miami field division of a Federal Bureau of Investigation (FBI) organised crime unit, while going to the University of Miami law school at night. Earnest, hardworking, aspirational and dedicated to the job and his long-term girlfriend, Mary, he was a handsome man: like a blonder, shorter, stockier version of Mark Hamill from *Star Wars*. Always armed, when suited up he made a point of carrying a SIG Sauer P229 9mm; in polarised sunglasses and Bermuda shorts, a Ruger SP101 five-shot stainless .38 Special. He'd narrowly missed catching Luis in Mexico and had gathered more than enough intelligence to bring him in.

'I had a lot of crap going on in those years,' says Harley. 'They were the busiest years of my life, between 1993 and 1999. That's when I really worked the most.'

He wasn't about to give up now.

2

The Venezuelan Job

So Luis instinctively knew Robert Harley and USCS, the DEA or US Marshals could break down his door any minute. This awareness didn't help his stress levels. He rarely got enough sleep. He was also deeply unnerved by the paper trail being left behind by the Venezuelan job, the biggest smuggle of his career; an elaborate criminal enterprise he'd been working on for nearly a year.

Luis's assignment in South America that August was to oversee the departure of the Maltese-flagged bulk freighter *Suerte I* from Puerto Ordaz to Rotterdam, the Netherlands, and then Antwerp, Belgium. Puerto Ordaz is a big port on the Orinoco River and part of the city of Ciudad Guayana, where ships load up with cargo then navigate through 180 kilometres of winding, jungle-choked waterways and mangrove swamps to the Atlantic Ocean.

From The Plains (Los Llanos) region in Colombia, bales of cocaine would be airdropped over the border to pre-arranged locations in the remote Orinoco Delta, a vast wilderness in eastern Venezuela. For landing planes, Los Mellizos also had a mile-long runway on a 5000-acre farm called Doble Uno, less than 100 kilometres from Puerto Ordaz.

Once the *Suerte* was out on the open sea, 30 miles off the coast, it would rendezvous in the dead of night with a fleet of *pangas*, or fastboats, commanded by Jorge García aka 'Cuñado' (Brother-in-Law), a fit, lean Colombian in his late 20s who wore dental braces and since March 2000 had headed up the cartel's operations in the jungle. He had been directly responsible for supplying the cocaine to the *Suerte*.

From these boats Jorge and his men would onload over five tons of coke, conceal it in hidden compartments on the so-called customised 'mothership', and the *Suerte,* with *cuida cargas* aboard to guard the load, would set off for Europe.

When the ships reached Spanish territorial waters, local criminal clans with direct links to the Eastern European mob would intercept a consignment of the cocaine off the Galician coast on fishing boats.[37] From there it would sail for the English Channel, where another consignment would be offloaded to another fishing boat for eventual sale and distribution in Great Britain.

If everything went smoothly, five tons of coke would be successfully delivered to the cartel's mafia customers in Albania, Spain, Russia and England and the boat would dock at its final destination, Antwerp, completely 'clean'. There would be nothing for any cop or narc to find.

*

It was a brilliant, watertight plan. But something was skewiff in Caracas. Luis could feel it in his bones. There'd been whispers among cartel members something might be going down, but the order hadn't been given by the leadership of Los Mellizos to abort.

'It was getting screwy. I was very nervous. I kinda felt there was a little heat on us; that we were being watched. Caracas was already turning a little sour with [Venezuelan president] Hugo Chávez coming in the previous year. I had been planning to meet my family and my sister and her kids in Barcelona in July, but I couldn't go because my Mexican passport was missing.'

Patricia had turned up in Spain with Juliana, six, and Santi, three, as her husband had requested, but without a passport to travel on from Venezuela, Luis hadn't shown. It was going to take some arranging for his counterfeiter, a woman called Natalia Hoyos, to travel 2600 kilometres from Guatemala City to Caracas with a replacement.[38] Luis had many fake passports to choose from – over seven – but hadn't thought to bring a spare to Venezuela. The one he wanted Natalia to bring was another Mexican passport, this one under the name 'Louis Anton Naviansky'.[39]

'I always tried to keep the same initials because that way I didn't have to change my shirts, because all my shirts were monogrammed. I had them made at Mario Pelizza, the tailor for the Mexican president. It's more expensive to change your wardrobe than get a new passport. The *Suerte* was supposed to have arrived a lot earlier, it was delayed, so I just couldn't leave Venezuela without a passport and without the *Suerte* having arrived. I figured once the *Suerte* docked, we'd loaded the shit and it was gone, I'd have Natalia come in from Guatemala with my Naviansky passport.'

So, instead, it was simply easier to have the whole family fly to Venezuela. Not the most normal thing to do in the middle of a major international drug conspiracy, but Luis couldn't see any other way around it and he was desperate to see his kids.

*

Patricia, who'd been furious at Luis's no-show in Barcelona, had already left for a pre-arranged holiday with her Italian boyfriend. So it was left to Luis's sister, Laura, to drag her two teenage sons, Andrés and Martin, as well as Juliana and Santi all the way from Europe to Caracas.[40]

'I was upset with Luis because all my pre-arranged travel plans got messed up,' says Laura. 'I was also upset because it wasn't till the absolute last minute that we found out he wasn't coming at all. I had to cancel a trip to Paris with my children. Patricia had dropped off my niece and nephew on my second day in Barcelona, and Luis never showed up to pick them up. I had to travel to Venezuela to take the kids to him.'

It wasn't, however, a straightforward procedure getting them through immigration. Juliana arrived without the right visa, leaving the already harried Laura to plead with officials to let them into the country.[41]

'It was incredibly aggravating and stressful. Juliana had a Colombian passport with no Venezuelan visa. It could have ended badly, but having lived in Latin America for many years, I knew a few hundred dollars would go a long way in solving the problem.'

Luis had to wait outside the terminal with his driver while all this was going on, wisely refusing to come inside because of the police presence. (He knew Juliana would say *Papá* if she so much as saw him, and they had different passports.) In the end, once the bribe had been paid, they were allowed to stay on a 30-day visa and Patricia cut short her trip in Italy and travelled to the Venezuelan embassy in Colombia to sort out the paperwork.

Naturally, when Laura met her brother outside the airport and offloaded Luis's kids to his and Michelle's care for a few days, she was livid. But not as angry as Patricia was when she eventually turned up from Colombia to take them back home to Mexico City. As far as she remembers it, there would be no introductions to Luis's buxom blonde lover. Michelle was keeping her distance, perhaps wisely. All the same, Patricia had a sense she was close by.[42]

'I knew Luis had a new girlfriend with him in Caracas because she did something to Juliana's hair. She put in highlights [*laughs*]. *Imagine*. My daughter was six years old.'

As for the kids, they were blissfully unaware anything was going down and had no idea their father was even involved in crime. Laura's 16-year-old son Andrés, however, was starting to have suspicions about the man he called 'Uncle Lou', who'd booked rooms 1116 and 1117 at the Gran Meliá.

'I'd never seen him in worse shape,' he says. 'He was fat, stressed, smoking cigarettes. He looked like hell. He was always secretive. We'd order room service and I'd go to sign the cheque, and he'd say, "*Don't* sign your name!" But he'd always been a bit eccentric, so I didn't question it. There were always stacks of cash and bags of money around. He never had a cell phone. My uncle was always in a payphone booth or standing by a payphone, making phone calls. He'd be like, "Come with me, I've got to run a few errands." But running a few errands with Luis was to watch him stay on a payphone. I was like, "I'm bored. I'm not coming with you anymore." That was his office.'

3

Midnight Run

THE *SUERTE* HAD LEFT Greece with a Ukrainian crew and captain in April, gone to the Black Sea to pick up a legitimate cargo and then sailed to Lagos, Nigeria. From there it was supposed to travel on to Brazil to pick up sugar but instead went straight to Venezuela and reached the mouth of the Orinoco on 4 August 2000. It arrived in Puerto Ordaz the next day, where it loaded up with iron ore.

Now a week later, the boat's Ukrainian captain and crew were being sent home. They'd left Puerto Ordaz and were staying at the Tamanaco, where they settled their 'back pay' or bonuses in cash – tens of thousands of dollars in US currency – with Callisti chairman and fellow hotel guest Angelos Kanakis.[43] Luis, with a room nearby at the Gran Meliá Caracas on Avenida Casanova, had been visiting Kanakis over two nights.

An entire replacement crew of nine Filipinos and six Bangladeshis, along with a Filipino captain, Néstor Suerte, had been recruited in Chittagong, Bangladesh, by Luis's diminutive, 40-year-old Bangladeshi-Colombian colleague Jamil Nomani aka 'Indurain'.[44] After flying into Caracas from Dhaka via Amsterdam on Dutch airline KLM, the new crew was getting ready to leave that night from Puerto Ordaz for the *Suerte*'s midnight run to Rotterdam.

From the mid-1990s Los Mellizos had been moving massive loads of cocaine, hundreds of tons, on freighters from Central and South

America to Cuba, North America and Europe in one of the biggest narco conspiracies of all time. They even sold 'a lot' of coke to the Hells Angels in Canada, who were 'a big client'.[45] Some ships were intercepted but others made it. In fact, Luis estimates the cartel had successfully smuggled ten times the amount that was ultimately seized by authorities: 'About 200,000 kilos, definitely, in a short period of time. Probably ten, 12 freighters got through, *easily*. There was a lot of merchandise that made it.'[46] Jorge García had even bought an Antonov cargo plane to courier dope to Albania, from where it would be distributed by the Albanian and Russian mob for sale on the street in Eastern Europe.

But this drug run was different because the *Suerte* was coming *from* Greece, then going *back* to Europe on a route the cartel called 'Los Quesos' – The Cheese. It was so named because it ended up in the Netherlands, the home of edam, maasdam and gouda.

*

The cartel had 25 tons stored at its base in the jungle, ready to be sent out to sea. But with a single vessel only able to successfully conceal five to six tons, it was going to take the better part of a year to get it all to Europe. Which was why Luis had thought to bring the structural, architectural and engineering plans of two new ships he was proposing to buy with his Greek smuggling partner, Callisti Maritime owner Elias Lemos.

Callisti Maritime had, according to Luis, a 'very ambitious plan to buy a lot of ships' with the end goal being for four vessels to operate at any one time. The going price for a freighter was '$2 mil, $2.3, $3 mil, some $3.5'. Luis was deep in discussions with the Colombians about where they were going to build the stashes on the vessels to hide the dope and wanted there to be no disagreements or misunderstandings.

'I was in South America so the Mellizos could see what they were buying. "Are these plans good for you? Can you see that you can put in a nice stash unit in these ships? Are they adequate? *Yeah?* Everything cool? *Okay.*" And they hand over seven, ten, 12 million dollars in Europe for us to buy these two ships. We were actually looking at three ships but I took the plans for two.'

Iván de la Vega Cabás, a gopher for Los Mellizos, was his contact when he got to Venezuela from Milan that June. What Luis had expected would be a two-week trip to South America instead turned into two months. Iván, in turn, would pass the proposal on to the Mellizos' *oficina* in Bogotá, which would then send their men to board the ships and weld the tailor-made compartments to hide the cocaine.[47] But the decision to hire a whole new replacement crew for the *Suerte* in Bangladesh had irritated Luis.

'I was always against it. I said, "Fuck this shipping bullshit. We're all going to go down the drain because of the paper trail." That's the thing I always told Jorge García, who was Iván's boss: "This is going to come back and bite us in the ass." Jorge was head of operations, head of logistics, head of shipping, coordinating the shipping of merchandise to Europe. Jorge reported directly to Los Mellizos. He was the one who brought me into the Mellizos organisation.

'I said to Jorge, "Listen, this is bullshit. We'll do this freighter thing and we'll buy a couple of freighters but we've gotta buy fastboats. We should be transporting 5000 kilos on 80- or 90-foot open fishermen [boats] with three inboard diesel Caterpillars with four islanders from San Andrés that nobody knows from Adam, and if they do get busted they don't know jack shit. There's no paper trail. All they have is 5000 kilos, a big boat and four crewmembers with nothing to say.

'I knew exactly what I wanted to do: build offshore fishing boats in Brazil, bring them up the coast, park 'em up in Fortaleza, park a couple in Trinidad, and use those. If we have to, we fucking sink the boat after we give the Spanish people the dope and fly the islanders back through Cape Verde and there's no paper trail. We cannot have *crews*. We cannot have 15 fucking Ukrainians and 20 fucking Filipinos. You can't be big in an evil business and have offices like we had in Greece, in Mayfair in London, in Milan. I say to them, "Here we are dealing major amounts of cocaine and we've got *shipping offices*? We're all going to get busted." I realised later that all of this was going to fuck us up and get us into a heap of trouble. We got away from our basic roots.'

In an ideal world, Luis and Jorge wouldn't have been shipping coke out of South America at all.

'Our plan was to start plantations in Africa and avoid having to cross the Atlantic by boat and having to pay that freight.[48] Looking back now, it had all the ingredients of a clusterfuck with the Africans; too many volatile characters, too much power, money, ego. It would have been been crazier than humans could handle efficiently.'

*

The Orinoco Delta, all 43,646 square kilometres of it, full of Warao Indians, jaguars, anacondas and crocodiles, was a cocaine smuggler's paradise. The cartel had picked just about the remotest part of it: the Mariusa National Park (*Parque Nacional Delta del Orinoco*) in the centre of the delta.

'The eastern part of Venezuela was actually not even Venezuela, it was Guyana. But the Venezuelan Government claims Guyana or a big part of Guyana [the vast Guayana Esequiba or Essequibo region west of the Essequibo River, roughly 40 per cent of the former British Guiana]. The Orinoco Delta, that is *huge*. It makes the Everglades look like a little fucking backyard. There are tribes in there that are so remote maybe they haven't even seen white men. We had a "fishing station" with dugouts and fastboats; not fastboats like cigarettes, big *pangas* – 34-foot, centre console, two Yamaha outboard engines – so the merchandise would be airdropped to that area where we had that fishing station. We called it a fishing station or fishing camp because supposedly that's what they were. People there at a fishing camp, *fishing*.'

The cocaine, in hundreds of bales of 30 to 35 kilos each, would be hidden in rectangular, waterproof plastic barrels shaped like phone booths, wrapped in fishing nets and anchored under the surface of the water. To any surveillance aircraft overhead, nothing appeared out of the ordinary. The fishing camps would await their instructions to move the merchandise out to sea once boats had left the delta.

'The ships used to come into Puerto Ordaz and drop off sugar or whatever they picked up in Brazil or brought from Africa, and they would pick up aluminium, iron ore, whatever, and if you look at the mouth of the Orinoco, once you're out of there you're already into the Atlantic. It avoids that whole hot spot, which is from Panama all the way to Venezuela. That's why that area was so good.'

The operation had an apartment with a radio in Puerto Ordaz to communicate with Jorge García and his men at the fishing camps in the delta. Calls would be made in the early evening or early morning.

'The merchandise would be airdropped into the fishing camps and when you airdrop merchandise you put a little neon glow stick on the bales. So we were on the radio one day and they get on the radio from the fishing camp. We're like, "How did everything go, did you receive the airdrop? Was everything good?" And they go, "Yeah, the only problem is some of the locals, the [South American] Indians, were startled when they saw lights coming from the sky." These are Indian tribes that are very far removed from civilisation – simple Indians. They see lights falling from the sky.

'And the answer to the people in the fishing camp from the apartment, from their boss in Venezuela who worked with us, was, you know, "Give 'em aspirins, give 'em aspirins for their headache." That means *shoot them all*. So they went and killed them. It was not my decision and completely out of my hands. It's one thing to kill someone in the business – you *choose* to be involved in it – but killing totally innocent people? *No.* That bothered me. It hurt my soul.'

4

The Cab Ride

L UIS PUT OUT HIS cigarette and nodded to the bellhop that he was ready
to get inside the taxi, a yellow Mazda sedan. The bellhop opened
the door and Luis got in. He asked to be taken to the Gran Meliá, ten
minutes away. The driver turned on the meter and pulled away from the
Tamanaco. They'd gone only three or four blocks through bumpy, rain-
slicked streets when he decided to speak to Luis. He was of Portuguese
descent, not a *mestizo*, in his late 40s, early 50s. He'd been watching his
well-dressed passenger in the rearview mirror the whole time.

'Hey, didn't I pick you up last night?'

'Yes, I think you did.' Luis had noticed when he'd got in but hadn't
said anything.

'Listen, my friend. Something really weird happened to me last
night after I picked you up. They stopped me, the *Guardia Nacional*,
and interrogated me for three hours about who the fuck you were.
They said they think you're involved in some kind of *narcotráfico*.'"

Drug traffic. The *Guardia Nacional Bolivariana* (GNB) is the
Venezuelan National Guard, well known for its torture of prisoners.

'*Whoaah*. I freaked out. Seeing that taxi driver twice in two nights
was a thing of fate. It was unbelievable.'

In his line of work, Luis never used a regular driver for one good
reason: 'Whenever you have a designated driver he knows there's
some designated bullshit going on.'

He had to think fast.

"'*Man*," I said with my Mexican accent as I was Mexican at the time, "no, that's a mistake. I'm a Mexican entrepreneur here doing business in Caracas, that's an insult, that's crazy." But by now I was really scared. I could feel my blood pressure was going up. "Please stop the cab. I'm going to get off. I need to walk and get some air." I gave the guy 50 bucks, *boom*, and got out of the cab. I then called Michelle at the hotel and all the time I'm thinking to myself, 'We're being watched. We are *fucked*.'

*

It was a Code Red Antonio. How had he been clocked? *Who* had clocked him? Was the DEA in Caracas? Had someone in the cartel ratted on him? Right now, in a state of high panic in a phone booth somewhere in the teeming Sabana Grande shopping district, was not the time or place to work it all out. There was no time to even go collect his things. He just needed to fucking run.

'Call the front desk, call downstairs, tell them you're having a bunch of people coming in from out of town,' Luis told Michelle from the payphone. He was frantic but still trying to work all the angles.

'What the hell's going on, what are we . . .'

'Listen, Michelle, listen carefully: you're having some Mexicans coming in and you want to reserve a table for 12 at the restaurant. Tell them you want to make sure you have all the best champagne on ice. You might want to hire some *mariachis*. Do they know any *mariachis* in town?'

A *mariachi* band is not the first thing that comes to mind when trying to evade police but that's Luis Navia: he was thinking ahead. They were doing a classic runner.

'I knew the hotel would parlay that information to the DEA right away and then they'd be thinking, "Oh shit, the Mexicans are coming, the big guys from Mexico, this and that," so they wouldn't make a move on us right away. They'd be so caught up on this whole thing about this party that they'd be like, "Wow, this idiot's gonna bring the fucking Mexicans over, this is gonna be great, now everybody's gonna get nailed."'

Luis continued directing Michelle: 'And you come out, you give the bellhop 50 bucks. You tell him to go get roses, go get whatever. And then you say you're going to do some last-minute errands. Do *whatever*. You walk out of the hotel and walk towards the avenue and I'll pass by in a taxi and pick you up.'

'I can't believe this.'

'Shut up, Michelle. Just go with the flow. You don't understand the seriousness of this. Do as I say or we're *fucked*.'

'What the fuck, Luis? I'm leaving all my stuff back at the room, my ring, my . . .'

'You can put the ring on your finger or in the bag. Bring nothing else. *Period*. Okay, maybe your clothing. That's it.'

It was a wise decision.

'Sure enough, *boom*, I pass by in the taxi and Michelle gets in, *boom bam*, we switch taxis three times, I knew that we were being followed, and from a couple of payphones while we were switching taxis I called Iván.'

It was now approaching midnight.

'We're fucked, Iván. We are *fucked*. You have to get out of your hotel. We need to meet up and you need to get the fuck out of here. They're onto us. This is *exactly* what happened, Iván. The taxi driver told me this. You gotta understand this is *real*. A taxi driver doesn't come up with this shit just off the top of his head.'

'*Wha* . . .' Iván was still half asleep and hadn't processed the full enormity of what was going on. He just sort of groaned back at Luis, like he was crazy.

'Listen to me. The taxi driver told me. That's *it*. You can do whatever the fuck you want but I'm out of here. You can either come with me or not but I'm outta here. I'm gone.'

'Okay, okay.'

Soon enough, Iván too began panicking. There was barely enough time to get his things together. He arranged to meet Luis on the street.

'So Michelle and I picked him up and switched taxis again, *boom*, then the three of us headed down to Maiquetía.'

5

Flight to Maracaibo

CARACAS LIES AT AN ELEVATION of 900 metres. Simón Bolívar International Airport at Maiquetía is situated 30 kilometres north on the Caribbean Sea at 72 metres. Container ships are visible off the coast not a far distance from the runway. Normally it's only a short descent to the airport via four-lane highway, 45 minutes, but the trip ended up taking hours because of mudslides. Venezuela had declared a national emergency.

'At the time there had been torrential rains and unbelievable boulders, *huge* boulders, six foot, eight foot, had come down from the mountain into the port town of Maiquetía. There were boulders in the middle of the fucking town. It was a natural disaster–type situation. So we had to take some side roads to Maiquetía.'

There were no planes to catch as it was now 2 or 3am, and in any case Luis had no passport because it was missing. Not the best situation for fleeing the country.

'The way it all happened was very fucking strange. I just don't lose passports. *Never in my life*. I'd realised it was missing a few days earlier but didn't really give it much thought, although I was worried. It wasn't like me to lose my passport like that. Something was wrong. It was in the back of my head but at that point I hadn't made a decision as to what to do there yet. I was already too far into the smuggle; there was too much pressure in getting that boat loaded and out of there,

23

so that overrode everything else. So I put it behind me but I realised they – not the DEA, the *Guardia Nacional* – must have come into my room at the hotel in Puerto Ordaz and stolen my passport. They didn't take my wallet. That's where I was before coming to Caracas.'

He'd have to wing it without his passport and try using his Mexican driver's licence. Iván knew there was a flight at 6am. Luis was already nervous enough about airports.

'An airport is a shopping centre with a runway and a police station. *Period*. I avoided airports like the plague. We found out there was a domestic flight to Maracaibo, which is closer to the border with Colombia. My plan was to go to Bogotá and go talk to the Mellizos, the owners of the merchandise. Go back to Colombia. Try to get away from these guys. There was nowhere open at four o'clock in the morning so Michelle and I check into this sex motel and open the door and the first thing I see is like this wooden horse, with stirrups and the whole nine yards. A wooden horse, for you know, getting, you know, *weird*. And I don't know what happened but Michelle and I were so, I don't know if it was the adrenalin or the fear, I don't know what got into her, but we began fucking like crazy. Three, four, five times a day when we were on the run.'

*

The trio arrived at the ticketing counter and said their names without showing identification. Maracaibo was a one-hour flight west from Caracas, just over 500 kilometres. Maicao, a few clicks past the border in Colombia, was another 130 kilometres, a two-and-a-half-hour drive in a taxi.

While they'd been fleeing Caracas, the *Suerte* had left Puerto Ordaz for its rendezvous with Jorge's *pangas* 30 miles out to sea from the Orinoco Delta. Luis had no way to get in touch with Jorge García in the jungle or Indurain, his recruiter in Caracas.

'All the time Iván and I were heading towards Maracaibo, and for those days that we were in Maracaibo, nobody [in Los Mellizos] knew what was going on with us. They didn't know what we knew. Nobody knew.'

It turned out Jorge and Indurain, on 12 August, the same day Luis had caught the taxi at the Tamanaco in Caracas, had already given the order to load the *Suerte*, which had sailed to its offshore location. However, the next day, a patrol boat of the Coast Guard Command of the Bolivarian Navy of Venezuela, thinking Jorge was smuggling contraband sugar, attempted to stop his *panga*, the *Orca*, with 3000 kilos of coke packed tightly inside along with an accomplice called 'El Negro', and another *panga* carrying 2200 kilos, Jorge's brother 'Kike' or 'Kique' and a man called Paul Perez.

The Coast Guard vessel had no idea the *Suerte* was already being monitored by the GNB, which had been patiently waiting for the cocaine to be taken aboard the ship before arrests could be made. A gun battle ensued between the Coast Guard and the *Orca*, Jorge began throwing bales overboard and with his small band of men he escaped into the mangroves, paying off indigenous people to find their way out of the Orinoco Delta. The 3000 kilos in Jorge's boat was never recovered but the second *panga* and its 2200 kilos was seized, along with six more boats, plus the cartel's communications equipment.

A five-day chase followed, with over 40 GNB soldiers pursuing the five escapees in the most difficult conditions, with tidal changes, endless mud and rising swamp water. Two cartel members left behind by the group were arrested at the fishing camps, and 16 altogether were arrested on the ground in connection to the Orinoco smuggle. If anyone could find his way out of the wilderness it was Jorge, who could fly a helicopter and was a skilled navigator. But the GNB's operation was blown. After waiting 14 hours for the drop-off that never came, the *Suerte* set course for Trinidad and Tobago with nothing aboard but iron ore.

'That's why Jorge went out [from the fishing camp] to deliver the merchandise. If he had known the extent of the fuck-up, obviously he wouldn't have been going out on a boat to deliver the merchandise to a ship that he knew was compromised. Those two days that everybody lost touch, nobody knew what the fuck was going on. Iván and I knew what was going on but we didn't want to call it in yet. We didn't want to fucking drop that pill on the Mellizos.'

Which was understandable. The GNB, led by Brigadier General

Antonio Alizo Castillo, Colonel José Antonio Paez, Division General Gerardo Daniel Briceño García and Captain Nelson Aguilar, ended up officially recovering 8800 kilos (just shy of ten tons) of cocaine in hundreds of bales from the Mellizos' fishing camps.[49] In dollar terms, about $440 million worth of blow, and that's a conservative valuation. What happened to the remaining 15-and-a-bit tons stashed in the delta is anyone's guess. The Twins were going to be mightily pissed – and Jorge, as the load's organiser, would be held personally responsible.

Either he made up the shortfall or he was a dead man.

6

Into the Black

A N OIL TOWN OF two million people with a heavily polluted lake from hundreds of oil wells, Maracaibo, in Zulia state, didn't have a lot to recommend it, but for 260 nights a year electrical storms roll in at the mouth of the Catatumbo River that empties into the 5000 square-mile Lake Maracaibo and put on the world's greatest lightning show.

Luis and Michelle weren't doing any sightseeing. They checked into another sex motel and didn't do a whole lot but eat *cazuela de mariscos* (seafood stew) at a local Peruvian restaurant while Luis waited for the Naviansky passport to be hand-delivered by his counterfeit passport lady, Natalia Hoyos. She had to fly from Guatemala City to Caracas to Maracaibo, a trip that involved a lot of connections and delays. Natalia duly arrived, Luis paid her, and she went back to Guatemala. It was disgustingly hot, August, the middle of summer, ten degrees north of the equator.

'Maracaibo's a fucking ugly city, the worst taxis with no air conditioners; it's as hot as a motherfucker. It's always hot in Maracaibo.'

Luis thought he'd successfully given the GNB the runaround and everything was still salvageable now that he had his passport, which is why he'd held off trying to contact Jorge or Indurain to abort the loading of the coke. He had no idea Jorge had been involved in a gun battle or Indurain had let the *Suerte* leave for the Caribbean.

'I knew we were hot but I thought we were going to pull it off. I was just concerned with getting my ass to safety. I was ready to cross the border.'

Back in Colombia, The Twins knew nothing, either. Or so at least Luis thought.

On their second day in Maracaibo, Iván told Luis he had run into Heiner Arias Gómez aka 'Julián', a hitman for the cartel.[50] Iván called Luis to meet him on a park bench down by the lake. He'd already organised a taxi to the border for the next day. He was scared.

'I think they're going to kill us here.'

'Listen, nobody knows what the fuck's going on,' Luis replied. 'If Heiner was going to kill you, you wouldn't be here telling me that right now. You'd be dead. And I'd be dead. We'd all be dead. We wouldn't be having this conversation.'

But if Heiner wasn't going to kill them, there was every chance the GNB would. And who else was coming for them? Luis also suspected Iván knew more than he was letting on.

'Iván was shitting in his pants because I think he knew more than he wanted to say. He didn't want to scare me that much. He knew we were fucked. He didn't want to be the one to call it in and tell the Mellizos that the whole thing got blown to pieces.'

Rattled, Luis then made his fatal mistake: calling Elias Lemos. What he didn't know was that the two calls he made from a phone booth at Galerías Mall on Avenida La Limpia were not going to Elias's mobile phone in Athens but to Paris, France. Their conversations, under three minutes, were being tapped by the authorities. Elias, already under arrest, was being told what to say on the phone.

'I had to say *something* to Elias. I had to say, "This is going to be aborted. We're fucked." I didn't know how big this thing [Operation Journey] was. The phone was on roaming. So every time I called, [the DEA] grabbed the phone call and they realised I was in Maracaibo. That first time I called, they mobilised a bunch of people to Maracaibo. They traced it from Europe. They didn't know where Iván and I were. We could have gone anywhere, we could have gone towards Guyana, we could have gone south towards Manaus on the Amazon, we could have gone towards Valencia, Venezuela. They had no idea.

'The second phone call was to tell Elias, "You're not going to hear from me for a few months, I'm crossing, and I'm going under the radar; I'm going into the black." That was my last phone call. But that one they were ready for. They really triangulated that one; they triangulated it to the phone booth at Galerías Mall.'[51]

*

It was 16 August. Luis had been on the lam, running from arrest, in Venezuela for all of four days. From the phone booth he and Michelle had gone to kill some time at the cinema.

'We were at a movie theatre and I saw some really weird activity. I saw some people at the exit doors.'

Unsettled, he went out into the lobby to get some popcorn, to see what else was going on. There was another guy who seemed to be watching him. After the movie was over, Luis went to a currency shop and bought a Bank of Scotland note because it had a whisky distillery printed on it, and Luis liked whisky. Michelle went off to do some shopping. They tried to act as normal as possible.

'I then went to the barbershop and sent Michelle to change some dollars. It was at the barbershop that these people came up to me. I was shaving my beard but keeping my moustache for a change of look for the crossing to Colombia. I was relaxing, I had my eyes closed and suddenly this guy says, 'Hey, *queda quieto. Guardia Nacional. Está detenido por sospecha de narcotráfico.*'

Translation: Hey, stay still. National Guard. You are being detained on suspicion of drug trafficking. It was the chief of security of the mall, a retired *Guardia Nacional* officer, who advised him he was about to be handed over to the six GNB officers standing behind him in khaki commando gear and armed to the teeth with machine guns.

The barber was frozen with fear. Luis had to grab his hand to stop the tremors.

'He was literally *shaking*. I thought, "This guy's going to cut my jugular." And I go, "*Narcotráfico?*"'

Luis surrendered without being handcuffed. He didn't want to make a scene. But before he was escorted from the building, he motioned to the GNB officers to come with him to a laundry room out the back of the shop where there were two washing machines.

29

'Listen, this is a mistake,' he said, walking backwards into the room and raising his hands in protest. 'Let's not make a scene here and let's talk. I'm a Mexican entrepreneur. I'm here on business. I don't know where you got your information but I'm sure we can clear this up. I'd like to talk to the attorney at the Mexican embassy.'

It was all a stalling tactic, of course. One of the washing machines had its door open and in his back pocket Luis had the smugglers' codewords scrawled on a piece of paper. As he was talking away, somehow he managed to slip it in unnoticed.

'If they found the piece of paper I'm no fucking Mexican businessman.'[52]

7

The Gringo

THE GNB WAS VERY interested to know more about the missing Jorge García. Iván had already been arrested and Michelle, who had wandered off in the mall when Luis was apprehended, had gone back to the sex hotel. The GNB suggested Luis call her and they picked her up. All three were being detained at the police station but were kept separated.

The *Suerte* had by now been stopped by a US Navy (USN) vessel off the coast of Grenada while refuelling en route to the Netherlands, and handed over to the USCG. It was later escorted to Galveston, Texas, where it arrived early that September.[53] No cocaine was found on board. Another ship in the Mellizos' conspiracy, the *Privilege*, again with an all-Filipino crew, had left the Orinoco for the Adriatic with a load of asphalt on 16 August and, as the target of a smaller Spanish operation called *Operación Ostra*, would be raided 650 kilometres southwest of the Canary Islands in Spain. As it was in international waters and flying the flag of the Democratic Republic of São Tomé and Príncipe, the Spanish first had to get permission from the Africans to raid the vessel.

The *Privilege* was found not to contain any cocaine, even though it was pulled apart for three weeks by the *Armada Española* (AE or Spanish Navy), *Servicio de Vigilancia Aduanera* (SVA or Customs Surveillance Service) and *Cuerpo Nacional de Policía* (CNP or

National Police Corps) on the orders of a Spanish National Audience Court judge, Baltasar Garzón, on 31 August. Over 100 people were involved in the search but could not locate the five tons they believed was on board, even though some reports suggested the cocaine had been found.

The police interview began. Luis was handcuffed to a metal chair that was bolted to a cement floor in a bare white room with blood stains on the walls. His interrogators threatened to cut him up with a scalpel, a *bisturí*.[54]

'You could *see* the blood on the wall. It didn't faze me. I mean, I was *concerned*. You know, something comes over you that just nullifies [sic] you. You're in fucking limbo. You realise your life just went down the complete drain but you're in limbo. Because if you really swallowed the whole pill of what was happening, I think you'd fucking overdose and die. But sometimes I think your body has defence mechanisms that won't let that happen. Someone with chronic high blood pressure, now that could be a situation where his pressure could go to 230 over 130 and he'd fucking croak. That didn't happen. I took it pretty good.

'The Venezuelan police were saying, "We're going to cut you up into little pieces if you don't tell us where the money is." I didn't really care. I didn't believe they were going to cut me up into little pieces and all this shit. They were playing good cop, bad cop. There was a Colombian cop who was the nice cop. The Venezuelan cop was the bad cop.'

With Luis refusing to play ball, he was removed again and put in the back of a black Suburban outside the police station. The air-conditioning was on full bore. The Colombian cop was in the front to his right, the Venezuelan to his left in the driver's seat, saying nothing, completely nonchalant. It was late afternoon and still hot as fuck, but the car wasn't moving.

'Then suddenly I looked to my right and I see this pair of fucking white skinny legs, long legs. The guy's knees were up to almost the window. And he was in shorts. And then I saw like a Hawaiian shirt, and I said, "This is it. I'm fucked. This is it. We're dead. We're *fucked*. The Americans are here. It's over. The *gringos* are here.'

For Luis Antonio Navia, 'El Senador', 'The Greek', the man with seven passports who'd been on the run for over a decade, it really was over.

He just had no idea how.

PART 2
ROCK 'N' ROLL DRUMMER

8

Silver Platter

'I'M THE LAST GUY in the world that should have gotten involved in this business, because I had no reason to. I had a great family background, a great, *great* education. I went to Georgetown University. *Jesus Christ*, you can't get better than that. I had great business opportunities. El Chapo had no other option. It was either this or he would never get rich in his life. But what happened is I got involved with cocaine in such a highfalutin, can't-say-no way that it was put to me on a silver platter. I didn't have to go out and deal with gangs, selling shit. From day one it was just put on a silver platter for me on a very big level. Such a big level we used to ship 2000, 3000 keys. You think I ever saw a key? I *never* saw a key. It was just a phone call. It was like trading on Wall Street.'

*

Luis Navia came into the world at the private clinic El Centro Médico Quirúrgico (The Surgical Medical Centre) in the leafy upmarket neighbourhood of Vedado in Havana, Cuba, on 27 August 1955. Vedado was the most exclusive part of town and his parents, Luis Navia y Cuscó and María S. Bonavia, had a huge apartment, a whole floor, to welcome their first child. But three years later, with the addition of a sister, Laura, the Navia family had an even bigger spread, upgrading to a 5000 square-foot two-storey house at

Calle 194 entre 15 y 17 in Biltmore, a new residential area north of the city.

The sale price of $280,000 was a lot of money at the time but still less than his father, Luis Sr, would earn each year in bonuses. María was charming, vivacious, good-looking, doting and much younger than her husband – 14 years younger. They were a beautiful and well-to-do Cuban family and hardly had to lift a finger with eight full-time employees, including three maids, two chauffeurs and a butler. The two kids even had their own individual nannies.

It was a charmed existence for Luis Sr, befitting someone who was the right-hand man to legendary sugar magnate Julio Lobo y Olavarria, very likely at the time the richest man in Latin America with an estimated fortune of $200 million.[55] Lobo's flagship company, Galbán Lobo Trading Company, was the largest sugar-trading concern in the world in a country whose backward, agrarian economy depended on the price of its sugar exports.

The 'sugar-wolf of Cuba', as newspaper *The Panama American* called Lobo in 1956, owned over a dozen sugar mills; had offices on Wall Street; a huge portfolio of assets in land, telecommunications, insurance and shipping; an enormous art collection; as well as arguably the world's best private collection of Napoleon-related items; and even boasted his own bank, El Banco Financiero SA.

Luis Sr was less flamboyant in his spending than Lobo but equally cultured, with an appreciation for good tailoring and the finer things in life, a trait that would be deeply ingrained in his only son from an early age. Born in 1908, Luis Sr had risen to his lofty position as Lobo's confidant from a lower-middle-class background, starting at Galbán Lobo at 13, qualifying as an accountant, and becoming vice-president by 1957. He also served on the boards of the Bank of Nova Scotia and the Royal Bank of Canada. He had impeccable English because he was often sent to New York for work.

'My dad was the real person behind the everyday business that Julio Lobo trusted with making intelligent decisions; not his relatives by blood who didn't have brains that were caught up in their high-society shit. My earliest memory is in the kitchen in the house at Biltmore with the employees. I've got pictures from the day I was born. The photographer that was in charge of taking pictures of me and my sister built a house on what my mother paid him just to take pictures of us.'

It was an idyllic childhood in mobbed-up, swinging, pre-revolutionary Havana, and Luis spent many days playing and swimming at Playa Varadero, east of the capital, or dancing around the living room to standards 'El Manisero' and 'El Bodeguero'. But he was too young to be aware of the political and criminal dimensions of doing business in Cuba.

*

In 1956, notorious East Coast mobster Meyer Lansky, friend of Charles 'Lucky' Luciano and Benjamin 'Bugsy' Siegel, famously known as the 'mob's accountant', sent his emissary, Boston lawyer Julius E. Rosengard, to Cuba to get part-financing for the 21-floor, 378-room, $14 million seaside Havana Riviera on Malecón and Paseo, complete with casino.

Cuban dictator and Lansky's friend Fulgencio Batista through the country's national development bank, *Banco de Desarrollo Económico y Social* or Bank for Economic and Social Development (BANDES), was underwriting most of the construction costs. Batista had made Lansky an advisor on gambling reform in 1952 and, like the true crook he was, was getting paid off in millions of dollars in bribes a week. The hotel and casino opened on 10 December 1957.[56]

Rosengard, one of Lansky's inner circle, an accountant and Lansky's 'gambling representative' according to the FBI, was also treasurer and a board director of the Compañía de Hoteles La Riviera de Cuba SA, the front company for the project. Bugsy Siegel posthumously sat on the board. So Julius was duly referred to Luis Sr and the financing he sought was arranged, including an injection from Lobo's bank, Banco Financiero. The American and the Cuban went on to become good friends. So good that Luis Sr loaned Julius $120,000 of his own money over two instalments in 1957 and 1958, an enormous sum, to which Julius stumped up his wife Emma's jewels as surety.[57]

'Julius and my dad developed a strong friendship aside from their business dealings. My mother and Emma also became very close. My dad was never involved in any illegal activity or had any association whatsoever with Meyer Lansky and he didn't need to. He never mentioned any funky business. Julius and my dad bonded because of the type of people they were: extremely discreet right-hand men behind the scenes. This is my thinking. You know, you gotta keep somebody clean. If not, it's a clusterfuck.

'Julio was the outgoing speculator; my dad was the conservative administrator making sure things didn't go out of whack. My dad was a very conservative man. He was always well cashed. He didn't go out with hookers. He didn't have gambling problems. He was a clean-cut, hardworking guy. He was totally dedicated to Julio Lobo and Galbán Lobo. He was of impeccable moral structure.'

Either way, the timing of Luis Sr's business dealings with Rosengard was unfortunate. By New Year's Day 1959 Cuba was a communist state in the hands of revolutionary leader Fidel Castro. Batista had fled with his cronies to the Dominican Republic and then Portugal, along with planeloads of loot. The party for the mafia in Cuba was over – as was Julio Lobo's sugar empire.

'The last sugar mill Galbán Lobo bought was the Hershey Corporation mill outside Havana. I have letters written by my dad of him telling Julio Lobo not to buy the Hershey mill because of the trouble with Fidel.'

Lobo wasn't having it. He had even sent money to the left-wing rebels in their early days, not knowing how much he was accelerating his own demise.

'Navia,' said Lobo, as he referred to his friend by the patronym, 'that kid Fidel we will manipulate like a puppet.'

'No, Julio, you are wrong. The situation is worse than you think, and it's too late to handle that puppet.'

Luis Sr was right. Castro, Che Guevara and the guerrillas rolled into Havana on 8 January 1959 on their US Army–surplus military jeeps. Casinos were trashed. The writing was on the wall for Galbán Lobo. Soon, the hotels and casinos that had sprung up all over the capital in the 1950s were nationalised by the state and Lansky's prize jewel, the Havana Riviera, was wrenched from him. Gambling became illegal. By early 1960, Luis Sr had made up his mind and booked a flight to Boston.

'My dad left to have a doctor's check-up for a heart ailment and never came back. He claimed he'd had a stroke. He conjured the whole trip as a ruse to leave Cuba without raising suspicion – he wanted to start setting things up in the States for the eventual exile he knew was coming. Julio stayed in Havana a little longer. My dad knew at that point they were fucked.'

That October, Lobo rejected an offer from Cuban Central Bank president Guevara to become Minister of Sugar in exchange for all but one of his mills and his residence. The Hershey Corporation mill Luis Sr warned him not to buy would be appropriated by the state, like practically everything else privately owned in Cuba.

'Fidel Castro was never a communist. He was just out for himself. Julio knew that he was going to be offered the position by Che Guevara and discussed it with my dad and whomever was giving him the backing he needed at the time. And they both had decided to refuse. They knew that a meeting was scheduled but no date and time was given. Suddenly Julio gets a call at two in the morning and goes to the meeting and refuses Guevara's offer.

'Guevara had received him in his office with his boots on the table, wearing the green military pants and a "wife beater" T-shirt, which Cubans call a *camiseta*. Julio was shocked because he had no regard or respect for the stature of the man he was receiving. Julio took a heavy hit – from [a fortune of] $200 million down to maybe $20 to 30 million he had offshore. That's what I've heard. Batista was the big one; since he knew what was coming, they say he took $300 million out of the country.'

Two days after his meeting with Guevara, Lobo left Cuba for good, leaving most of his possessions, including his Napoleonic collection, behind. He would end up dying in 1983 with comparatively very little in an apartment in Madrid.

9

Tom Sawyer Land

A FTER A FEW MONTHS of being settled in Miami along with 100,000 other Cuban émigrés, Luis Sr called for his family to follow him. Luis estimates his father managed to get out with about $600,000 to $750,000 in cash, plus various accounts held in his name in foreign banks.

On 22 May 1960, María, Luis and his lookalike 15-month-old sister Laura flew to Florida on Pan-American Airways accompanied by two maids, and booked into Cabana 41 at the Key Biscayne Hotel and Villas. At the time Key Biscayne, a paradisiacal island connected by a causeway to Miami, was an area largely made up of World War II veterans and dotted with retirement villages, but is now one of the most expensive residential areas in the United States, with some homes worth tens of millions of dollars. What used to be a favoured destination for senators and presidents is now a hub for rich South Americans.

It was quite the introduction to American life. In Cabana 40, right next door, then Vice President and Republican candidate Richard Nixon would recuperate from his close 1960 electoral loss to Democratic candidate John F. Kennedy. On 14 November that year, less than a week after the poll, President-elect Kennedy visited Nixon at the hotel. Luis Sr and Nixon had come to be formally introduced by Cuban-American Bebe Rebozo, Nixon's best friend and the owner of the Key Biscayne Bank. The three became friends, Nixon later bought two homes next to Rebozo, and the Navias attended the 1968 presidential inauguration of Nixon, the same year Luis's parents became American citizens, conferring those rights on their two children.[58]

When not in Miami, the Navias holidayed with the Rosengards in Hyannis Port, Massachussetts, not far from the Kennedy family compound. María was afraid of flying so they would catch a train from Miami to Boston, where they were picked up by the Rosengards' uniformed chauffeur in a black Cadillac Fleetwood limousine. Luis's memory of those days vacationing with the mob lawyer is a fond one.

'Julius and Emma had a house on the shore of Nantucket Sound in Cape Cod. Julius's pastime in Cape Cod was painting and he had his studio he called "Camp David", after his son, in the back on the house. They gave me one of those little red wagons called a Radio Flyer and we built it with one of the nannies that they had at the home.'

But throughout Luis's childhood his father remained a distant parent. Luis Sr was busy all the time, travelled a lot for work, was not quite present when he was at home, and put an emphasis on education and study rather than play. Of course, this meant that Luis both idolised and feared his father, who enjoyed fine Scotch whisky but was never drunk. He carried himself as a total gentleman at all times and always wore impeccable attire. Galbán Lobo's New York trading office, Olavarria and Company, kept an apartment year round at the five-star Sherry-Netherland on Fifth Avenue until 1962.[59]

'Always the best suits in New York. Tailor made. Ties from A. Sulka or Countess Mara. Shirts all monogrammed. Handcuffs. Not handcuffs, cufflinks [*laughs*]. With me, they had to handcuff me. My dad always stressed an education. Never did he mention money. My dad never spoke about money. *Never.* It was my mother who always put a lot of value on money. That I got from her. Greed was instilled in me by my mother. My dad was a very serious man. He had a great sense of humour but I am very much like my mother. Probably a little bit too much.

'If I would have had my dad's seriousness I would have been better off in life. My sister's totally like my dad. She demands respect. I'm like my mother. My mother used to joke around all the time. I was a fucking pain in the ass. If she said be home by six I'd be home by eight, because I was out swinging from trees into Pines Canal, spearfish hunting in the flats, riding my bike with my friends. I was always out there. I never did homework. My mother used to come after me, hit me, throw something at me. Are you kidding? My dad, all he had to do was *look* at me.'

*

In 1962, Luis Sr and a group of exiled Cubans partnered with local American sugar growers to form the Glades County Sugar Growers Cooperative in Moore Haven, Florida. The coop had 50 members, 280,000 acres of land under ownership and 150,000 cultivated with sugarcane. Luis Sr was comptroller (chief financial officer), vice-president and head of marketing for the refinery, Moore Haven Sugar House.[60] Its success earned the attention of the local mafia, but old connections made in Havana put paid to any extortion.

'They were going to market refined sugar all over Florida, which they did under the name Sunshine Sweets. Green Brothers was the exclusive broker to distribute the sugar. [Florida mobster] Santo Trafficante Jr wanted some kind of "in" because obviously this was a big deal. My dad really didn't want that whole situation, didn't want that weight on his shoulders, so he asked Julius for advice and Julius went to Meyer Lansky, obviously, and went to bat for my dad so that there was no involvement from the mob in Tampa.'

Back under the swaying palms of Key Biscayne, Luis was enrolled at Key Biscayne Elementary School and Laura at Little Island Playhouse Pre-School. The Navias had bought a house at Harbor Court near the yacht club. Luis was spending a lot of time in the pool learning how to swim from Dick Cutrera, a local swimming instructor.

'The first thing Cutrera tells me is, "Never go off the high board. Don't even go off the *low* board." Sure enough, first thing I did was I went off the high board. You tell me not to do something and I would find a way to do it.'

At school he was no less rebellious. One incident saw him sent to the principal's office.

'One guy was picking on me in third grade. Lynn Morris. We were eight years old. I was always a little guy. I never had problems with anybody, because I was a little guy but I got along with everybody. My personality was my sword; it has always been my sword. I could use it to gain and I could use it to defend. But one day Lynn Morris was bothering me, *really* bothering me, so, you know, back then you had to ask permission to go to the teacher's desk to sharpen your pencil. So I asked permission, I got up, went, sharpened my pencil, Lynn Morris was sitting in front of me, and as I was walking back from the teacher's desk I went *whaaaack* with my pencil and stabbed him in his left leg, in the shin. The pencil went inside his leg. *Boom.* That was like, shocking. He never bothered me again.'

Luis wasn't expelled. Along with his friends he took out his frustrations on the local wildlife.

'We would have been reported to the Humane Society. We used to take like lighter fuel and throw it on frogs and light them on fire. We used to take lizards and hang 'em and light them on fire. We used to go hunting rabbits, snakes, racoons. They call it animal abuse. It was just normal back then. We were living on Key Biscayne. It was wilderness. We always had BB guns and slingshots. We'd ride around on bikes with BB guns and shoot somebody's window. It was like growing up in Tom Sawyer Land.'

10

Grams in Georgetown

L UIS EARNED HIS FIRST dollar putting up chairs for $5 at the local church, but in the ninth grade at the all-boys Belen Jesuit Preparatory School, age 14, he first learned the economics of supply and demand.[61] His parents thought he was being 'an entrepreneurial young man'. The priests didn't agree.

'I would take a couple of dozen sandwiches from home and make seven, eight dollars. Back then that was a lot of money. Every day. Ham and cheese, and some were more expensive, so I put in a *croqueta*, which is a Cuban croquette. I used to sell those things for like 50 cents. Between 35 and 50 cents, you'd come home with eight bucks. Then the priests busted me and they didn't let me sell any sandwiches anymore. So then instead of taking ten sandwiches I'd take five and charge more for those five.

'Belen was a great school. My dad had the money to pay for any university I wanted to go to. But I never liked studying, I was never turned on by studying, I never thought study would get me anywhere. I didn't see myself as an accountant, attorney, doctor. I just saw myself as a businessman. I was a disciplinarian's nightmare. Without studying, without doing any homework, without doing jack shit, I got Bs, Cs, a couple of Ds, like in math, because I really hated math. Algebra, I never understood that shit. If I'd done an hour a night, I would have been Bs and As, without a doubt.'

Around the tenth and 11th grade Luis began growing out his hair, playing drums, and smoking high-grade marijuana from dealers who had smuggled it in from The Bahamas. For summer-vacation money, he worked at AAA, the emergency road service, taking calls. He and his friends would spend weekends getting stoned and watch the sunsets over Biscayne Bay. Music was a big part of his life. The first record he ever played on a phonograph was 'I Want to Hold Your Hand' by The Beatles.

'What impressed me about The Beatles wasn't really their music or anything; it was just the fact they were young and they were millionaires. The thought that 20-year-olds were *millionaires*? That really got me into it. "Playing drums should be a good thing." So I started to play drums. I was always into hard rock. Santana. Pink Floyd. Jethro Tull. The Who. Kinks. Led Zeppelin. The Beatles. Rolling Stones. Cream. Blind Faith. Jeff Beck. Rod Stewart. That was my thing. I never went for Barry Manilow.'

He wasn't much of a reader, but Mario Puzo's *The Godfather* left an impression.

'Man, that really grabbed my attention. I said, "This is where it's at. This kind of fucking life, this kind of *power*, this kind of money." It thrilled me.'

His first official girlfriend was Claudia Betancourt aka 'Clau', a 'hot item' with 'a great body and dynamite ass' from one of Key Biscayne's Cuban families who he'd met at the yacht club, around the age of 12. They spent their afternoons and weekends in paradise, waterskiing on Biscayne Bay or boating with Clau's father, Omar, to The Bahamas.[62] But a girl called Liz Francis claimed his virginity at 15.[63] She had green eyes, looked 'like a little Liz Taylor' and they went together to the senior prom.

'The Cuban girls didn't put out. Liz lived five blocks from me. She was more liberal about having sex and I was getting more action from Liz. I always worked my personality big time. I wasn't a super-good-looking guy. I wasn't tall. But I always had a girlfriend. I never had problems in that department.'

By the end of high school, he was back with Clau. When she turned 20, it happened: she finally put out.

*

Luis graduated as a senior from Belen in 1973 and was accepted into the University of Miami to study business and accounting. His proud father celebrated the achievement by buying him a 1973 Chevrolet Malibu. Luis Sr, still sensing there was some hope for his son, promptly took his only boy to New York to meet the law firm Milbank, Tweed, Hadley & McCloy, 'the top lawyers in the nation, the lawyers for the Rockefellers'. They stayed at the St. Regis on 55th Street and Luis Sr would take Luis for veal scaloppine alla marsala at his favourite restaurant, L'Aiglon.

'No matter who I've ever dealt with in the drug business, none of these guys measure up to the people my dad dealt with. He dealt with ambassadors, Wall Street, big people in the sugar trade. He was in a whole different ball game. Even though I was in an evil industry, cocaine, I dealt with the most powerful people in *that* industry. That's a power trip. Let's say you're in the computer business and you deal with Bill Gates or Steve Jobs. Or you're in finance and you deal with Warren Buffett. In my world every day when I woke up the people that I dealt with were the leaders of that industry.'

The following year, 1974, Luis enrolled in his first classes at UM and took to collegiate life, even running for senator, a student government position nominally representing 1000 undergraduate students. He lost by two votes. But any studiousness was shortlived.

'I took a snort with my older cousin. We were at his house for Thanksgiving and we went to the back where the pool was and he said, "Try this." It was definitely a picker-upper but the reason I mostly enjoyed cocaine was the euphoric-type feeling I got when you drink and snort. The cocaine counteracts the drinking, you wake up and you can drink more. When I started snorting I stopped doing the pot.

'Your mind is a lot more complicated than your body. That's why coke is so amazing. Forget your body. It's your *mind*; that's what it really takes over. People don't understand that because they don't ever get enough good coke. Coke really hits your mind; that's why Edgar Allan Poe snorted. When you snort the real shit you actually get to a state of euphoria or as close as you can to euphoria.'

Luis's parents hadn't lost hope. A Cuban historian friend of theirs got Luis into prestigious Georgetown University in Washington, DC in the summer of 1974, through the proverbial back door.

'There was an opening in the Portuguese department. It hadn't filled its quota. So I sneaked in through the Portuguese department and ended up mostly taking business courses, which is what I liked. So I was a Portuguese major but taking mostly accounting and business courses.'

Luis never went to Portuguese class and to this day doesn't speak Portuguese. But speaking Spanish at home each day in Key Biscayne had made him bilingual. At Georgetown, he made his first coke deal.

'I had a connection in Miami and I knew a guy that sold in Georgetown. I had a friend of mine bring up nine ounces [255 grams] and I sold them. Back then that was an *amount*; not everybody had nine ounces. I made $700, $800 an ounce. I didn't cut 'em or anything. It was just a straight handover.'

He also dropped out. He was 20 years old. The Malibu had been totalled in an accident. He'd stayed in Washington all of a year and a half. It was 1976.

'It was such a fucked-up major that classes were at 7.30 in the morning. Back then I was smoking pot with my roommates from Ecuador and shit. Who the hell was going to wake up at 7.30 in the morning? Like an idiot I partied and hung out with my friends. Everybody around me was becoming a professional. All my friends were very grounded; they knew what they wanted to do and the direction they were going in. I didn't have a solid compass pointing to where I wanted to go.

'I was never convinced that schooling was the answer to my success. My grades weren't that great so my dad called me back to Miami: "No more Georgetown for you. Come back because you're not taking full advantage of what you should and you're just out there on your own. Time's up."'

11

The FM Scam

HIS DAD WAS RIGHT. Options were fast running out for Luis and so were his chances. He took some accounting courses at Florida International University (FIU) but failed to graduate. He did, however, show some aptitude for selling drugs, both at FIU and his first adult job, assistant bookkeeper, at Top-40 radio station WMJX Stereo FM or 96X. It serviced the Miami–Fort Lauderdale area. His business card read, 'Luis Navia, Jr, Accounting.'

'I would buy the ounces in Miami for $1200, cut 'em, and send 'em up to Boston to my friend who used to pay me $1800 for 'em. At 96X, I would log in the commercials, and the [air] times, and then the bookkeeper would price it and invoice it. As assistant bookkeeper, they would give me the log sheets for when a commercial ran [on air] and I had to log it in to another sheet. But I was never at my desk for the bookkeeping and I was always inside the music-production part of the radio station with the DJs and the station program manager, because that was the fun part. I always fulfilled what I had to do but I spent a lot of time with the DJs.

'I'd buy a pound of pot for $300 and then ounce it out and make $600, and then sell those ounces to the radio station employees, DJs mostly. I went to see Led Zeppelin with one of the managers and when Robert Plant came out on stage we had like a fuckin' ounce of cocaine with us and we were right there, and *boom*, that was unbelievable.

We were the only people with fuckin' cocaine like that. We had a dozen girls with us.'

On weekends he was partying out. Luis and a group of friends had taken a six-month lease on a house on Key Biscayne in front of the Sonesta Beach Resort. A young Andy Garcia, who'd go on to be a Hollywood star, would drop by.[64]

'We had a big 96X party at the house with the 96X band and we bought these large garbage cans and we filled them with all kinds of liquor and Kool-Aid and we put acid in there and fuckin' next day there were fuckin' people spread out, passed out in the neighbour's yard, people passed out all over the fuckin' neighbourhood. I found a chick in my closet a day later. She was still passed out. It was crazy.'

*

At the time, 96X, '100,000 Watts', was trailing behind competitor Y100 (WHYI) in the ratings and the pressure was on to lift listener share in order to be able to charge more per minute for commercials, which was how radio stations delivered profits to their owners. Then Luis got involved.

'96X lost their licence because of me. The station ran some contests that weren't actually living up to what they claimed to live up to. At the time, radio stations were rated in their market according to the Nielsen Audio [Arbitron Radio] survey books.'

Over 2700 such books were mailed out to random addresses in Miami–Fort Lauderdale each ratings period by Nielsen, asking households to fill in their radio-listening habits and then mail the books back. One afternoon, Luis's very good friend and former Belen classmate Jorge Lopez called him at the station.

'I received four Nielsen books. What the fuck is this? You must know: you work in a radio station.'

Jorge's whole family lived with him and they'd received not one but four April–May survey books at the one address. His mother listened to classical music, his dad to Cuban music, his brother to hard rock.

'I said, "What? From *Nielsen*? Oh, my God, Jorge, this is fucking *gold*." So I went to the station and I said, "Hey, my friend has four Nielsen books. He's willing to put down that the whole fucking family listens to 96X from morning to midnight." What I wanted out of the deal was I asked for $5000 and I think I got $3500 in cash; quite a bit of money. Jorge got a rug and furniture for his house; we got a bunch of [free] Marantz amplifiers. We sold some of the Marantz amplifiers so I walked out of there with $6000. When people asked, Jorge said that he won a "contest".'

The four adulterated survey books actually made a difference. The Lopezes wrote down that they listened to 96X around the clock and 96X went from a 3.2 listener share to 5.7 in the survey and #1 in the Top-40 category. From charging $40 a minute for commercials, 96X FM's owners Bartell Broadcasting could now ask for $120. It was a perfect scam.

'Then suddenly the rumour started to spread that Nielsen had jigged up the books, and sure enough it came back to the station. Bartell owned six stations and Bartell was owned by Charter Broadcasting, a public company. The general manager that ran 96X was Mort Hodgson; his father was one of the founders of Charter, a really rich family from Atlanta. So he never got fired but he had to call it in that there was funky shit going on with the books.'

Hodgson, who was general manager, blew the whistle on his own station on 14 August 1978 to the Federal Communications Commission (FCC), the national body that regulated American radio broadcasting and which had already been investigating 96X for ethical breaches since 1975. On 18 January 1978 a preliminary decision had been made not to renew 96X's licence for 'repeated misconduct in nine contests over a two-year period'. An FCC administrative law judge had labelled 96X's contests and giveaways misleading and deceptive. This was the last straw. Luis was fired, along with two senior executives. In September, industry magazine *Record World* reported a 'part-time bookkeeper' was the culprit. Nielsen reissued the surveys and ordered they be taken again.

'I thought they were going to come down on me with some kind of FCC charge because they found out it was me. I was the one who rigged the whole thing, so that's when I left to fucking Ecuador for a month with my friends from Georgetown. I went to Guayaquil and, *fuck*, what a great place to go. On Holy Week we went to

Lima, spent a week there, partied our brains out and came back to Ecuador.'

An unforgiving FCC finally revoked 96X's licence on 14 February 1981. The last song it played on air, amid the DJ's tears, was The Beatles' 'The Long and Winding Road'.

12

Deathtrap

AFTER THE 96X FIASCO and his Sundance Kid getaway in Ecuador, Luis had landed a job as a salesman for New England Mutual Life Insurance of Boston and things were looking up. So on 25 August 1978, two days before his birthday, Clau decided to throw her boyfriend a welcome-home party.

'I was just sitting on the sofa, had a drink in my hand, and in through the door comes this girl. White. *Stunning*. Red curly hair. You know, *whoaah*. Bra-less. Fuckin' great tits just looking atcha. Gold chains, gold Rolex, beautiful green Thai silk dress . . .'

The whirlwind's name was Bia Gálvez: 28, a mother of two with an exotic accent, a head of tight ginger curls, arched eyebrows, a perfect nose, a strong bust and a wide smile: like a young Susan Sarandon.

'I mean, *wooow*. Just *sexual*. She was off the fucking wall. Bia was about six years older than me and we started talking and before you know it, we said to each other, "What are we doing here? Let's get out of here." And she left behind her date, Carlos, and I left behind Clau, and we went straight to her apartment on Brickell Key.'

Just walked right out. They didn't emerge for two days.

'The first thing I fell for was his sex appeal,' Bia remembers. 'Luis was a very smart man, fun to be with, a gentleman, a great lover.'

'We woke up the whole fucking neighbourhood,' laughs Luis.

'Went into the shower, broke the showerhead, broke the soap tray. She was too much for me to handle; too much at the same time. It was a pretty fucked-up thing to do [to Clau]. The next day Carlos was like, "I'm going to get that son of a bitch." But when he found out who Bia was and who protected her, he definitely calmed down real quick. We never heard from him again. I don't really know what I told Clau. It is what it is. Shit happens, man. It was instant fucking lust with Bia. It's a big wound for Clau. I feel real bad about her. I don't know how to ever make it right to her.

'I grew up a bit of a spoiled child. I was a rich kid from Key Biscayne. I was always frivolous about what I was going to do. I wasn't set in my ways, like, "I want to be a lawyer or a doctor." I wasn't the happiest camper. I was selling *insurance*. Not taking advantage of Georgetown was a complete fiasco. My life was a trainwreck. But then I met Bia and it was instant love and lust. Later it was money. The lifestyle, the coke, the exoticness. I was the perfect candidate to be swept off my feet and derailed. She was a deathtrap and a lovetrap at the same time, and I don't regret any of it.

'Back then, my mother thought Porfirio Rubirosa was the ultimate playboy. He was a Dominican who married Ava Gardner. He lived off rich women. So here I am, living the young man's dream to meet an older woman with a lot of money that's gonna teach him sex and you're gonna learn life through the eyes and in the arms of an older woman that's *experienced*. That's a dream come true. Three years after I met her I already had $5 million.'

*

'I need to go to San Francisco,' Bia told him in bed. 'Will you join me there?'

'I've got work but I figure I can skip a few days. So sure, yeah.'

'You don't need to pack anything, Luis. We'll buy whatever we need there.'

Bia hailed a cab to the executive airport at Palm Beach International, 120 kilometres north of Miami, and Luis went along for the ride, promising to meet her out west in a few days' time. A Learjet was waiting when they arrived.

'I saw some big, round, football-type things wrapped up inside the plane. Bia said it was "raw emeralds" from Colombia, still embedded in the rock. I had never seen a kilo before. I only dealt in ounces.'[65]

It wasn't the time to ask any questions.

When Luis flew to San Francisco on a later commercial flight, Bia, as she had promised, dressed him on arrival, buying suits and ties from expensive boutiques. They got a room together at the St. Francis, a five-star hotel in Union Square. In the city, Luis met a man called Brian Livingston, a wealthy *bon vivant* in his early 30s who liked to get stoned on weed and buy properties up and down the northern Californian coast. Brian, who Luis describes as 'a gentle soul, like a big teddy bear, a very good man', gave them a Dodge Magnum to drive at their leisure.

After a couple of days, Bia took Luis out to Sausalito, where they parked in front of the Golden Gate Bridge at dusk. Eddie Money's 'Wanna Be a Rock 'N' Roll Star' was playing on the radio. They had a bottle of Dom Pérignon and a couple of champagne flutes. By now he'd twigged as to what was really going on.

'Listen it's not emeralds. It's cocaine,' Bia told him. 'This is my business. Are you willing to stay with me?'

Luis looked out at the lights on the bay before turning to face her. His life was about to take a critical turn.

'Bia, I always wanted to be a rock 'n' roll drummer and, fuck, this is a lot better than rock 'n' roll.'

And that was when Luis, just 23 years old, a failed career in radio behind him, a fledgling salesman for New England Mutual Life Insurance, fell in with the Medellín Cartel, the most violent criminal organisation in the history of the world.[66]

PART 3
BISCAYNE BANDIDO

13

La Mona

BIA AND LUIS ENDED up staying a month in San Francisco, flitting between their hotel in Union Square and Brian Livingston's apartment in Sausalito, with its collection of museum-grade Persian rugs. Their host had a background in Thai stick and hash, but after the mid-1970s like a lot of marijuana dealers he realised there was far more money to be made in cocaine.

By the end of 1978, he was not just one of the Bay Area's biggest cocaine dealers – he was a pipeline to the insatiable coke market on the West Coast, where profits were even better than Florida. Brian was also about the best contact it was possible to have: he had a solid reputation for being an honest operator, he wasn't violent, he paid on time and he paid well.

'If Brian would have been a typical coke dealer,' says Luis, 'this thing could have gone sour real quick.'

Everyone was making money. Luis's new girlfriend was making so much money that when he suggested to Bia that it might be time to go back to his day job at New England Mutual – as he explained, technically he hadn't taken leave or given notice and they'd be wondering where he was and what he'd been up to – she bought a $1 million life-insurance policy right on the spot so that he wouldn't have to go back empty-handed to Miami after being out west for a month. The premium was $30,000 a year and she took two years on a monthly payment plan.

'This should tide you over for a while with these idiots,' she said.

When eventually Luis returned east, he duly got a trophy and was named Salesman of the Month – ironic for a man who was selling life-insurance policies to the Medellín Cartel. New England Mutual sent him to its headquarters in Boston to do a special course. He even managed to sell another million-dollar policy to a Jewish businessman from Panama. He was on a roll in his personal and professional life and it had all started with the most fatal of attractions.

*

Bia Gálvez was born in 1949, grew up in the islands of the Netherlands Antilles, was of Dutch-French background mixed in with Venezuelan, and descended from a long line of liquor and cigarette *contrabandistas*: smugglers. To this day there's a boulevard in the capital of Aruba, Oranjestad, named after her grandfather who made the family fortune.

Her father, Roland, according to Luis, 'owned a bar in some whore town called San Nicolas in Aruba' and Bia admits: 'Our relationship was not so good. He was very conservative and old-fashioned; though a very good man with a good heart.'

But her formative teenage years, the 1960s, had been spent in Colombia's second biggest city, Medellín, with her mother, three sisters and brother. According to Luis, Bia was a wild child, totally 'off the charts', who'd gone to school with nuns but now she was in league with the devil: the Medellín Cartel.

'When I was 13 I went with my twin sister, Andreina, to a boarding school in Medellín,' she says.[67] 'My mother and the rest of the family moved there later on when my father bought a house. I stayed four years in that boarding school and after I finished school we lived at my father's house. It was there I began meeting people [from the drug world]. We were the generation that tried to change society: Jimi Hendrix, Janis Joplin. We used to escape from our home in Aruba to go to parties.'

After graduating from school Bia moved back to Aruba for a period, then returned to Medellín, marrying a Colombian called Manolo Varoni when she was 19. She bore him two children within two years. The relationship didn't last but in Medellín Bia met an American marijuana dealer, Peter Sharwood, who was dating her sister.

Sharwood and his business partner, Marcos Geithner aka 'Sy', later became customers when Bia moved to San Francisco in the mid-1970s and 'began working with Fabio Ochoa Vásquez and some other guys' selling cocaine. All she will say about her introduction to Ochoa, one of the most powerful narcos of all time, is that they met through a 'friend'. Her two kids stayed behind in Aruba with her family. At the time the going rate for a kilo of cocaine was roughly $65,000 in California and from Bia the pair 'bought a lot'. On each kilo she was making $5000 profit clear, so half a million dollars on each consignment of 100 keys.

The man she worked for, 'Fabito', wasn't just anybody. Not only was he one of the five most powerful figures in the Medellín Cartel (alongside his two older brothers Jorge and Juan David, Pablo Escobar and José Gonzalo Rodríguez Gacha aka 'The Mexican') but Luis says Fabio and Bia were close.[68] They became even closer when Brian Livingston joined her client list out west, along with his business partner David Patten.[69]

At 28, Bia moved to Miami. Fabio Ochoa was living in Coral Gables in southern Miami and Bia began dating one of Ochoa's first cousins. When they broke up, she was introduced through another 'friend' to a fresh source of supply or 'SOS': Oscar Peláez Monsalve aka 'El Poli' (The Cop).

*

About 173 centimetres tall, light skinned, handsome, solid and muscular, with a broad nose, straight brown hair and deep-set, dark-green eyes like a clean-shaven Waylon Jennings, Poli was a mysterious cartel figure from Medellín who'd got his nickname in that city for a number of reasons: he'd actually been a policeman, killed a lot of people as a policeman, and, after retiring and joining the cartel in the mid-1970s, he killed even more people, including policemen. He and Bia began working together immediately.

'He called me "La Mona". I was Poli's distributor, not his friend. But with the Ochoas there was some friendship.'

Poli, like Pablo Escobar, wasn't a pure narco: he was a rarer breed of criminal: a *bandido*, a bandit or outlaw.

Says Luis: 'Pablo Escobar never said he was a *narcotraficante*: that's what TV said he was. Pablo always said, "*Soy un bandido*." And he *was* a true *bandido* in the good sense of the word: a very tough motherfucker. But Poli was a known *bandido* in Colombia before Pablo. Poli had a few years on him too. The attitude of a *bandido* is: "If it's out there and I want it – I'm *getting* it." These guys [like Pablo] were just playing at being narcos. If you aren't born a criminal, you're never going to become a criminal. You may do criminal activities, but deep down inside the real criminal's a criminal from the heart, not from his activities.

'A *bandido*'s a guy who'll kidnap you, kill you, *whatever*; he's just a badass. He doesn't need money to be a badass. He's a badass because he was *born* a badass. The people that were in the cocaine business back then were the lowest of the lowest of the lowest. You had to be a fucking criminal motherfucker to be in that business.'

And Poli more than made the grade as a fucking criminal motherfucker. Coming from a 'full-on Medellín' background – a broken home in a low-class *barrio* – Poli got into cocaine circa 1975/'76. When he first arrived in Miami in 1978 as an illegal immigrant off a boat from Bimini, he was doing piffling kilo deals with Cubans. Bimini, a chain of islands in the western Bahamas, was the cartel's favoured jumping-off point to Miami, because Colombians didn't need a visa for Panama, and from Panama they didn't need a visa to get to The Bahamas. It was also only 92 kilometres away from the United States: an easy trip for people smugglers.

'At that time in the late 1970s, cocaine still had not reached the elite American consumer. It was dog eat dog. Poli survived that business in Colombia, came to America, and started dealing with the Cubans. They'd try to rip him off and he'd kill them. He was not psychotic; he was just very determined and possessed a functional mind. He had very strict rules and you didn't cross the line on his rules.'

But after meeting Bia, he was selling 100 keys in California to Brian Livingston. It was a mutually beneficial arrangement. Poli supplied and protected Bia. She provided him with a client that couldn't get enough merchandise. He didn't need to be moving more. Poli's style was to keep a low profile, kill a few people, remain a *bandido* and stay under the radar, all while making serious money.

'He'd hit the fucking jackpot,' says Luis. 'Poli was just cruising. He was not giving coke to any Cubans. In Miami back then, there were a lot of ripoffs and piece-of-shit types willing to rip off anyone – even Poli – to make a fast buck. They'd be king for a week or a month at max. He didn't need to be dealing with Cubans in Miami, or Colombians for that matter.'

Bia was also the ideal middle person. For Poli, she meant 'less heat or no heat'.

'We were never close,' she says. 'Poli protected me because I made money for him. That's the biggest reason. My life was completely separated from [the cartel]. Poli was only a supplier, not a friend. He was a real gentleman to me. But he always protected me from everything; he didn't want heat on me.'

For an emotionless killer with an iron grip, Poli had a tremendous sense of humour and loved to laugh. Having grown up in Medellín, Bia had a tough personality and could fend for herself, but Poli wouldn't allow any harm to come to her and would kill anyone who tried. Even so, she knew the business relationship had its limits – and drawbacks.

'When people knew Bia was working with Poli, nobody wanted to work with her, because they knew they could have a problem with Poli,' says Luis. 'You didn't fuck with that guy. He was a different breed. His look and the way he carried himself just let you know that he was not a person to mess with.

'It was like that scene in *Hannibal* when Hannibal Lecter picks up the FBI agent Clarice Starling in that pig pen surrounded by those Italian man-eating hogs, and the hogs just back away from him. Poli had the same presence as Hannibal Lecter; he instilled fear. So Bia never went to work with him on a daily basis. She knew that with Poli you should hang out with him for maybe five minutes, ten minutes, then count your blessings that you didn't get fucking shot up while you were with him.'

14

Sucking Tit for Milk

THE END OF THE 1970S and the beginning of the '80s was the high point of the market price of coke in America, and nowhere more than California. The US–Mexico border had yet to open up to cocaine smuggling and allow the future Mexican cartels a direct pathway from Tijuana to Hollywood.

By the time Bia was selling to Brian Livingston, a consignment of 100 kilos was fetching over $60,000 a key. That in turn would be broken up into half-kilos and sent to other dealers in all corners of the United States – Nevada, Hawaii, Alaska – where it would be cut multiple times to amass enormous profits once it reached the street. As an example, a kilo that cost $3000 in Colombia could be worth $250,000 once it had been cut. For that $6.2 million of cocaine, Bia paid Poli the wholesale price of $55,000 a key. That worked out at $700,000 profit for Bia from just one plane trip.

Poli in turn was getting much of his coke at cost price of $45,000 plus freight from José Antonio Cabrera Sarmiento aka 'Pepe', a major mover of merchandise in Florida, as well as having Pepe bring in Poli's own merchandise at $2000 to $3000 a key plus freight. Pepe would routinely load up his Merlin with 500 keys and fly from Colombia to an airstrip in Okeechobee, a two-hour drive from Miami.[70] As a high-ranking member of the Medellín Cartel, Pepe was one of the richest cocaine smugglers of the era but, fatally for him, one of the most indiscreet. He wore a bracelet that had 'PEPE' spelled out in diamonds. He paid for Rolls-Royces and yachts in cash. This flashiness saw him come up on the radar of US law enforcement and he spent most of the early 1980s being arrested, skipping bail, indicted, on the run or in jail.

'Pepe was under the umbrella of Medellín,' says Luis. 'He had his own cooks in kitchens in Colombia where they produced the coke. He was 47 years old back then. Poli was in his 40s too. So both men had been around for a long time [in the business] and were independent branches of the cartel. Poli had his own tailor-made cocaine manufactured in Colombia and he would bring it in Pepe's plane. His stuff was marked "357" because of the .357 Magnum he carried.

'So if we sold 150 kilos, 75 was Pablo Escobar's, 50 was Pepe's and 25 was Poli's, because Pepe also transported for Pablo. When Poli hooked up with Brian, he was selling a lot of Pepe's merchandise. But Pepe's loads were usually around 500 to 700 keys because he had a Merlin and he'd come straight in. On those he was doing 250 to 300 for Pablo and 50 for Poli. Pepe would take Pablo's shit and give it to Pablo's own distributors in Miami and just charge them a transport fee.'[71]

One of the cartel's distributors was Griselda Blanco Restrepo aka 'La Madrina' (The Godmother), a sociopath made famous by various documentaries and films. She would eventually be gunned down outside a butcher shop in Medellín in 2012 after being deported from the United States.

'Griselda came from very low on the social totem pole. At the beginning she was a distribution/sales arm for Medellín; an important sales outlet. But I'm sure she brought in some units of her own on the trips they sent to Miami, and she had other ways of bringing her own merchandise through other contacts she had that had routes into the States. Not too many people had transport routes. The Medellín Cartel and the Cali Cartel had the routes [into the United States] and anybody else that had transport was transporting for them. The people that were running transport from the northern coast of Colombia were mostly doing it for Medellín. There were not too many independent *oficinas* at that time.

'Then as Griselda grew and the volume of sales grew, she started feeling she owned Miami and the people in Medellín started to cut her off. She created her own sales and distribution organisation here in the States. She was head of a complete organisation with sources of supply in Colombia. The money got to her head so she started problems with other groups and came into conflict with Pablo. Then she killed a cousin of the Ochoas: Marta Saldarriaga Ochoa. Griselda made a lot of money and when you invest your money in problems and in conflicts, your problems and your conflicts are as big as what you invested in them – if not bigger. She invested a lot in creating havoc and vendettas.

'In truth, she was built up to be more than what she was. Griselda was scared shitless of Poli and his group. She knew that before she was even born, Poli had already killed 22 people in Medellín, half of them cops. Griselda wanted no part of Poli. *Nobody* wanted any part of Poli. If he went right, she went left. It was like a contest between a fucking tiger and a tied-up donkey. She knew she was on the losing end of that one. She may have the most violent, the most psychopathic [of the narcos in Miami], but Poli had further reaches into old Medellín; deep, *dark* Medellín. She knew that no matter how many people she hired she could not get to Poli. But he could get to her. She respected him. They both came from Medellín, but he was already killing when she was sucking tit for milk.'

15

Blue Boxes

THE MEDELLÍN CARTEL IS thought of in the west as having always been under the centralised control of Pablo Escobar, but in reality it was a loose agglomeration of suppliers and transporters, all of whom were ferrying loads for each other to the United States.[72]

'It was a bunch of entrepreneurs *from* Medellín,' says Luis. 'The moneymakers in the Medellín Cartel were the Ochoa brothers, The Mexican, Fernando "El Negro" Galeano, Gerardo "Quico" Moncada, "Mono Abello" [José Rafael Abello Silva], Pepe Cabrera, Carlos Lehder, Pablo Correa, and the Pereira group, which was Octavio Piedrahíta – a transporter for Medellín who owned a football club in Pereira – Fernando "Marulo" Marulanda and "Mono Lopera" [José Vallejo Lopera]; I worked with all these guys. It was loosely knit but it was tight between Pablo, the Ochoas and The Mexican. The others were transporters or earners.'[73]

Escobar, as was his arrangement with Cabrera, would simply request a certain amount of weight be carried on routes to the US mainland. Escobar freighted his own coke on his own planes – the cartel was said to have as many as 55 planes at its disposal – but he also muscled in on other smugglers' routes and, if they didn't cooperate, he had them killed.

'If someone had a good route Pablo would go to them and say, "Take 200, 300, 500 kilos of my merchandise on your route."

You're not going to say no to Pablo. I was doing it with El Negro Galeano. He was my main contact and introduced to me by a friend of mine [from the cartel], Luis "Miki" Ramírez.'

Ramírez was an earner for the Medellín Cartel. He'd started out in the late 1970s/early '80s buying coke from Leticia, the southernmost city in Colombia and the capital of the department of Amazonas. He was also a close associate of Leticia cocaine heavy Evaristo Porras Ardila aka 'Papá Doc'.[74]

'Obviously part of that merchandise was Pablo's. When you got to be a certain size [as a trafficker], you got a phone call. Pablo was *Pablo*, don't take anything away from what he did. He was feared and he was a hell of a guy. But there were people that were there in Medellín before you even mentioned the Medellín Cartel.'

Like Bia's supplier, Poli. Says Luis: 'He was the only guy who ever defied Pablo.'

This was not an insignificant thing. The cartel's Jorge Ochoa once told PBS television program *Frontline*: 'You couldn't confront Pablo Escobar, because you knew what would happen: you would die.'[75]

'When the heat came down on Pablo, he called Poli to help him on a job,' explains Luis, who heard the story secondhand through an intermediary. 'This was later, in 1991. What I heard was Pablo wanted Poli to kill somebody for him and he had no reason to kill the man. Poli said, "No, you've got the wrong guy. I'm not for hire like that." Pablo started to get a little feisty and Poli said, "You know what? Let's end it right here. You take mine" – and he gave him his gun – "and I take yours and let's go for it. Right *now*." And Pablo says, "*No, no, no, no, no. Tranquilo*, settle down." So that was that. Pablo almost got offended but he still respected Poli.

'Now the way I see it is that Poli did that just to remind Pablo, "You can't have me kill for you with all your bodyguards and all your money. Remember who I am, because with me, it's one-on-one. If that's the way you want to go right now, that's the way it is with me. It's *you* and *me*. Forget about all these fucking bodyguards. For you to be at my level, it's got to be you and me if you want to do it like a man.

'Now if you want to do it like a fucking pussy or a chicken, then you can have your bodyguards kill me. But if you want to do it the way you know it's done, the way you know I've lived my life, then we're going to die under the rules of my life, which I know you understand is *our* life: the life of a *bandido*." Anybody else, Pablo would have fucking shot him right then and there. But he had too much respect for Poli. Being a *bandido* is a whole other culture.'[76]

*

The amount of money being made by the cartel was staggering. Production costs on a kilo of cocaine were minimal, about $1200 to buy 500 kilos of coca leaf from farmers in the Andes to turn into paste, then base, then refined cocaine or cocaine hydrochloride in its kitchens. In 1978/'79, a million or a million-and-a half pesos would buy you a kilo of pure cocaine in Colombia, around $3000. Getting it to the United States cost another $5000 per key. But once in Florida, it sold for upwards of $40,000, much more if you got it to New York, Los Angeles or San Francisco. By 1980, the price in Miami was $50,000 and each year it seemed to be getting higher. So there was astronomical profit to be made even before the cocaine was cut.

'Pablo Escobar, the Ochoas and The Mexican formed a group: The Mexican was the military arm of Pablo; Pablo with his cousin Gustavo controlled a lot of routes and under them were Pablo's partners Fernando Galeano and Gerardo Moncada; and then the Ochoas established the first distribution networks in the States. The first cocaine that arrived in Miami came wrapped in duct tape in the shape of soccer balls. If they were airdropped they'd be put in a plastic-type condom and also wrapped. Geometrically that's not the most efficient way to pack.

'The Ochoas came up with the idea to do boxes, which packed neater and maximised space on any plane or boat. So Pablo handled part of the organisation, the Ochoas handled the distribution, and The Mexican handled a lot of the kitchens and labs and the military part of it. And then they each *grew* themselves. The Mexican had clients, routes and suppliers of his own. Pablo also had suppliers and kitchens of his own, which he shared with the Ochoas and The Mexican, just like The Mexican shared his kitchens with Pablo. They were all interwebbed but they each had their own private routes that they didn't share with anybody.'

In 1984, after the cartel saw its processing plant in the jungle, Tranquilandia, burned to the ground in a Colombian Government raid, The Mexican started his own kitchens, making the purest cocaine available anywhere.

'The Mexican probably had more money than all of them at one given time. He was a fierce, *bad* motherfucker. He was worse than Pablo. He had very good cocaine. Each brand [of cocaine] belonged to a different group and these brands gained recognition because of how good they were. The Mexican had "Centavo" and "Reina"; those were marks of cocaine that hit the market. They were *fantastic*. So then [the cartel] all went under the Centavo brand. Of maybe 3000 kilos of Centavo, a thousand belonged to Pablo, a thousand belonged to The Mexican, and a thousand belonged to the Ochoas. The Medellín Cartel had the blue boxes, *las cajitas azules* – everybody wanted the blue boxes. In fact, blue boxes were so in demand other groups started to pack their merchandise in blue boxes. They were all having a great run and the market got flooded.

'Medellín wasn't the only cartel but it was the *major* cartel. The Cali Cartel was functioning but not as heavy as it did in the late '80s, early '90s. In the early '80s it was the Medellín Cartel, without a doubt. The Mexican was going to nail Cali. If they didn't shoot him first they had to bring in United States helicopters to get rid of him.[77]

'What made Pablo really wealthy was his association with the Ochoas, which opened up the cartel's distribution. You can't do everything yourself. The best example of a group that ran their business with administrative skills and business acumen are the Ochoas. They were the most level-headed and smartest. They didn't let the money go to their heads in a totally reckless way. They were able to make the money and keep it. Since Fabito had come to the United States and lived in Miami, he initiated the distribution inside the country and he had a lot of contacts for the sales. But then since everybody wanted cocaine, after a while *everybody* had cocaine contacts.'

16

Stalin in the Flesh

L UIS WAS IN WAY over his head surrounded by such hardcore criminals, but he didn't care. He was having the time of his life being Bia's live-in companion at Brickell Key while miraculously still holding down the insurance job.

When one day Poli brought 100 keys to Bia's apartment in a bunch of suitcases, he met Luis for the first time. They got on immediately, Poli enchanted by Luis's trustworthiness and sense of humour, Luis in awe of Poli's confidence and swagger.

'He was a very dangerous man. Poli wasn't serious; he was *very fucking dead serious*. I thought it was *fantastic*. Hang out with really cool people that have the power of life and death over other people? Make millions of dollars? Fucking pretty cool. I never got scared with Poli and killing people. Not that *I* killed people, but I knew that he did that. I didn't know exactly *when* he was killing people. It wasn't my call.

'I'm not going to kidnap kids but if we had to kidnap someone because he didn't pay, yeah. Poli killed people because they owed him money, because they did something wrong. He wasn't just randomly killing people like a psychopath. If you go to him, and you take five kilos from the man and you don't pay him, you know, you *should* be shot. You knew *exactly* what you were getting into.'

Not everyone in the cartel liked Luis, though. Bia had made an acquaintance called Joel (pronounced *ho-el*), yet another ex-cop from Medellín who was very close to Poli and also working for the cartel in Miami. Luis describes him as 'a volatile person, a wildcard, a wild, crazy sonofabitch. Those guys in Medellín were the scum of the earth – fucking killers. They'd whack people every day. They were from the low end of the totem pole and had risen on that totem pole by not being nice guys. At that level nice guys end up dead.'

Poli wanted Joel accompanying Bia on her trips out west and she wasn't happy about it, but they began travelling together by plane. Cocaine would be sent from Florida to California by car, and they would fly over to arrange sales and collect money. Joel was primarily there as 'protection'.

'I had seen Joel in some places in Medellín,' says Bia. 'We were not friends but he used to go sometimes to discos that we went to. It was a surprise to see him in Miami. I never knew his last name.'

Tensions boiled over on a selling trip to Los Angeles.

'They got to the LA Hilton one day,' says Luis. 'Joel was a good-looking guy, always well dressed, with expensive clothes, but he was rough around the edges and he spat on the rug of the hotel. Sometimes he was whacked out of his fucking brain [on cocaine]. But no matter how whacked Bia was, she never lost her cool. Bia got pissed and she told Poli and Joel got mad. One day [during the trip] Joel was high as a fucking kite and he left behind a fucking briefcase with $250,000 in the lobby. The bellhop had to retrieve the briefcase for them.

'So Bia had certain complaints against Joel: that he was a pain in the ass to travel with because he got a little drunk on the plane, sometimes a little obnoxious, a little loud. So Joel told Poli, "Why don't we whack Bia and we keep the client?" Poli said, "By no means." He told Bia, "You continue working with Brian and Joel will also work with Brian, but *separately*."'

What Luis wasn't to know was that when Bia had bought the life-insurance policy from him, she'd done it not just to help him out but because she actually believed she was going to get killed by Joel to take over her connections on the west coast. He found this out much later through Bia's brother, Arturo. In truth, the only thing truly stopping Joel killing Bia was Poli, who was even scarier than Joel – if that were possible.

'Joel was a very low-class person,' says Bia. 'He dressed sharply but he had no manners and I told Poli that I didn't want to travel with him anymore. Joel didn't like it but Poli told him if he did something to me he was a dead man, so I never heard from him again.'

*

The way Luis describes being with Bia, life – and Miami itself – opened up to him like a pop-up book.

'It was like a dream. Nothing in my life was mediocre. Suddenly everything's possible. You want a fucking house in Monaco? We can have a house in Monaco. Just got to do a couple of trips. Everything was possible. What made life difficult was no longer a problem, which was *money*. Money was never a problem. Anything you wanted, you bought. You never had to ask the price. When you don't have a budget, it's amazing. Gifts. Watches. Jewellery. Clothing. You hopped off the real world. Miami in the '70s and '80s was restaurants, nightclubs – Regine's, Ménage, The Mutiny, Alexandre, Faces in the Grove, Scaramouche, Cats, Ensign Bitters – champagne, cocaine, dancing, disco, *fucking*. It was like another planet. I hopped on this fucking spaceship and went to another planet.

'Miami was *crazy*. There was a side to Miami, the "cocaine cowboys" shit, and I was right in the middle of it and didn't even know it. I'd lived a very sheltered life. I didn't even know black people. I didn't even know Hialeah. I was hanging out on Key Biscayne with Key Rats [a term for people who grew up in Key Biscayne]. Then I met the most beautiful girl, the richest one, and the most dangerous guy. These guys, Poli and Joel, were real gangsters. Money's money whether you rob banks or hijack planes. It's your *business*. But Poli was worse than all of the other cocaine cowboys put together. Bia told me, "This guy has a reputation *from* Colombia."

'Poli wasn't just some fucking idiot that hopped on a boat and came to Miami and killed a couple of guys the other day because they stole a couple of kilos. No, this motherfucker had killed a lot of people *in* Colombia. He'd killed a lot of policemen because the most corrupt people in Medellín were the cops. He was feared *in* Colombia by the people that were feared *in* Colombia. So I knew that with Poli I was with, fuck, Stalin himself in the fucking flesh. And that gave me such a *feeling*.

'He was one hell of a fucking guy. Poli's word was his bond. You make a promise to God, and you fail it, lightning hits you. He was the cat's meow. He feared nobody. He'd pull out his gun and if you were quicker, all the power to you. If not, you were down. And he'd just leave you there like nothing had happened. He did not fool around. If you owed money 11 o'clock Tuesday and it didn't come around, he didn't give a flying fuck about the money. Poli always had money; he could take money from someone else. You can keep your fucking money. You're *dead*.'

17

Disco Champagne

L UIS HADN'T BEEN WITH Bia for long, just a matter of months, but his long-suffering parents had come to accept their long-haired, tearaway son was lost to the dark side. It was the early months of 1979 and there would be no salvation in the insurance job for Luis. Their attitude was to embrace him rather than disown him altogether.

'[*Sighs*] They kinda, you know, they kinda *suspected*. They knew something was going on. I wasn't doing a 9 to 5. But they felt it was better to keep me close than throw me out of their house. I was never a well-grounded person. I didn't ever have strong convictions: I want to study hard, I want to be a doctor because I plan to have a family and get married and I think by the time I'm 45 I should have my own practice and when I'm 60 I'm going to retire because I want to buy a yacht. *No*. I wasn't thinking about *tomorrow*.

'So they were worried, very worried, obviously. They didn't know the extent of it, by no means. Not even the fucking law knew what we were doing. So they knew I was being kept and that I was living with Bia. She helped disguise it a lot, put it that way. Nobody figured that Bia, a woman, could be a big-time cocaine dealer. She was just a rich girl from Aruba, and I was with her.'

The law, however, did catch up with Luis.

'I was in a black Porsche 911 SC Targa with a guy called Randall Ghotbi in a backstreet in Coconut Grove, going to Brickell to Bia's apartment.[78] We were partying in The Grove. Randall was from one of the richest Jewish families in Iran. The Shah had just been kicked out, the Ayatollah came in and the Ghotbi family came to Miami and to New York. They pulled $400 million out of Iran.

'Bia and Jorge Lopez were in one car, and Randall and I were in the other. And I get pulled over by the cops and we had, like, an ounce of coke on us. I gave it to Randall and he dumped it out his window. I got taken in for DUI. So Randall goes to Bia's and tells her and Jorge that I'm at the station, and that's when Bia opened up a briefcase with like $300,000 in it – bundles and bundles of hundreds in rubber bands – and sticks her hand in and gives Jorge a wad of cash, "Get him out." *Boom.* Jorge goes down to the station and bails me out, but then we have to go back to that area in The Grove to look for the ounce of coke. And we found it.'[79]

*

It wasn't long before Luis managed to fuck up a good thing with Bia because of his major weakness: women. Bia was out west in San Francisco and had left him the keys to her place at Brickell Key.

'She found out that I fucked this real-estate lady. I rented an apartment for Poli close by on 1450 South Bayshore Drive and Brickell, and I invited her to Bia's apartment and Poli was there. We were having a party, snorting coke and drinking, and Arturo Gálvez, Bia's brother, ratted on me: he told Bia that I was having a party at the apartment and fucking a girl. Bia dumped me.'

It was their first fight but Bia, to be fair, was entitled to feel aggrieved: Luis had had sex with another woman, his real-estate agent, in Bia's own apartment. They got back together briefly but the relationship was too high octane on a daily basis for it to survive long term.

'There was a lot of physical sexual attraction so that always kept things going. We argued over petty stuff but mostly we were just enjoying our partying together. We would go to dinner and drink and then come home and continue drinking and snorting and have great sex. Then the next day we would be hung over and then relax. It's not like life was hectic and we had a lot of things to do all the time.

We'd just wake up and do whatever we wanted. We were constantly shopping for her kids, who were living with their grandmother in Aruba. We were enjoying life all round and travelling to New York to San Francisco to LA to Aruba.'

Bia found another boyfriend, a cocaine trafficker from Santa Marta in northern Colombia, and ended up moving to Lake Tahoe, on the border of California and Nevada.[80]

'I always wanted to keep Luis out of all that, as well as doing drugs,' she says. 'Mostly it was a good relationship but I ended it because he drank too much. I loved Luis but I couldn't handle the trouble he created. My life and business were completely separate. There were too many dramas due to alcohol. I always had a soft spot for Luis in my heart, but couldn't accept the way he drank and got crazy. Then there were the incidents at Xenon in New York and Faces in Miami. He got kicked out from both clubs.'

For Luis, his nightclubbing life is all a bit of a blur. He went with Bia to the world-famous Studio 54 on West 54th Street in New York before it closed in 1980 but says, 'I got bored and I went to sleep in some bleachers they had upstairs. Everybody who ever went to Studio 54 makes a big deal out of it, but I really didn't see it as that big of a deal: it was just a disco like any other disco. Great music, lights flashing and weird people walking around. What I really wanted to do was fuck Bia in the balcony area and since Bia didn't want to fuck I decided to sleep. I think I'm the only guy that ever went to Studio 54 and took a nap.'

Luis can't recall what happened at Xenon (like Studio 54 a supertrendy nightclub but on West 43rd) yet remembers what happened at the private Faces in the Grove at Mayfair Mall, Coconut Grove, south of Downtown Miami.

'We got so whacked out on Dom Pérignon, well, I did, that I started dancing on the dancefloor, took off my shirt, start swinging my shirt. Then suddenly I go to our table, I take the fucking bottle out of the champagne bucket, put it on the table, and take that bucket in the middle of the dancefloor, and just go, *whhhaaa*, threw all that ice on the dancefloor and everybody starts to slip and fall. It was raining disco champagne.

'And they suddenly turn on the lights and the bouncers come in and they grabbed a friend of mine, Jaider Esparza, and they just picked him up and threw him against a brick wall [*laughs*] and he had nothing to do with it.[81] Bia and I slipped out like nothing.'

She was singularly unimpressed.

'I don't like that type of behaviour. I don't like scandals. That was the main reason our relationship ended. At Xenon Luis got kicked out for the same reason as Faces: he threw the champagne bucket with ice-cold water and ice to the dancers to cool them off. After I left him and he began to work with Poli, he began to do drugs.'[82]

'Two party animals cannot blame it on each other,' says Luis, trying to remain philosophical about a woman whose primal sexual fire haunted him for decades. 'Bia broke up with me because, for a person like me, it's not good to be with a person like her. For a person like Bia it's not good to be with a person like me. We just fed into each other's craziness. That's *reality*.

'So I moved out of Bia's, took a studio apartment at 2100 South Bayshore Drive and went to work with Poli. He was actually *with* me when I was fucking the real-estate lady. *He* wanted to fuck the real-estate lady. I said, "No, no, this is my girl." He said, "I want to tell you something. Friends are to keep. Girls are to share." The bodyguard who was there with us, he thought Poli was going to shoot me, because I had denied him the right to fuck this girl.'

It was the start of the best training Luis could ever get in the coke trade.

'I never changed as a person. I guess I was always amoral when it came to money. But I never thought about it. When I met Poli, if it would have been anyone less, maybe I wouldn't have gotten into the business. In a way I was enchanted by his sense of "strictness to a code" – *you don't pay you die*, for example.

'A life of extremely high danger among extremely dangerous people comes with some magnetism. I was romanced by the danger but not *part* of the danger. These people put me in a *trance*. And it was the basis for the 25 years that I was never scared and never thought I would get arrested. I thought that feeling was going to last forever.'

Bia's new boyfriend, meanwhile, got busy with a pair of scissors.

'The guy turned out to be complete fucking idiot,' sneers Luis. 'He was so jealous that he went through all Bia's photo albums and cut me out of every photo she had. Every picture of Bia and me together, he cut me out. You know how many girlfriends I've had in my life and they've had ex-boyfriends? You think I ever cut a girlfriend's ex-boyfriend out of a picture? What a fucking *asshole*.'

18

Drive, He Said

W ORKING FOR POLI AS a chauffeur was a straightforward job. He needed someone who spoke English, had a driver's licence, owned a car and 'didn't look like a lowlife thug'. But Luis's new boss wasn't Miss Daisy. If Poli ever got pulled over by the police, Luis explains, 'There would have been a shootout immediately. He wouldn't have handed over his licence. He would have given them a .357 fucking Magnum bullet in the head and driven away.'

It was a tense time to be a drug trafficker in Miami. At 2.30pm on 11 July 1979, two Colombian assassins in a 'war wagon', a Ford Econoline van with gunports, painted with the words 'HAPPY TIME COMPLETE PARTY SUPPLY' on the side and filled with weapons, bullet-proof vests and ammunition, pulled into the parking lot of Dadeland Mall in Kendall, in southern Miami, got out and coolly walked into Crown Liquors, where Luis and Bia used to 'buy two, three thousand dollars' worth of liquor for the apartment. Cases of Château Haut-Brion 1964; I mean, *unfuckingbelievable* wine.'[83]

They immediately opened fire with machine guns, killing Colombian fugitive Germán Jiménez Panesso, 37, and Dominican bodyguard Juan Carlos Hernández, 22. Morgan Perkins, 18, a store clerk caught in the crossfire who attempted to escape, was again shot in the car park while the gunmen were making their getaway. It was a bloodbath. Dade County assistant medical examiner Dr Charles

Diggs told *The Miami Herald*: 'I started counting bullet holes in one of them – and gave up.'[84]

Bia, knowing Luis was already becoming intoxicated by the business, had a word to Poli to protect her former boyfriend and not let him get killed.

'She asked Poli to take care of me. She felt, *fuck*, if I was going to be out there [in the coke business] it might as well be under the wing of a guy that's not going to let me get taken for a ride.'

So Luis, behind the wheel of a four-door silver Lincoln Continental, became a driver in a three-piece suit 'like an insurance salesman' with his New England Mutual card on him at all times. If he had to talk to the cops, 'I was an innocent-looking guy.' He remembers his first day.

'I picked up Poli from Charter Club [condominium] on Biscayne Bay, where he was living. He had just gotten up. He had showered, was in his boxers, and he had one of the girls putting talc on his feet, like a valet, helping him get dressed. He was very pampered. "La Rola" was his best friend; she was his confidante.[85] He trusted her with his life. But he had young girls with him all the time; they were sex companions.

'Poli would dress, like, *unbelievable*: a blue suit with an open silk shirt, a vest, and a fucking gold chain with a solid-gold jaguar with two emerald eyes. He'd wear one of those blue velvet hats; a Patek Philippe thin gold watch with a nice gold ring, a diamond pinkie ring. Almost dressed like a pimp. Not my style. You see this guy, you'd say, "What the fuck?"'

Each subsequent day followed a loose routine: Luis picked up Poli at 10am and they had a typical Colombian breakfast – a thin *arepa* (flatbread) spread with a little butter and a sprinkle of salt and accompanied by a drink of hot chocolate – in whatever apartment he was staying in.

Poli kept apartments in Charter Club, Key Biscayne and South Bayshore, alternating constantly for safety. He was well aware the heat was on him. Florida's biggest law-enforcement agency of the time, the Dade County Public Safety Department (later the Metro-Dade Police Department), had recently formed, albeit only to shut down four weeks later, an 18-man Special Homicide Investigation Team – the

'SHIT Squad' – to probe 24 drug-related homicides involving Latinos going back to November 1978.

A Latino policeman from the unit known only to Luis by the name Poli gave him – 'El Colorado' (The Red One or Red), for his red hair and Irish looks – was causing trouble and had raided one of Poli's apartments, hauling everyone inside for questioning down at the station – including Poli's children and the maid. It was all part of a Miami-wide police harassment policy, but Poli was apoplectic at this mortal affront to his dignity. It was now personal between him and El Colorado.

Armed with nothing but service-issue .38 calibre revolvers or .45 Colt semi-automatic pistols – unlike the movies, there were no long guns or shotguns stored under blankets in the trunks of their cars – Miami cops were poorly equipped for a war with Colombians toting machine guns, but all the more determined.

'I knew Poli had a battle with a Dade County cop called El Colorado. Colombians back then would hire lawyers after being arrested or taken in for questioning, but Poli never hired a lawyer after El Colorado hauled him in. He must have been so humiliated he ordered a hit on El Colorado instead. Poli moved every three months. He slept in one place one night, another place the next night.'

After breakfast, it was off to a meeting.

'Poli was never on time. If you told Poli, "Listen, we'll meet at McDonald's on 79th Street at 11 o'clock," he'd show up at one. It's because by being late for so many meetings he avoided getting killed so many times. He never hung out with a lot of bodyguards. He was very smart that way. He knew that alone he'd hide better and he'd keep a lower profile. He kept it "small" and that's part of the reason he never got killed in Miami. It was hard to find Poli.'

Lunch was usually at Mike Gordon's Seafood Restaurant, Joe's Stone Crab or The Forge 'and we'd spend $1000, $2000 like nothing', staying for hours and sometimes ordering four bottles of Château Lafite. Luis would have a couple of toots with his boss after lunch and they might go shopping.

'Poli would go into clothing stores and buy $8000 worth of clothes. He just said, "Drive," and I drove.'

When it was time to drop off Poli, they'd have dinner together and hang out a bit before Luis went home to sleep. He'd come by the next day and start all over again. When he wasn't chauffeuring Poli, he'd run errands.

'He once had me go to the airport to pick up some fucking duffel bags in a locker that were full of grenades and silencers and machine guns. So I went to the airport, looked around, made sure everything was good because I'm not a fucking idiot, I know it's not fucking Bibles, I opened up the locker, pulled out the duffel bags and here it is. There were no metal detectors. It was 1979. You could walk in an airport with a gun back then. I made sure nobody followed me on the way back. He said, "Did you look inside?" and I said, "No." And he asked me, "Didn't you wonder what I was sending you to pick up?" I said, "I don't wonder." My job was not to wonder. That was a big test.'

Other times Luis would work as a drug mule in tandem with Bia's brother Arturo and a third person (whoever was available) on cross-continental commercial flights. They'd take three kilos apiece when there were small quantities of merchandise to move out to Brian Livingston. There were no sniffer dogs to contend with. It wasn't the age of sophisticated airport security, even though a quarter of all seizures of cocaine were happening at Miami International Airport.

'California was the ticket. It was just as profitable as bringing it from Colombia to Florida. We would take keys on Eastern Airlines in suitcases and in hand luggage to Brian. Anything we got [from Poli], 12 kilos, 15, 20, 30, we'd send to California. If it were a low amount, he'd send me and Arturo and one more [mule], each of us with three, four kilos, on a plane, hand luggage, *boom*, nonstop to San Francisco, we'd give Brian 12 kilos.

'Arturo was white, a good-looking guy, *young*. Poli wouldn't put on a [South American] Indian-looking dude or nothing like that. We flew separately, Arturo and me, although the same flight, different tickets. On the plane we acted like we didn't know each other. I always dressed sharp, trying to look like an insurance guy. Coat and tie; I would use a blazer. You wear a blazer and people think you're an Ivy League guy. A blazer's the best disguise. You can do anything with a blazer. You wear khakis and a blazer and you can rob banks.

You don't even need a mask. They'll just look at the blazer. They don't look at your face. Blazers are amazing. If you ever want to do something criminal, wear a blazer.

'Back then you could just wrap the shit up, like if it was a Christmas present, in your carry-on bag and take three kilos and put it through the X-ray machine and you'd continue. We put it through the machine, and that's it. I was never afraid. Went to Miami airport, Eastern Airlines, hopped on a plane, put it through, *boom*, gave it to Brian, checked into a hotel, waited three, four, five days for him to pay us the money and we'd come back.

'While we were in San Francisco, we'd go to restaurants, party and wait. If I was nervous I wouldn't have done it. It was just the right time, the right place. If you did that five years later, you'd be fucking shitting in your pants. But back then nobody knew about this shit. One time coming back from San Francisco, I had $230,000 in a box that I checked in as hand luggage, and [airport security] looked at it, they put their hand in, they saw it was money and they let me go. It was another *time*.'

19

Ballad of a Well-Known Gun

LUIS WAS ALSO SAMPLING Poli's own product: by the key. After following such a set routine with his employer every day, he developed a coke habit of his own: sharing eight to ten grams a week between four to six people. This was not street cocaine; it was the best of the best in Colombia. He'd only been working as Poli's driver for a matter of months, but already made a few hundred thousand dollars.

'It was pure, it was there and it was part of our lives. We would never run out. It was just shit you took out of a kilo. Grab a bunch, put it on something, chop it up, *let's go*. It was part of our going-out routine, drink, next thing you know, you're doing a couple of bumps.[86] It was great for sex. You do lines when you buy shit off the street and it's so cut you gotta do a line. Poli would never, *ever* do a line. That's bullshit. That's shitty coke. We would *never* do lines. We were taking it right from the kilo.

'Poli would take it with his two fingers, go like that [*sniffs*], that's it. One in each nose [*sniffs twice*]; that was pure shit. You don't care if you drop some on your shirt. You just shake it off. Or if there was some shit on a table because we were partying, a little spoon or a little knife, and the tip of the knife [*sniffs*], that's it. I never saw anyone roll up a [dollar bill] and do a line. Fucking do a line of that shit and your fucking eyeballs would pop out.'

And even though he and Poli were around each other constantly, and came to consider each other as friends, Luis was made to never forget who he worked for.

'Sometimes he was tough with me. The day I dropped $100,000 playing poker with him, I told him, "I'll pay you this afternoon," and it was like three in the fucking morning when I said that. The afternoon was in what, like, *nine* hours? And sure enough, Poli didn't go to sleep. Enrique, his brother, came by my apartment that morning to tell me, "You'd better get your ass over there with 100 grand. Oscar hasn't gone to sleep. He's waiting for you. For him a gambling debt is more *sagrado*, sacred, than any kind of cocaine debt. He is fucking furious, Luis. If you don't get there this afternoon like you promised he's going to fucking kill you." And I go, "You're kidding me?" He said, "No, I'm not. That's why I'm here. Don't think I'm here because I want to be."

'When I got to the apartment, Poli was in bed; not sleeping, *sitting* in bed. I went to shake his hand, he didn't shake my hand, he just said, "Leave it there." It wasn't until the next day that he called me. But at the same time he trusted me with his life because I was the only guy who knew where he slept. I rented him his apartments. To people like Poli, when you lay your head on your pillow at night, nobody can know where you do that. Nobody can know where you sleep. Because then you really don't have a life. And they'll kill you while you're sleeping.'

*

When Poli felt like a change of scene, he and Luis would go to nightclubs, Poli bringing an arsenal of weapons with him in his Antioquian 'man bag', a *carriel*. But they never went to The Mutiny in Coconut Grove, Miami's most notorious nightclub, an annex of the hotel of the same name.

'Poli would stay away from those places. He was too hot. The Mutiny was not for him. Cops used to hang out there just to see who was there. He was way beyond all that. They were just a bunch of wannabes.'[87]

One night they went to the nightclub Alexandre at the Omni International Hotel on Biscayne Boulevard.[88] The Omni was where Pablo Escobar stayed when in Miami.

'Poli always had his *carriel* with his machine gun, his MAC-10 and his .357, but on the way out of the disco he gave me the *carriel* with the MAC-10, the .357 and a 9mm.[89] When he put it on my shoulder, my fucking shoulder almost fell off. We walked out of Alexandre, took a cab, like *nothing*. I was oblivious to it. I was so into the lore.'

Though Luis estimates Poli killed 'at least' eight people in Miami, he only saw him fire his gun once.

'A .357 will never fail you. It'll never jam. It's a revolver and it's got a bang and Poli was a great fucking shot. If he pulled his gun, somebody died. One morning, I picked him up at his apartment at like seven o'clock. Which was strange; he wasn't an early riser. He was *pissed*. He got in the back seat and says, "Let's go here," and we drove to Fontainebleau Park, these apartments in the west part of Miami. So we go up to the apartment and inside that apartment was Oscita, his son, and a kid called El Negro.'

*

In the mid-1970s Miami had been a pot-smuggling hub, but with the explosion of the cocaine trade and a resulting problem of oversupply there was reduced demand for marijuana by decade's end. Cubans controlled the distribution of coke in South Florida, routinely ripping off Colombians who supplied the product and cutting pure cocaine to be on-sold at massive markup to other cities around the United States. Fed up, the Medellín Cartel had started sending its own people to Miami to take over the entire business by force. Every day, assassins were being smuggled in by boat at $1500 a head. It was war.

'Cubans have an ego that's bigger than the Colombian ego and the thing is when you've got two egos like the Cuban ego and the Colombian *coastal* ego they're the same thing: they're two coastal peoples. But the Cuban ego came up against the Colombian–Medellín–Antioquian ego; and *paisas* are smart.[90] They don't just have an ego; they have an ego *and* a brain. That's why the Colombians had to send people over to Miami just to kill the Cubans. These were not mellow Cubans. They were hardass Cubans; as bad as the Colombians. But the Colombians always had the upper hand because they had the element of surprise. They bring in some guy from

Medellín nobody knows on a boat from Bimini, he whacks somebody, he goes back to Bimini. They don't live here, so they have the home-turf guerrilla advantage. That was why Poli had brought Oscita and El Negro from Bimini to kill somebody, a Cuban that owed Poli money from an old debt and that Poli had a war with, but the Cuban wasn't dead.'

Oscita and El Negro, only 17 or 18 years old, had already been in Miami for three or four days to carry out the hit but nothing had happened. Poli was furious.

'He thought he had given them clear instructions to go out and kill the Cuban. Then he starts to realise the reason these motherfuckers haven't gone out to kill this guy is they've started smoking base, *basuco*. He sees the towel on the back of the door, so the smoke doesn't go out. Poli was so pissed that he was *blinded* by how pissed he was. I'm just sitting on the sofa and I'm holding his *carriel*. He had a gun with a silencer, a MAC-10, the fucking thing with a couple of extra clips weighed 20 pounds. Suddenly he starts walking around, and he says, "*Loco* [*sniffs*], do you smell something?" I go, "No, no, I don't smell anything."[91] He starts walking around and he sees little drops of shit on the floor.

'And they opened the bathroom door. "We have a dog." They didn't want him to see the dog. And a puppy comes out. These guys were so based out they didn't bother to take the dog out to shit. Poli was so pissed, he said, "Fuck this," sat down right next to me, reached down into the *carriel* and went, *fttt fttt*, fucking killed the dog with a silencer. And that's when I said, "*Okaaay*, this is going to be a hell of a day." What a way to start. Basically Poli told those motherfuckers, "Listen, you pieces of shit, you either take care of this or I'm going to take care of it, and I suggest you take care of it." It got taken care of, because I never heard of it again. Oscita and El Negro went back to Bimini the same way they came in.'

*

At the end of 1979, Poli abruptly left Miami with the hit on El Colorado not executed. Luis had spent just three months driving for the taciturn Colombian but their time together left more of a lasting impact on his life than Miami University, Georgetown, FIU, or anything Luis's parents ever said to their son.

Rolling Stone that September had published a piece called 'The Cocaine Wars' by *Miami Herald* reporter and future bestselling writer Carl Hiaasen, about Dadeland and the battle between cops and cocaine cowboys in Miami. What had been a problem confined to Florida became an issue of national concern.

'I saw that article on top of the coffee table in Poli's apartment in South Bayshore Drive. It's not like Poli hung out at a bookstore. I was the only guy besides his sister and another family member that knew where he slept. I just walked in and they were packing a suitcase and I saw they were putting in a couple of .357 Magnums, Poli's weapon of choice. His sister Estella said, "Oscar's going back to Colombia, this whole thing's got too hot with El Colorado." He left Miami because of that article. He knew his time was limited if he stayed. He was as hot as a pistol when he left.'

PART 4
THE
NETWORK

20

Navia's 11

AFTER POLI WENT BACK TO COLOMBIA, Luis decided he'd had enough of driving cocaine cowboys to lunch and wanted to branch out into the business on his own. Bia had stopped selling to Brian Livingston after she met Manolo Varoni, so there was an opening to sell cocaine directly to Brian, with Enrique Peláez Monsalve, Poli's brother, coming in as his SOS, source of supply.

The San Francisco honeypot couldn't last forever, though, and Luis was smart enough to realise it. To get seriously rich and become a major player, what he needed to do was diversify his client base, broaden his supply chain and distance himself from the city's drug wars as much as possible.

If 1979 had been bad for drug violence in South Florida, 1980 was worse with the heightened tension created by street riots in Miami that May, then the 'Mariel Boatlift' from April to September when over 125,000 seagoing refugees from the port of Mariel west of Havana, including inmates from prisons and patients from mental hospitals, swamped the city.

Fidel Castro had allowed anyone who wanted to leave Cuba to reunite with their families in the United States and taken the opportunity to clear out Cuba's jails and asylums. A tent city sprung up under the I-95 overpass. Groups of *Marielitos* were joining the cocaine trade, buying weapons and causing mayhem. The crime rate in Miami went up 89 per cent, murders 20 per cent. A local TV station was broadcasting public-service announcements about what to do if you got caught in crossfire during a gun battle. At seafood restaurants down by the Miami River, DEA agents and dopers would often be sitting at adjoining tables, and if a load were successful the dopers would send over a celebratory bottle of Perrier-Jouët champagne to the agents. It was Little South America.[92]

'What really shook me up was when the Mariel Cubans came over in 1980,' says Luis. 'They were completely out of their minds. One of them, a debt collector, had the Grim Reaper tattooed on his chest and in Spanish it said: *Matar es mi vida. Muerte es mi destino.* Killing is my life. Death is my destiny. When he closed his eyes one eyelid had *te* and the other eyelid said *veo*: I see you.

'I wanted nothing to do with Miami. I was already going a lot to LA and avoiding Miami as much as possible. I knew how these Cubans were. I didn't want to sell cocaine to them. I was slowly transforming into Colombian. I was living with Colombians, my friends were Colombians, I was around Colombians on a daily basis. Bia never sold cocaine to any Cuban.

'There could have been good Cuban buyers in Miami, but I didn't know any of them. Anybody will knock anybody off, steal from you. The Colombians were suppliers; they weren't clients. I thought, "Why should I have to deal with Cubans when I have a decent American I'm dealing with in Brian Livingston?" I had a good thing going in San Francisco. These *Marielitos* in Miami weren't honest Cubans like my dad. They were fucking street guys who were out to cut your throat, steal your coke and let you get killed by the Colombians.'[93]

But to go national, he couldn't do it alone. So Luis started to build a handpicked team of suppliers, transporters and dealers to get the product into major cities across North America.

First, he began bringing in cocaine through new suppliers in Colombia. Second, he hired Bernardo Palomeque and Javier Mercado, two former *marimberos* (pot smugglers) from Cuba who were the antithesis of Mariel Cubans: they had a glamorous touring-car operation in Miami called B&J Racing. Bernardo and Javier, behind the wheels of Chevrolet Corvettes, Ford Mustangs, Chevrolet Camaros and Porsche 911 Carreras, had competed in high-performance races such as the Daytona 24-hour and Sebring 12-hour.[94] In turn, they sub-contracted their Colombian associate, Francisco Moya aka 'Juanchi', a fellow *marimbero* from Santa Marta.

Third, Luis employed a driver, Diego Forero, for transporting loads out west by road. Diego was Cuban-American but 'totally Americanised' and spoke impeccable English: a huge asset if he were ever stopped by highway patrol. Fourth and finally, he recruited Leif Bowden aka 'Arlo' in Santa Cruz, Terry Wozniak aka 'Landshark' in Los Angeles, Roger Lisko in Orlando and Brett Spiegel in Tucson as buyers, with additional sales connections in Boston and Minneapolis–Saint Paul.

It was like putting together a team of bank robbers for one last job, just like in the movies. Along with his existing client Brian Livingston in San Francisco, Navia's 11 effectively opened up Luis's cocaine to seven cities and five states and laid the foundations for what would become a small- to mid-scale 1980s cocaine empire.[95]

*

The Colombians that began supplying Luis were the most crucial part of his powerplay.

Octavio Piedrahíta, a transporter closely affiliated with the Medellín Cartel, would become best known as the owner of football clubs Deportivo Pereira (of the same city) and Medellín's Atlético Nacional. But secretly he ran a profitable cocaine route with an airline called *Transportes Aéreos Mercantiles Panamericanos* or TAMPA, a cargo carrier from Medellín.[96]

'The Piedrahítas had a lot of merchandise in Miami and their main distributor was their cousin, Elkin 'El Negro' Mesa.[97] They had thousands of kilos distributed in Miami and I was one of the guys that sold merchandise for them. Each group had a *recibidor*, somebody who received merchandise. The distributor for the wholesaler was called a *repartidor*. *Repartidores* were nobodies that they sent from Colombia to Miami. They received the merchandise and distributed it to whomever they were told to. They'd didn't make money off the sale. A lot of them took a monthly salary. They'd come to Miami, the cartel would rent them a house and they'd receive $10,000 a month. Sometimes when things were slow or delayed they didn't have much work but they'd still receive their monthly salary.

'The ones that got the salary were usually the *caleteros*; all they did was stay and "babysit" the merchandise at a *caleta* or stash house. They would come with their family and all and look normal. They'd just sit at home and watch TV. *Recibidores* had opportunities to make more money; the office would send some kilos in their name at cost, pay freight and sell through the office's distribution network.

'The Piedrahítas became big. Octavio had many brothers and they sometimes worked independently of Octavio. I worked a lot with Fernando who was partnered with the other brother Orlando. Fernando was stationed permanently in Miami – and he received merchandise from Octavio and Orlando who were on the production and shipping end in Colombia. But Octavio was the brother with the most merchandise and the wealthiest. As a family, they weren't exactly good-looking people. They were mixed: [South American] Indian and black. Octavio was the best looking of all of them, like an Indian with green eyes. They invited me to their home in Medellín. I met their mother and all the brothers and spent a couple days as their guest.

'Nevertheless Octavio started doing well for himself since he was running the TAMPA route plus other routes; he'd smuggle shit into the United States and made a lot of money really quickly. He was a very wealthy guy in Medellín. His brothers had their own access to cocaine in Medellín and sometimes they used Octavio's transport and sometimes they used other people's transport.

'Sometimes Octavio was in good with Pablo Escobar, sometimes he wasn't. I think Pablo kidnapped him once and it was like a joke in Medellín that every time Pablo needed a little extra money, he would kidnap Octavio – until he finally killed him. I don't know if it was over a mess they got involved in or just for the hell of it. I guess Octavio was getting too big for his britches; acting too much like a big shot. He was flashy. A big gold chain and a Mercedes, all that shit.'

Luis's other SOS were two upper-middle-class Medellín families he met through Bia, relatives of the Ochoas of the Medellín Cartel. Their coke came branded as 'MM' (for Medellín and Miami).

For security reasons they cannot be named, as they are alive and well in Colombia and not known drug traffickers.

'They all knew I had contact with Bia's main connection, Brian. But they did not want to supply me while Poli was supplying me. They were very cautious. They came from a high status – not the "elite" Medellín class at the time, but they had *class* status. Poli on the other hand came from the most dangerous and violent neighbourhood of Medellín – either *barrio* Antioquia [Trinidad] or Guayaquil, which are both very tough places. So they didn't want to be anywhere close to what they knew was a very dangerous situation. They knew that any conflict or discrepancy with Poli, the outcome was death. It was as simple as that. So after Poli left Miami they started to supply me. For a while one of these Medellín families was my main supplier.'

*

By the end of 1980, Luis was about to make his first million but had the humility to realise none of it could have happened without Poli and Bia.

'I kind of expanded really quickly. I built up a sales network, quite a business, in a short period of time. When people realised that I had been Poli's chauffeur, driven him, sold his coke, moved coke for him with Brian, lived with him, been his trusted confidant who was with him every day, the offers came flying from the Ochoa brothers, the Piedrahítas, *everybody*. But we got more merchandise from Fernando and Octavio Piedrahíta than we did from the Ochoas' relatives and Poli's brother Enrique put together.

'Poli was so feared that when he went back to Colombia and I was a free agent, they figured I must be a good guy to work with if I'd survived working with him; for them it was a hell of a resumé or a great credential. They really believed in me. They knew I came from class and wasn't some rat right off the street, and they respected that I grew up with that code of honour that I learned from Poli. I worked with Poli all that time and there was never a penny missing. If there would have been any missing, I wouldn't be alive to tell the story.

'It all went back to Poli. They really respected that. That opened big doors and then people started giving me a lot of merchandise.

Nobody would dare approach me when I was with Poli; to them, they thought Poli may take it as, "Oh, you're trying to steal my client." That's the last thing any of these motherfuckers wanted to happen: Poli thinking they're stealing the client. They didn't want to have any issues with Poli, or *potential* issues. With Poli, any sort of problem, certainly you were going to get whacked. So people didn't exactly want to get whacked that much; they kinda stayed away.'

Cocaine, ultimately, was no different to any other franchise.

'I realised this business was great. I liked it. I was constantly moving merchandise. I wasted no time. I was moving anywhere between 100 to 200 kilos a month, which is a lot, and the business was growing. I started taking from Enrique, the Piedrahítas and the Ochoa relatives. They knew that I would sell 100 kilos for Poli so they started offering me 100, 200, 300 kilos. That's when I started to develop Landshark and the other guys. With all that merchandise I started giving some to Brian, some to Arlo, some to Landshark, some to Roger and some to Brett. You build up a client base. That's my entrepreneurship. I build you up. I make you competitive in your market with good price and good quality. I was receiving cocaine fucking *pure*. I only ever cut it once. I cut 80 kilos and I made 100. And I never did it again.'

Luis could have been forgiven if he had; there was so much money to be made. By 1979 the wholesale price of coke was $51,000 and, through 1980 and coming into 1981, Luis was selling a key for $58–60K to Brian and $57–58K to Arlo and Landshark. A kilo sold for about $55K in Miami. A typical key might then be cut into three lots by a buyer and resold for significant profit.

'Being a narco was a business to me. I wasn't a killer, I wasn't a bad guy; I was a businessman. Everybody gets into the business to make money. Nobody gets into the business to kill people. What happens is the business changes them and they become killers. What kept me alive was my ability to turn a profit for everyone. It wasn't a gun in my pocket, it wasn't that I had 50 armed guys, it wasn't that I was a badass motherfucking killer; it was my ability to get shit from point A to point B.

'I stayed true to the essence of the business, which was making a buck. Everybody veers off. Because they make a buck, they buy fucking weapons, they hire bodyguards and they go crazy and they kill people. If you stay true to the business, it's to make a buck. It's not to kill nobody.'

*

But, still, he also had to know when to turn on the gangster persona.

Terry Wozniak was a blond, blue-eyed, very good-looking Canadian from a wealthy background who had gone to the prestigious St. Andrews College in Aurora, Ontario. He had got the nickname Landshark for his acumen as a smooth-talking salesman and hustler. Before he met Luis, he'd been a nobody out on Key Biscayne buying from small-fry suppliers who simply didn't have what he wanted: 30 or 40 kilos to sell out west. He kept badgering Luis to let him have some of his coke and Luis was becoming irritated.

'Okay. Listen, motherfucker. What is it you can do?'

'I can sell it in California, Luis.'

'I'll start you out with a kilo. But, let me just tell you, if you lose it you're gonna die. You better come back with the money, otherwise you're going to have a serious problem. That's who we work with. We are fucking *killer* Colombians. I'm not going to kill you, I don't believe in that. But I do believe in it if you steal. So I won't be doing any killing but you will be killed. They will kill your family up in Toronto. I'll take a chance on you. It's up to you. You either sell and live or steal and die.'

'Yeah, sure, no problem, Luis.'

It was the start of a beautiful business relationship. Landshark would buy hundreds of kilos every few months.

'He kept up his end of the bargain and really expanded sales. He was pumping out some serious weight for a while there. Then he decided to retire and go to Costa Rica and married an Eastern Airlines stewardess that used to take kilos out west. In the cocaine business you've got to kill. It's the only way. If people are bad, if people think they can take you for a million dollars and live, they'll take you for a million dollars. A million is a very powerful incentive. And if people think they can get away with it, they'll do it. In that business you've got to kill them.

99

'Landshark ended up owing me $300,000. So in the end he did fuck me but I had made so much money by then it didn't matter. If I can absorb the loss and it's my money, no one gets killed. But when it's the Colombians' money, they will kill you. You pay for it with your life. You crossed their line, not mine.'

21

Dirty Work

IN NOVEMBER 1980, JOEL, who had stayed in America to keep selling Poli's product to Brian Livingston, was killed in San Francisco by a gang of Peruvians. There are no known newspaper records of what happened, but according to Luis the Peruvian group had tried to muscle in by selling to Brian and there was a confrontation, which ended up with Joel dead.

Furious, Poli brought in a new enforcer for his precious cocaine pipeline: Evangelista 'Mario' Navas Villabona, a Colombian from Bucaramanga who had been paroled from an Oklahoma federal prison the previous month on a marijuana- and cocaine-trafficking conviction and issued with a deportation order back to Colombia, which somehow he'd managed to skip. He was in his late 20s, tall, dark, skinny, moustachioed, reasonably good looking, and dressed flashily in gabardine pants and silk shirts.

'Mario came to whack the Peruvians. Dangerous guy. He'd put one right between your eyes, no problem, real quick. He just showed up one day as Joel's replacement. Joel had been very close to Poli; there was no way Poli and Mario were not going to avenge Joel's death. Take *vengarse* – revenge.'

The problem for Luis having such a hothead in his midst was protecting his own access to the prize client they were sharing. Mario had taken over from Joel in handling Poli's product in California; but with Poli back in Colombia and not overseeing day-to-day operations, what was stopping Mario taking out Luis and keeping Brian all for himself? It was a volatile situation with potentially fatal consequences. Luis instinctively knew he was dealing with a cold-blooded killer who would murder him without a second's thought for exclusive access.

'Poli shared the goose that laid the golden eggs with his brother and myself. But with Mario coming in, it could've been a situation where greed and the sheer amount of money being made could have caused me trouble. I don't know if deep down Mario was happy, but he was totally comfortable with killing people and had no doubts at all when it came to having to eliminate somebody. But I felt safe somewhat because Poli simply would not have allowed anything to happen to me.'

Even more uncomfortably, Mario had moved into the same apartment complex at Venetian Islands in Miami where Luis was then living and wanted Luis to vacate.[98]

'He said, "You're heating up *my* building. I want you out of here as soon as possible. We both can't live in the same building."'

What saved Luis was the same thing that saved him every time: his fast-talking. Even when Mario decided Luis owed him $400,000 for no reason, he found a way to sidestep certain death.

'Mario said I owed him $400,000 because I took one load out [to San Francisco] and I gave Brian 100 kilos and I gave it to him at 58 [thousand] a key and Mario was selling it to him at 62. And because of me he had to lower his price to 58 and it cost him $400,000.'

Cocaine-dealer math is not like any other math. A meeting to iron things out was arranged one night at Luis's apartment.

'We started to drink and snort. I had a kilo at the apartment. We were listening to The Police album *Reggatta de Blanc* over and over again and snorting coke. And that's when we started getting sentimental. I said, "*Wait*, you know, Mario, I've always respected you and Poli a lot, you know, and I know how much you love guns.' And I had just been in San Francisco and had bought this fucking antique gun. I don't how much it cost me. I don't know if it was $5000, $7000, $10,000, but the fucking gun cost me some money. And I thought, "*Shit*, I'm going to make up with Mario. This whole thing with the $400,000." Usually when you owed Mario $400,000 you died rather quickly. With me, it was different. He let it ride. Mario liked me. I was no threat to him. I was a cleancut kid.

'So I gave him the gun. We were all coked up and everything. When he opened the fucking case, he went, "*Woooow*. You're incredible. I knew you were a good man. You've become a real friend." But, you know, when somebody gives you a gun you gotta give 'em one in return; it's just the karma. So Mario reaches in his back and he pulls out his 9mm Browning, 14-shot, he kept it locked and loaded, and he gives it to me and I didn't know what to do with it. So I put it in the closet. And then he says, "Hey, but this doesn't mean you don't owe me the 400; you still owe me the 400, but we're a little better now."'

The next day the gun went off.

'Sure enough, I went into the closet, *boom*, the fucking thing misfired. That's the real reason why I left the fucking apartment. I didn't know where that bullet went; probably through a dry wall into somebody else's apartment. You could trace the bullet to that gun that killed I don't know how many people. For sure it killed more than one.

'When I next met up with Mario, a few days later, he asked where I had been. He hadn't seen my car around the building for a few days. I said, "Don't you remember? You *asked* me to leave. Out of respect for you I left." I think that impressed him. He was never to know I'd really left because of the missing bullet.'

*

As long as Luis didn't step on Mario's toes, selling cocaine out west was a straightforward process. It was so easy, on one occasion a female friend of his did a mule run on a private Learjet from Miami to Seal Beach, northern California. She and her male companion pretended to be newlyweds with coke stuffed in their suitcases. They had confetti and champagne aboard the private plane to give the impression they were on their honeymoon – the works. Luis was a man for fine details, which is probably why he lasted so long in the drug-trafficking business.

'When I was in California I worked at maintaining a look, a *stature*. I always went to Wilkes Bashford, which was a very high-end men's clothing store, and that's where I bought all my Brioni suits. I met Sharon Chase there, a fashion designer. She was friends with Gordon Getty and Danielle Steel. She knew all the top chefs: Jeremiah Tower, Alice Waters.

'We used to go out to all the best restaurants; the greatest restaurants in America were in San Francisco. Back then was when the California *nouvelle cuisine* was taking off. Sharon gave me a lot of legitimacy, being with her. Hotel suites, the opera, champagne at all times, a Cadillac limousine with a chauffeur – over the top. We were a great couple. When I went to LA I would stay for a month at the Beverly Hills Hotel and take a bungalow in the back, take two bungalows; one of my guys would take one, I would take another and our bills there were $30,000, $40,000 a month, like easy.

'What saved me was my low profile; I look innocent. There's a guy I knew, Joey Ippolito aka "Joey Ipp", who later sold coke to O.J. Simpson.[99] But he wasn't doing it like I was. Joey was taking 50 kilos, selling it out west, with O.J. Simpson, the Playboy Mansion and James Caan. He was in a limelight situation. That's not what you're supposed to do when you're dealing dope. You're supposed to keep a low profile.

'I never hung out with those crowds that I knew would only bring heat. My double life was being a criminal, an outlaw, and not trying to get captured. I could not bring heat to myself by hanging out with O.J. Simpson and James Caan and being the guy that sold them coke. Are you kidding? How long was that going to last? It's like asking to be arrested. I would never do it like that; being out there in society and everybody knows I'm an Italian guy in the dope business like Joey Ipp.'

*

The real dirty work was being done getting the coke from Miami to point A (Jacksonville) to point B (Santa Monica) and driving back again: the Interstate I-10 corridor from northern Florida to California, a punishing round-trip of almost 8000 kilometres. Through a mechanic called Helios, who was married to Enrique's and Poli's sister Catalina, Luis had a two-passenger Ford pick-up truck customised with a hidden compartment for his Cuban-American driver, Diego Forero. A 'fucking beauty', it was designed to hold 400 keys but usually stored 220 to 250 for better concealment.[100] It had a flatbed in the back with a raised floor or false double-bottom.

'Helios was good at working with metals and was a welder and had once mentioned to Poli to buy a small welding shop in Hialeah so they could make silencers. The truck had a motorcycle in the back, always kind of dirty and full of mud so it looked as if Diego was doing motocross circuit, going cross-country with his motorcycle.'

Diego would pick up the merchandise in a designated parking lot. The Colombians would leave behind a car containing the coke, which Diego would then drive to another location, where he would switch once again (with the coke) into another car.[101] He'd then drive to his vegetation-shrouded home in Coconut Grove to a covered garage and unpack the merchandise during the night. There the truck would be loaded up for the big journey.

'He'd always have some girl go with him. He had a girlfriend called "Red" and she was a big girl. Not a pretty girl but not ugly. She was a hairdresser. Diego was a really stupid-looking, withdrawn, reserved, laidback and not very talkative guy – definitely had a peculiar way about him. Tall – not fat or muscular. Just long limbs and on the thin side. He didn't look like a cocaine transporter. You would never think he was involved in anything illegal. He was the perfect man for the job and the stash was so well made, if anyone grabbed it they would have to bring the dogs because you couldn't figure it out.[102]

'The I-10 went from northern Florida and cut through Alabama, Louisiana, Texas, New Mexico and Arizona into California. Diego used that road when he delivered to Landshark in LA. Diego delivered a few times to Brett in Tucson, but a lot of times Brett would come up to LA and pick up his stuff. Brett had a big farm in Georgia and sent some of his people down to Miami a few times to pick up and take back to Georgia. He had a distribution ring going all the way up to the Carolinas. Roger would also come down to Miami from Orlando with his own people. He was very careful and we would give it to him here and he would handle taking it back up north.

'When Diego was taking merchandise to Brian he'd take a more northern route, going up to St. Louis [Missouri] and cutting across west. Most smugglers from Florida took the easy route, which was the I-10, but that became very hot and it also became hot for bringing money back.

'The northern route put us right into the Santa Cruz area where we had Arlo, and a lot of times we would divide the merchandise between Arlo and Brian. Sometimes we took a trip specifically for Brian or sometimes we took a trip specifically for Arlo, but those were the two main clients I had out there: both big players, each moving 100 keys a month. At $60,000 a key, it was a lot back then. A large shipment of coke from Colombia was 500 keys. It wasn't like now when they're bringing up 20,000 keys at a time.'

*

Getting coke out west was a cinch. It was bringing the money back east that was proving tricky.

'Diego was stopped on his way back from California, somewhere in Alabama or Louisiana, and the local sheriffs confiscated $160,000, and it was *my* money. In reality, it was a ripoff scheme because all he got was a citation that such and such police station is holding $160,000 and he has 90 days to claim it, and if he doesn't it will be forfeited. I'm sure that piece of paper never got officially filed anywhere and the cops kept the money. They confiscated millions of dollars that way and kept it for themselves. They would just keep the form in their top drawer; nobody ever came back to claim the money when it was drug money, so the confiscation was never really recorded – it never existed. But that was typical. The sheriffs in that area knew that a lot of vehicles passing through were coming back with money from California to Miami.

'Last time I transported money back myself, I had bought a 1981 Mercedes 300 TD in Miami, brand new, yellowish beige colour. I loaded it up with about 90 kilos and Diego drove it out west to give to Brian. I had about $6.2 million that I had to bring back to Miami. And I loaded it all up in that fucking Mercedes, in the trunk, it was about five or six suitcases, small ones, big ones, with some idiot named Coca Bear from Miami, and I said, "Fuck, me having to drive with this fucking idiot and this money," but I didn't want to drive alone and

I had nobody else, and Diego had already driven the coke out west and he wasn't available.'

Coca Bear was a large-framed, buck-toothed, mixed-race Cuban dealer from Little Havana in Miami. He spoke loudly, was easily agitated, and had a heavy coke habit: hardly the ideal driving companion. Kind of like a stoned, strung-out version of the John Candy character in *Planes, Trains and Automobiles*.

'So I hopped in the car with Coca Bear, who was a complete jerk-off – we barely spoke – and leaving San Francisco on the way to Reno I almost drove off the fucking mountainside. I'm not the best driver in the world. Scared the shit out of that motherfucker [*laughs*]. Dumb sonofabitch fucking turned white. So he says, "I'll drive from now on."

'We went to St. Louis and then made it back to Miami. There was so much money being accumulated out west from my sales that I said to the Piedrahíta brothers, "I can't be transporting that money back to Miami anymore. I'm not going to do this anymore with Learjets, either. You need to set up a banker out west to take my money from now on. From then on, the money we made from sales was always laundered in LA.'

Many years later Luis discovered that the dopey Coca Bear – in cahoots with a dealer accomplice in Miami – had been planning to kill him sometime during the trip so he could steal the $6.2 million in the trunk.

'It was only when they found out some of the money was headed for the Piedrahítas that they decided to abort.'

22

Dead-Shark Eyes

HE MIGHT HAVE BEEN getting richer, but the more coke Luis handled, the more he was putting up his own nose.[103] He had given up on Santana albums and recreational pot and was bingeing on his own merchandise. Doing cocaine 'was just part of my life'. He liked to play tennis when not on drug business and was partying heavily two or three times a week with his usual trinity of stimulants: blow, alcohol and hookers. He was already a multimillionaire, both through illegal means and legitimate business, and living it up.

With the help of his father and in partnership with Bia's cousin, Ernesto Gálvez, Luis had started a trading company/sugar-packing operation, Caribe Packing, in Aruba. Luis Sr had long ago cashed out of his Glades County and Moore Haven sugar interests and diversified into shipping companies Ship Operators of Florida and Florida Lines, registering ships in The Bahamas and Mexico. Lobo-Kane Inc., a New Jersey-registered company with links to Luis Sr's old friend Julio Lobo, had the licence to use the Hershey name in the Caribbean. In partnership with Caribe, Lobo-Kane's Hershey sugar was shipped from New Jersey to Aruba. Ernesto would distribute the sugar in Curaçao supermarkets and other stores throughout the Caribbean.

Caribe Packing was a chance for Luis to go straight and his father was right behind him, all the way. It was the only reason he got involved.

'He wanted me to be more conservative with my money, be more disciplined, not party so much, and the whole Aruba sugar thing was set up for me to expand on it. He really enjoyed Aruba; he loved the place. But it's like that old saying: You can lead a dog to water but you cannot make him drink.'

*

The real truth, kept from his father out of shame, was that Luis was a functioning drug addict who had graduated from snorting coke to smoking it with a beautiful neighbour from Key Biscayne: Katie Brooklyn, a willowy, slightly drugged-out 22-year-old brunette with a Mia Farrow–style *Rosemary's Baby* pixie cut.[104] Luis's driver Diego introduced them, much to Diego's dismay when the two instantly hooked up.

'Diego was kind of a hanger-on, my wingman is some ways,' says Katie. 'But he was the one who connected us. Luis was somebody I'd been aware of because he was a Key Rat, so I knew the name "Luis Navia". We grew up on the island together. Diego was also from Key Biscayne but he was different to Luis: there was a tenseness underneath; anger boiling under the surface. He liked being around all that stuff; the danger. Diego came from a good family. He liked to have pretty girls around him and everybody liked him, because he was a nice guy; he was funny, he was always very free with his cocaine. But I think he was extremely jealous and resentful of people like Luis, who were the real deal and got all the babes.'

Which was easy, with his endless supply of coke.

'Luis and I had a great time together. I loved that life. It was limousines. It was just like being rock stars but it was all drugs [*laughs*] and a lot more money. Most of our time was spent partying, going places. It really was like the Wild West in Miami: shootouts in the streets. Every day you would hear about mass murders; it was really nuts. The streets were just clogged with these bright red Porsche Carreras with these big fins on their back and [on the water] there were the giant cigarette boats. All these dealers didn't care who knew who they were. Nobody hid their money. They flaunted it and bought these really expensive things. It was a crazy time. We even bought a horse called Rocky.'

Luis laughs at the memory: 'We bought a fucking saddle that was worth more than the horse. We paid $7000 for the horse and $15,000 for the saddle. And the riding boots from Hermès, this and that. And then we forgot we owned the horse, we were so based out, we didn't pay the bills for the hay for the horse. The bill for the hay was $4000. They repossessed the horse.'

In return for all of Luis's largesse, Katie taught her boyfriend how to smoke freebase or, in their case, high-class crack.[105]

'Luis would boil some water, get a test tube, put some coke in it to heat up in the water, making sure to turn it frequently, and once the coke was melted he'd add baking soda. The coke then turns into rocks. You put it on a plate, stick it in a water pipe, take a suck, and smoke accumulates.

'Oh, my God,' recalls Luis. 'Your heart feels like it's going to fucking pump right out of your chest and your mind goes like a slingshot to the fucking *moon*. The feeling of euphoria is just *booooooosh*. Then that's the feeling you continue trying to chase the whole night; you'll never get that same feel from the second one. But you keep basing and it does a number on your head. When you're young and basing, sex is fucking pretty wild too. It's degenerate. You come up with all kinds of weird shit. I never got into homosexualism [sic], but we would always have lesbians, two or three women, shows and stuff like that. You sit there for a while and then you just talk shit for hours. You're solving the world's problems. High, fucking, talking about sentimental shit, the world, *anything*, you name it you'll talk about it.'

By mid-1982, Luis was freebasing 'all the fucking time' with Katie.

'We would go two, three days staying up, smoking the stuff; that's what it does to you,' remembers Katie. 'One time at Luis's apartment, his mom turned up and saw us totally strung out and started screaming at me, calling me a *puta*. Really, *really* embarrassing. His mother was shrieking at me, "You come from such a good family, what are you doing?" She knew my dad and my mom.'

Luis was also experimenting with a variation of freebase, what Colombians called *basuco*. You take some coke, put it in a sock or coffee filter, put acetone in it, heat it up with a blow dryer, and what's left is base cocaine. You mix it with tobacco out of a cigarette, light it, it melts a bit, and you take a hit.[106]

'When I was with the hookers and the girls, it was mostly cocaine. It was with Brian that we would smoke freebase in a glass pipe. Base was nasty. Brian was completely hooked on base.[107] When he was on base he could hardly talk; his eyes were just wide open, kinda paranoid. Mario loved *basuco*. Poli would usually do a snort but he would also do some *basuco*.

'When you start on that shit, you do not stop. I can tell you that when I smoked base you hallucinate, without a doubt. It gets to a point where you start hearing things, you start seeing things, you get super-paranoid, especially since you're already in a paranoid state because of what you do for a living. One time I was out in California, north of San Francisco, at Diego's house and we're smoking base and he took a machine gun with a silencer and just fired right into the fucking bushes. There was a forest behind the house. He was convinced there were people out there coming to kill us.

'Another time Brian had a house on a golf course and it was made of wood with a wooden, steel-type roof. A fucking golf ball hit the roof of the house. *Fuck*. It's a miracle we didn't die of a stroke. We used to take turns peeking through the blinds.'

*

Katie had started freebasing in 1980, well before Luis, and was making it with baking soda. By 1982 she admits she had a 'very big addiction problem'.

'I really knew how to do it. When I had access to cocaine that's how I wanted to do it; I didn't want to snort it. When you could freebase it, why would you want to snort it? So much better. *Oh, my God*. It's like your brain gets hit with a freight train. It just is so powerful. That's why people love crack. It's the same thing. It's a really great high; I don't recommend trying it [*laughs*].'

And even though everybody was getting wasted, Mario and Enrique decided that she was a bad influence on Luis because she'd taught him how to smoke freebase. It was okay for them to do base, just not Luis's girlfriends. They gave her an ultimatum.

'One day they told her she can't go out with me anymore. That if she does, they're going to kill her.'

She didn't think twice: 'Luis and I were never real serious. It was all drugs, really. We hung out maybe close to a year, then the Colombians kinda freaked out because Luis didn't do base prior to me and now he was doing all the product and not being as reliable. I had to get out of the relationship or be killed. It was in this really nice apartment out on Key Biscayne. I had been partying with Luis and Mario and a bunch of other guys came in. They were like shadows. The feeling that came off of them was so negative and dark and scary. They had dead-shark eyes. Black, bottomless eyes like sharks.

'I hate to say this, but they all look the same, the Colombians: real dark. Black eyes, black hair, dark skin. I didn't really want to look at them long enough to really take in who I was looking at, because I intuitively knew that this stuff I should not be observing; that these guys could kill me. They didn't care. They would kill people without even thinking about it. It was *zero* respect for human life. You just didn't want to meet their eyes. Plus, being a good-looking American girl, I didn't want to give the wrong impression. I was just real cautious with them. I did not like them.

'The atmosphere in the room changed when they came in. If you're in the water, a dark ocean, and suddenly a giant shark went by you, and you feel the cold current – that's how I felt with these people. They took a look around and they pulled Luis into this other room and left the door open. They're talking in Spanish and English and I heard Mario tell him, "If you don't break up with her or get rid of her, we will. You can't do this."

'Mario was nuts. *Scary, scary, scary.* When you're on coke you're a bit paranoid, right? Hearing that and feeling that, and I really do feel I could have been killed that day because these guys were crazy, I left. I needed to get out of there. If I hadn't, the guy was so unstable he might have just shot me or killed me right there. They were very, *very* bad people.

'I had no shoes on. My heart was racing through my chest and I was all the way on the east side of Key Biscayne and my family's house was on the west side, so I was walking across the island which is a couple of miles, and the sun was out, and after being up for days on cocaine and just that feeling of incredible humiliation and abject terror that they were going to come after me and I was going to be killed, it was horrifying.

'For days afterwards I was afraid one night somebody was going to come through the window and just quietly slit my throat because I knew too much or whatever. I was very scared. And then I couldn't get in touch with Luis. He had stopped taking my calls. And I now know it was to protect me. He needed to totally end all contact with me or they would have come after me. Luis is very spacey and stuff but he's a really good guy. Everybody loves Luis.'

As for Luis, he was told in no uncertain terms: *This shit is over. Pack a bag. You're out of here.*

'And they took me and sent me off to San Francisco, to the Miyako Hotel, a Japanese hotel.[108] Enrique came with me. He respected my father and did not want to see him suffer watching his son's life flushed down the toilet. The place had paper sliding doors, wooden floors, Japanese food. Back then it was very unknown. A small but very cool place. All the rooms had saunas. So these motherfuckers stuck me in a sauna for a month and dried me out till I didn't want to smoke base no more. There were no withdrawal symptoms; maybe there was an urge to go out and have some drinks because that's what initiates everything with me. Never in my life did I do coke if it wasn't after three or four drinks. Same with freebase: it's drinks, coke and hookers, in that order. They cleaned me up and Katie and I never saw each other again.'

She completely quit cocaine one day in 1986.

'The night before, I was smoking freebase with a guy and clearly heard a voice saying, "One more hit and you are dead." I stood up and walked out of that house right then and there, even though there was still quite a bit of cocaine left. That voice, which I now think was God, of course, terrified me. I went into rehab that morning. Later I found out that the guy I was smoking with died that night of an overdose.'

23

Night Train

M EANWHILE, MARIO WAS BUSILY preparing to assassinate the Peruvians. Luis's $400,000 debt hadn't been paid. He was still happily going out to San Francisco, safe in the belief he didn't owe Mario anything. Or so he thought. His new *lavador* or money launderer in LA, a Colombian called Vicente Blanco who had become a close friend, freaked when he found out.

'Are you fucking nuts, Luis?'

'He's my friend. Nothing's going to happen.'

'*No*, man. With a guy like that you don't even argue.'

Vicente gave Luis the money for the debt immediately.

'I mean, I would have paid Mario eventually, but time went by and I always told him, "It's not like I owe you 400. You didn't *make* 400; it doesn't mean I *owe* you 400." That went on for a while. If it weren't because he liked me, he would have killed me.'

*

Luis got a call to go a stash house in Kendall and pick up 180 keys of cocaine from the Piedrahítas. 'El Tigre', a Piedrahíta family member, was taking care of the merchandise. When he arrived with Diego, they found a room with no furniture and a bedroom. Inside were 80 kilos marked with one brand, 100 kilos marked with another, and about 300 more kilos also marked differently. It was a sizeable lode of coke.

'And I said to myself, "*Whoaah*, this is fucked up." I'm a good guy but, fuck, I know where all this merchandise is. I could pick up my 180 kilos and talk to a fucking *bandido* and tell him, "Hey, I know a house where there's 500, 600 kilos, go hit it." Sure enough, a few days later, El Tigre was found dead in that house and they stole the merchandise.'

Mario was called to 'clean up the body, clean up the mess and make sure that El Tigre's body went back to Colombia for the funeral'. He was also paid $250,000 to 'recoup the merchandise', which meant killing the people who killed El Tigre and getting a percentage of the value of the missing cocaine. Mario had already taken care of the Peruvians. Nine dead bodies in San Francisco and LA. All dispatched while he was as high as a kite.

'It's not a lightweight job there. Well, fuck, you know, the Peruvians shouldn't have killed Joel. Why the fuck would you want to kill Joel? And you think you're going to *live*? Humans are fucking stupid. I know Mario killed the Peruvians. I remember we had to go get him out of a fucking motel room where he was holed up with hookers and he was beating them up.

'Here's Mario, all fucking strung out, based out, with no shirt, in the room. I walk in, he's got a fucking gun strapped on to his hand with duct tape and smoking with the other, and a couple of hookers are all banged up. Somebody got the call, I think it was Diego, to go get him some more shit because they were running out of it, and when Diego walks in there he sees a whole scene with Mario having beat up the hookers. He comes back to me and Brian and tells us, "This guy's fucking out of control. The cops are gonna come down on that place. We gotta get him out of there. This guy's gonna burn us to hell."

'Mario wouldn't allow anyone to go in there except me, because he didn't feel threatened by me. So I had to bring him some more shit, some fucking liquor, started drinking with him and gave him some Valium to calm his ass down. He paid off the hookers, let them go and I just sat there and talked with Mario for seven hours till it got darker and he calmed down completely and went to sleep.'

*

In March 1982, Luis invited Mario over for an early Easter ham dinner at his parents' place. It was awkward. To say his guest was a little rough around the edges was an understatement. Being a Colombian too in Miami at this time carried something of a stigma in certain social circles, so Luis introduced Mario to Luis Sr and María as 'a friend of mine from Venezuela'.

Mario was emotional at how he was being treated. Used to being seen as an outcast, it meant a lot to him to be accepted by a family from a different socioeconomic background to his own.

'I can't believe you invite me to dinner, Luis,' he said quietly, turning to him while they were seated next to each other at the table. 'You don't judge people by who they are. We're friends. Equals.'

Luis was just 27 and a millionaire five times over when his father died that September. A pimple had come out on his nose that turned cancerous and it spread quickly to his lungs and pancreas. He died 17 days later. Luis Sr refused care. He went quickly. Luis went to the hospital every day while he was sick but wasn't there when he died. He was selling a car and collecting some money – just going about his normal everyday business – which he regrets to this day.

'The only two friends of mine from the cocaine business that ever met my dad were Mario, Poli's brother Enrique and Fernando Piedrahíta. Enrique and Fernando were both ushers at my father's funeral and helped to carry the casket. My relationship with my dad was always good; not super-affectionate, but he was a good man. He went the way he wanted to – *quickly*. He never needed any taking care of. I couldn't see my dad any other way.

'My dad was always working; my mother also believed that money is the solution to all things in life. My mother was very materialistic. I was not brought up correctly; I was not *led* to bad things but I was not straightened out. You put braces on people to straighten out their teeth. They should have applied heavy braces on me – and they didn't. So yeah, I regret not being there when he died, but that was me being very immature. I've been badly structured, badly trained. I was let loose to do whatever I wanted. But I'm not the kind to blame my parents. It is what it is.

'I lived in a society that was *super*-superficial; money was everything to the people on Key Biscayne. We grew up thinking money was *everything*. I saw nothing morally wrong with smuggling. A lost kid anywhere can be snatched up by anybody. You can lose your son or daughter if they're not well structured and a little weak. Nowadays with drugs, you start out doing a little drinking, going to South Beach, a couple of discos, you get in with the wrong crowd and you're *gone*. That's what happened to me.

'You've got to be totally out of your mind to be thinking like I was thinking at the time. My priorities were messed up. Where's this person going with all this? I was never grounded, and I think that's what shocked my dad. But then, what was he going to do? There was no stopping me. I was buying Ferraris, Porsches, running with major, *major* motherfuckers that disrupted society, killed cops, killed people. But I should have just forgotten about everything else and just been concentrating on my dad.'

I feel for the first time in our conversations that Luis, the tough-guy narco, is showing me a side of his personality he rarely shows anyone. He's truly opening up. I want to push him more. So I put it to him directly: Your father was such a strong figure in your life but in a sense I'd argue you betrayed his values by entering a life of crime.

'Without a doubt. And I completely tarnished the last name. It was a complete fuck-up.'

Luis pauses. There's a real note of emotion in his voice.

'I don't think about it, because if I thought about it I'd be so guilty that I wouldn't be able to function.'

Laura, whose manner in person is strikingly different to Luis – calm, measured, discreet – doesn't quite buy her brother's account of his parents not having straightened him out properly: 'Luis was very rebellious and overall he had a good relationship with our parents; he loved them very much. But Luis was his mother's favourite. She would protect him on many occasions and help him hide the truth from my father. My father was always very frustrated with Luis. He squandered so many opportunities that were given to him because he wanted to party. My father was an earnest, respectable and honourable man. Luis was the complete opposite in terms of temperament.'

*

At 10.40pm on Thursday, 7 October 1982, in Jacksonville 555 kilometres north of Miami, Mario boarded the *Silver Star*, the Amtrak No. 82 service to New York City, under a false name, armed with a Browning semiautomatic and a MAC-10, and holding $5000 in cash. With him were his 24-year-old sister, María Isabel Navas Villabona Ramírez, and his sister's two children, nine-month old Juan Fernando Ramírez and three-year-old Zuli Ramírez. They had a six-by-ten-foot first-class sleeping compartment and Mario went to sleep in the top bunk.

Before dawn the next morning the train was just outside Raleigh, North Carolina. The compartment was dark, the blinds were closed, but Mario was hallucinating on cocaine, possibly after smoking base. He thought he saw hands under the blinds. He was hearing voices. He was startled by some coloured lights. An argument broke out between him and María. In his own mind, he saw the compartment door open and twice opened fire at the door with the machine gun, thinking he was under attack. The conductor called ahead for police and, after stopping in Raleigh and evacuating the other passengers, the carriage was detached by Amtrak employees from the rest of the *Silver Star*, which eventually went on to Manhattan.

For the next three days Mario, firing his weapons periodically and unpredictably for no apparent reason, was at the centre of the biggest siege outside a prison in American history up to that date: with Raleigh police officers, snipers, news crews, Special Weapons and Tactics (SWAT) teams, firefighters, emergency personnel, county sheriffs, highway patrolmen, state investigators and two dozen FBI agents, including Frederick Lanceley, who taught the hostage-negotiation course at the FBI Academy in Quantico, Virginia, all massed outside.

Agents Gary Noesner and Spanish-speaking Raymundo Arras from the FBI Crisis Negotiation Unit, communicating through a speaker that was installed outside the door of the carriage, had offered Mario food and water but got no response. It was stiflingly hot during the day, freezing cold at night. Mario, naked or dressed only in shorts, either remained silent or was cursing to himself. He was suicidal. When he did talk, amid the crying of Zuli, he gave his name as 'Mario Rodríguez'.

Attempts to get intravenous fluids into the carriage via a tube passed through a bullet hole in the compartment door failed, because it wouldn't fit through the exit cavity. When food and water finally got to the hostages it was too late to save the baby boy, who died on the Sunday after two days without water. María had been shot in the forehead above the left eye on the Friday by her completely based-out brother. Her putrefying corpse smelled so bad it was attracting flies.

The stand-off ended close to dawn on Monday, when not long after midnight Mario passed Zuli out the window to agent Arras after 33 hours of negotiation in Spanish. After consulting with the man he called his *padrino* (godfather), New York attorney Paul Warburgh, who was speaking to him through a bullhorn, Mario surrendered. He emerged at 5.45am from the train dressed in a black leather jacket, maroon satin shirt and blue jeans.

'My understanding was that he started smoking base sometime after the train left Miami, and by the time they were in North Carolina he was whacked out of his mind,' says Luis.[109] 'Base makes you very paranoid when doing too much of it. You start to hallucinate – especially when you live a life where you have cause to be paranoid, like Mario's. Base puts you in a very dangerous state. At first it's euphoric, then it gets weird, and you don't stop until there is no more – and when there is no more you've got to knock yourself out with booze and Valium. At least that's what I did. If not, the withdrawal is nasty. Mario was a casualty of addiction while Joel was a casualty of war.'

Mario, then 29, was charged with two counts of first-degree murder and one of kidnapping. At trial, in 1984, it emerged he had been to jail in October 1974 and was convicted for trafficking under the name 'Mario Navas' in New York in July 1976.[110] The defence in the Amtrak case claimed Mario was an insane schizophrenic but it wasn't accepted and he was sentenced to life, convicted for first-degree murder of baby Juan and involuntary manslaughter of his sister. The prosecutor, District Attorney J. Randolph Riley, had sought the death penalty. When the jury foreman announced he'd been found guilty, Mario blew them a kiss.

In prison, fellow inmates would taunt Mario by mimicking the sound of a steam train.

*

Luis was talking on a payphone in San Francisco to his mother back in Miami.

'She'd told me to open up a newspaper, so I went to a newsstand. Mario's picture was on there. He had half his body hanging out of a window with a machine gun in his hand or something.

'"Hey, isn't that the guy you invited to dinner?"

'I was freaking the fuck out. I was thinking this could be a major problem here. I didn't make a big deal out of it.

'"No, Mom. He looks like him. My friend's Venezuelan and the newspaper says this guy was *Colombian*. *No, no, no*. That's not the same guy."

'"Oh, *okaaay*."'

PART 5
WILD WEST

24

Santa Marta Gold

IN OCTOBER 1982, FOLLOWING Luis Sr's death, Laura Navia, 24, married her brother's *lavador* Vicente Blanco, 40, in a small wedding in Panama City. Luis had introduced the pair to each other over dinner in Miami and they'd fallen in love. The newlyweds went to live in a penthouse in a 20-storey luxury apartment building in Santa Marta on La Costa Caribe, the Caribbean coast in Colombia's north. That Christmas, they invited Luis and his grieving mother, María, to stay for the holidays.

A picturesque but sprawling historic city of half a million people in the tropical banana-growing department of Magdalena, Santa Marta has five beautiful aquamarine bays, boasts scores of white-sand beaches, and is hemmed in by the snow-capped Sierra Nevada de Santa Marta, all of which makes it a popular place for tourists. It's also a major hub for drug trafficking and has been since the 1970s, being situated smack-bang in South America's most storied region for high-quality marijuana cultivation.

Coming not long after the death of Luis Sr, Christmas and the New Year should have been an opportunity for the Navias as a family to come together, pause and reflect on the passing of the great man. But Luis had his mind elsewhere.

Caribe Packing, a company that had started off as 'a clean, small deal', would after Luis Sr's death and Luis's buying out of the partners, be used as a front for cocaine trafficking to the US Virgin Islands and Puerto Rico. Luis would bring in refined sugar from Colombia, pack it, export it to the rest of the Caribbean under the Hershey brand and 'put some merchandise inside the sugar' that went to Saint Thomas (in the Virgin Islands) and Puerto Rico.

'Caribe had *been* legitimate. We bought used packing equipment from the Lobo-Kane operation in Pompano Beach, Florida, and set it up in Aruba. The plan was never to transport coke. I never did anything criminal with sugar while my dad was alive. Lobo-Kane was no longer involved. I only did it once or twice, then I got really scared. It wasn't much because I was trying it out. We only did one shipment to Puerto Rico.

'I was gone a lot. I was living in San Francisco most of the time, LA. I thought I had God by the beard. I thought I had hit the jackpot and was on my way to becoming an international fucking millionaire entrepreneur, and I was completely mistaken. But I was making money. I had some nice cars and I lived in nice places and I travelled.'

He was also eyeing an altogether different deal, the first and only pot smuggle of his career: 35,000 pounds or 17.5 tons of 'Santa Marta Gold', the best dope in the world, for which he stumped up $150,000 to Javier Mercado as starter capital for the purchase of the weed in Colombia and to organise transportation to the United States.

Javier and his American partner, Bernardo Palomeque, had already pulled off their first coke smuggle from Santa Marta for Luis: 160 keys purchased direct from the Medellín Cartel's Miki Ramírez, a close confidant of Pablo Escobar and Fernando Galeano.[111] Javier and Bernardo, sailing from Miami, picked up the load on a Defender boat called the *Happy Hooker* off Santa Marta, then came back through The Bahamas and into Miami, mooring it at the marina of the Rusty Pelican restaurant, right at the entrance of Key Biscayne, which overlooks the Miami skyline. It was hardly the world's most incognito smuggle but this was the early '80s.

Their Colombian liaison, Francisco Moya aka Juanchi, had taken six to eight months to deliver the merchandise from Miki Ramírez, and in the end it had been more hassle than it was worth, but it was a momentous event: Luis's first independent smuggle into the United States. This time Juanchi was promising a quicker turnaround.

As a *marimbero*, pot was his bread and butter and he had connections to the Dávila family, arguably the most successful and powerful marijuana traffickers in northern Colombia.[112] A steel-hulled 100-foot fishing trawler called *Cristal* was ready to go with an Ecuadorian captain who'd been paid $35,000, while Javier's crew in Miami was all set to receive the goods 200 miles off the coast of southern Georgia, north of Florida. They'd pay the balance. For $10-a-pound cost price, the pot would sell wholesale in America for $200 a pound, so 35,000 pounds would bring in $7 million minus $2.5 million for expenses: a $4.5 million profit.

'I had never done pot [as a smuggle] before in my life,' says Luis. 'My end of the deal was I put up the money to buy the pot, to come up with the expense money to get the show going. The pot was going to cost about $350,000, but $150,000 would get us going and do the trip.'

Finding the cash wasn't a problem. Luis had millions stashed away in safety deposit boxes in Aruba and Miami, half a million secreted in the attic of his dead father's house, another half a million packed in a mid-sized Zero Halliburton suitcase in a spare bedroom, more in small fire-resistant safes, and $250,000 on his person as play money. He was so flush he bought an apartment in Grove Isle for $250,000 in cash, with everything in it, sight unseen, when an indicted neighbour needed to get out of town quickly. But he had an important caveat stumping up the money for Juanchi.

'I actually wanna *see* the shit. I've never seen pot like that. I want to go.'

Juanchi and Javier thought he was crazy, but they acquiesced and Luis, dressed in blue jeans and a double-pocket khaki shirt with Lucchese cowboy boots, was picked up in Santa Marta by two or three of Juanchi's sidekicks to be driven to the jungle. Leaving Santa Marta, they travelled 100 kilometres south to the town of Fundación and then wound 165 kilometres east to just south of the city of Valledupar.

'It was no man's land. We were far in the middle of fucking nowhere is where we were. They didn't know where the fuck they were going.'

From there they were close to Venezuela and the Sierra de Perijá. When the road stopped they switched from the car to mules, getting higher and higher into the mountains, crossing rivers in areas controlled by groups affiliated with *Fuerzas Armadas Revolucionarias de Colombia – Ejército del Pueblo* or Revolutionary Armed Forces of Colombia – People's Army, better known as FARC. Inevitably, they were ambushed and held for ransom.

*

To give some historical context, there is an importance difference between the Colombian guerrillas, probably the best-known guerrilla group in the West being FARC, and the Colombian paramilitaries or *paras*.

'The guerrillas are left wing, "We're doing it for the liberation of the people," which is a fucking bunch of bullshit because they've murdered innocent people. The paramilitaries are right wing, *against* the guerrillas. It was Carlos Castaño Gil who started the paramilitaries when the guerrillas killed the Castaño brothers' dad.[113] The victims are the innocent *campesinos*, the peasants of the countryside. The guerrillas go into their town and they've got to feed the guerrillas. And then the guerrillas leave and the paramilitaries come in and they find out that they fed the guerrillas, so they kill them for feeding the guerrillas. They're both complete, total pieces of shit. But the group that kidnapped me never identified themselves as FARC.

'In Colombia there was a time called *la época de la violencia* or *La Violencia*, which was the conservatives against the liberals, and it was nasty. There were a lot of killings.[114] So Colombia has a long history of political killings. And from that era the guerrillas were born. They wanted a government free of the grip of the oligarchs, established families and right-wing money people.'

And in the process of loosening that grip, they opened up huge swathes of Colombia to cocaine production: land that the national government in Bogotá simply had no control over.

'For 50 years Colombia has been plagued by FARC and other guerrilla groups kidnapping politicians and businessmen and killing people. The major cocaine cartel in Colombia is FARC; they sell to *everybody*. They have a huge presence in Peru and Ecuador; they supply the cartels. They've been working directly with the Mexicans for years now. Ecuador is *flooded* with guerrilla cocaine. When I lived in Colombia I could never go from Bogotá to Santa Marta by car, because in the middle you'd get stopped by the guerrillas and kidnapped or killed.

'Then the paramilitaries with their drug money created armed militias and each one of those groups had 6000 men armed to the teeth, controlling certain areas. The paramilitaries claimed that they were never involved in drug dealing, but they were exporting tremendous amounts of product out of the Urabá area. If you think I've exported shit, they've exported 30,000 times more than me: millions of kilos. They've killed *thousands* of people.

'During the time of Andrés Pastrana Arango, the worst president Colombia ever had, he gave FARC an area of about 42,000 square kilometres, like the size of Switzerland, a no-conflict zone; it was a peace territory.[115] And all FARC did was set up cocaine labs and produce cocaine that supplied them for the next fucking 20 years. It was one big fucking cocaine lab.

'FARC supposedly disassembled but they just franchised their cocaine-growing areas and their labs through smaller criminal groups. They didn't reintegrate into society.[116] South America is still fucking the Wild West. Nobody's done a Netflix series on the Colombian guerrillas. They're the major suppliers of cocaine to the world.'

*

Luis handed over $20,000 in cash – it was all he had – but realised he could make a deal with the *comandante*, whose name was Camilo.

'One thing I clearly remember is that the people I was with told me that theirs was a non-violent group, so it was probably a mellow offshoot of FARC. I got in survival mode and said, "Let's make something good out of something bad." If I had just frozen up and melted down, they would have buried me out there. I said, "*Comandante*, we're here to buy pot. I don't need to buy it from them. I can buy it from you. We can all make money here."'

'Okay, let's talk,' Camilo replied. 'How much are you looking for.'

'Thirty-five thousand pounds.'

'By all means.'

The contract was thus sealed verbally and Luis and Juanchi's men were released.

'When I got back to Santa Marta, I told Juanchi and Javier, "The good news is I'm back. The bad news is we're not buying your pot. We're buying the pot from the guerrillas." I traded in my cowboy boots for some rubber boots the *comandante* had. That sealed the deal. I came down with red eye from being up there in the fucking jungle.'

The smuggle went ahead as planned, the boat being loaded up at night, and there was an entourage of a dozen people in three boats who wanted to be there when it happened on the water, including the owners of the load and their assistants. But Luis was told not to come due to a problem he had with a swollen knee, an injury from skiing and tennis. Juanchi thought it best he stay behind and manage the radio in Juanchi's apartment with Juanchi's wife. For him, it was another fortunate twist of fate.

'When they were loading in the ship at night in Bahía de Cinto, Juanchi went to the onload of the merchandise. A bunch of my friends went in three open fishermen to help. Santa Marta has five bays but there are very rough, ragged, sharp rocks at the point of each bay; it's surrounded by rocks. It was too rough, the waves hit. So two or three of the boats tipped.

'Everybody was in the water. One of the boats sank. The smart people were the ones who stayed in the middle and didn't try to go into land, because the waves were so rough that you would get banged up against the rocks. There's huge fish in there; not so many sharks, but huge groupers, and a lot of these people when they got cut up by the rocks obviously got eaten by the fish.[117] Five people died that night.'

The *Cristal* carrying the 35,000 pounds of marijuana managed to make it out of Bahía de Cinto and sailed north to the Windward Passage between northwest Haiti and eastern Cuba to The Bahamas, but the USCG cutter *Dauntless* intercepted the load east of The Bahamas and impounded the dope.

The fact the load never got to the drop-off point in the ocean off Georgia didn't matter to the guerillas. A deal was a deal. A furious Juanchi was forced to hand over to the guerrillas the $150,000 Luis had originally given him and come up with the $200,000 balance. It had been an expensive disaster.

'That's when I decided to continue doing only coke. It was too risky to send boats loaded with pot; they were too slow. It was better just to airdrop 500 kilos of coke and be done with it.'

25

The Spaghetti Incident

S URPRISINGLY IT WASN'T THROUGH the two impeccably lineaged
Medellín families connected to the Ochoas that Luis got the
biggest break of his fledgling drug-trafficking career. Rather it came
through their practically unknown narco associate Camilo Zapata
aka 'El Halcón' (The Hawk), an independent operator who was using
the smaller Pereira Cartel, a syndicate based in the city of Pereira,
west of Bogotá, as his SOS.[118]

It was through Halcón that Luis was introduced to Pereira duo
José Vallejo Lopera aka 'El Mono' or 'Mono Lopera' and Fernando
Marulanda aka 'Màrulo', as well as the unaffiliated Alberto Barrera
aka 'Paco', a transporter who was sourcing a lot of his coke from the
Medellín Cartel.[119]

Halcón, Mono, Marulo and Paco were not household names in the
drug business in Colombia, but they were all major players inside or
intimately connected to Medellín, the crucible of the cocaine industry,
all four men having squared away tens of millions of dollars, if not
hundreds of millions, in Swiss bank accounts. Working with Bia and
Poli, Luis had been a couple of degrees removed from the top players
in the cocaine trade. He'd got a degree closer with the Piedrahítas
and the two Medellín families, who'd started supplying him while
Luis was still in Miami. But now he was dealing directly with cartel
heavies on their home turf on a first-name basis.

The South Florida Drug Task Force, an interagency initiative set up in 1982 by President Ronald Reagan and helmed by Vice President George H.W. Bush, had been tremendously successful, at least initially, in stopping loads from Colombia, and practically shut down The Bahamas and the rest of the Caribbean as a viable route into Florida. In just over a year, cocaine seizures went up 54 per cent, some eight-and-a-half tons being interdicted.

Much of that was down to an expansive radar system – radar balloons, mobile radar on USCS boats and planes, military radar including airborne early warning and control system (AWAC) aircraft, conventional aviation radar – but it was not foolproof: low-flying small planes and small boats could still evade detection.[120] The states further west along the Gulf of Mexico (Alabama, Mississippi, Louisiana, Texas) and unradared Mexico, not yet a narco state but ripe for exploitation with its corrupt police force and military, seemed like a much better back door into the United States, so the cartels were ideally looking for a transporter who could get their merchandise over the gulf and across the 3145-kilometre US–Mexico border with a minimum of fuss, loss and wastage.

Luis was their man. But formalising business deals with the cartels often required lunch dates and one such occasion required Luis to come to a ranch or *finca* outside Pereira. When he got there, the unnamed cartel boss, a large man dressed in an untucked polo shirt, was serving spaghetti with tomato sauce; not slow-cooked tomato sauce but the bottled commercial variety. It was just Luis, the cartel boss and a couple of his henchmen.

'Spaghetti and a bottle of fucking ketchup: Colombian ketchup. I was shocked but *fine*. We're eating; we finish lunch. Then he taps me on the shoulder, "Hey, I want you to come look at something." So we went out to a shelter with metal roofing behind the dining room. They'd park tractors there, farming equipment. And I see a guy being held down on a concrete floor by two or three guys. His legs were tied. One guy was holding his legs, one guy on each arm and shoulder, and one guy pouring water on his face. He was being waterboarded. I go, "What the fuck is going on here? What did he do? Did he steal a thousand kilos?" and he goes, "*No, no, no.* He stole beef.

He's a cattle thief." Stealing cows was a serious business in Colombia back then. In the Wild West, if you stole cattle they'd shoot you or hang you on the spot. In Colombia I was in the Wild West. I was back in 1865 USA.'

The cartel boss took Luis aside to explain why the cattle thief was being tortured. A young man in his mid-30s, he'd claimed he'd been stealing cows for a restaurant that was owned by one of the cartel boss's friends. But when he brought this friend to meet the cattle thief, the cattle thief was asked to identify him and couldn't. He got caught in a lie.

'It all started going south for him after that,' says Luis, matter-of-factly. 'I said [to the cartel boss], "Listen, I really don't need to be here looking at this. This is not my business. We just had lunch." He never insinuated that if I ever lost a load it would happen to me, but they ended up waterboarding the guy a little more. Then he said, "Take him away."

'By now they'd tied up his hands as well and they threw him in the back of a Toyota truck and they took him out into the field and put two in his head. They weren't going to shoot him there and get blood all over the truck. They buried him somewhere on the farm. Then we went back to the dining room and talked about doing some trips.'

Though he remains somewhat disturbed by what he saw that day, Luis shrugs it off as part and parcel of running a cartel in Colombia in the 1980s.

'It did put me off buying farms and having cattle. I didn't want to deal with farm managers. I didn't want to deal with employees who stole cows from me. If you stole cocaine from me, I just turned you on to the fucking owner of the cocaine, the *oficina*. I didn't want to complicate my life. But to me that kind of torture is nothing. If I would have been in that [torturing] business I don't believe in "partial" shit. I'd just grab the guy and fucking cut his leg off. "Okay, motherfucker, your leg's gone. You want to lose another leg?" That captures your attention real quick.

'Waterboarding is CIA bullshit. Waterboarding is fucking Boy Scouts. *Come on.* If I were ever to be tortured, waterboard me. That's the best torture in the world. Bad torture? Imagine some guy grabs you, another guy grabs your right arm, and they take a fucking chainsaw and just go *whaaack* and cut your fucking leg right at the knee. That's the first thing they do. No waterboarding. No *nothing*. You lost your leg and there's blood coming out. You tell me. What do you prefer? That or waterboarding? It's just what they use when they don't wanna leave any marks. Real torture? They take a fucking chainsaw and just chop your leg off. Or they put a fucking piece of fucking steel right up your ass and put you on a barbecue and they fucking twirl you around until you fry to death.'

26

Kilo of Thorns

THROUGH HIS DEALER FRIEND ARLO, Luis had been introduced to an American called Greg Lazzara, who'd run charter boats in Hawaii before falling in with Arlo and his doper crowd in Santa Cruz and becoming a sort of errand boy. Luis also would later use Greg for collecting money from his clients in California and Florida. While out west, Greg had made a contact with an American called Pino Fatone.[121]

'Greg was from New Jersey,' says Luis. 'Rough around the edges; kind of a heavy-breathing, hyper, very intense guy that nobody wanted around. Greg had a friend, Pino, a dope dealer, who introduced me to a guy called "The Doc" and he had the connection to Rafael Caro Quintero [aka 'El Príncipe'] and "El Cochiloco" [The Crazy Pig, Juan Manuel Salcido Uzeta] of the Guadalajara Cartel.[122] The Mexicans were just starting to get into coke. You see it in *Narcos: Mexico*. I was never introduced to Caro Quintero personally but we've been in the same room in Puerto Vallarta.[123]

'It was all arranged through The Doc. He worked with Caro Quintero big time. *Weed*. Then they started working coke with me and this was apart from the [Miguel Ángel] Félix Gallardo group. I only met The Doc once, in Tucson. Some other smuggling was done with a group I met through my brother-in-law, Vicente, who never got into drugs. His sister, Andrea, who was also a money launderer,

Luis Antonio Navia and his parents, Luis Sr and María, photographed in Havana a few years before the 1959 Cuban Revolution. Luis Sr was the right-hand man of sugar baron Julio Lobo y Olavarria. *Courtesy of Luis Navia*

Luis Sr and María with Meyer Lansky's 'gambling representative', lawyer Julius E. Rosengard, and Rosengard's wife Emma at Lansky's Havana Riviera hotel. *Courtesy of Luis Navia*

The impeccably attired Navias step out in Havana in the 1950s. Says Luis of his father's style: 'Always the best suits in New York. Tailor made. Ties from A. Sulka or Countess Mara. Shirts all monogrammed.'
Courtesy of Luis Navia

Luis and his sister, Laura, at Hyannis Port, Massachusetts, circa 1962. They were photographed inside 'Camp David', the art studio of Julius Rosengard.
Courtesy of Luis Navia

Luis, Laura, Julius and María, Hyannis Port, circa 1962. Julius's chauffeur is in the background.
Courtesy of Luis Navia

Luis graduated as a senior from the all-boys Belen Jesuit Preparatory School in Miami in 1973. He can be seen in this page from the yearbook at right in the top-right photograph, wearing a Coca-Cola styled 'Cocaine' t-shirt.
Courtesy of Luis Navia

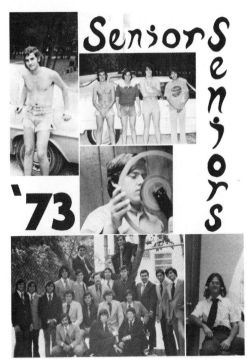

Luis was being groomed for great things in the world of business by Luis Sr. He took his only son to New York for a meeting with the law firm Milbank, Tweed, Hadley & McCloy, 'the top lawyers in the nation, the lawyers for the Rockefellers'.
Courtesy of Luis Navia

Luis during his short stint at the University of Miami.
Courtesy of Luis Navia

Luis with Latin American roommates Pablo and Iván at Georgetown University, Washington, DC, where he first sold cocaine: nine ounces or 255 grams.
Courtesy of Luis Navia

Luis was first introduced to the Colombian cocaine cartels through his Aruban girlfriend, Bia Gálvez, who had high-level connections in the Medellín Cartel. *Courtesy of Luis Navia*

Luis: 'It was instant fucking lust with Bia.' *Courtesy of Luis Navia*

Luis at a hotel in Beverly Hills, California, circa 1980/'81. His cocaine-trafficking career had just begun. *Courtesy of Luis Navia*

A newsprint picture of the arrest of Colombian enforcer Evangelista 'Mario' Navas Villabona after the deadly Amtrak siege in North Carolina of October 1982.
Photographer unknown

A candid photo of the late Oscar Peláez Monsalve aka 'El Poli', reputedly one of the few men in Colombia who ever stood up face-to-face to Pablo Escobar. This photograph was recovered from one of his *caletas* or stash houses by Miami-Dade detective Roberto Diaz in 1979. *Courtesy of Roberto Diaz*

In an attempt to go straight and emulate his late father, Luis briefly owned/ leased 22,000 acres of sugarcane in Florida. But he became involved in a fraud that sparked a United States Customs Service investigation, Operation Bittersweet, and ended up walking away from the sugar business altogether. *Courtesy of Luis Navia*

Luis's friend Lucchese crime-family figure Joey Martino was executed by his mob colleagues, encased in a cement-filled drum and dumped in a canal. Luis: 'I had a lot of dealings with the Lucchese group: somewhere around 6000 kilos. We used to have breakfast with 'em in Miami every other day. We used to sit down, typical mob style, you have nothing to do, you sit down for breakfast like Meyer Lansky did with his buddies. Coffees, Danish, this and that, and come up with something.' Their smuggling route to San Francisco was called 'Tony Bennett'. *The Martino Family*

Luis partying in the late 1980s with friend Richard Booth and girlfriend Lisa Cushing, who went to live with Luis in Colombia but didn't adjust well to life in South America. Lisa was later killed in an air accident. *Courtesy of Luis Navia*

Luis looking sharp in Bogotá, Colombia, 1989. He was now a pure narco but a man permanently on the run. *Courtesy of Luis Navia*

introduced me to a guy they called "El Tío", The Uncle.[124] Like "The Doc", I never knew his real name.'

Moving from pick-up trucks and fishing boats required a bigger capital investment in transport, so Luis bought his first plane, a 1977 beige Fairchild Swearingen SA26-T Merlin IIB twin-engine turboprop, for $500,000 out in Los Angeles, with Paco taking a 50 per cent share.

'The Merlin was a huge fucking plane; it stuck out – like it was bigger than the hangar. It stood real high. It looked like a fucking spaceship. It was not your typical smuggling plane: more an executive type, a big turboprop for private business. Most of the coke transported on the Merlin was through Paco. He had a lot of routes. His main sources of supply were Marulo and Mono through Halcón, and Pablo Correa of the Medellín Cartel.'

Luis kept the Merlin at small airports in Burbank, California, and Fort Lauderdale, Florida, and had two pilots, a *gringo* called Gordon 'Goo' Gray and a Colombian called Alejandro Álvarez, fly it to airstrips at Montería, southwest of Cartagena, and Aguachica, a flatlands rice-growing region northwest of Bucaramanga, to pick up the dope.[125] They'd also make occasional airdrops in The Bahamas. Each load from Colombia was about 600 to 700 kilos. The Mexicans handled the crossing logistics. The Doc took care of things once it was over the border.

'We started doing Rafael Caro Quintero's airstrip at La Peñita de Jaltemba, north of Puerto Vallarta, through a connection I met through Vicente Blanco. We hit that strip between eight and 12 times. We also used the Merlin to do some airdrops in Cancún to some of [the Medellín Cartel's] people. We hit Cancún eight to ten times with Miki Ramírez's merchandise. We also landed the Merlin a few times in Spanish Cay in The Bahamas. Alejandro flew into La Peñita and Spanish Cay.

'Goo was The Doc's and Pino's pilot. He was a crazy American, a great bush pilot. He was a great fucking pilot. *Period*. People in Colombia found out about how good he was as a pilot. He had to abort a mission, a Douglas DC-6 he was on; he landed off Cabo San Lucas in Baja California and he was stranded in the sea and he ended up in hospital. We did a few runs where Goo would airdrop in The Bahamas, come back in the morning, restock and refuel and fly out to Mexico – a 12-hour trip each way. Eventually problems arose between me and him and Greg Lazzara, but as a pilot he was amazing. Best bush pilot I've ever seen.'

*

And so quite by accident, Luis, using Puerto Vallarta as an operational base, became a pioneer of moving coke through Mexico in the early 1980s. A lot of Americans had been smuggling grass since the '70s, of course, and pot in Mexico was still a very valuable export. During one work trip he was introduced to a pot-smuggler *gringo* living up in the mountains of Puerto Vallarta, a friend of Rafael Caro Quintero whose marijuana-growing skills were made globally famous in *Narcos: Mexico*.

'He was a connoisseur of pot. He was like a hippie, a throwback from the '70s. I didn't catch his name. I went up there with my brother-in-law, Vicente, and this guy gave us some cookies to eat and he said they had marijuana in them. Brother, on the way back I started to hallucinate like I would have taken acid. I looked next to me, Vicente was driving, and I saw my father. I looked down at Vicente's legs, I saw my father's legs.

'Not too many smugglers were doing what I was doing; that I guarantee you. Nobody really had a plane like the Merlin. The Colombians, yes. The Mexican [José Gonzalo Rodríguez Gacha] and Pablo Escobar had a fleet of planes. [The Honduran narco] Juan Ramón Matta Ballesteros was already in Mexico working with Pablo, and bringing coke up to the Mexicans, and his partner was [Cuban narco] Alberto Sicilia Falcón.[126] But I was the only independent smuggler doing it.

'But to tell you the truth, each trip on the Merlin when I was dealing with Greg, Pino and Goo was a fucking royal pain in the ass. The trips I did without them were fine. The plane was great. On one trip these idiots fucking landed somewhere in the middle of the desert up in northern Mexico and had some mechanical problem, and I had to send two Mitsubishi MU-2 airplanes, "Rice Rockets", small little jets with turboprops, with mechanics from Miami with spare parts to fix the Merlin.[127]

'They had to jack up the plane and the whole thing was high risk, because how do you explain being in the middle of a desert fixing a plane that had no flight plan? It was either that or burn the Merlin. You know how much those fucking repairs cost me? About $100,000.'

*

The Doc was also using smaller piston-engine planes to airdrop in the Arizona desert. One particular airdrop had gone awry, some of the merchandise literally hitting cactuses on the way down. The cartel was not happy and had the punctured bags returned to Medellín.

'That was through Mexico with a crossing in Arizona; final delivery in LA. The bottom line is that we delivered in LA but some bags had cactus thorns in them.'

A meeting was arranged at El Pomar, the ranch of the SOS, Pablo Correa Arroyave, who became 'very wealthy and moved a lot of cocaine, *huge*' before he was killed by Pablo Escobar in 1986.[128]

Luis believes that Correa at one point was moving more coke to the US than Escobar and it had become an intolerable situation for the Medellín Cartel boss. When it came to coexisting with Escobar, 'you got too big, then bye-bye'.

'Correa told Paco he wanted to meet the man responsible for the route. So I went to meet him in Medellín. I booked into the InterContinental and was picked up by some of his guys. It was a very nice retreat he had on the outskirts of Medellín that had a professional cycling track: *pista de ciclismo*.'

It was then that Luis claims 'El Patrón' himself, Pablo Escobar, who also had some of his cocaine being transported, turned up. Los Pablos, the two Pablos, were in the same room with Luis. [129] The Cuban kid from Key Biscayne who'd sold croquette sandwiches for 50 cents a pop had come a long way.

'You can't have kilos with fucking thorns in them [*laughs*]. That's the power these people had: a kilo that's out in the desert. They took it back to Colombia just to show me. Pablo's coke was on all the trips but we never had a personal business relationship. So Pablo came in with ten fucking Suburbans and Jeeps with a bunch of his guys. Then the first group of his guys came in, then the second, and then he came. He always had what they call *anillo de seguridad*, which are security rings. The first group comes in, the second group comes in, you never know what car he's in.

'When Correa told me Pablo was on his way up to his office it was like nothing; he received a call on his radio and he said Pablo was coming up. I told him not to say anything about the thorns in the coke because I was kind of embarrassed, and worried if Correa did say something Pablo would say, "*Thorns?* What kind of fucking transport guy is this?" But Correa said, "*No, no, no. Tiene nada que ver con nuestra conversación.*" It has nothing to do with our conversation. Pablo was not there to see me; he was there to see Correa and I was not involved in the meeting that they had. But we shook hands when he came up and then they went into Correa's office.

'Most people from Antioquia, I don't know why, do not have a super-firm handshake. Pablo's handshake was medium-strength but firm. He was wearing jeans, tennis shoes and a plaid shirt with a pocket and a little notebook and a pen. The notebook fit in the shirt pocket.[130] He was courteous and I was courteous – "Pleased to meet you" type of thing.

'I was working with top people in Colombia at the time but just because Pablo Escobar walks in the room you don't try to make unnecessary conversation; you follow the lead. He was not there to see me and there was no reason for me to try to make it anything different. Of course, I knew who he was but Pablo back then was not the mythological figure he is today. At that given moment Correa was not Pablo's equal but he had a very significant amount of cocaine in the States. He was definitely a major player in the Medellín Cartel. I can forever say I was in a room with both of them. Two Pablos and a kilo full of thorns.

'That night Correa invited me to be his guest at the best disco in Medellín at the time, Kevin's, and then we went back to one of his houses with some girls and he assigned a few bodyguards to me.[131] The name of the head bodyguard was Chocolate. The next day one of Paco's private planes picked me up and took me back to Bogotá.'

*

As for the troubled Merlin, it eventually met its inevitable death in the blue waters of the Caribbean. It had simply run out of gas.

'The last time it flew Alejandro was shitting in his pants and so scared that he took off from Spanish Cay before they could top off the fuel tanks, so he had to land in the water. We call it *acuatizar* in Spanish. The plane is now part of a fucking reef off a Haitian beach.'

27

River of Blood

LOSING A LOAD OF marijuana or cocaine didn't necessarily mean certain death, as it's often made out in Hollywood movies about drug trafficking. It was far from a murderous free-for-all – or at least it wasn't till it devolved into all-out war in Colombia between Medellín, Cali and the government in Bogotá in the late 1980s and early 1990s. There was a degree of tolerance exercised among the cartels when it came to seizures, water landings or other screw-ups – of a sort, anyway. It was part of the business.

'You know the base of it, how it really works? You've got to keep your word, pay your bills and never lie. Anybody can lose a load. But you have to face up to it. There's a saying in Spanish: *La cara del santo hace el milagro.* The face of the saint makes the miracle. You lose a load, you go right to the owner and tell them, "Listen, I lost a load and it happened like this. Right now I've only got $700,000 but here it is; that's good money. The rest I'll pay back." That builds up your goodwill.'

No amount of goodwill, however, can save you when you steal a load, are *suspected* of stealing a load or someone simply wants you dead. Especially when that someone is Pablo Escobar. He might have dressed like a computer nerd and been awfully polite to Luis when they met at Pablo Correa's home, but Escobar was a mass murderer directly linked to the deaths of two of Luis's closest friends in the cartel: Mono Lopera and Paco Barrera.[132] Both men dreamed of a life outside the drug business: they wanted to go to live in Paris, for different reasons. But El Patrón would never let them leave Colombia.

*

Mono, who was 'early 40s, very good-looking, well built, blond, blue-eyed, almost six-feet tall', was cooking super-high-grade cocaine under the brands 'Cocos' and 'USA' in Ecuador and 'making a lot of money'. He owned a Spanish abode in La Candelaria, the colonial part of Bogotá with its narrow cobblestoned streets. Mono's home, a kind of retreat, had an unassuming entrance with two large wooden doors. Behind it were manicured gardens, rooms filled with antiques and exquisite furnishings, butlers, maids.

'You would walk the sidewalks and see these huge wooden doors and not realise that there were beautiful palatial homes behind them. Inside it was like another world. Back in the 1980s nobody really took a liking to that, but Mono did because he had that sense of art in him, so he bought one of these homes and completely renovated it. He used to just go there and hang out and get away from it all; it was like his retreat. It was just a great feeling to be behind those closed doors in the cool weather of Bogotá and listen to the sounds of the birds and the peacefulness that he had created there.

'Mono's idea was to one day leave Colombia, go to Paris and study French for a couple of years, take his family. That was his dream. He had some beautiful farms in Pereira, one called Marruecos [Morocco] with a large yucca plantation. The yucca fields were totally manicured. At that point he was a serious player in the cocaine export business. He was shot when he was visiting Medellín. I was told Pablo killed him. Either shot in the head or in the kidney. He was not taken hostage and tortured. A typical thing Pablo would do is hold you and you would have to basically beg for them not to torture you and ask for a quick death. He would take a good chunk of money from you before that happened.

'All I ever heard was that Pablo did not like that Mono was growing so big so fast and from knowing of his desire to educate himself more, his love for the finer things in life and his love for the arts, wanting to go to Paris and learn French, that was probably too much for Pablo to swallow and he did not see eye to eye with that.

In the end it could have been envy. But Mono was somewhat involved with the Cali people and maybe that's why Pablo killed him. Pacho Herrera became Pablo's main enemy.[133]

'Pablo was an even-tempered guy but when he got something in his head he was determined to carry it out. I have friends with strong ties to the old groups of the Medellín Cartel and the general word is that Mono was getting too big and his death was a result of differences with Pablo. Some personality differences must've come into play. I can see a situation where Pablo started taxing him a little more and demanding certain conditions and Mono said no and that's why he was killed.'

*

But it was the murder of Paco that shocked Luis the most for its sheer brutality. Paco, from Bucaramanga, was killed on a farm in Magdalena Medio Antioquia. His right-hand man, Pedro Pablo, had told Luis what happened. Luis had eventually bought Paco out of his share of the Merlin before it was ditched off Haiti, and together they did a bunch of trips from an airstrip in Montería, Colombia, airdropping in the Florida Keys and Cancún.

'With Paco I must have done close to 20 tons; that's a *lot* of trips. He became my main partner in Colombia. Paco accumulated about $140 million in a short period of time but he wasn't a badass or prone to violence. He was one of those guys that had it in him to better himself, to learn another language, to study. He said to me, "It gets to the point where you have that much money, you have to be ready to kill to protect it, and since I'm not ready to kill I'm going to retire."'

Like Mono, he'd already bought an apartment in Paris and was planning to move there with his girlfriend, Viviana, to get away from the cartels altogether.

'If you're gonna retire you should *tell* nobody you're gonna retire. They never let Paco retire. He would accumulate merchandise from a lot of people. And then he would just shoot it out on the different routes he had and then he would call you and tell you, "Listen, tonight, 300 of your kilos are going to Miami," for example.

'But a lot of the time he would take 300 kilos and not tell you they were going to Miami. And he'd send them to Miami, sell it there, and then with that money he would buy merchandise and replace your 300 kilos. That's a no-no. You're finagling. That rumour went around and it caught up to him. It's not like he owed somebody $20 million but Paco was riding a very fucking thin line. He was in somebody's scopes.

'People just got a little bit too jealous of him, and that's a problem also. And that's why I always made sure not to come across as too educated or an *I'm-better-than-you* type. A lot of people didn't like that about Paco. "Oh, so he can come, he can make $140 million, and he finagled a little bit, and we gave him a pass on that, and now he's just going to retire and go to fucking Paris, and now he thinks he's better than all of us?" *No, no, no, no.* Somebody may not like that.

'So when he called a route and people found out their merchandise was being sold in Miami because it all has markings [on the coke], Pedro Pablo in combination with somebody else kidnapped him. I've always suspected he had a hand in and profited from Paco's death. Rumour said it was Pablo Escobar [who ordered the hit] because Paco had finagled the merchandise. Since he was not a violent man they took most of his money. They took $80 million. And he gave it up. And they said that they were going to let him go. And they never let him go. I remember Pedro Pablo telling me about what had happened. They picked up his ass, they tied him up, they took all his money, and they killed him. The day they told him, "Okay, you can go," he went to wash his face in the river, and the guy who was there, when [Paco] bowed down to wash his face, *thwaaack*, chopped his head off.

'Think of it: in the mountains, in Colombia, in the middle of nowhere, a river running, and Paco, after days of being kidnapped and paying the ransom, going to wash his face and the guy next to him just pulls out a machete from its sheath. I can picture the guy with the machete, and *whooom*, the head just floating down the river. The ugly part is it takes more than one whack with a machete; it's not a katana and the person doing it is not a trained samurai.

'Every day is a thin line between life and death. In that business you can be dead the next minute. You look at somebody the wrong way. You say the wrong thing. You come across the wrong way. You think you're better than they are. There's so much planning: they can either whack you then and there or wait six months and whack you.'

28

Sugar King of Palm Beach County

Perhaps Luis realised his own longevity in the business wasn't guaranteed, so, as he had done all his adult life, he kept one foot in criminality, the other in respectability. The defining characteristic of his drug-trafficking career to this point had been walking this tightrope of self-identity. It still ate away at him that he hadn't proved he had the nobler makings of a real businessman to his father when he was alive; someone who could make it in proper commerce, not the illegitimate alt-world of cocaine smuggling.

Even in death Luis Sr continued to define how his son thought of himself; matching up to him seemed impossible to Luis through crime. But if he could somehow get a foot in the door of a real business and give it time to grow, he might actually stand a chance of proving he was a worthy inheritor of the Navia name.

Luis's ticket, or so he thought, was taking a stake in Wall Street sugar-trading company Lobo-Kane, run by Julio Lobo's nephew Gustavo Lobo and an Irish-American called Gerald J. or 'Gerry' Kane. Before his death in 1982, Luis Sr had introduced Gerry to his son and Lobo-Kane was already involved in the Navia family's concern in Aruba, Caribe Packing. Gustavo and Gerry didn't know, however, that Luis was using Caribe to traffic cocaine in the US Virgin Islands and Puerto Rico.

'I had given Gerry about $400,000 and the idea was to buy

50 per cent of Lobo-Kane. I think the contract was for $1 million. They thought it was money that I inherited from my dad. My father was known as a person that brought a lot of money from Cuba – and he did – but most people thought he brought over a lot more than he actually did. My dad was a very conservative man. He built up his sugar reputation over many years of hard work. I didn't inherit a lot from him. I inherited his name. But after he died I got the big idea of, "I'm going to invest in Lobo-Kane."'

Problem was, before he knew it, Luis was back to his old tricks – only this time he was playing 'the whole sugar game'. His impulse control was clearly poor.

'My original plan had been to become a legitimate businessman and get out of the other business. But I met this black guy from Trinidad called Mike Laburd, a businessman who lived in Toronto.[134] When I went to visit him he had his office on Bay Street, which is the Canadian equivalent of Wall Street. He was involved in international commodities trading and had some kind of plan to falsify paperwork after we imported sugar and left it in the States. He needed someone to sell it in volume for him, which was where Gerry came in.

'I thought it was a great idea. We weren't hurting anybody; it's not like we were lending people money and putting people in debt on mortgages that you knew they wouldn't be able to pay back and then you would have to come around and take their homes. It was a business where really there were no victims; the only victim was the US Government not getting their share of tax.

'I do not have that line [sic] of what's good and bad in business; business is business and government tariff laws are more crooked or more corrupt than anything else, so I had no reservations about contrabanding sugar. Compared to what I did every day for a living it was like nothing. I made a mistake playing international businessman after my dad died. He would never have gone for any of it. Apart from it being illegal, he would have told me how rough the sugar business is. But we were making more money doing the fucking sugar than the coke.'

*

The scam worked like this: in the early 1980s the United States Department of Agriculture (USDA) heavily subsidised the sugar industry through the federal price support program. A pound of raw American-grown sugar was worth 22 cents to a farmer in the US when sold to a refinery. Once refined, the wholesale price was 28 cents. But outside the US, a pound of raw sugar was only worth four or five cents, sometimes as low as three cents. So it was against the law to sell imported raw sugar in the US – if it came into the country, it did so under the strict condition it was refined and re-exported within 90 days. Importers would then claim a generous rebate or 'drawback' on the duty they paid to bring it in. This system kept American refineries in business and safeguarded the livelihoods of American sugar growers.

Luis saw an opportunity for Lobo-Kane to make a few easy million. He and his partners would buy dirt-cheap sugar in the Dominican Republic, export it to the US and pay the 2.8-cent-per-pound duty set by USDA, have it refined at Godchaux-Henderson Sugar Refinery in New Orleans (costing them no more than five cents per pound), then re-export it to the Caribbean and claim a 99 per cent rebate on the original duty and any export credits.[135]

Only his sugar wasn't actually being re-exported. Lobo-Kane falsified papers, passed off the sugar as American-grown, and sent it to a company called New York Bakeries which bought it at 21 cents a pound, seven cents cheaper than the going rate for American refined sugar. Lobo-Kane would pocket both the rebate and any credit on the falsified bills of lading (documents showing it had been sent for export by ship), plus the 12 cents difference between the cost of the imported refined sugar and the sale price to the bakery.

'Mike handled the sugar export and re-export part. I hooked him up with Gerry, who handled the selling of the sugar part and keeping the books. They started to put the whole thing together and they needed a capital infusion from me – $3 million – to get it going.'

Godchaux-Henderson was a subsidiary of Great Western Sugar Company, Dallas. They had bought the refinery from Luis's father's old friend, Julio Lobo, when he was offloading assets after the Cuban Revolution. Access to the refinery was limited and lucrative.

But because of the Cuban connection, the Navia name carried some weight.

'Drugs are the fastest way for poor people to make money. I did the sugar contraband thing only because I had a structure of sugar behind me that cost millions and millions. Wherever I went, smuggling followed me. Here I am trying to go legit by getting into the sugar business, but tempting situations are put in front of me. Everywhere I stepped, I was stepping into a smuggling pond. It's like Mr Magoo; everywhere he went he was surrounded by accidents and came away without so much as a scratch. I was the smuggling Magoo. So I went to Louisiana and personally met with the president of Godchaux-Henderson. It's not easy to get a slot in a refinery; they're reserved for the big players in the sugar industry. You can't just be anybody and go to Godchaux-Henderson and ask them to refine 10,000 tons of sugar for you.'

*

While Luis was buying Lobo-Kane a sugar company called L-Bis Industries fell in his lap.[136] L-Bis, based in Lake Harbor, Palm Beach County, Florida, had been started by a man called Lambert Bisonte who was the son-in-law of Thomas Vilgrain, 'one of the pioneers of the sugar business in Florida, a Florida cracker'.[137]

Bisonte had got into financial strife after borrowing tens of millions from banks to funnel money into another business he had, a goat farm in Darby, Montana, and began defaulting on his payments. He was now looking for a partner to come in and buy a stake in L-Bis. The deal involved 22,000 acres of sugarcane, half of which would be owned outright, the other half leased long term.

'Lambert believed in the future of goat cheese. He was trying to sell L-Bis because the banks were going to take it. He'd milked the company and put the money in the goat farm in Montana. L-Bis was a sugar-growing operation but it "rested" the sugar land by growing rice. So it had a rice mill and the rice it produced and milled was mostly exported to Haiti. It was $60 million in debt.

'While people in Miami were buying raceboats and thinking about hookers and going to The Mutiny, even though I was completely fucked out of my brains doing drugs and drinking and partying like an animal, I still had some kind of vision of what I wanted to be in life: which was to follow my dad's footsteps and be a legitimate businessman. So I went to Lambert and said, "I'll buy it. I'll give you $400,000 under the table for you, and we sit down with the banks, you back me up on everything and I'll commit to the banks and put in $5 million in new capital to restructure the company."[138]

'The deal with Lambert was to buy the business and take him out of the equation. That way he would be free of all obligations and debts that L-Bis incurred under his ownership. I was down in Florida busy with the whole L-Bis acquisition and my smuggling operation, so I let Gerry and Mike handle the sugar smuggling. But I needed somebody to help me out with L-Bis.'

The man Luis chose was Jaider Esparza, who'd been thrown out of Faces in the Grove in a case of mistaken identity when Luis had decided to dump a bucket of ice cubes on the dancefloor. Jaider was a short, skinny Cuban with beady eyes who made a habit of drinking a bottle of Crown Royal whisky every day.

'I needed Jaider because he knew how to work with banks. He was ex-CIA; one sharp dude. He'd got shot in the leg in the Bay of Pigs invasion and was a "player", although not in the drug business. He spoke with a Cuban Southern accent and wouldn't hesitate to shoot you. He was armed at all times: a gun holster on his ankle and some kind of self-defence knife in his left pocket.'

He was also a conman wanted for fraud.

'He started a computer-leasing company in North Carolina in the late '70s/early '80s when large-capacity computer systems were very expensive. He would lease these computers to big companies and it turns out he was scamming banks for huge amounts of money. He would offer the computers to companies that were doing payroll services, for example, leave them the computers and use those leases to get money from the banks to buy more computers, and I think a lot of those leases were false – it was like a Ponzi scheme. From what I heard, a lot of these leases didn't exist; he just pocketed the money. He was hiding from his problems in Miami and owed the IRS quite a lot of money. But he was an agile guy business-wise.'

So Luis and Jaider hit the road in Jaider's Cadillac or took planes. Luis made sure to bring plenty of cocaine with him for his personal use.

'I did not know the extent to which he was indebted to the banks and in trouble with the banks, but I said, "You help me buy this operation and I will help you solve your problem with the IRS." So Jaider was key as a front man for wheeling and dealing with these North Carolina and Florida hicks. We went to Charlotte and met North Carolina National Bank [NCNB].[139] We sat down with First Bank of Clewiston, Florida. There was another bank in Dallas. Using my dad's good name they thought I was the heir to his sugar interests in Miami. They refinanced $60 million in loans and we bought L-Bis Industries. The banks gave me $60 million – and I was a coke dealer, a smuggler.

'In Charlotte, after Jaider and I closed the deal in Memphis, it was like I was the leader of the Boy Scouts. I had 20 girls following me everywhere I went. *Everybody* wanted my cocaine. I ended up getting laid with three, four chicks in the room; we fucking had a great time.'

Luis was now the part owner/part leaseholder – at least on paper – of 22,000 acres of prime Palm Beach County sugar country.

'I went up to the mill various times, of course, and rented an office but was hardly involved in the business at all. I was drinking a lot and snorting a lot. Jaider and I were doing a lot of partying. Over-the-top spending money and living large.'

But almost as soon as he'd got into the sugar industry, Luis decided to get out. If he couldn't do justice to his father's name in his father's business there was no other option. For him, it was simply a matter of honouring Luis Sr's legacy, a point of integrity.

'Smuggling was my territory but sugar was *his* turf. When it came to sugar, I had to be like my dad – honourable and impeccable – or not be in it at all. The minute I had to walk *his* turf in *that* sugar land, I had to walk it like he walked it. Which wasn't my style. Not being corrupt. Not smuggling. I had to do it the right way; not be flashy or associate with shady Trinidadian businessmen from Toronto. So it was a great plan but I had a lifestyle that was incompatible with it. Carrying out the plan and my lifestyle were on a collision course with each other.

'It hurt me a lot to have to turn my back on it. Looking back, I was crazy not to have dedicated myself to L-Bis. My dad used to drive to Clewiston and stay three, four days a week. I should've moved up there, bunkered down and been an everyday, present, hands-on owner and learned the sugar business and been involved.

'I put together that whole L-Bis acquisition because it was a big deal to me: so I could say to myself I was as big as my dad and he would be proud. My intentions were good – they *were*. I wanted to get into sugar and get out of the coke. It was because of his name that we got that land. The only time I've ever felt guilty or reflected on what's right and wrong is when it comes to my dad. All my life I never gave a flying fuck about anything else. Of course Lambert wanted it back so I returned the company to him and never looked back.'

Yet not before using the last days of his ownership of L-Bis to launder money.

'I took full advantage of the situation at hand. Buying L-Bis gave me the opportunity to move other monies around. I laundered what was a good chunk of change – $4 million – to Aruba using some of the other companies that I owned independently of L-Bis. I also paid Jaider what I owed him. Back then people were not really that in tune with money laundering, and me having a sugar operation in Florida, being partners with a Wall Street sugar brokerage firm, and having a packing operation in Aruba associated with one in Pompano Beach created the perfect climate for me to launder.'

*

But for the first time, the feds were circling. While Lobo-Kane was scamming drawbacks in New Jersey and offloading contraband sugar to New York Bakeries, a long-running USCS investigation into the sugar industry called Operation Bittersweet, based out of New York, Baltimore, Miami and New Orleans, was wrapping up.

Lobo-Kane hadn't been the only sugar company fiddling the books: in fact, the practice of defrauding the US Government through bogus rebates and bills of lading was widespread: dozens of companies had been complicit. Some 250,000 to 500,000 tons of foreign sugar had being dumped, tens of millions of dollars had been stolen, and

Lobo-Kane's creative accounting had led to a tip-off, which resulted in Luis receiving his first subpoena. He hired a lawyer, Tom Wolfe of Miami law firm Shutts & Bowen.

Lobo-Kane was indicted for 'aiding and abetting, false claims, false entry, smuggling and uttering false bills of lading', and Luis was summoned to appear in a courthouse in New Orleans before a grand jury. But not before Gerry Kane, just 54, had a heart attack and Mike Laburd fled to Trinidad.

'The subpoena came in the mail and Gerry dropped dead on his front lawn in Staten Island. Thank God, because if not he would have blamed me for everything and I would have been indicted and gone to jail. I would have been *fucked*. Mike ran. He flew the coop. They never caught him. If they had, he would have fucking electrocuted me too.'

Luis said he gave $30,000 for the purchase of the sugar when the real figure had been $3 million. Lobo-Kane would eventually plead guilty to five counts of illegally importing 1.4 million pounds of sugar. Gustavo Lobo claimed innocence and agreed to an early plea deal while the Kane Estate admitted wrongdoing, Gerry's pension fund being garnished to pay fines.[140] Overall, Operation Bittersweet nabbed 12 companies and 11 officials in what amounted to a $50 million nationwide fraud on sugar import fees.

In hundreds of newspapers around America, Associated Press ran with the story of Lobo-Kane's downfall.

SATURDAY, AUGUST 3, 1985
SUGAR CONCERN ADMITS FRAUD
NEW ORLEANS -- A New Jersey concern has pleaded guilty to five charges of fraud in connection with the 'Operation Bittersweet' crackdown on illegal sugar operations. Lobo Kane Inc. of Linden, NJ., entered the plea in federal court. Customs agents said the company agreed in plea bargaining to return to the government $250,000 in illegal profits.

The company also was fined $30,000. The indictment said Lobo Kane bought millions of pounds of sugar for export, filed false claims that it would be exported and then diverted the sugar back to the United States for resale at the higher domestic price. Lobo Kane was charged with submitting at least 45 fraudulent claims, resulting in $250,000 customs duties being refunded to Godchaux-Henderson Sugar Refinery.

The government said Godchaux-Henderson had nothing to do with the scam.

As for Luis, no further actions were taken against him, because with Gerry and Mike gone, there were no witnesses to corroborate the government's case.[141] Caribe Packing was shut down and he walked out of the sugar business being owed millions (his share of the contraband profits that Gerry had kept) but a free man. To celebrate, he went drinking with Tom Wolfe on Bourbon Street in New Orleans.

'The first thing I did when I got out of the grand-jury room was I told Tom, "Let's go hit a bar." And I said, "I need to buy something as a reminder of this." So I bought a beautiful painting of the Mississippi River. I flew home with that painting as a reminder of that grand jury. It's still hanging in my sister's apartment. And I never contacted Gus Lobo or any member of Gerry Kane's family again.'

PART 6
WAR
ZONE

29

Five Units of Fercho

B Y HIS OWN ADMISSION, Luis 'got spooked by all the sugar legal shit' and threw himself back into something decidedly less dangerous – cocaine trafficking – with a new sense of purpose. He'd found his groove as a smuggler and barely had to lift a finger to make a lazy million: the systems were in place, the right connections had been made, his Colombian suppliers were eager to move more of their product, and demand in the United States was at a peak – despite inroads made against the industry by President Ronald Reagan's war on drugs.

From Pereira, Montería and La Costa Caribe in Colombia he was moving thousands of kilos through Miami, Mexico, The Bahamas and Jamaica. Luis, now one of America's major drug smugglers yet unknown to law enforcement, had perfected the art of the route – though not without taking considerable risks. The Achilles heel of any cocaine-transport operation is unreliable personnel, someone flipping. Or it's volume – smuggle too much and the chances are you're going to be noticed.

'But for every load that gets caught, 50 make it through. It's ridiculous. You're in this business for so long that you just find the right person in the right place. You develop all kinds of friendships all over the world. You go wherever you have those friends. You've just got connections. Your whole network in life is dedicated to the export and trafficking of cocaine. That's how it is. Time, dedication and reliable contacts, like any business.'

*

Luis's main client was now El Tío in Mexico, who started moving big weight. After receiving Marulo's coke from Colombia he crossed it over into San Diego through Tijuana in Baja California. Another Mexican contact, Eduardo Fonseca, known by the moniker 'El Compadre', The Godparent, smuggled into McAllen, Texas, from Reynosa in Tamaulipas.[142] He was working directly with the Mexican federal police, the *federales*.

'Tío turned out to be a fucking goldmine. He had his own connections at the border. He had cars cross over and paid off officials. I had lost the Merlin so we rented a plane, a Cheyenne, and a pilot, 'Romerito', from Vicente Wilson Rivera González, one of the original cocaine producers from Leticia.'

Each load was 700 keys and Luis did 30 trips, nearly half of them to Guaymas, Mexico. And that was just one plane. He ended up operating a fleet of seven private planes, some bought, others leased – a Rockwell Turbo Commander, Beechcraft King Air, Piper PA-42 Cheyenne, Piper Navajo Panther, Cessna Titan, a Cessna Conquest and a Learjet 25 – and would variously keep them in hangars in Venezuela, California, Mexico and Colombia. In total, he moved more than 55 tons, or over 50,000 kilos, on small aircraft from Colombia to the United States in the late 1980s.

Fernando Marulanda would emerge as one of Luis's chief suppliers during this period.

'Marulo was a big, heavy-set guy, bald, about six-feet tall; he must've been 250 pounds. By any standards he was definitely on the heavy side. His nickname was "El Gordo", The Fat One, though I never heard anybody use the term *gordo* about him in the bad sense. As was his nature, he was always "moving with a purpose" – 24 hours in a day wasn't enough. When we first met he'd just come back from Ecuador, where he had been kidnapped and tortured by the police. He was hung by the tip of his thumbs and beaten bad. They'd discovered one of his cocaine labs. His partner Mono Lopera had arranged for the ransom to be paid and everything to be taken care of.

'Marulo was always buying farms and converting them into beautiful cattle ranches or places where he kept his showhorses; they were unbelievable.[143] He was known in Colombia for having beautiful *fincas*, just like the Ochoas. After Mono died Marulo became the top dog in Pereira and somehow he managed to keep out of harm's way. On one trip we airdropped off The Bahamas and there was like 400 units [keys of cocaine] on that trip. It wasn't a lot. But Marulo said that there were also five units of something he'd marked "Fercho", which is a nickname for Fernando – and he made it very clear to us that it was different; it was heroin. We took it and we gave it to somebody in Miami on his behalf. We never did it again.'

Did that bother you?

'I don't think about it much – heroin wasn't my daily business and Marulo just put those units on the trip. It was meaningless. I was not interested in opening a market for that and I don't think Marulo did too good either on the selling end or on the supply side. Cocaine is just as bad as heroin; it's just a different high. The only difference being cocaine was the drug of all the successful New York bankers and Hollywood movie stars; all the discos were full of cocaine people: dancing, having a great time. Cocaine was equated with discos and outlandish lifestyles. Heroin was equated to some junkie shooting up in an alley. But you can get just as addicted on freebase as you can on heroin.'

*

Having successfully kicked his own freebasing habit after his enforced self-isolation at the Miyako Hotel in San Francisco, Luis had turned his energies to spending his own money on the things he loved: cars, hookers and fancy hotels.

'At one point between Miami and San Francisco I had 14, 15 cars. I had a blue Bentley, a black 1981 Ferrari 308 GTSi, a 1957 MG, a 1965 Mustang, a 1962 Corvette, a four-door Vanden Plas, a couple of Jaguars, three Porsches, three Mercedes-Benzes. I kept most of them in storage, one at Diego Forero's and one at my parents' place.

'I'd give hookers $15,000 like *nothing*. Me and a friend of mine, Richard Booth, a salesman for Southern Wine & Spirits of America, would call up Moonflower Escorts in Miami Beach and they'd send girls over. I was the only customer who had credit. After one three-day spree with a dozen hookers we paid them $45,000. One day we threw $60,000 down the trash chute because $30,000 were false bills and we didn't want to get caught with them. We made a mistake and instead of ripping up 30 we ripped up 60 and threw away $30,000.[144]

'Nobody *ever* paid for dinner. I never went out to a dinner that was less than $900. I always picked up the bill. Every day I'd pick off something I liked in a boutique, like a $400 shirt. One day I walked into a store and I said, "What the fuck is this?" It was a cane made out of rhinoceros dick. "Wow, cool. Let's take three of those." They were $500 each. I'd go to San Francisco and buy all kinds of weird art. In Tucson, we'd stay in hotels for *months*. To pay a $50,000 bill at a hotel was nothing. You just spend money recklessly every fucking day, plus all the collateral expenses for your entourage.

'I had a friend called "Dave the Slave"; he was our gopher. He had a daughter. So for the birthday present, the baptism, we gave him a kilo of coke. But the truth is the craziest thing I ever wasted money on was just paying bills for trips where merchandise went missing. They were losses that I assumed so that people weren't killed. And we weren't making money like Pablo Escobar who *owned* the merchandise. We were only making a percentage on the transport. We weren't making $10 million a trip; we were making a million.'

*

Luis might have had money to burn but one of Navia's 11, Javier Mercado, was living way beyond his means on Star Island in Miami and looking to bring more coke into the United States to fund his extravagant lifestyle. To do so he was cutting some important corners in the process.

'Javier and his partner Bernardo Palomeque had made a lot of money and they retired for a while. They were both hitting it hard in the late '80s. Bernardo had a Gold Rolex with diamonds and his name engraved on it, a gold bracelet with his name, a chain with diamonds and a fucking flying eagle on it. He had a long-stretch Mercedes with a bar in the back. He was out of control. Then he started snorting coke, drinking a lot and hanging out with this young Cuban girl. It fucked up his marriage.

'Javier was a really good-looking guy, suntanned, tall, green eyes, a really bright guy; he used to date the most beautiful Venezuelan beauty queens. He'd had a very successful pot run with Bernardo and Juanchi and was a reckless motherfucker. He had everything going for him, but I think he was so desperate and so burnt out he was making a lot of bad decisions without thinking. He overextended himself. He was almost bankrupt. So after not seeing each other for a while, I ran into Javier and told him that I had just bought a Conquest II for $850,000 in Oklahoma. He suggested we keep the plane in Venezuela where he had connections with ex–Venezuelan Air Force pilots and commercial pilots.

'The Conquest for its speed and size – not being big and easy to keep on the ground – is probably the best airdrop-smuggling plane ever. Not as comfortable as the Merlin for executive comforts, but a lot better for airdropping. I would take care of the SOS in Colombia after moving down there and he would take care of the operations in the States, which included the airdrops to The Bahamas as well as the receiving of merchandise in California from El Tío and El Compadre. That's one thing I told Javier. "El Tío doesn't even know our name – we send merchandise to him and he pays us. That's the best-case scenario. Anybody has a problem, nobody knows who's who." The worst thing you can do is work with a person when he knows your name.'

*

The pilot Javier organised to fly the Conquest was actually a co-pilot, a Panamanian-Chinese called Chang aka 'El Chino'. Javier's regular pilot had never flown a Conquest and Luis's group didn't have a certified Conquest pilot who could step in. El Chino had recently been sent to flight-safety school to learn the aircraft's systems. Different types of aircraft have their own landing gears, hydraulics and instrumentation that require familiarisation before flying. Javier assured Luis that El Chino knew these systems and was ready to go. There was no time to waste. They needed a good bush pilot and quickly. The problem was that El Chino had never passed the course.

'Sure enough, the fucking plane lands in the desert outside of Monterrey, Mexico, they unload the merchandise, the merchandise leaves, suddenly the blades of the plane they feather, they go sideways, and you have to pull a switch under the seat to unfeather the blades so that the plane can go forward, so it can have grab.[145] These motherfuckers, El Chino and his co-pilot, they couldn't find the switch to unfeather the blades. The engines ran, everything was on, but they could not unfeather the blades and couldn't move forward.

'Supposedly if you go to flight-safety school you know the systems and it's the simplest of all things. It turned out to be a little switch under the pilot's seat. The Mexican Army was coming down the road. El Chino and his co-pilot were like, "We cannot leave this plane here." So they burned the fucking plane. The army arrested some of the Colombians and Mexicans receiving the load; they were put in jail. It was a complete fuck-up. The only good thing was we saved the merchandise. But I lost my plane.'

So Luis simply went out and bought one in better condition in Missouri. Every fledgling business needs its equipment.

'I bought the second Conquest with my own money and paid a little over a million with some odds and ends to bring it to $1.2 million. Obviously I was pissed but there was so much money coming in from the merchandise, we could always afford to buy a new plane.'

30

Body in a Barrel

M ANY TIMES DURING THE writing of *Pure Narco*, Luis referred back to *Wiseguy* by Nicholas Pileggi. It was clear he identified very much with Henry Hill, a low-level hood in the Lucchese crime family, one of New York's 'Five Families' of La Cosa Nostra, who after decades in the yoke of the mob went into federal witness protection to save his and his family's life.

'The reason Henry Hill had to rat those people out is the minute he gets arrested, the first thing they do is they don't support his family, they don't give his family the pension that you deserve, because if you're sitting in jail and your family is religiously getting $10,000 to $15,000 a month with no problem, you don't rat nobody out.

'The American mafia used to have some very honourable, business-minded people involved. They laundered their money in America and they made America great. The mafia was little when New York was little: New York grew, the mafia grew.[146] They went into Las Vegas and created casinos. But real honour is when somebody gets busted and somebody goes and says, "This is your pension. You will have this for the rest of your life." That's why it's so incredible when you work for a company like FedEx or Coca-Cola for 30 years. You retire and they give you a pension, they give you a pay cheque. They're *there*. Even the US fucking Postal Service has a better retirement plan than crime.

'But these guys in *Wiseguy*, they think they're going to get ratted out, they even tried to kill Henry's wife; [the scene with] Jimmy the Gent [played by Robert De Niro] in the Garment District. So that's what it is. That's what I would tell people. The mafia ain't no fucking company. They're a bunch of cutthroats. There's no honour. There's none of that.'

Luis knows this not from the movies but from personal experience, after going through one of the strangest interludes in his drug-smuggling career: when he worked for the American mob in South Florida and met a man called Joseph Martino aka 'Joey', an 'earner' for the same Lucchese crime family Henry Hill was forced to rat on. Martino had become Luis's good friend after being introduced by Javier Mercado and Bernardo Palomeque.

'We hit it off right away. Joey was not a highly educated man; he just had a great personality and all he wanted to do in life was make money and live as well as possible. With Joey it was always coke, but I know that before he was involved in pot. He didn't do anything all day. All he did was plan his small goals: go to breakfast, visit with his girlfriend and then go to dinner with his wife, Joyce, hang out at Turnberry Isle during the weekends and suntan next to the pool. A ladies' man.

'You could say it was a shallow life but that's who he was: a very outgoing, very funny guy. He was happy living between his apartments in Miami and New York City. He was a great-looking Italian: black straight hair, clean-shaven. He was always well dressed, but kept it casual: he would wear those sports jogging sweatsuits a lot of the mob guys used to wear, with nice white tennis shoes.

'Joey hooked me up with the Lucchese group. Anthony Accetturo and Frank Suppa were the heads of the Lucchese family down in Hollywood, Florida.[147] We started working the Jamaican route. I had a lot of dealings with the Lucchese group: somewhere around 6000 kilos. We used to have breakfast with 'em in Miami every other day. We used to sit down, typical mob style, you have nothing to do, you sit down for breakfast like Meyer Lansky did with his buddies. Coffees, Danish, this and that, and come up with something.

'We called it "Tony Bennett", this trip that we were doing to

San Francisco. I met quite a few of the Italian guys. I was bringing in loads for them. But I wasn't connected to them like Joey was, because that was all he did; that was his thing. The Lucchese group used a small twin-engine plane, piloted by a guy named Bob, a Florida hick. They had a refuelling stop in Jamaica and I would load 'em up in Montería and we did a bunch of trips right into Fort Lauderdale Executive Airport. They had it paid off and they had local Hollywood police in their pocket also. When Paco was still alive we did eight to ten runs. The other guys I did that route with were Halcón and the Ochoa relatives from Medellín.'[148]

But in January 1988 Martino and a fellow mobster called Steve Cassone were arrested in possession of 20 keys. In exchange for a lenient sentence, Joey pleaded guilty and got ten years. Cassone got five. That June, while on bail, Joey left his home in Turnberry to go out for breakfast and get a shave at a barbershop, stopping his Mercedes at a phone booth outside a drug store in North Miami. He felt he was being watched. He made a phone call, his beeper went off, and he returned to the phone booth again. It was a short conversation. He waved at whoever he thought was watching him and then left west on 183rd Street. It was the last time he was seen alive.

'Joey got arrested because he started dealing with an undercover cop. He was set free on bail and when the Lucchese group read the indictment, they realised he was selling the merchandise to this undercover cop at 16 and he only told them 13.[149] So between that and the fact he was gonna sell 'em out and turn state's evidence, [the Lucchese group] invited him to a meeting where they killed him. They clubbed him over the head with an ashtray, I believe, something like that.[150] They put him in a 55-gallon barrel and they dumped him in the river at Hialeah.'[151]

It wasn't until 1994 that what was left of Joey's body was discovered, FBI divers fishing out the drum from its resting place in 15 feet of water. His skeleton was wrapped in plastic and his feet had been encased in cement. He could only be identified through dental records and the watch he was wearing. They'd entombed him with his gold Rolex.

*

Joey's death deeply shook Luis; not just for its savagery and clinical execution but the fact it exposed him to a greater risk of being double-crossed or even eliminated himself.

'The Lucchese group wanted to continue working with me, because they reached out after Joey went missing. The Italians, they always wanna have their fuckin' hook into you.[152] I was always with Joey but I'm not part of no fucking mafia. That's your deal. I'm an independent contractor. I'm not part *of* the Medellín Cartel. My back-up and source of supply is Medellín, different people. I ain't no fucking Yakuza, I ain't no fucking mafia, I've got enough troubles. That's why I let Joey Martino deal with them.

'These guys all want a piece of your hide. One tries to kill the other one, one's trying to cut the other one out. If you just turn your back for a minute they'll take your clients. You're dealing with the sort of people that if you slip up and they have the chance to kill you and gain advantage from your death, they *will* kill you. And if they don't kill you they will steal a load if they can get away with it.

'Joey always told me to "Cover your ass, cover your back, because these guys are ruthless" and he was right: he ended up dead. So I figured without Joey being there these guys are *bad*; they would not hesitate to kill me. I'd send them a trip and they'd kill me, they'd keep the trip, and it's *over*. I was looking at it from a business point of view: I had no guarantees of any kind, no security, it didn't feel right. After Joey was missing a week, two weeks, I said, "He's *dead*." His wife was going crazy. I said, "I'm gonna get the fuck outta here. This is just going to get bad."

'I bought myself a little time and didn't send them the trip. Then, since they had nobody to work with, they started reaching out to some other group and I heard they all got popped in Louisiana. There's no honour in the mafia anymore. They're a bunch of fucking conniving hoodlums, thieves, no-gooders. Pablo Escobar killed his partners, the partners killed other guys, everybody's killing everybody. It's a bunch of bullshit.'

31

Going Down

JOEY MARTINO'S DISAPPEARANCE ULTIMATELY convinced Luis to leave Florida and the United States for good. He wouldn't live in Miami again for nearly 20 years. A traffic incident that got out of hand simply confirmed his decision.

'Around the time Joey went missing I was living in Grove Isle, Miami. I had a two-door Jaguar XJS. I was with a woman called Annette Soudry, driving out of La Crepe St Michel restaurant in Coral Gables. Annie was a French-Moroccan model: skinny, tall, crazy hair. She spoke French. Her English was all French style so that even added more to the exotic. Annie was in the front seat and a guy called Billy Basto was sitting behind her and Annie's sister, who was Billy's girlfriend, was sitting behind me on the left-hand side of the car.[153] Billy was a Vietnam vet. He had issues with authority figures.

'So we drive out of the restaurant and I get pulled over. I hardly ever had a licence; it was either suspended because of speeding or it was expired, but sometimes back then you could talk to the cop and pay a fine on the spot. I had driven without one for so many years that it was very much of a pain in the ass for me to go stand in line and get one. So I'm talking to this cop nicely, handling the situation in a nice way, and this guy, Billy, pushes the front seat forward, gets out of the car and hits the cop's partner – the other cop that was there.

'All hell breaks loose and they just start pounding on Billy with nightsticks, and in the matter of a minute, another squad car was called and Billy's ear was almost completely torn from the side of his head. So they held us both in custody. I remember being fingerprinted. I got out right away because I posted bail and there were no real charges against me, but Billy got lost in the system for three or four days before his family found him and bailed him out of a Dade County holding facility.'

*

Moving to Los Angeles seemed a wise idea. Luis flew west, brought over his new girlfriend, a pocket-sized blonde heart attack called Lisa Cushing, and for something different decided to open an art gallery, Navia Gallery on 665 North La Cienega Boulevard, West Hollywood. His plan was to hold an exhibition of Colombian art as its maiden show.

'I felt that Joey's partners had something to do with his death. So it was a good time for me to get out of Miami. It was always my dream to own a gallery because I was into art. I'd been buying art since 1979 when I first went out to San Francisco. It was also a good way to launder money.

'Money laundering is nothing to me; more than anything you're just avoiding taxes on what you sold, because obviously what you're selling is not legal. And that's what I did for a while until I had to close it. The gallery wasn't open that long but for the time it was open I laundered $6 million, $7 million. All this shit [drug money] that I got from El Tío, it could have been $10 million, $12 million, easily.'

The scam, like all of Luis's scams, was simple enough. At the time the Colombian artist Fernando Botero was hot on the West Coast.

'You have a guy in Colombia make a replica of a Botero for $500 and sign "Botero", and you buy a bunch of emeralds that are worth $500 and you bring them into the country, bring it through customs, and you declare your Botero painting at $300,000 and you declare the emeralds at $2 million. It was mostly emeralds that nobody could really put a value on. Who would say they were not real back then in 1987? You're at the airport, clear customs, fill out the forms for the high amount of money, you hire security services transport to take it from the airport to the gallery the next day and then you "sell" [the painting] for $500,000, $700,000, whatever, and you sell it to somebody in the Philippines.[154]

'Ferdinand Marcos had just been overthrown and back then there were a lot of Filipinos coming into LA. You insure it and you send the fake painting in a very secure insured transport service to the Philippines to, er, "Joaquín Wang Pie". These people didn't exist. Who was going to find out if Joaquín Wang Pie walked into the gallery, paid me cash, and he left to the Philippines and I sent him his painting? Or Joaquín Wang Pie bought his painting and left? Where's the painting? I dunno. I guess in Joaquín Wang Pie's apartment in Malibu Beach. Back then you could do all that shit. You can't now.'

But any sideline in fine art was going to be shortlived under the circumstances. Joey's disappearance, legitimate fear of the Italian mob putting a hit on his life, and the unfortunate traffic incident with the police in Miami had all been dramatic enough. What tipped Luis over the edge were murmurs of a DEA operation in the southwest.

'That's when the feds indicted 132 people along with The Doc in Tucson. Greg Lazzara and Gordon Gray were really worried and were convinced we were going to get indicted – typical Greg getting overexcited; he was a borderline nutcase and a social misfit – but I took the situation seriously enough and saw the possibility was there. I was already planning to move to Colombia but that put the lid on the bottle. I left for South America sometime around late August 1988, and Greg and Gordon came down after me. I never got a clear answer on how bad that got or how close it was going to get to me.'

Luis wasn't going to take his chances. He instructed his Miami-based corporate attorney Reid Constable, who'd represented him in his sugar dealings, to start offloading the bulk of his substantial property portfolio – million-dollar lots in Mashta Island, Key Biscayne; a house in Bayshore Drive, Coconut Grove; two apartments in Grove Isle and one in Turnberry; four rental apartments; and a vacant lot in Vail, Colorado – and missed his own party at the gallery. A Honduran woman and later lover of Luis's called Daniela Villareal managed the gallery in his absence.[155]

'I wasn't able to go. I was already in Colombia. From there I sent a bunch of painters to do that first exhibition but I have a *photo*. People drinking, hors d'oeuvres and bullshitting.'

*

When Luis touched down on an Avianca flight at Matecaña International Airport in Pereira, he had specific instructions from Fernando Marulanda: carry a soccer ball as your carry-on luggage. That way, a paid-off policeman would know who he was and yank him out of the line for passport control.

'I never went through immigration. I never registered as coming into Colombia. A couple of Marulo's guys picked me up at the airport and I stayed at a hotel in Pereira for two or three days.'

From there he went straight to Bogotá, moving into an entire-floor apartment on Calle 1A, right next to the American's ambassador's house on Avenida Carrera 3 in the posh neighbourhood of Los Rosales. His living room looked into the ambassador's backyard: an ironic choice of address for a man running from stateside justice, even though Luis didn't necessarily see it that way.

'I thought of it as living in a foreign country. It wasn't "on the run" like these Americans who write these books – "I had to live in a fucking apartment and share it with five illegal immigrants" or anything like that. When you're at a certain level in society, when you've got money, you *blend* in. You've got high-level friends, no one suspects you, everything's easy. You transfer from one country to the other. You just have to get the right paperwork.'

He even brought down his girlfriend, Lisa following him on a separate flight along with her pampered bulldog, Floyd.

'She had green eyes and she was wild. *Playboy* wanted her to do a centrefold, but she turned it down and she was with me at the time, so really didn't need the money. Fuckin' rock 'n' roll to the max. I mean, this girl would put on boots and a miniskirt, dance, *fuck*. Talk about a head-turner. She was a cool chick.'

But Lisa with her elaborately moussed and sprayed 1980s hairdo was not quite made for Colombian life and nor was Floyd. She only lasted four months.

'I felt protected down there, definitely. There was no extradition and Pablo Escobar was fighting for no extradition. Pablo declared war on a country because of no extradition. He said, "I prefer to have a tomb in Colombia than a jail on the other side."[156] They had to fight that war but it got out of control. It became a real war. In Pablo's eyes it was like when the Americans fought the Germans or the Arabs. You blow up planes, you blow up cities. It was a crazy time. The whole country suffered.

'So Colombia was definitely not for Lisa and there was not the kind of strength in our relationship to keep it together in a place that was foreign to her in every sense and not to her liking. The dog was accustomed to Evian water, so he gets to Bogotá and we go to one of the farms in Represa del Sisga, northeast of Bogotá, and he drank some water from a creek or something and he got a stomach infection. He died really violently. When Floyd died, Lisa said, 'I'm not happy here," and I said, "I understand." And that was it: she left.'[157]

Luis was nearly 33 years old, newly single, exiled and living far from home in what was effectively a war zone, with a dead bulldog on his conscience. He had all the money he'd ever need and still had an appetite for partying and fast women, but something was missing from his life. It was time for him to get serious and stop messing around with models, hookers and *Playboy* centrefolds. All wayward men, fugitive coke traffickers included, need to meet a nice girl sooner or later.

32

The Night They Shot Galán

IN THE FIRST SIX months of 1989, there were 2338 murders in Medellín and the cartel was arguably at the peak of its destructive power. Pablo Escobar, who had made *Forbes* magazine's list of the world's billionaires for three years running with a personal fortune of over $3 billion, was doing whatever he could to stave off the threat of the Colombian Government reinstating extradition – and that meant incredible levels of violence.

His biggest threat was a popular politician called Luis Carlos Galán Sarmiento, the candidate for the PLC or Colombian Liberal Party (*Partido Liberal Colombiano*), who was running on a platform of no mercy and a return of extradition for the narcos who were destroying the country from within. Escobar's beef with Galán was also personal: in 1983 Galán had pushed for Escobar's removal from Colombia's Congress, ending his political career before it had even started.

Luis's plans that northern summer were just to relax, so he headed up from the cool highland climate of Bogotá to the drier Santa Marta for some sun and sand.

'I went for a vacation and to see my sister. So I'm at the beach at La Cangreja and I see this young, beautiful, blondish Colombian girl getting into the water from the back side. Beautiful figure, cinnamon-white skin. I said to the guy I was with, "If I were to go for a Colombian girl, it's going to be somebody like that." I waited for her to come back out and she sat down with her friend.'

Her name was Patricia Manterola, she'd just turned 20 and was on spring break from her marketing and publicity studies at a college in nearby Barranquilla. Luis was about to deploy an early version of the pick-up art of 'negging'.

'I was tanning,' Patricia remembers. 'And the guy said, "Hi, does somebody have sunblock?" He came right up next to us. I took the one that I had, the Hawaiian Tropic, and passed it to him. And he said, "No, no, no. I want the *other* one." He took it! The Bain de Soleil. It's French, more expensive.'

Says Luis: 'I just started putting that shit on, all over me, using up half the bottle [*laughs*]. And she complained I was using up all her suntan lotion. I really liked her. She didn't like me at first but I just kept hitting on her.'

Patricia: 'I'd never seen this man in my life. I was like, "My God, he's Cuban, *whatever*." He went off to the water with my suntan lotion and I never saw him again. He was so . . . oh, my God, I don't know. I should have turned . . .' she pauses, reflecting for a moment. 'No, *no*. Everything happens for a reason. The next day I was at this house party and another friend of mine came up to me and said, "I want to introduce you to somebody from Miami." It was him: the guy from the beach who took my tanning lotion. I was like, "I cannot believe this." Luis was something *different*. Maybe that attracted me. It wasn't easy for him to get me.'

But he wouldn't be deterred.

'Patricia was a beautiful girl – a *knockout*.'

*

Patricia Manterola was born in Barranquilla, Colombia, on 19 July 1969 to Juan and Gladis Manterola. Of Spanish descent, Juan was a well-known attorney while Gladis's wealthy family ran farms on huge estates on super-prime land in and around Santa Marta: avocado, rice, banana, African palm, cattle ranching. In fact, they were one of the original families who started the paramilitaries, the *Autodefensas*, against the guerillas. Extortion was always a problem in the wilds of northern Colombia, and the Manterolas were not only personally well armed but hired private security guards.

'Since the time of my grandfather, who was a cattle rancher, we always carried a gun in the Jeep, along with a radio. Every car had a gun. We had to defend our land. So a lot of people like my grandfather, my uncles, the family of my grandmother, with other landowners we had to pay people to protect us from the guerillas. They always wanted more money; they killed people that worked for us.'

Says Luis: 'Patricia was a very clean girl from a good family, which I really liked. Her parents had divorced when she was six. She had two brothers. She didn't do drugs and didn't have an alcoholism problem. Juanchi, who also came from a good family in the area, knew of her and told me, "Man, you picked a real doozy there. But her uncles are going to kill you." Patricia was a clean kid from another generation. She's 13 years younger than me. She didn't grow up in that whole cocaine era.'

'I never did any kind of drugs,' she insists. '*Any*. I saw all the drugs in the world but I never tried it. Everybody knows that I don't do drugs. I went to the best high school in the city and one of the best colleges in Barranquilla. My friends were far from that business and there were no cartels in Santa Marta.'

*

On one of their first dates at La Escollera, a disco in Santa Marta, Luis turned to Patricia at about 10pm apropos of nothing and asked her to come with him to a farm called 'Panorama', owned by local marijuana-smuggling identity Juanchito 'Juancho Caterpillar' Noguera near Aracataca.[158] It had a well-known illegal airstrip, a 'hot' place for law-enforcement interest.

'"Patricia, would you accompany me?" I said. "I've got to go see a friend of mine about something." Gordon Gray had taken off in the new Conquest a few hours earlier and was airdropping in The Bahamas. I wanted to get on the radio and see if everything was good.'

'I said okay,' she recalls. 'I didn't know what was going on; I knew something was going on but not exactly what.'

The way she tells it, Patricia had no idea at that stage Luis was involved in cocaine. He planned to have her home by her father's curfew of two in the morning. They got in their car with a chauffeur and one of Juanchi's bodyguards and drove, with another car containing two more bodyguards tailing behind.

'So we're on our way to the farm and suddenly we hear on the fucking radio, "They just killed Galán."'

*

It was 18 August 1989. At 8.30pm at an open-air rally in Soacha in southwest Bogotá, Pablo Escobar's political nemesis, Luis Carlos Galán Sarmiento, had been assassinated on the orders of Escobar and other conspirators.[159] Up to 18 *sicarios* had been lying in wait. The military were going to any farm that had an airstrip and were on their way to the entrance of Panorama. It was a state of emergency and the cartels were firmly in the government's sights. Escobar's greatest fear, extradition to the United States, was immediately legalised by President Virgilio Barco Vargas. In the coming weeks, tens of thousands of people would be arrested, cocaine kitchens destroyed, and countless weapons, vehicles and aircraft seized.

Says Luis: 'The whole country had gone into lockdown. It was martial law. The fucking army started putting up roadblocks everywhere and we were outside the city limits of Santa Marta on the way to this farm in the backlands. We were past the point of no return; we couldn't turn back. They were arresting everyone on the highway. So we just had to get into the farm and, *fuuuccckkk*, we were stuck at the farm.

'Goo was on his way back from airdropping and there was nothing else we could do. We couldn't ask him to go somewhere else and land. What the fuck are we going to do with the plane? If we'd stayed the army would have hit us at the farm, we would have all gone to jail, they would have confiscated the plane, we would have been royally fucked. From above, if they'd had any army helicopters they would have spotted the plane *immediately*. We had to get the fuck out of there quickly.'

Luis and Patricia were parked next to the runway at Panorama and twiddling their thumbs in banana land in the middle of nowhere. Nothing was happening. It was an anxious wait and fog had rolled in.

They burned some tyres in barrels to get some fires going so Goo could see the dirt strip. Soon, dawn broke.

Luis: 'Goo comes back from the airdrop and it's daybreak and he's trying to land and the ceiling is too low.[160] He's trying to come down to spot the strip and it's very dangerous, because when the ceiling is that low and you're going that fast, you're coming down and, before you know it, the fog clears and you're so low that you may hit the ground or the treeline. It's like being in a fast-moving vehicle blindfolded, then suddenly the blindfold gets removed and there's nothing but the ground, trees or hillside in front of you. A pilot's worst nightmare.

'So it takes a very good pilot to land when there's a low ceiling and fog. We were on the radio guiding him in, giving him references because it was extremely dangerous even for an experienced bush pilot like Goo. We were all on edge as there was a good chance he wouldn't make the ceiling and land – and he *had* to land the plane. There was no other option. He was out of fuel and there was nowhere to go because of the situation with the military. If it would have been five more minutes, ten minutes, that he couldn't land because of the ceiling being too low, he would have crashed and died.

'He followed the instructions of one of the guys who handled the airstrip there and knew the area. Goo was flying 95 per cent by radar. "By radar" in the sense of what this guy was telling him, not what the radar was telling him. He couldn't see shit while coming down to land. Miraculously, he managed to pull it off. The plane came back with no seats or anything, because when you airdrop you take out all the seats so you can put in the extra fuel.

'A guy called "Moñón" Dangond had a strip called "La Y" in Ciénaga so we asked him if we could go from Panorama, make a little hop over to Ciénaga [26 kilometres sou'-sou'-west from Santa Marta], and keep the plane in one of his hangars.[161] We had to make it a short hop. We couldn't be flying around and we needed a place where there was a hangar so we could hide the plane, put the call letters back on, get our Venezuelan pilots who'd flown it to Colombia back on board and get the fuck out of there.[162] It took a lot of convincing for him to agree but he was close to Juanchi and our whole group. He said he'd let us do that for a few days but that was as much as he could allow, given the circumstances.'

'Luis was afraid; everybody was really worried,' says Patricia. 'But I didn't really care; everything back then was an adventure.'

Luis: 'I think I was more scared than she was. I feared for my life. So here I am with Patricia [*laughs*] and she hops on a fucking plane that just came from airdropping 800 kilos in The Bahamas and smells like gas [petrol]. Goo was like, "Who the fuck is she?" I said, "She's my girlfriend." And then I hear, "I'm *not* your girlfriend!" [*laughs*]'

Eventually Luis and Patricia got to the airstrip in Ciénaga, they took a car into the city and Patricia was able to return home to her worried father with a ready-made story: they'd been stuck all night because Galán had been assassinated.

'It was a hell of a way to start a relationship,' says Luis. 'This was like our first date. It *was* our first fucking date.'

Patricia still can't believe it either: 'I never imagined I was going to be Luis's girlfriend, let alone his wife.'

33

Two Toucans

PATRICIA'S ATTORNEY FATHER JUAN MANTEROLA was a traditional man who wanted to know the parents of the man his daughter was dating, and if he didn't like the sound of them, he simply forbade her from dating. That was that; this was rural Colombia, after all, where people sometimes get shot over family squabbles.

Her two polo-playing uncles, Fabio and Antonio, were also fiercely protective of their niece and well known in Santa Marta for settling differences with bareknuckle fists, rather than guns. If they found out that she was going out with somebody 13 years older, a man not from Colombia who nobody knew, least of all an international cocaine-smuggling felon, there could have been a major scene. The only solution for the star-crossed lovers was to pretend nothing was going on.

'We had to hide the relationship from my family,' says Patricia. 'They knew *everybody* in Santa Marta. Nobody knew about us, not even my close friends. Only Luis's friends knew about it. At the beginning I didn't have any clue of what he was doing; at that time the only problem I could have had was with my family about his age.'

While newly installed US President George H.W. Bush was telling Americans in his first televised address from the White House that 'victory over drugs is our cause, a just cause', Luis moved to Barranquilla to be closer to Patricia's college dorm in front of Parque

Washington and into a newly built high-rise hotel called Dann on Carrera 51B. The Colombian national football team stayed there during qualifiers for the 1990 FIFA World Cup in Italy.[163]

'We stayed in Barranquilla for about nine months. There was a lot of movement and action at the hotel. I'd see the players in the dining room and invited them to dinner. It was a great time in my life. I was in my early 30s, I was in Colombia, I had the Conquest, and I was working with Juanchi in Santa Marta and his group while renting the plane out to different drug-smuggling groups and making very good money. Juanchi and I were moving heavy weight.

'Patricia had a lot of guys after her so I wanted to make sure I discouraged that activity. I always had the concierge delivering stuff to her: flowers, teddy bears. Making sure she got home from school. Sending her food from the hotel if she wanted to eat something. Other guys knew who I was, so it wasn't like they were too anxious to get involved with Patricia.

'I used to hang out by the pool and one day I bought a couple of toucans and just built a big white cage in the lawns of the hotel to put my birds in there. I had a welder come over and put together the whole fucking thing. *Bam boom ba.* Back then you could buy toucans on a street corner. I used to do whatever I wanted. It was like my backyard. The owner came up to me and said, "What are you doin'? You're turning my hotel into a fucking zoo now?" I didn't ask permission. I was spending $3000 a week staying there, which was a lot of money in Colombia. I was the king of the hotel.'

But Patricia still wasn't sure Luis was the right man for her.

'I almost broke up with him. My behaviour was like a child's. "I don't want this, I don't want that." So one day I was in a corner fruit store in Barranquilla and I said, "I don't want you anymore." I turned around and started walking away from Luis and he was so mad he took a tomatillo, a small tomato, and he threw it, and I don't think he meant to hit me, but it hit me in the back. I screamed. The guy from the fruit store, who knew me, came at him with a machete. Luis went running down the street [*laughs*]. I was so angry with him but I was more worried that the guy from the fruit store would catch up to him and kill him.'[164]

*

From Barranquilla, Luis and Patricia moved to Bogotá at the height of the cocaine wars, with Pablo Escobar fighting the Colombian Government and the Cali Cartel on two fronts.

Luis had a front for his cocaine operation, an office at the World Trade Center on Calle 100 under the name *Asociación de Macadamia de Colombia* ('Macadamia Association of Colombia'), a sly nod to a 700-acre macadamia farm in Costa Rica he'd bought as an investment in the early 1980s. He had a personal secretary, Clara Macias, and an assistant, David Santos.[165] Patricia got her own apartment in case her family ever visited, while Luis stayed in his next to the ambassador's residence. She spent most of her time, however, over at Luis's. His bright idea was to buy her a $10,000 mobile phone (they were dear at the time) for when her dad called.

'My father always called me at seven in the morning and I couldn't stay in Luis's apartment because my father would call,' Patricia remembers. 'So he bought me this phone and got me another one for my car. I could then answer my phone in his apartment so my dad would think I was at home. We had a life like "normal" people. We moved around in the art community of Bogotá. We were neighbours of the United States ambassador; the view from our apartment was the ambassador's garden.'

Says Luis: 'We lived in Bogotá when the bombs were going off.[166] At no time did I say to Patricia, "Let's leave Bogotá," because of the bombs. We were in it and we could have run away from the violence just like anybody else, but we stayed. I just never thought it would happen to me. Thank God nothing ever happened to us.'

Patricia only realised something was not quite right in Luis's affairs when he told her they couldn't go to Miami.

'One day he told me he couldn't go back there. I think Luis always felt like he had to be on the run. But I was more aware about Luis's situation than he was; he liked to think that he spoke good Spanish in Colombia, but he didn't back then. He likes to think he is Colombian but he's not. He always looked and behaved like a foreigner and had the accent to go with it [*laughs*]. People were always asking him, "Where are you from?" And, you know, you didn't want to have that kind of attention when you had a fake identity and were living in the country illegally. My friends, my closest friends, maybe they suspected Luis was in the business but we never behaved that way or gave them reason to think that. But some people knew, for sure. If we got invited to things like weddings, we'd go but we'd just go to the party and that was it. It's not like we were going to dinner parties every week.'[167]

Their age difference was never an issue early in the relationship but on a chartered flight to Cuba, they were handing over their passports to military police who had boarded the aircraft to make immigration checks. Patricia collected the passengers' passports and handed them over.

'Who is Luis Navia? Where is he?' said the policeman. He was flipping through the pages of Luis's fake Colombian passport.

'He's *there*,' Patricia replied, nodding in the direction of the seat where Luis was drinking Scotch and laughing with his pals.

'Lady, get your daddy to come here.'

34

Death at Dog Rocks

MEANWHILE, LUIS'S MILLION-DOLLAR CONQUEST was a workhorse. He would bring it down to Colombia from its base in Caracas and do four trips at a time – two to Mexico, two to The Bahamas – to minimise flying times in and out of Venezuela.

'That plane probably did 15 trips, maybe 18. We made about $12 to $15 million with the Conquest alone. We always made money in Mexico. But on a few Mexico trips we were selling merchandise at $8000 a key when the price was 12.'

Deep in his own financial straits, Javier Mercado came forward with a proposal.

'Luis, Tío is taking too long to cross the merchandise [over the border]. We send the shit up to him in northern Mexico and he takes 30 to 45 days to cross?'

'It's fine. He always comes through.'

'We can do it much better. Let's work with Juanchi. We can airdrop in the Florida Keys, have my guys pick up and we can have our merchandise in a week. The next day we're in Miami.'

Luis was against the idea because smugglers from Santa Marta were 'disorganised'. But he gave in because he trusted Javier and wanted him to continue running operations in the States.

'He was a very able, intelligent and well-seasoned smuggler and knew how to solve problems. But we lost six trips back to back and I took a heavy hit. Even if you lose the merchandise you've still got to pay the pilots.'

Javier became increasingly desperate for a successful load. When the Conquest got to Pereira from Venezuela for one of Marulo's loads, he got on as a co-pilot when the designated co-pilot wouldn't make the trip because of safety concerns over failure reports (an aviation term for engine or system problems with the plane).

'When the engines reach certain hours of flying time you need to bring them in for scheduled maintenance; you should not push that. Javier hadn't spent adequate money on maintenance as required by the hours the engines had on them. So when the Venezuelan pilots got off, they said that the engines had some mechanical reports. The Colombian pilots got on and after a few minutes of checking out the systems, the co-pilot said he would not fly on the plane with those reports unchecked and pending. That's when Javier said he would go as co-pilot and somehow convinced the Colombian pilot, Junior Dangond aka "El Gordo", to go along with him.'

Luis got on too, just for the hell of it. The departure was timed for mid-afternoon so they would arrive in The Bahamas after sundown. The waiting boats would then pick up the cocaine during the night.

'Just out of pure adventure, I said, "Shit, I'll go with Javier. I'll go in the back; I'll go as a kicker."'A kicker is the passenger whose job it is to drop the merchandise out of the aircraft. 'And in the back of the plane, there was a black skinny guy from Barranquilla, a mechanic called Noel Cervantes aka "Kaliman".'

The four men were ready to take off when there was a commotion on the tarmac. El Gordo turned off the engines. Fernando Marulanda, who was there to supervise the onloading of the merchandise, wanted Luis off the plane and sent over his enforcer, Carlos Arturo Patiño Restrepo aka 'Patemuro', to forcibly remove him.[168]

'Get *off* the plane, Luis.'

'What the fuck, Fernando? Why? What's the problem? Javier's going.'

'If you die, who's going to pay me?'

'Okay, *okay*. Yeah, I guess you're right.'

And so Luis got out of the plane and watched his Conquest with

700 keys on board fly off into the skies above Pereira, bound for the Caribbean.

'A plane has to be in perfect shape when you're going to go down to airdrop. Planes aren't designed to go down, slow down, pull back the power, open the back door and throw shit out the back. Sure enough, they went down, they slowed down the power, the engine failed, *boom*, the fucking plane cartwheeled it right into the ocean at Dog Rocks in The Bahamas and all three of them died: El Gordo, Javier and Kaliman.

'Some of the merchandise was retrieved; they handed it to us in these fucking pails full of saltwater and cocaine. Javier's brother was down there, coordinating the receiving end with the boats on the water. He was on the radio and heard the whole thing. That was the last plane I owned. In the end, because of all the bad decisions Javier made, because he was so desperate, he fucking died. Desperate people do desperate things that result in fatal consequences. You don't hop on a plane that the co-pilot hopped off, although I was crazy enough to go along for a ride. I lost my Conquest that cost me a million dollars and another million in my share of the merchandise. But Marulo saved my life. I'm alive today because of Marulo.'

It was also the day Patricia found out what Luis really did for a living. He was a broken man. He'd lost $2 million in two planes, as much again in coke, and another friend was dead. Somehow, through it all, he was still alive. It was as good a time as any to get married, the couple formalising their relationship at Notaría 45 in Bogotá. There was no ceremony but they celebrated afterwards at an Italian restaurant.

'In Spanish we say, *nos casamos a escondidas*: we got married secretly,' says Patricia. 'I just sent a message to my dad and my little brother that I was married and that was it. Nobody in my family knew about Luis's business; only my brothers suspected it later on. Luis never looked or behaved like people who were in that business, we had friends who weren't in that business, and he had a really nice cover with the office in the World Trade Center. That's the funny thing: if you knew him at the time you would never have believed that he had something to do with drugs. Luis *never* talked about cocaine. But the day Javier died he was crying. He was completely destroyed and drunk. He told me everything. We were together by then. I was in love.'

PART 7
SCARFACE

35

Felony Favours

IN 1991, THROUGH AN INTRODUCTION by Fernando Marulanda, Luis began working for a Colombian drug lord called Luis Hernando Gómez Bustamante aka Rasguño, one of the heads of the North Valley Cartel – what Luis calls 'Northern Valley' – a criminal organisation that would become world renowned as the usurper of the Cali Cartel. Rasguño had only started out in 1987 but within three years was a major player, with up to 800 men working for him at any one time. His personal cocaine brand was Rolex.

'I moved merchandise for Rasguño to the Caribbean – airdropping off Tampa, as well as The Bahamas and into the Florida Keys, as well as water transport in fastboats into the Cancún area in Mexico for delivery to Houston.[169] We moved a lot of merchandise for Northern Valley and I became key transporter for that cartel.'

They also became unlikely friends, Rasguño borrowing one of Luis's aliases in Colombia – Julio Guzmán – for himself.

'Come January, everybody [in the cartels] changes his name, because you start the year with a new name. You don't want to be the same guy who got hot last year. So we were talking, I was ready to leave for the airport, and Rasguño says, "Oh, by the way you can't use Julio Guzmán anymore. I said, "What? [*laughs*] Er . . . *okay*." What are you talking about?" He goes, "Yeah, that's going to be my name this year. Dr Guzmán." I was like, "Okay, I'll call you later and tell you who I'm going to be this year."'

Picking a name was no laughing matter. You needed to keep up to date with aliases in the cocaine business – or you could lose your life.

'When he was still alive, The Mexican, Rodríguez Gacha, moved about 2000 kilos to La Guajira. Some [South American] Indian guy at the strip where they received the 2000 kilos was like, "Who the fuck is this? Who is sending this shit from the interior? Some fucking idiot called Andrés? Who the fuck is *Andrés*? Fuck this guy." So they plotted to steal the 2000 kilos and they did. It just so happens that that year Rodríguez Gacha changed his name to Andrés. And sure enough, when you steal 2000 kilos from Rodríguez Gacha, the military arm of the Medellín Cartel, he sent his fucking group to La Guajira and they just killed, I don't know how many fucking Indians, 40, 50, 60, 70 fucking Guajiran Indians. "Who the fuck is Andrés?" *Okaaay*. Here we go. They found out who Andrés was real quick.'

*

Rasguño, born in 1958 in El Águila in the northernmost part of the Valle del Cauca, 'El Valle', was based near Pereira in and around the city of Cartago, and got his nickname, which means 'Scratch', for the scar on his left cheek which was left behind from a bullet that got way too close; according to folklore, Rasguño had laughed it off as only a scratch.

North Valley was probably the third biggest criminal syndicate in Colombia, behind Medellín and its original overseer, Cali, but would eventually attain complete dominance of the Colombian cocaine trade in the mid-1990s. At its height it accounted for 60 per cent of all cocaine transported to the United States, moving 500 tons in total.

It wasn't an easy time to be a drug trafficker in Colombia. Pablo Escobar was on the run from Colombian and US special forces, kidnapping high-profile targets and terrorising the main cities with car bombs and assassinations. His Medellín Cartel partner The Mexican was dead and the Ochoa brothers had given themselves up to the Colombian Government and confessed to criminal activity, in exchange for no extradition and imprisonment on heavily reduced sentences. In the vacuum left behind by the rapidly disintegrating

Medellín Cartel leadership, Cali and North Valley began thriving. Business was booming for Luis.

'Northern Valley was Orlando Henao Montoya, Rasguño, Iván Urdinola. The three of them ruled that whole valley and they were a very violent group. Rasguño had a hell of a reputation for being extremely violent and volatile, though I never saw that violence first-hand. Everyone in Colombia feared Rasguño big time, just as much as Pablo Escobar. He *was* the Northern Valley Cartel.

'While the [Cali Cartel's] war with Pablo was going on, Rasguño controlled the entrance to El Valle from the northern point at Cartago. He had to filter out all the people that Pablo may send into Valle del Cauca through Cartago, the gateway to El Valle.[170] You know how many people were killed coming in from Medellín through Pereira into Cartago to go into El Valle? Fucking *hundreds* of people died. Every day someone died. Kidnappers would be chopped up – *ba ba ba ba ba ba* – stuffed in burlap sacks and thrown down the Río Cauca. Rasguño had everything [audio] taped. The whole fucking city was phonetapped. A taxi driver picked up some guy who didn't look right? *Boom.* Dead. It was like nothing.

'Rasguño was very organised, not off the wall, not crazy, had everything calculated. That's why these narcos become so powerful and so successful and why they last so long. Anybody that does business with Rasguño you knew what you were getting into. He didn't say he was a saint. He was very honest, strict and upfront and you knew it. You fuck up, you pay or *die*. I highly respected him.'

*

Marulo's introduction of Luis to Rasguño was no small thing. In fact, introducing colleagues to each other in the drug business carries a great deal of responsibility, danger and financial risk.

'You don't do felony favours.[171] For somebody to do that, there has to be a lot of trust and confidence that the person's going to perform. There's no upside for them if you lose a load; they'll get charged for it. If anyone fucked up a load it could have been massive.'

Luis had a smuggling route with El Tío from the department of Risaralda, Colombia, into Tabasco, Mexico, with Rasguño providing the merchandise plus a pair of valuable Beechcraft King Airs.

'King Air 300s cost $4 million each in Colombia. So $8 million in equipment, plus, say, $5 million in merchandise, you're talking $13 million if the shit hits the fan. To us it was one more deal. Those planes Rasguño had, they left right from Pereira International Airport: each plane loaded up with 1300 kilos. They didn't leave from a fucking clandestine strip or nothing. You paid off the tower, *boom*.'

Fucking up a load involved a heavy hit indeed.

'El Tío lost a 400-kilo load and I paid up $2.4 million, just not to have the hassle. We handed it to them in LA and Rasguño's people lost it. They got busted, somehow, whatever. But still, he didn't like to lose. So Rasguño charged *me*. He charged me $6000 per kilo, not at cost; I already had some transport expenses factored into that $6000. So $2.4 million.

'The smart thing to do is pay the man and continue working with him. If I didn't pay him, Rasguño would either have ended up killing El Tío or they would have grabbed him, then El Tío would have said, "Let's get Luis out of the way; how much do I owe you, $2.4 million? Okay, we'll work direct now." Or they would have grabbed me, forced me to pay and got me to tell him El Tío's name and how to get in touch with him. He sends his people to talk to El Tío, hooks up with him, starts working with him, tells him I didn't pay, so El Tío has to pay, then Rasguño collects from both ends. That's how people are – not necessarily Rasguño, mind you, who was always honest with me. But it's a fucked-up business.

'So sometimes you take a loss because you're going to make more in the future. You've got to play it smart. You've got to realise that against these big animals a little rabbit has no chance. I just didn't want to be in a bad situation. I analysed it and realised that paying up would be better, and in the end at least I continued working with El Tío and made my money. There's a lot of things you know after so many years of working with people.

'But the great thing about this business is that on one trip a hundred units can yield a million dollars: $10,000 profit per unit. We really started to hit Belize heavy on the airdrops in 1989/'90 with Miki Ramírez and later on with Rasguño. I was doing a lot of airdrops off Tampa as well as Mexico trips. We were hitting it *hard* in '91. The Gulf War had broken out so [the US military] moved out some of those AWACs to the Middle East and we just banged those lighthouses a lot with Rasguño, with Miki who was getting his merchandise from Fernando Galeano. Pablo Escobar was still alive at that point.

'That was when we started doing the boat trips to Cancún. I opened up Cancún to Rasguño; I created that route. By "opening up", I mean I gave Rasguño the idea and he financed the buying of the first boats and the set-up of the operation in San Andrés. We were taking 700, 800 units per trip. That was my route, my people, my idea. I invented it. I bought the boats with Rasguño's money, I had the contacts, I took San Andrés captains and crews to Pereira to meet him. I was already doing a lot of airdrops to Cancún, but airdrops became a little dangerous because of radars out of Panama and stuff, so we decided to go by water.

'These boats were undetectable. They were almost like submarines, they'd be so low to the ground. Two trips we lost because we got with a storm and he didn't charge me for those trips, but he kinda kept it on the back ledger. But Rasguño's guys did go in and rough up the crew to make sure it wasn't bullshit and the loads had actually been lost.'

36

The Wake

B Y MID-1991, PABLO ESCOBAR had surrendered conditionally to the Colombian Government, agreeing to imprisonment at his own $5 million custom-built prison in Medellín called *La Catedral* (The Cathedral). It was a sweet deal: the jail was patrolled by guards he controlled on land he owned, on the guarantee he would not be extradited to the United States. In June, Colombia had passed a law in the Constituent Assembly to rule it out once again. The drug lord's sentence would be five years but he would last only 13 months before breaking out in farcical circumstances.

Escobar's jail was less a penitentiary and more a functioning luxury clubhouse for playing soccer and screwing whores. More alarmingly, he was using it as a base to continue directing his crumbling but still very powerful criminal empire with total impunity. And that meant having senior figures in the cartel visit him in person, including Luis's friend Fernando 'El Negro' Galeano and Galeano's partner Gerardo 'Quico' Moncada.

On 3 July 1992 the pair went to visit Escobar over the issue of 'taxes', or kickbacks, to the big boss but never came back.[172] They were shot, their corpses dismembered and then burned to ashes.[173] A day later their brothers, Francisco Galeano and William Moncada, were also killed. The already erratic and paranoid Escobar had lost the plot.

'There were three people who were supposed to go visit Pablo when Galeano and Moncada got killed: Galeano, Moncada and one other. I can't name him. Bad motherfucker. He used to buy all our merchandise from the trips we did up to the States with Miki Ramírez, Galeano and Pablo. Plus receiving thousands of keys a month from other groups. He's a billionaire. He was selling all of Galeano's merchandise before Galeano died.

'Anyway, he didn't show up to that meeting. He was supposed to go. He was smarter than that. He never went. He's one that fell through the cracks. Everyone says that he's been working with the DEA for many years, doing some kind of shit that nobody even knows about. Some people say he's an asset for Mossad [the national intelligence agency of Israel], a very rich and connected person. He's definitely very tight with the US Government, some kind of aid to antiterrorism; he's a wearing a super-bulletproof coat. He is a totally different animal.'

Luis's friend Miki, a powerful figure in the Medellín Cartel, who himself was due to visit Escobar, turned up at Luis's and Patricia's apartment in Bogotá upon learning of what had happened to Galeano and Moncada. He ordered a band of *mariachis* play while he mourned.

'Miki cried for El Negro at my apartment with *mariachis*. He had *mariachis* there for fucking almost a day and a half. The *mariachis*' lips were bleeding. We were drinking, he was crying. It was like a wake.'[174]

Remembers Patricia: 'He wouldn't allow the *mariachis* to stop. The *mariachis* could not sing anymore. And I had to speak to Miki and say, "Please, let them rest. I'm going to order food so everybody's going to eat." I was the only woman in the house and I had to get some [food] orders. And he said, "Okay." The *mariachis* stopped, everyone was relieved and nobody knew what to do. He was in pain. He'd just lost his friends.'

Luis: 'After that, Pablo called Miki and said, "Come see me." He had to go talk to Pablo at *La Catedral*. He was at my apartment in Bogotá before he left and he told me, "I may not come back." He was freaking out. You can't say no to Pablo Escobar. If you say no they're going to come kill you anyway. Miki was always very concerned. Everyone used to go and visit Pablo up there. He had to pledge his allegiance. You were 100 per cent with Medellín or you were going to traffic with Cali. Obviously he said Medellín.'

When Miki returned from the 400-kilometre journey to Bogotá he went straight to Luis's and Patricia's apartment. He was shaken.

'This is getting very fucking crazy, Luis. It was very dangerous. I didn't think I was going to make it out of there.'

Later that July, with Colombians up in arms at the killings of Galeano and Moncada, the country's new president César Gaviria ordered Escobar be moved to a military prison in Bogotá. There was a major stand-off and Colombia's deputy justice minister was kidnapped while attempting to negotiate Escobar's surrender. When Gaviria dispatched special forces to raid the prison, Escobar cut the electricity and used the subsequent confusion and chaos to stage his famous 'escape' from *La Catedral* to become a fugitive from justice yet again. It was so easy he practically walked out with his band of loyal *sicarios*. He was making a mockery of everyone.[175]

And that was precisely when Miki and his friends, including Galeano's brother Rafael and paramilitary leaders/brothers Fidel and Carlos Castaño Gil with funding from the Cali Cartel, decided to form the vigilante group Los Pepes, *Perseguidos por Pablo Escobar* or People Persecuted by Pablo Escobar.

Los Pepes wanted to take down Pablo for good.

*

Effectively a state-sanctioned death squad or terrorist organisation and beginning in January 1993 and running through to the end of that year, Los Pepes killed over 300 people either closely or loosely connected to Escobar (including total innocents who had nothing to do with him at all) yet allegedly had the full support of the reorganised and US-trained Colombian police special-operations units known as Search Bloc or *Bloque de Búsqueda*.[176]

Hunted on the ground and surveilled from the air, the corpulent, unkempt Escobar retaliated with more killings and car bombs, but he was in a dragnet from which there was no escape. It was the beginning of the end of the Medellín Cartel, the criminal organisation that had given Luis his start in cocaine. Miki himself, who Luis says 'worked two sides of the coin' – the cartels and the police – stood to directly benefit.[177]

'Miki was definitely at war with Pablo and had full government support: bodyguards with all the credentials and machine guns. The sort of weapons only government agents can carry legally. We were handling a lot of Fernando Galeano's merchandise and I was close to Miki, but I never felt I would ever be a target of interest to Pablo.

'Miki is actually a *fantastic* guy. He's a better salesman than I am and I'm a great salesman. He's fat, gregarious, he puts you in his pocket immediately. He's a fantastic, lovable con artist. Legal business, illegal business, *sideways* business, whatever business, he's just one of those guys. He's always been a great friend to me.'

He also gave Luis his narco nickname, 'El Senador' (The Senator). They were at Luis's apartment and were about to make reservations at a local restaurant when Miki said, "There's no need to make reservations, we just go." At the time, Patricia was pregnant with her and Luis's first child. Luis remarked that if he ever had a son, Senador Navia would be a good name. So Miki called up the restaurant and made the reservation under the name Senador Navia, they got in, and the pair had a good laugh about it. It was that simple.

'Nobody really knew the real reason why Miki called me "Senador" but I always dressed well. I usually dressed in khakis with a white or blue shirt and always threw in a pink; always did like pink shirts. One day I met Orlando Henao's brother Arcángel, "El Mocho", and Rasguño at Rasguño's office and I was wearing a really nice off-white linen suit and a white linen shirt, with a Dunhill blue-and-beige tie with perfect matching shoes. Mocho and Rasguño didn't dress so great.'

El Mocho had got his nickname, which means 'The Amputee', because he was missing an arm due to a birth deformity.

'Mocho goes to Rasguño, "Look at this guy. *El Senador.* He looks like a senator. We look like we work for *him*." And then Rasguño goes, "I know, I *know*. Don't remind me. I may have to kill him if you remind me twice." Rasguño was always kidding around: "I'm going to kill you, motherfucker." But they were words of endearment. He would never say that to anybody else. He'd just kill you.'

*

Affection had its limits. One day Luis made a terrible *faux pas* with Rasguño from which he was lucky to escape with his life. Rasguño was a portly man who enjoyed his food. After his own appetite, whatever goodwill Rasguño had for Luis was always going to be a secondary consideration.

'We shared an apartment together in San Andrés. San Andrés is a free-trade zone 150 kilometres off the coast of Nicaragua.[178] There you can buy American canned goods, Campbell's Soup, all the shit that you can't in the Colombian interior because there are no taxes on the island. Patricia would sometimes come over and cook for them. They'd get really bored in San Andrés with the food there, since they weren't at their farms with their servants, wives and cooks.

'So I come in and someone had bought all this Latin food, Colombian canned goods. Rasguño wasn't there. He was out. And I go, "What the fuck is all this Colombian food? We should be buying American food. We're in San Andrés." So I threw away all that Colombian food and I bought American food but it was *his* fucking food. Who in their right mind throws away somebody's food, let alone Rasguño's?

'So he came back to the apartment and saw I had thrown away his food; imagine, the leader of Northern Valley Cartel blowing off his top to the max. He put the word out: "Bring me that motherfucker right now. I'm going to kill him. This time for real I'm going to kill this motherfucker." Juanchi went looking for me. He finds me and says, "You're dead. Ras is *fuming*."

'So I get back and Arcángel Henao is sitting on this La-Z-Boy, looking at this whole scene of Rasguño chewing me out to the max. Red, ready to fucking bust a fucking chair over my head. Mocho is laughing. Rasguño is blowing his top. Everybody was just like *shaking*. They figured he was going to shoot somebody. You're talking about people that have killed thousands of people. And you know what he said? "So now I know why they call you Senador. You're so fucking high class you can't eat Colombian food because you're in San Andrés. Okay, motherfucker, you're not going to be El Senador no more. You know who you're going to be? You're going to be 'El Emperador'. You're not a senator, you're a fucking *emperor*.'

'Don *Ras . . .*'

'What I'm going to do, from now on, *every fucking boat* that leaves from this island I'm going to tell the captain your name. And the boat's not going to be named *Esmeralda* or *Quico 1* or *Mary 2* or *Island Girl 4*, it's going to be called *Emperador*. It's going to have your fucking name on it and I'm going to tell the captains that the owner of the merchandise is Luis Navia, El Emperador. If by any chance on any of these *El Emperador* boats we lose the merchandise, I'm going to charge you for it. So maybe that'll get you going when you've got the fucking *gringos* on your ass again.'

'Man, don't do that.'

'Sure enough, Rasguño put "El Emperador" on the boat. From then on, *El Emperador* hit like ten or 12 times. Usually those boats would go with 1600 kilos: of that, 1000 were Rasguño's, 600 were Mocho's, but 200 of Rasguño's were Orlando Sabogal's, "El Mono", who was Rasguño's right-hand man. He hated me and wanted to kill me. He would not have hesitated putting three in my head. He was jealous of my friendship with Rasguño.

'So Rasguño was like, "If they lose a load, everybody's going to charge their percentage on the boat to this man right here, The Emperor!" Now I'm saying yes to everything Rasguño is saying. I'm not going to go against this guy, being who he is. In the end, no *El Emperador* boat ever lost the merchandise. It's a miracle that I threw away Rasguño's food and I'm alive."

*

But Luis still felt like he was trusted and liked enough to be able to call on Rasguño for personal favours. After Escobar's escape, a meeting was arranged in Cartago between Rasguño, Luis and three major traffickers: Hernán Prada Cortés aka 'Papito', Silvio Bernal and José Orlando Sánchez Cristancho aka 'El Hombre Del Overol'.[179]

'They asked me to take them to see Rasguño. Papito was originally a member of the Medellín Cartel, but when people knew that Medellín was going down he asked me to set up a meeting with Rasguño. So I took Papito and Silvio to see him and Orlando tagged along. Papito and Silvio had the same worries and wanted to secure a right-to-live ticket after the war was over.

'Papito and Silvio were partners and shipping huge amounts to Mexico, 6000, 7000 kilos at a time, hundreds of thousands of kilos; at that time they were worth $500 million each, easily. Silvio used to be a gem trader in New York in the early 1980s; very elegant, educated, sharp, one of the smartest guys I ever met. He had a very successful relationship with a group of Mexicans affiliated with Arturo Beltrán Leyva of the Beltrán Leyva brothers, a very big cartel group in Mexico.[180]

'So Papito and Silvio didn't want any trouble and were open to working with Northern Valley. They knew the intimate friendship I had with Rasguño and that I was not the type of person that would set 'em up, take 'em to Rasguño and they'd all end up getting tied up and killed. That's a move, where if you wanted to double-play anybody, they'd all end up dead. You'd take 'em to a set-up. They trusted me as a loyal, honest, non-violent intermediary. They put their lives in my hands.

'These people aren't dumb. They're extremely wealthy, very powerful drug people. And they chose me to go talk to Rasguño. In life, generally, I've always been able to deal with people. Either the worst or the best, I've always had a pleasant demeanour for both. When I'm around you can put your guns down, we're here just as friends. They met with Rasguño, everything was cool and everything went forward. Rasguño started to work with them, being their SOS on these big loads.

'They were all in Rasguño's pocket. All the guys from Pereira, like Patemuro, Marulo's bodyguard, became very rich. He made hundreds of millions of dollars. I mean, think about it. You send 1500 kilos. After you transport the dope for your clients, you end up with 400 kilos free for yourself after the Mexicans take their cut. Four hundred kilos, you just made $6 million, $10 million. They did that five to ten times a month. Rasguño would do *ten times* that much.'

37

Real Crazy Motherfuckers

PABLO ESCOBAR AND RASGUÑO weren't the worst of the narcos Luis got to meet in Colombia. In fact, they were lightweights compared to some of the demented serial killers getting about in the cartels of the early 1990s.

One of them was Jairo Iván Urdinola Grajales aka 'El Enano' (The Dwarf), an evil cocaine and heroin trafficker from El Dovio in Valle del Cauca, who was once described by DEA agent David Tinsley in *The Washington Post* as 'the most feared trafficker in Colombia and worldwide as far as Colombians are concerned. He may be the most violent criminal on the face of the earth. He has an insatiable appetite for violence.'[181]

Urdinola was certainly renowned for butchering people in the most horrific manner possible: chainsaws, the works. In the Valle del Cauca he was responsible for the decapitations and mutilations of hundreds of victims, whose bloodied, mangled corpses regularly flowed down the Río Cauca as a warning to his rivals. Their fingertips would be burned or cut off to prevent identification.

For that reason, even Rasguño, who wasn't shy of chopping up somebody on a whim but better humoured than most cartel leaders, didn't want anything to do with Urdinola. However he was okay with Luis working with him, as long as he was kept out of their affairs. Luis and Urdinola set up a meeting in a car dealership that Urdinola owned in Cali.

'Iván was a very powerful person that you did not want to fuck with. He used to charge everybody for every loss. He never took a loss. Even if it was his fault, it was always *your* fault. I knew he was violent and vicious, a dangerous guy, but it was a dangerous business. Most people I dealt with were like that; I mean, with the most powerful SOS cartel leaders and such, you don't become that way by being a "nice guy". It was an *adventure* to deal with them. If you were in the dope business and you weren't dealing with psychopaths, then you weren't really in the dope business. That's what made it exciting; at least to me it was really exciting.

'There are no words to explain the adrenalin of doing business with these people, talking to them on a daily basis and dealing with them when they're in a good mood and when they're in a bad mood and knowing how to handle those situations. That's extreme living, to say the least. You are never tougher than the Mexicans. You are never tougher than the Colombians. You always have to remember that. You are just an idiot, a fucking bug that they can just swat any time they want.

'When I was in Mexico, I always told myself: I am in the land of Mexicans. They are the bosses. You can never act as a bigger shot than your hosts. You are nothing compared to these cartels. I was very sure of what I was doing and I knew that if I were to have a problem with Iván it would not be through dishonesty or leading him to believe one thing and doing something else.

'Still, you're dealing with volatile personalities and you never know: you can be very honest, suddenly have a problem, and one of these maniacs gets up on the wrong side of bed and just decides he doesn't want you around anymore and that's the end of the story. But if you sat around and thought about that all the time, then you're in the wrong business.

'Wall Street bigshots don't sit around all day thinking about how much they could lose; they think about how much they're gonna *make*. Losing cannot be part of the formula when the stakes are so high. It's like a profession and you decide what your specialty is going to be. My specialty was big numbers and when you deal with big numbers you deal with big sources of supply, and most of the time the big sources of supply are extreme-personality types.

'I got used to that. Very few Colombians would deal with someone like Urdinola on a one-to-one basis like I did and work huge numbers that would scare the hell out of most people. I always thought the bigger the better. It gets to a point where you're too big to fail. You'll probably be killed quicker for losing 50 kilos than you will for losing 5000. It's like the big banks; they're too big to go bust.'

But as is the way with many killers, Urdinola had a soft side. He could also be generous. After the meeting in the showroom was over, he spontaneously handed Luis the keys to a brand-new BMW M535i. A chauffeur drove it for him from Cali back to Bogotá. Luis was happy to accept the modest gift.

'Not long after that I did a trip to the Florida Keys for Iván in one of his planes – 600 kilos, but the fucking coke hadn't been packed right. There had been a mix-up where my waterproofed coke was sent to Mexico and the unprotected coke was sent to the Keys. So we did the airdrop and *boom* – the coke got splattered all over the Caribbean Sea. But Iván didn't charge me for it. It was unheard of. He made somebody pay for it or replace the merchandise; I guarantee you. The bags were all ripped open. The cocaine was full of saltwater. My connection in the Keys, Jorge "El Gordito" Cabrera, had to pick that shit up and put it in pails to give it to these people who received it as proof.[182] But, sure enough, I talked to Iván and he said, "I don't want to listen to you anymore. I'm not going to let you whip out a pencil, because the minute you whip out a pencil we all lose. You know what: give me back my car.'

'Oh, shit. You know, *er*, the car's a little beat up.'

'You lose my merchandise, now you tell me my car is beat up?'

'Iván, you won't believe it, man.'

*

Luis told him the embarrassing truth. There had been an incident in the car park of a condominium in Bogotá, outside the apartment of his pilot friend Gordon 'Goo' Gray.

'I went there to hang out with Goo. He's a good cook and he made dinner and we started drinking and snorting. Patricia wasn't totally pleased but she knew I liked to get together with my friends and drink and have a few snorts and talk shit all night. Goo's wife, Phoebe, had a really good-looking friend and she was trying to hook me up with her but she wasn't at the apartment that night.[183] The next day Patricia called and said, "Okay, time to come home."'

'When Luis didn't come home and I woke up in the morning I was so worried,' she remembers. 'I started calling everybody. "Is Luis at your house? Is Luis with you?" And Phoebe called me. She said, "Hey, don't worry, Luis is here, he spent the night here with Goo, and they were drinking. They're asleep now and then they're going to eat something."'

'There was no jealousy; other women don't bother me in the least. I was sure nobody could stand him like me [*laughs*]. I was tired because I was taking care of Luis all the time. I was just a child but I was always like, "Please don't drink too much. Please don't do the coke." He *lovvves* coke. He didn't want to stop doing it. I always wanted him to stop.'

Luis continues: 'Being my usual rebellious self, I said, "No, I want to stay." So Patricia drove up to come get me and I kept saying no, that I wanted to stay and continue partying with Goo. When she got there, she called from downstairs from the guard house and she must've told the guard something because the guard let her in, so she was still pleading with me on her phone to come downstairs.'

Patricia: 'Luis didn't want to leave. I was really tired. I said, "Hey, let's go. It's enough. It's not your house. You can continue drinking and doing whatever but in your *own* house."'

Luis: 'I kept saying, "No, I'm not going." Patricia knew Goo had the penthouse and it had a balcony. So she was like, "If you don't wanna come downstairs, come out to the balcony and see what it's going to cost you for being such an asshole."'

Luis went to the balcony clutching his phone.

Patricia: 'And I was *soooo* mad, I took the keys of my car, I saw his car and I smashed into it. I completely destroyed his car [*laughs*]. The worst part was I destroyed mine too.'

In fact, Patricia was so incensed she rear-ended Urdinola's BMW four times with her own BMW, while Luis was watching on aghast. Hearing the story told in full, Urdinola let out a big laugh.

'Give me the story again, Luis. It sounds like my wife. Just fix the car up and send it back to me. That's the funniest story I've ever heard. You're one crazy sonofabitch.'

Luis's wife didn't find it so funny. Patricia was so upset she left Luis for a month and, in her own words, 'hid' from him at a friend's apartment. His drinking and coke habit had become too much for her to handle and she was over it.

'He waited for me every day while I was there, and I was like, "I don't want to know anything about you anymore, Luis. *Anything*. I'm tired. We're done." But a friend of ours got us together. When I came back I needed a drink: I ordered a Buchanan's on the rocks and told him: "You know, you have to take care of me." Luis promised he wouldn't drink for a year. And he did it. That's why I went back to him and our relationship survived.'

*

In early 1993, around the time Gilberto Rodríguez Orejuela and Miguel Rodríguez Orejuela of the Cali Cartel began negotiations with the Colombian Government to surrender peacefully and stop trafficking, in exchange for reduced jail time and keeping their spectacular wealth, Luis began working with a blond, blue-eyed Cali figure called Claudio Endo aka 'Mono Endo'.

'A fucking psychopath, a *maniac*. You talk about maniacs. Claudio was known to be a fucking psycho killer. That motherfucker would go and chop you up with a saw himself. He was nuts and wired. His eyes were always bloodshot, so they were red, white and blue. I just had a knack for dealing with nuts, I guess, I don't know. What I did was completely insane, but it was perfectly normal for me to go to Cali and work with someone like that. He was regarded as even more of a psychopath than Iván and more volatile.'

'The Cali Cartel was trying to cut a peace deal with the government and part of the peace plan was to stop working, so they asked everyone to stop working.[184] Claudio said, "Fuck you. That's easy for you to say; couple of fucking old geezers that already have $10 billion. I'm still making my money. I still need to work." So he continued working. I did five or six trips with Claudio to Cancún to my people, 5000 kilos, when nobody was doing nothing. That's a lot of merchandise. We just whacked it like nothin'. *Boom boom boom*.'

That's when he got a phone call from Miki Ramírez.

Pure Narco

'Senador, *please*, I beg you, stop working with Mono Endo. You're my friend. I don't want to see you die. Believe me, with Mono Endo you're going to end up dead. With me, there's no problem; you can lose a load. You're my friend. You're not his friend.'

'I agree.'

'So come home, come back to Bogotá, and I will open up the *oficina* just for you. I will give you what you need. But *stop*. Stop immediately with Mono Endo.'

It was sage advice. Endo was targeted and killed a year later by the Cali Cartel, who had sent a gang of *sicarios* to assassinate him at his *finca* outside Jamundí in the Valle del Cauca, just south of Cali. He was depicted being killed in season three of *Narcos* being dragged behind a car on the orders of Cali's Hélmer Herrera aka 'Pacho'.[185] The incident never happened. Instead Endo was shot between 50 to 100 times with machine-gun fire at close range. But the end result was the same.

'They just came in and shot him up in the bathroom of his farm. He locked himself in there and they just whacked him. Real crazy motherfucker.'

*

As for Iván Urdinola, in April 1992 he was arrested on a trafficking charge following a raid of 300 police and sentenced to four years and seven months' jail (an initial, much tougher sentence of 17 years was reduced because he confessed to sending cocaine to the United States). His equally feared younger brother Julio Fabio gave himself up in March 1994.

Urdinola was all set to walk free two years into his sentence but he was then rearrested and charged in relation to the August 1991 acid torture and brutal murder of an army officer called Ricardo Petersson, who'd had an affair with Urdinola's wife Lorena Henao Montoya, the sister of Orlando, while in Cali. Petersson was slit from his stomach to his throat and thrown in the Río Cauca, like most of Urdinola's victims. Still behind bars, Urdinola was murdered by poisoning in 2002.[186] Ten years later, Lorena was assassinated by *sicarios* on a motorbike.

There are few happy endings in the drug business in Colombia.

38

The Prisoner of Cartago

IN MAY 1993, LUIS did lose a load: a small but significant one in the scheme of things and for those who impounded it, when a boat called *Top Gun II* was intercepted by the US Navy hydrofoil USS *Hercules* some 200 miles west of Key West, Florida, with 375.5 kilos of 94 per cent–pure cocaine aboard. The two offloaders were detained and delivered into the custody of the USCS.

That year Luis was getting most of his work transporting for Rasguño, but was involved in a sideline as a supplier with his old smuggling friend from Santa Marta, Francisco Moya aka Juanchi. They'd rendezvoused the previous year in San Andrés with a group of smugglers Juanchi knew from the Florida Keys, but to Luis they were strangers and this had made him nervous. Juanchi's contacts were using a fleet of vessels from the Keys city of Marathon to pick up Miki Ramírez's cocaine that had been airdropped off the west coast of Florida, then bringing it back to the Keys and taking it to Miami for distribution. The *Top Gun* smuggle was the ninth and last.

'We had sent Juanchi's cousin to oversee operations in Miami and Tampa and receive monies and make sure merchandise was distributed, and he'd come running back to Colombia because he got hot. So we knew we were already hot. We were hitting the South Florida area from three angles: the east side, airdropping in The Bahamas; the west, airdropping off Tampa; and then from Cancún we were also sending merchandise up to Mississippi and Louisiana. At the same time we were working the Mexican border and delivering merchandise to LA.

'*Top Gun* was a trip that we did from Colombia to Cancún,' says Luis. 'It was a double offload. We had a large blue twin-engine inboard fastboat that Rasguño had bought in Buenaventura. And we loaded that boat with about 1200 kilos, dropped off 800 kilos off Cancún, received more fuel and continued to drop off 400 kilos more a little further north to Scorpion Reef [Arrecife Alacranes], north of the Yucatán Peninsula. The captain really didn't want to do the second leg of the trip and I don't blame him. After the two guys on *Top Gun* picked up the load, they were chased by this *huge* hydrofoil. It was like a building behind them. And they were busted.

'That was a logistical mistake. I should never have done a double smuggle. When you get to a place and you're handing off merchandise, that's it; the crew wants to go back. You should just deliver and go back but with a double smuggle you can pick up heat doing the first load and not know it, so you're already on fire on your way to the second drop-off.'

Luis was rightly spooked by what had happened.

'I was concerned, obviously. I knew that these people were going to talk. But I was living my life as if I had already been indicted. I knew I was hot; I'd been hot for years. What I did not know was that these people knew my name. Those fucking idiots that came to San Andrés from the Keys, I didn't know them. Juanchi knew them. I was not too happy meeting these people. I think one of them was already undercover.

'Juanchi got high and fucked up on coke and shit and my name must have slipped out. When you're drunk and high on coke, you talk about this shit, you think this guy's your best friend, and sure enough I told Juanchi, "Why the fuck are you working with these people from the Keys who know your name, when we are working with El Tío from Mexico? He doesn't know who we are. He doesn't need to know our names. He knows that if he steals from us he's going to die. Yeah, he might take 30 days to pay us but he pays us and he doesn't know our *names*."'

Luis didn't know it yet but his cover was blown.

*

Things, however, were about to get a whole lot worse. Patricia was five months pregnant and staying at the Ritz-Carlton in Cancún. Andrea Blanco, the sister of his brother-in-law, Vicente, was also with Luis in Cancún but there was a problem.

'Andrea was losing her mind; she ended up in a psycho clinic. Basically she started talking shit about me. She didn't say that I was stealing but worse: that I was talking bad about Rasguño, that I was downplaying him, saying I was the boss and he was a gopher for me. Imagine – totally ridiculous. Never in my life have I ever done that. I respected Rasguño and it was an honour to be working for him.'

'She was a little bit nuts,' says Patricia. 'Andrea left a message for Luis with the front desk of the hotel, "The DEA is after you." And Luis and I took everything and we ran. And we went to Playa del Carmen as a precaution and nothing happened. But we didn't know that nothing was going to happen.'

The damage had been done, however, and word got to Rasguño that Luis had been badmouthing him. Luis got a call from Juanchi.

'You should fucking leave the country, right now. He's going to kill you. He's fucking pissed.'

Luis was mortified; they might have had their differences and business was business, but above all else he considered Rasguño a friend. So rather than fleeing to Southeast Asia, he jumped on a plane to Colombia and met the head of the North Valley Cartel at his *oficina*. Instead of talking things out, Luis was kidnapped and kept for 21 days at a *finca* outside Cartago.

*

'When they grabbed me, they put me in the car with a policeman from Pereira, one of Rasguño's bodyguards and some other Ras guys. On the drive over I was looking out the window to the pastures of the Valle del Cauca and my vision was going past the horizon and taking my mind away from the situation I was in. I was in a state of limbo. What's going through your head is that you're going to die. If you are taken in – you never walk out alive. What are you going to do? Turn into a Walter White?[187] That was very fictitious, that *Breaking Bad* shit. You took your lickings and you kept on ticking. I never for one minute thought that they were going to torture me; none of that stupid stuff, no. I just thought they were going to put a bullet in my head and it's over after you pay.'

Based on nothing more than a rumour, he'd been kidnapped and Rasguño had a legitimate pretext for doing so; but Luis believed there were overriding strategic motivations at play.

'They were already planning to do it, to take over my route and all this shit. Rasguño never takes somebody in, holds them, and lets them go. That's not good business. He wouldn't have let anybody else live. The reason he let me live was I wasn't a violent guy. That's what saved me.'

In other words, Luis wasn't the kind of trafficker who could do a couple of trips, make $20 million, and use part of that money to avenge his kidnapping. Rasguño was after a ransom: calculated through loads for the cartel that had been lost and cocaine Luis had bought himself on credit. It was an expensive tab sheet.

'He told me I couldn't leave until we squared off accounts. That's when everybody thought I was going to get killed. Even if you clear your accounts, you die anyway. The only thing you hope for is that they don't torture you. Rasguño did a complete audit. Believe me, if he would have found out that any of the shit that was said by Andrea was real, I'd be dead. I'm alive because I didn't steal from him.

'I had merchandise on different trips I had bought on credit and the merchandise that was en route hadn't been *coronado* yet – which means to get it to its destination and get paid. Rasguño's bill came out to $4 million. Cartels don't have fine print in their contracts. Money's a very powerful tool; you need to use it. I'd rather pay up than see somebody killed or be killed. If you don't pay, you die.'

*

Coming up with that kind of money quickly took some doing and fast-talking. Luis paid what he could in property deeds to apartments he owned in Bogotá and land he owned in San Andrés, plus cash and stakes in future loads, while his wife offered land she owned in Santa Marta, her car, art collection and jewellery. Juanchi also had to pay Rasguño but wasn't held.

'For a week I was in a daze,' says Luis. 'I didn't know what the fuck was going on. It was a nice farm with a pool. Rasguño's people would bring in some books in English. For the first three days I was handcuffed to a bed in an apartment, but the rest of the time I just stayed by the pool at the farm.

'I volunteered all my assets and my money and everything. I was the largest landowner in San Andrés. I had incredible lots down by the water where I was going to build a marina, I had lots on Santa Catalina, lots in Providencia – and that's what paid part of the $4 million.[188] They went to my apartment in Bogotá. They were very decent with Patricia. When Rasguño snatched me, she was seven months pregnant. Patricia said, "Take my paintings, take my jewels." They were worth a lot of money. His men said, "*No, no, no*. We don't want nothing of yours." Then they let her see me.'

Patricia, just 24, displaying a courage belying her years and not knowing whether she would be killed herself, met the cartel's lawyer in a café in a Bogotá shopping mall called Centro 93 to make arrangements for the payment of the ransom. Then 15 days after Luis had been taken, she flew to Pereira and fronted up at the *finca* in Cartago with 'a long list' of how she and the father of her unborn child were going to pay: properties, land, paintings, cars. Luis's personal secretary Clara Macias was with her, having helped put together the list.

'Rasguño was so ashamed when he saw me. All of them were.'

'When she showed up,' adds Luis, 'they couldn't believe it. No one does that. Patricia went to Cartago seven months pregnant. They were embarrassed because they'd never have expected a woman to show up. In most of these cases when that happens to someone's partner or husband, the women and everybody start hiding all the assets. They don't want to give up anything. They say the exact opposite of what Patricia said. Which was, "Take everything but just give me my husband back." She's got her grandfather's balls. Rasguño really liked Patricia. Rasguño's people thought she really didn't deserve me; that she had to put up with a lot of shit from me. They saw that she was a straight shooter.'

Patricia remembers it vividly: 'Rasguño told me, "*No, no, no*. Take your car. I don't want *your* things. That is not necessary." He promised me that he'd respect Luis's life and I explained to him, "He's not from Colombia, he doesn't have a brother, he doesn't have cousins, he doesn't have a family, he only has a sister and a mother in Miami who are never going to come to Colombia to ask what happened, so you can never expect *represalias* [retaliation]." No one was going to avenge Luis or do something like that. That's why I was there and they knew me. I really wasn't afraid because I think they are people with honour. They have this code that nobody really understands. They do respect some things.'

*

Any thoughts of escape were crushed when Rasguño's cold-eyed number-one henchman Orlando Sabogal Zuluaga aka 'El Mono' or 'Mono Sabogal' paid a visit. He made the situation very clear: Luis would be killed if he so much as even contemplated escaping. If El Mono had his own way he would have turned Luis into a colander from bullet holes, but Rasguño wasn't allowing any harm to come to him.

'El Mono *haaaated* Luis,' says Patricia. 'I cooked for El Mono and Rasguño in San Andrés. I'd always been nice to them and showed them respect. Luis and I were the opposite of the kind of people you normally see in the business. We were well educated. If you understand a bit about the social classes in Colombia you will know that some people don't treat each other with respect. I was never like that. My grandfather and my great-grandfather came from Spain and they taught us to respect the people who have less than you or work for you. You don't have any right to mistreat those people. So I always was very polite; more than polite. I tried my best. So because of the way we treated Rasguño and El Mono, they treated us with respect in the moment we needed it.'[189]

Eventually Luis felt confident enough to break the ice with the three *sicarios* who were guarding him.

'I got bored with the rice and beans every day and we used to send out for pizza. The old me came back. I created an ambience around me of laughter. Everything was a joke. Then that led to the hitmen taking me out to the pizzeria and Rasguño found out because he owned the pizzeria. Then taking me out for phone calls to my attorney Reid Constable about my macadamia farm in Costa Rica, and Rasguño found out because he had the phone company tapped. Then taking me out to get a driver's licence, and Rasguño found out because he had the motor registry tapped. I'd been in the country so many years I wanted a Cartago driver's licence, for the hell of it. Rasguño had that whole town wired.'

The three hitmen even came to like Luis and asked him for work.

'They were like, "Señor Navia. Don Luis. *Senador*. Eh, what do you mean you want a driver's licence? Dead people don't drive; you could be dead in an hour. You may be delusional, but we really like you. Usually when it comes time to kill someone we're holding, they tell us, 'You do it.' And this time nobody wants to do it. We're gonna flip. We're gonna draw straws. It's a problem between you and El Patrón and if he calls the order, we're gonna do it. We're going to kill you but we don't want to do it."

'They knew I had great connections in Mexico and I told them that if I got out of this situation I'd probably just go to Mexico, and they told me that they would love to come work with me. I mean, who the fuck thinks of a driver's licence when he's handcuffed to a fucking bed and they're going to kill him any moment? Usually when you're tied up and you convince a bodyguard who's holding you hostage to take you out for pizza, when you come back you're dead and the bodyguard's dead. The three guys that were holding me, they were scared shitless. I mean it's a miracle Rasguño didn't fucking kill them all. But he knew I was innocent. I was so naïve that I was kidnapped and I still didn't realise I was kidnapped. I was thinking of pizza.'

*

On the third week of Luis's imprisonment, the reparation had been paid and he was free to leave.

'Bets were on in Colombia: this time he's not coming back from a kidnapping by Rasguño. It doesn't happen. Rasguño kidnaps you, then you've got to wish for a quick death, he takes as little as possible and he leaves your widow with something to live on. But I came back. It was like a ghost coming back. And when he let me go, most people would get in a taxi and hightail it to the next country. I took the taxi to the local hotel in Cartago that he owned and I checked in under his name. My bill was under him: *Luis Navia as per Hernando Gómez.*'

Luis requested a private audience with Rasguño and he came to visit Luis in his hotel room. Rasguño was carrying a Harley-Davidson branded black-leather briefcase.

'Man, you've left me broke,' he told the North Valley Cartel leader. 'I have no money. Can you lend me $100,000 in the meantime?'

'You know what, Luis,' Rasguño snarled. 'I'm going to give you what I have in my briefcase. Do me a favour. *Please.* Get the fuck out of town.'

Patricia had flown into Pereira and hailed a taxi to take her to collect Luis in Cartago.

'I felt a little bit afraid. If they were going to kill us, it was going to happen then. But everything was okay. Rasguño's bodyguards were like, "Good luck with the delivery of the baby," [*laughs*] and they hugged me. They told me they were going to miss Luis. When we were alone in the taxi back to Pereira, I was really scared. I thought: "They could kill us here on this road." I was only going to feel safe on the plane back to Bogotá. Luis never lived by the rules. Not even after he was released after being held for almost a month, he stayed in Cartago asking to talk to Rasguño. Anybody else would have left immediately.'

Inside the taxi, Luis opened the leather case to see what was inside. It was $50,000. When he got home, Rasguño called.

'*Motherfucker.* You didn't even pay the bill!'

'Well, it's *your* hotel, Ras. I thought the least you could do was put me up for a couple of days.'

*

On 2 December 1993, with nowhere left to run, Pablo Escobar was shot three times by the *Policía Nacional de Colombia* (PNC or Colombian National Police) on a Los Olivos, Medellín, rooftop at Carrera 79B #45D-94: one bullet in the back of his right leg, one in his back and the *coup de grâce* through his right ear. Photos of his bloated, shoeless body twisted in its last repose on a bed of blood-spattered, broken terracotta tiles went around the world. The Medellín Cartel was over.

Luis found out the news Escobar had been killed at Cartagena airport through a corrupt army officer.

Three weeks later, on 29 December 1993, at Clinica del Country private hospital in Bogotá, Luis became a father for the first time. He and Patricia had a daughter, Juliana, and she was premature but a healthy 3700 grams. He cut the umbilical cord.

'Patricia was there, you know, having the baby, *boom boom*, and I grabbed the baby and I tell Patricia, "Patricia, *wow*, this is amazing, this is beautiful, my God, she's beautiful, she looks just like . . . *me*." Patricia thought I'd said she looked just like her. When she heard that she looked like me, Patricia fainted [*laughs*]. *Boom*, they had to come in with oxygen and everything. That'll knock out anybody. So Patricia has the baby and we get home and we start getting presents in packages from [the mail company] Servientrega. Cartago is known for its embroideries.'

As Patricia unwrapped the presents, there were some unfamiliar names on the cards: 'El Diablo' (The Devil), 'El Búho' (The Owl) 'El Caballo' (The Horse). She was puzzled.

'Luis, who's Caballo?'

'Oh, that's the guy who first chained me up when I was kidnapped, but let me out the first night when I went out to have pizza.'

'*Wha?*'

'Yeah, he's one of the hitmen you met. He crucified one of his victims and skinned him alive and sprayed him with alcohol.'

'Oh, okay. Well, this nice embroidery is from him for our newborn daughter. Who's Diablo?'

'Well, that's another hitman who killed seven people when they tried to kidnap Rasguño.'

'Oh, well he sent a nice little pillowcase for our baby. And who's Búho?'

'Baby, you met them. These were all the hitmen who had me in custody.'

He still shakes his head about it today.

'These guys were fucking killers and they sent embroideries to my wife.'[190]

New Year's Eve was just days away and Luis had survived a true *annus horribilis* – the *Top Gun* bust, a kidnapping and extortion,

Escobar's death – and emerged somehow as a father. Yet, bizarrely, there is no residual animosity to the man who'd put him through so much: Rasguño.

'Once Medellín broke up and Pablo got taken down, Northern Valley kind of split from Cali. Miki Ramírez knew [the Colombian Government] were going after Cali, so he didn't know what was going to happen with Los Pepes. He knew they were going to come after his ass. The government took away his security. So when the DEA went directly after Cali, that gave Northern Valley a window. Rasguño was kind of the one that took over and Northern Valley became the biggest cartel in Colombia. But it was because of Rasguño I saw my daughter. It touches my heart and I'll always love him and I'll always do whatever I can for him.'

PART 8

BLAME IT ON CANCÚN

39

Fire in the Lake

KNOWING HIS NAME HAD likely been leaked and USCS or the DEA was onto him meant one thing to Luis: selling his remaining assets, packing up the family and leaving Colombia. His next destination, naturally, was Mexico. The cartels were being brought to heel in Colombia but in Mexico it was still very much anything goes and the perfect place to hide. He spoke the language, had been moving drugs into the country since the early 1980s and the *federales* could easily be bought off.

So in March 1994, he arrived on a Colombian passport in his own name transiting Mexico City to Cancún, a beachside city in Quintana Roo he knew very well. His wife, infant daughter and their maid followed him in June. He began openly living as Luis Navia, Colombian, but also had a Mexican alias and fake passport under the name Luis Novoa Alfandari. He even bought a coffee company, Café Koba, and started buying beans from local growers and roasting and blending them to supply the city's then-booming hotel sector and its American clientele. Luis was selling 20,000 kilos of coffee a month. But the main game was always cocaine.

'I never looked like a narco or acted like a narco. Juliana had just been born and I was thinking about the future, organising my future trips with my SOS, which was Hernán Prada. He had the merchandise but no sea transport to take the merchandise to Cancún, so I put

Hernán in touch with Alfredo or "Api", the brother of Mono Abello. Mono was probably the sixth most important member of the Medellín Cartel and also affiliated with the Coast Cartel.[191] Api had fastboats for transport in the Caribbean. Cancún became such a profitable port of entry for cocaine that everybody and his mother started to send shit there. It became one of the biggest if not *the* biggest route at the time. Cancún was fun and games by daytime, but by night thousands and thousands of kilos were coming in. We did a bunch of trips. We did three trips in the last six months of '94. We were back in business.'

Prada Cortés, a Colombian but US resident who was a big mover of merchandise in New York, had fled the country in 1989 after an FBI investigation into his cocaine distribution network resulted in a federal arrest warrant.[192] In Colombia his silent partner was Edgar Guillermo Vallejo Guarin aka 'Beto el Gitano' (Beto the Gypsy), a fellow ex-Medellín alumnus and major cocaine trafficker to Europe, and together they were getting merchandise from the department of Boyacá in Colombia from people unaffiliated with any cartel but associates of The Mexican, the late José Gonzalo Rodríguez Gacha. They sent over a *sicario* called 'Wálter'. It was the first and only time Luis ever had his own bodyguard.

'He actually looked just like The Mexican. The night we brought in the first trip the turtles were nesting in the sand. Wálter and I were there, eating Domino's Pizza. He had been a hitman for The Mexican but was a fucking awesome guy. Our suppliers wanted the maximum protection possible for me. We got along great. For Wálter it was a relief to be around a non-violent family guy. He felt very at ease. If he had to have it out with six Mexicans, he'd walk out alive and the six Mexicans would be dead. He was very good at what he did. After I'd made the first trip I brought Patricia over to live in Cancún and we never went back to live in Colombia.'

Says Patricia: 'I was so happy. Luis bought Café Koba and finally we were doing something different. In Bogotá a lot of people had bodyguards – armed escorts or *escoltas* – even people who had nothing to do with that kind of business had them; I had friends that had bodyguards and they were just wealthy, legal businesspeople. Back then kidnapping was very common. Before and after Pablo Escobar fell, there were militias that had all the structure but no bosses to follow and they became kidnappers, *secuestradores*. And we always had the guerrillas. I think it was the worst time to be in Colombia.

'So Café Koba was a good business and I helped in sales, expanding the business. Our partners were third-generation, very prominent coffee people. Luis played golf and was occupied with the coffee business and his macadamia farm in Costa Rica. Right now I feel like I'm talking about a world that has been completely trashed for the last 20 years and it might be hard for you to understand how me and Luis were able to live in that world and not be completely absorbed by the criminal side of it, but that is part of Luis's magic: he makes you feel like anything is possible.

'Everyone's concept of the cocaine business is that it's full of ugly people but it wasn't like that. I understand people who have never been to Colombia thinking that, but you'd find really nice, high-class people being involved. We never got involved in "ugly things". We never had a gun in my house, ever. *No*. Luis was always against guns. I don't think I've ever seen him holding a gun.'

'It was the best years of my life,' says Luis. 'We lived in a very nice house on the beach. We planted coconut trees in the big yard we had, went for beach walks every day, enjoyed life with my wife and my kid. South and Central America was my playground. I could go anywhere. I knew where to go, how to go, and as *what* to go.

'All the people that I knew in Mexico that were in the drug business, on the Colombian side, were all very well-to-do, high-level people. They had kids, the whole family atmosphere. It's different when you're an American with no cultural interactions. I wasn't a deadbeat. I moved in high society freely. To me it was no problem. We'd go somewhere and we were in like Flynn. That's an art that I had. A lot of people can't do that. They just can't adapt.

'Americans on the run in Mexico or South America have a hard time. But I adapted [*clicks his fingers*] immediately. The whole nine yards. The kids in school. The apartments. The car, the credit cards, the bank accounts, *everything*. Nobody in Mexico thought I was in the drug business. I was just a very rich Colombian guy who partied like an animal. That said, you have to be sharp and on your feet. It's not easy.'

Richard Booth, his old friend in mischief from Miami, agrees: 'Luis would always have to get up and just leave his belongings and move somewhere else. He really was a very bright guy at what he did to stay ahead of the game for 25 years.'

*

How to properly answer a phone call from a drug lord is one such skill only 25 years of experience can give you.

One day Luis answered the phone: it was Hernán Prada Cortés asking him about Alex DeCubas aka 'Coco' or 'Mario', a fellow Cuban-American cocaine trafficker on the run in Colombia. An ex-champion high-school wrestler with a hulking frame and connections to Félix Chitiva and Miki Ramírez, he was a fugitive from a drugs indictment in Florida, had recently left Brazil, and invested $2 million of his own money in a clandestine project to build a homemade narco submarine.[193]

'Hi, everything good, Luis?'

'Yeah, Papito. I'm good.'

A lot of people in the drug business get killed because people lie, badmouth their rivals, harbour jealousies, or completely make up stories to protect themselves and get other people killed instead. In the drug business every phone call is important. It pays to speak the truth, every single time.

'Hey, you know Coco?'

'Yeah.'

'What kind of guy is he? Is he legit? Does he know what he's doing?'

'Yeah, definitely. He knows what he's doing. He's been a smuggler all his life.'

'Would he steal?'

'*No.* Without a doubt he would not steal. If he has a loss, he'll own up to it.'

'Okay, because I was thinking of working with him.'

'He's an excellent guy. You're in good hands, Papito. He knows what he's doing.'

And that was that. But a few weeks later, Luis got a message to call Lester Delgado Cabrera aka 'Pinky', the cousin of El Gordito (Fatty),

Luis's Cuban *recibidor* in the Florida Keys.[194] He was in Bogotá. Pinky, also a Cuban, was a very relaxed, almost bohemian cocaine trafficker with a shabby dress sense and Harry Potter eyeglasses, who'd got his unusual nickname for the advanced case of psoriasis he had. He'd be shedding skin all the time.

According to Luis, before Pinky arrived in Colombia he'd been on the lam in the United States and then Rio de Janeiro, where he was sharing a house with DeCubas and a blond, blue-eyed American from Islamorada in the Florida Keys called Steve Smit aka 'Chepe', another fugitive. All three travelled on fake Dominican Republic passports.

Pinky's specialty was trafficking coke to England and mainland Europe on sailboats, usually 500- to 600-kilo loads, and using a Dutchman and Brazilian national called Godfried Hoppenbrouwers aka 'Pappy' as his logistical brains. Pinky and his Cuban-American colleague, DeCubas, got their coke from Pablo Escobar's former associate, Félix Chitiva, who in turn was getting his coke from Miki Ramírez and later Los Mellizos in northern Colombia.

'The three of them finally ended up in Bogotá because obviously they needed to get the work, and Colombia was where all the connections were. When they lived in Brazil, Alex would just hire hookers all day and Pinky used to put on his backpack just to walk and get away from that madness. I guess he was kind of depressed. He missed his mother a lot and knew that he wasn't going to be able to see his family anymore, being on the run. He could live off his backpack. When they got to Bogotá they again all lived in the same house. Alex started using his contacts to do his airdrops in the Keys and he also began building the submarine. Pinky concentrated on the sailboats to England and Chepe was very mechanically inclined and he worked with Alex on the sub.'[195]

'Hey, Luis,' said Pinky, down the line. 'I really want to thank you for what you did. You saved Alex's life.'

'What do you mean?'

'Well, when Papito called you, Alex was tied up. They'd had him tied up for a week or two. We lost a load in the Keys. It was a set-up. Papito wanted to see if you'd say Alex was prone to stealing loads.'

*

Wálter lived in the same apartment complex where Luis and Patricia had a townhouse/villa but Luis also kept a third apartment where they just talked and Luis would take his hookers. But the close proximity allowed him and Luis to get to know each other quite well, beyond their professional relationship.

'Wálter was at our villa on and off but he was always around; he never made his presence felt and he was a very respectful, calm person. He had a wife and daughter in Pereira. They owned a party supply store: ornaments and stuff for kids' parties, first communions. He felt they were safe there and he wanted to set himself up financially and get his family away from all the madness and live normally. He always carried a SIG Sauer P226 9mm; a great gun, easy to handle and accurate. He used to tell me it was special because it was German-made. I think it took 15 rounds. He also had an AK-47 hidden somewhere.'

But Patricia found out about the bachelor pad. She showed up, confronted Luis and left in a huff when one of his girlfriends was hiding in the shower. Wálter turned to him. He was about to teach Luis a very valuable lesson about the drug trade: it's all about protecting the business.

'Listen, I've been through a lot of things in life. And I've never been so scared as today. I am more scared of your wife than I've been of any man I've ever had to kill. This is not going to leave this room but let me tell you: this can never happen again, because if down south in the *oficina* they found out that I let you have a girlfriend and that in the process of you having a girlfriend your wife found out and we caused her any kind of emotional damage, they're going to kill me.

'Your wife is a very decent, classy girl. Believe me, I've seen it happen where these girls lose their fucking top and call the *oficina*. My lifespan would be the time it takes a hitman to come from Bogotá to Mexico City to Cancún and blow my brains out. After they killed me they'd probably kill that girl and dump her in the mangroves and get rid of the problem. You, they won't kill. You're not supposed to have girlfriends. You're supposed to be a family man because we're moving tens of thousands of kilos through here and there can be no waves. This has to be a very calm lake. There can be no fires in the lake.'

40

Chasing a Ghost

ROBERT HARLEY JR WAS born in Philadelphia, Pennsylvania, on 11 March 1965, the youngest of three children and the only boy with two older sisters. The Harleys were 'buffet Catholics' because they weren't especially religious and picked of Catholicism what they liked, while ignoring what they didn't like. Both his late parents, Italian-Irish mother Violet and Dutch-Irish father Robert Sr, were from the coal-mining region of Pennsylvania.

Violet worked for the US Navy while Robert Sr was an oilman for the Phillips Petroleum Company, so when his father got promoted they'd find themselves moving. Harley had a peripatetic childhood, switching between Pennsylvania, New York, Ohio, South Carolina and Florida. By 1979, when Luis began his cocaine career with the Medellín Cartel, 14-year-old Harley was going to St. Thomas Aquinas High School in Fort Lauderdale, 30 minutes up the I-95 from Miami, and working at a marina downtown called Pier 66.

'I was living in Fort Lauderdale when all this business really started taking off. South Florida in the late '70s was wide open. I graduated high school in 1983 and went to college at the University of Pennsylvania back in Philadelphia. My undergraduate major was in economics and finance. It doesn't make sense but I knew after freshman year that I didn't want to do that. I didn't know what I wanted to do for a living but I knew I didn't want to do *that*.

'Growing up in Fort Lauderdale I had a US Customs agent who lived two houses down from my family and I had an ATF agent – Alcohol, Tobacco and Firearms – who kind of lived diagonally from us, so I saw those guys fairly regularly.[196] And I liked being in Florida. I liked being on the boats, being around marinas and airplanes and all the rest of that, and I don't really remember exactly how it happened but in my junior year of college I started applying to federal agencies. I got interviews and went through the application process with multiple different agencies; I even got interviewed by the CIA at one point in Philadelphia.

'DEA actually offered me a job first in the fall of 1986 but at the time everybody was going one of two places for DEA: New York City or Puerto Rico. And I got an offer from Customs subsequent to the interview process from DEA. It was to go to Key West and literally that's how I ended up with Customs in Key West versus any other agency. It was about geography. Everybody starts at the same pay grade and goes through the grades at the same rate. In those years Customs and DEA was essentially the exact same job.'

By March 1987 Harley had enrolled in a 16-week course at the Federal Law Enforcement Training Center (FLETC) in Glynco, Georgia, to learn the ropes as a special agent. Six months later there was four weeks of 'boat school', where rookies were taught how to drive boats for interception.

Harley calls it 'FBI Lite because Customs wasn't nearly as regimented in those years as the FBI was. FBI agents in those days were still kind of suit and tie. Customs agents worked in the ports, airports and seaports. And you weren't ever going to wear a suit and tie doing that kind of casework. So the academy was a little more lax. Myself and one other guy in my class were the youngest by far. Most people were in their early 30s. We were both 22. So it was really unusual for them to take people that young, but there was a huge expansion because of what was going on in South Florida at that time.'

The Florida Keys had long been a hotbed of drug-trafficking activity with whole families of 'multigenerational smugglers', as Harley calls them, involved. There were so many smugglers in the Keys, agents would scour through high-school yearbooks picking out suspects. For the first couple of years as a USCS agent he was on the water.

'I was a boat driver. In those days there wasn't a marine officer position – the agents actually drove the boats when we were doing interdictions. It was two or three a week. It was very hectic in the beginning. By about '91 or so, because they put so many assets into the Gulf and the southeast coast of the US, it forced the smugglers into Texas, Arizona and southern California. There were still a lot of loads going into the Gulf of Mexico into '92 and '93. There was straight-on interdiction going on – boat patrols by Coast Guard, Customs, Fish and Wildlife, so there were coastal patrols, there were coastal radar installations on top of condominiums.[197] That's when BLOC, the Blue Lightning Operations Center [in Miami], was set up and that was starting to pick up the near-shore activity.[198] So you weren't having airdrops 20 miles offshore and the boats running it in.'

Instead, smugglers, including Luis and his *recibidor* friend El Gordito, were forced to make airdrops way out to sea. Serendipitously, cocaine bales float.

Continues Harley: 'There's a NOAA weather buoy way out in the Gulf of Mexico and it was outside of most radar range.[199] It was definitely outside of all fixed-radar ranges. And only if there were Coast Guard aircraft and other spook-type aircraft up would you ever know that an airdrop took place out there. That started probably in '91, '92. I think they called it the Coke Machine. That's a long trip, though. That's not easy smuggling for the guys doing the boat end of the deal. Around that time there were also a couple of airplane crashes and I think that had an effect on the willingness to do those long aircraft trips from La Guajira to the north side of Cuba and back, because you're kind of pushing those aircraft to the outer limits of their capabilities.

'In those years, to me, I felt interdiction was pointless. I don't think anybody knew exactly how much was coming in. Really, the way to stop it was to dismantle an organisation and it wasn't until '92, '93, when we changed our focus away from interdiction and towards actually working up the chain and dismantling organisations, *that's* when I think we really made a big impact.'

*

Pure Narco

In October 1991 Harley met Mary Adair, a shorthaired, tanned blonde from San Jose, California, while she was holidaying with her family in Key West. They fell in love.

'Her father was a captain of the Santa Clara California Police Department and he retired. One of his daughters lived in the Keys. They were there visiting. His youngest daughter, Mary, was there on vacation. And I met her through her father, Robert. We were drinking together at Fat Tuesday on Duval Street, Key West.'

Things really were that simple for Harley. He was like a fair-haired version of Mitch McDeere from John Grisham's *The Firm*, with the perfect girlfriend in tow. By 1992, he and Mary had moved in together. The same year Harley heard the name 'Navia' for the first time.

'We had a series of smuggling incidents where we caught the boatloads coming in. We prosecuted some of the folks on the boats and some of the boat drivers, the vessel operators, and a couple of those we were able to move up from them to the next level; kind of the mid-level brokers on the States side. It was myself and one or two other agents doing independent cases at the time that ended up intersecting when we started interviewing that next level of broker on the US side, not the foreign side. That's a different hierarchy. In the US a broker is not as important as he is overseas. It just means he's a guy who's got a contact that has cocaine. I can remember at least two or three different interviews where separate brokers gave us the name "Navia" and we were able to put it together. Eventually I put together "Luis Navia".'

Harley had a partner working with him called Carol Libbey. Originally from New Jersey, she graduated with a criminal justice degree from Northeastern University in Boston then joined the USCS in Fort Lauderdale in 1983, before transferring to Miami in 1989. As part of the Miami Investigative Drug Asset Seizure Group (MIDAS) she later worked as an asset forfeiture agent. According to Harley, her 'abilities to research things was excellent'. So excellent she turned up a photo from one of Luis's two traffic arrests in Dade County/Metro-Dade. These were the days when such records weren't automated.

'I said to Carol, "We *have* to find a picture and a way to identify the guy because otherwise we're chasing a ghost,"' says Harley. 'The worst thing that you can do is to chase a ghost, because you can never prove that this is the person you are talking about. It was critical. But Carol was very tenacious. She's a lot more serious and can be a lot meaner than I am.'

Libbey: 'Bob had an informant that told him that there was this arrest, so he had already looked in Coconut Grove's [law-enforcement computer] system and there was nothing, as well as the national system. So I decided to look in Metro-Dade's system, which at the time had jurisdiction over the entire county.[200] And I went down and went into their system and it came up with two arrests. It said [Luis's] name, the date, and next to one of the arrests it had a number. I asked what the number was and they said, "That's an archived file." So I requested the archived file.

'The next day Bob came with me and we went back, they pulled the file and there was really nothing in there except this picture. One of the arrest records was already destroyed. Every so many years they would destroy all their records. You didn't save it for anything. So it was an old snapshot. In the old days you would get your picture taken with a Polaroid camera. We had to take a picture of *that* picture.

'It took quite a few tries. It wasn't easy. All this digitalisation we have now was still in its infancy. They actually told us, "You're lucky because this should have been destroyed a year ago." You have to understand, back then DUI was not a big deal. DUI you would take the guy and you would put him in the drunk tank for the night and release him the next day. It wasn't like today, where it's "DUI, *ohmigod*, we have to arrest him and prosecute him to the full extent of the law." Nobody cared back then.'

Harley: 'We finally had a photograph of Luis. It was old, black and white, not great, from the late '70s. But we *had* a photograph. It was his arrest photo for a DUI. Then I could take it back to those brokers and do photo line-ups and say, "Point out Luis Navia to me." That's when we knew exactly who he was. That put a name and a face to a real person.'

*

By now Luis had been formally identified and indicted along with a group of other narcos in the Florida Keys and Miami, but the magnitude of what was about to come down on him was still a secret.[201] It was time to make a tentative approach to his family. So Harley and Libbey knocked on the door of Luis's elderly mother's house in Miami and introduced themselves. María, then in her late 70s, got the shock of her life but didn't come out. Luis's sweet-natured, softly spoken sister, Laura, who had divorced from the womanising Vicente Blanco in 1990, was also at the house and remembers meeting the two USCS agents outside.

Harley: 'They were very standoffish. It was non-confrontational. I was very polite and courteous. They took my business card and I was just telling them, "He needs to call me because I think things can go badly and I can make them better."'

Laura: 'I was quite concerned for Luis and my mother. As you can imagine, that situation was incredibly concerning.'

Libbey: 'They didn't like us. I know that's hard for you to believe because we're such nice people, but they didn't like us. They didn't tell us anything: "He's not here. Get off our property." [*Laughs*] Needless to say his mother and sister were not going to give us a picture. Luis had left the United States by then.'

Luis is vague about how quickly the news of Harley's visit got to him in Mexico, but he brushed it off as a mild nuisance and he kept the whole thing from Patricia.

'It's not like my mother and sister were completely oblivious. Laura married a Colombian and he was involved in money laundering but they were elegant, well-to-do, high-class people. *Everybody* was involved in cocaine back then. Like in Saudi Arabia, you know, most people are involved in oil. In Colombia, most people were involved in cocaine. Bob was hoping I'd reach out to him, cooperate and become a snitch. That's why they give you a business card. I was already acting like a fugitive. I had left the United States. I figured I was already indicted and a wanted man. Yeah, it wasn't the best news but it wasn't *news*.'

41

Dead in the Water

AFTER SURVIVING COLOMBIA DURING the hunt for and takedown of Pablo Escobar, living by the beach in Cancún was so uneventful and placid the most tumult Luis experienced was at night while he was asleep. He tossed and turned and would often talk while unconscious, waking with no memory of the nightmares he'd been having.

It would be a stretch to say this drug trafficker was haunted by the faces of people he'd known who had met violent deaths or with the guilt of shaming his family – Luis simply has no recollection of what passed through his mind – though it's possible. His physical health had also started to deteriorate.

'I took these herbal pills that were supposed to give you energy and cut down your eating habits. I was in pretty good shape, walking a lot, but I took these fucking herbal pills on the recommendation of a friend of Patricia's who was a weightlifter and bodybuilder and I had an allergic reaction with the joints in my body. Some days I couldn't even move. I couldn't get out of the car.

'It was really weird. It came to a point where they almost had to call for a wheelchair to get me out of the cab from the airport. In Bogotá I always used to stay at Papito's house; we were very close friends. He took me to his doctor who would analyse your physical being with pendulums. The doctor recommended all these fucking pills: chelated magnesium, shark cartilage, a bunch of shit.'

Around that time Luis was due to fly from Bogotá to Cancún via Costa Rica.

'At the last minute I was delayed for whatever reason and I had to change my trip and I flew via Cuba. *Boy*, when I got to Havana the state security agents really gave me the fucking treatment. They took me into a room. I have never in my life been so scared as I was there. I actually said to myself, "I may never, *ever* get out of here and nobody will ever know where I am," because I came into Cuba with a Mexican passport.

'A lot of Mexican *narcotraficantes* like El Señor de los Cielos, Amado Carrillo Fuentes, would meet their Colombian connections in Cuba.[202] I never met Amado, but we did some loads for him through an associate who paid us in Houston. The Cubans felt there was something fishy about me. They started giving me the tenth degree, and the 11th *and* the 15th.'

Luis explained he had just come from Bogotá, lived in Mexico City and owned a fledgling coffee business in Cancún. He was simply in transit and wanted to go visit one of the many coffee companies that operate in Havana. He'd prebooked a room at the five-star Meliá Cohiba Habana, right on the seafront.

'They interrogated me for about eight hours, till the morning. And I really thought I could kiss my life goodbye. Finally they let me go. The Cuban security agents drove me to the Meliá Cohiba, and they gave me a big presidential suite. And I knew it was totally bugged. They actually thought I was going there to meet with some kind of Mexican.'

The next day he toured Old Havana and went to a coffee business but he knew he was being watched.

'I was so scared the next day I went to the airport early. The plane took off at seven, I was there at five. I wanted to get home for Christmas. I was exiting [immigration], ready to get on the plane, and the lady who stamped my passport said, "So you're Mexican, *huh*?" And she said it in such a way that was like, "We know *exactly* who you are and we're letting you go but you can't fool us." I freaked out. When I got to Cancún, since I was running a day late because of the mix-up with Costa Rica, the guy that used to receive me in immigration wasn't there.'

Luis was about to learn a tough lesson. As former USCS agent Robert Mazur wrote in his book *The Infiltrator*, one of the cardinal rules of using a false identity is to 'stick as close to your real-life experience as possible in order to minimise the number of lies you have to spin'. Luis had strayed too far from his real-life experience.

'They could easily have discovered in Havana that I wasn't really Mexican; now I get to Mexican customs with a Mexican passport as "Luis Novoa Alfandari", and you know, you can fool someone with a Mexican accent if he's not Mexican but if he's Mexican it's pretty tough.

'I'd never lived in Mexico as a Mexican. I always had my Colombian passport. I was Luis Navia but Colombian. Mexicans thought I was Colombian. So I was in line as Luis Novoa Alfandari and a little upset from the whole episode in Havana, and the guy at the immigration desk starts talking fast. He asked me a question and I didn't really understand it, he was talking so fast, and by mistake I said, "*Cómo?*" And that was it. I was dead in the water. Mexicans don't say *cómo*, which means "what". They say *mande*.'

His weakness in Spanish dialects had finally caught up with him. A rapid-fire conversation ensued, with the officer trying to catch out Luis on his local knowledge. According to Luis's passport, he was born in Mexico City. The officer tripped him up quickly on a geographical question.

'What *delegación* were you born in?' he said, referring to the local word for borough.

'Polanco.'

'That's not a *delegación*, it's a shopping district.'

Luis had to think fast. His salesman instincts kicked in. But instead of making up a story like he would normally do, he did something totally out of character: he straight out confessed.

'Listen, you are right. I'm not Mexican. The reason I use this Mexican passport was simply for *commercial purposes* to expedite matters to avoid the lengthy visa process. I had no time to get a visa. I'm Colombian. I'm in the coffee business. I own Café Koba here in Cancún.[203] I live here. My wife is waiting for me outside. I am not in some weird business, as you may think. I just use this passport as it's easier to travel through Central America. So let's do this. Because of your time lost and all the inconvenience I've caused you, why don't you come to my house on the day before Christmas? I'm going to be with my family, have somebody come early in the morning, we'll work this out for 10,000.'

Luis laughs at the memory.

'He thought I meant 10,000 *pesos*.[204] When he came to my office at Café Koba, I gave him an envelope with 10,000 dollars inside and he almost flipped backwards. He offered me whatever I needed, a federal police escort to the Belize border, *anything* I wanted. He asked me if I could give his niece a job. After that, he was always there for me. But I'd been very lucky. I should have avoided the diversion in Cuba and turning up in Cancún without my immigration guy to receive me – all for trying to get home for Christmas. Always have your priorities straight when you're a fugitive. Your number-one priority is not getting caught.'

42

The Board Meeting

I T WAS THE SUMMER of 1995 and Luis was about to turn 40. He was living with his beautiful 26-year-old wife and infant daughter in a villa on a Mexican beach and had the best chance of his life to go straight. More than enough money was coming in from the night-time *panga* smuggles to finance his retirement many times over, Café Koba was doing well in Cancún, and a long-held passion project to build a multimillion-dollar 'binational macadamia operation' in Central America was starting to take shape. It was the perfect time to call it quits on crime.

'I had a great business in Café Koba. I would come home, have lunch, go out with Patricia and Juliana, go to the movies. Patricia had made good friends. We had a beautiful life.'

His 700-acre macadamia farm in the shadow of the Arenal Volcano in Costa Rica had proved a shrewd purchase for a block of land he'd only visited three times and Luis fancied himself as a Panama hat–wearing macadamia baron. But not being a hands-on owner had created problems. The way he tells it, some of his investors had been selling shares and stealing money.

'Costa Rica wasn't exactly my cup of tea. I always felt they were a bunch of fucking rats and Costa Ricans were too in bed with the Americans. I didn't like Costa Rica. The caretaker–manager was doing jack shit. I was living in Colombia at the time and I sent some

Colombian financial guys to look at what was going on down there. They came back and said, "You got a great piece of fucking land, it's all on a lake, it's worth a lot of money, and they're not working it to its full potential and this guy is basically skimming off the top. Whatever money you sent down there he's stealing part of it to live and part of it is going into the farm.'

Luis was so angry that for the first time in his life he contemplated killing a man.

'That would have come back to haunt me. That's it. I would have been *fucked*. Believe me, I wanted to. He stole from me, he deceived me, he lied to me. I put my faith in him. I thought this was going to be my way out of the cocaine business. I was planning to retire, that's where my future was, macadamia and coffee, and this guy backstabbed me.'

So Luis brought in his attorney, Reid Constable of Miami law firm Horan, Horan & Constable, to buy back stock and take a controlling interest in the farm and kick out the partners.[205] At the same time he commissioned a study of the macadamia industry in Mexico, initiated plans to build a processing plant, and had the grand vision of creating a Costa Rica–Mexico macadamia cooperative 'to open up Mexican macadamias to the world'.

Unlike his brief foray into sugar in the early 1980s, this time around he thought he was going to retire from cocaine for good, buy a turboprop, shuttle between his holdings in Costa Rica and Mexico, stick with coffee beans and macadamia nuts rather than coca leaves, do the right thing by his young family, and finally make good on the Navia name and do his father proud.

And then, just like that, it all fell away.

*

'When Reid went to a board meeting to present the takeover proxies and to exercise our control of the company, 51 per cent of the shares, an attorney that sat on the board of directors of Ilhabela Mac SA told him, "Did you know your client, Luis Navia, is indicted on drug charges out of Key West, Florida?" Reid had to leave that meeting. That was it. It was over.'[206]

Luis was on a payphone in Cancún when he got the news.

'Did you know that you were indicted by the US Government?' Constable asked him down the line from Miami.

'Reid, *Reid*, that's impossible. I've never been to Key West.'

'General Noriega had never been to the US either and he got indicted in Miami. I recommend you give yourself up.'

Luis didn't quite know how to react. He knew there was every chance he'd been indicted, but he'd not had it confirmed until that moment.

'I was freaking the fuck out. It was life-changing. I didn't tell Patricia right away. We had a baby. She kinda knew that I had an issue when I first left [the States], but we didn't talk about it, you know, it was just normal.'

This time he had no choice but to tell her about Harley.

'I wasn't angry with Luis,' she says. 'Just upset because I was really happy in Cancún. I had a one-year-old daughter and I thought we could finally make a life there as a family.'

43

The Firm

Robert Harley might not have left Key West but he knew 'almost exactly' where Luis was on a couple of occasions in Costa Rica and Mexico. The problem of bringing him in was a matter of interagency resources, along with myriad political and legal complexities.

'I did not go [down to Mexico] but [other] people did: DEA and Customs have people "in-country". But getting one of our agents in a foreign country to go run down a lead is not the easiest thing in the world, because they get a hundred of those a month. And convincing them that *this* lead is more important than all the other leads they need to run down is the trick. Attempts were made [to capture Luis], but I always felt they were a day late and a dollar short, each time. And it's just a function of getting people to do what you want them to do and they don't have to do.

'Keep in mind too, some places are easier than others to get people picked up and sent home. There are legal systems that are more complicated than others and legal systems that are more corrupt than others, and sometimes even though there's an opportunity you can't translate that into action. It's just not going to work.'

Instead, Harley had a better plan.

'We went a little more overt and went after his business records.'

*

'Carol Libbey's job was to identify potential assets for seizure and to exploit investigative avenues that you can get from assets,' says Harley. 'She really put the effort in. She was in the weeds. She is an excellent agent in looking at things microscopically, numbers and details. She was critical in putting together all of Luis's business stuff – like Ilhabela Mac – and then identifying Reid Constable as the resident agent for all of that.'

Libbey: 'I was in the Asset Forfeiture Group, which works with all the other [law-enforcement] groups in a parallel case to the criminal case [concentrating] on all the assets. We knew if Luis was involved with all these drugs, then there had to be assets, and that's how I got into it, trying to track him down through the assets.'

Harley: 'We found that Luis had assets and then he liquidated assets, bought new assets and then liquidated those assets, and it was because of how the business was going for him essentially. So Carol would come with the leads and then she and I, or me or some other agent, would take that [information] and start doing the interviews, questioning everybody and turning the heat up to see what would fall out.'

It was Harley who'd spoken to the directors of the macadamia plantation in Costa Rica and, as he puts it, 'shook up the world for Luis. I knew that, because Reid Constable just about passed out.'

More was to come. Harley paid a visit to Horan, Horan & Constable in Coral Gables, right near the University of Miami School of Law, and directly accused Constable of knowing Luis was a drug dealer and of laundering money.

'Reid Constable knew Luis was a dope dealer. He knew *exactly* what his client was. And Reid made money off Luis's business practices. He was the agent for the attempts to legitimise Luis's profits. Luis thinks that he was shielding Reid from it, but I've got news for you: Reid hired Vernon Dolivo, who at that time was one of the most expensive attorneys in Miami and they hung up all of the grand-jury documents that we wanted from that law practice.[207] We ended up with maybe a quarter of the documents that I knew existed that would have proved all the money laundering that had gone on.'

Libbey: 'This was a time when [attorneys] didn't ask questions: he had money, he hired me, I'm just going to do what my client tells me to do because he's paying. Whether Reid Constable fully participated in anything more than moving the assets and turning a blind eye, I don't know, but he definitely didn't want to know.'

Luis, however, maintains Constable knew nothing about his cocaine trafficking.

'He never suspected that I was in the drug business. Truthfully, he did *not* know and I will always maintain that Reid did not know; I cannot understand why Bob Harley doesn't believe that. I was just a rich guy because my dad was rich. Reid only knew about my money background from my dad's sugar business. He represented me in the buying of the 22,000 acres in Florida, so he was always exposed to sugar money. The one mistake I made was bringing him to visit me in Cancún. I should never have done that. Security-wise that was a big mistake. He should never have known where I lived.

'Reid played hardball with Bob. He didn't cooperate. He thought it was an abuse on Bob's part to be treating him the way he treated him; that he was an innocent victim, which he was, and Bob didn't believe him. Just because he didn't cooperate doesn't mean he's guilty. The government expects everyone to cooperate and if you don't and make them "work" for their information, they get pissed. It's a perfect example of the federal government's abuse of power. Reid did not know anything about any of my illegal businesses – at all. They treated him as if he did. They declared him guilty before ever proving him guilty and made him go through hell. If the federal government have a hard-on for you, they can destroy your life. And they destroyed his life.

'You know, they go in on riot mode, guns blaring, knock the door down, and they take all the papers in the law firm, your partners get freaked out; who the fuck wants a partner being investigated by US Customs? His partners probably thought he was money laundering for me and never told them anything and was making millions, which was not true. Bob unfortunately destroyed Reid's law practice in Miami, and Reid also suffered a heart attack. They destroyed him and then he had to scale down and move to Sarasota and open up a smaller law firm with his new wife.

'I don't know what the fuck happened there. Bob fucked it up for Reid. But then again, Reid fucked it up for himself. You're dealing with the US Government, the most powerful entity in the world. The chances of surviving a federal indictment are 97 per cent against you. They can say whatever they want and the burden of proof is on you. You know how much it cost the law firm to defend Reid? It was tremendous. Hundreds of thousands òf dollars.

'I feel very bad about what happened because I was a drug dealer. Reid was innocent. Bob came at him hard. It's one of those things that still haunts me. It's a nasty thing what happened to Reid Constable. That's one of the things I fucked up, that I feel really bad about and I wish I could someday make good on it and make it up to him.'

*

Harley won't hear a word of it.

'Reid Constable destroyed himself. Did he have a heart attack? Yes he did. Did he quit the law practice? Yes he did. He didn't die *destitute*. He retired from Coral Gables to, like, Fort Myers in a gated community and sold his partnership in an incredibly successful Coral Gables law firm. So that's no crocodile tears for anybody.'

You don't buy his story of innocence?

'*Never*. Still don't. One of the other partners ran interference for Reid. He's telling me, "I don't think Reid would have been involved in those kinds of things." I said, "*Really?* Where do you think Luis Navia, who couldn't come back to the United States to conduct business, was getting his money from? [*Laughs*] I mean, is that not in essence this bullshit that Reid didn't know? Your client can't come to the States and he's going there [to Mexico]?

'Reid knew Luis grew up on Key Biscayne. Luis was a US citizen. Reid travelled far to pick up money to go buy businesses for him. What did you think it was? There's no way that Reid Constable was in *any* way innocent of knowing what this was all about. And to this day I have no idea how much money the firm or Reid made off of all that transactional work, because those are records that they refuse to produce. They fought us tooth and nail about every document we asked for.[208] My argument was, "If you were innocent, prove it to me."

'Horan, Horan & Constable was a legitimate firm but they did illegitimate work and made a ton of money by simply turning a blind eye. And there's no way you don't know. So as far as I'm concerned, did Reid launder Luis's money? Yeah, he did. Could I positively prove he knew the source of funds? No, I could not. All I could prove was he had to travel foreign [sic] to conduct all of the transactions with a United States citizen. We're talking millions but not hundreds of millions.'

Luis doubles down in denying Harley's allegations: 'Reid did *not* know I could not come back to the United States. A lot of people decide to move to Mexico and are not fugitives. Reid never picked up money; I used transfers. Supposedly you are innocent until proven guilty, aren't you?'

*

Luis should have turned himself in to the authorities but going back to the United States wasn't an option. He just continued what he was doing and began taking the benzodiazepine Xanax to help him sleep and reduce his anxiety.[209]

'That indictment started in 1991.[210] The US Government has five years to pull the trigger. If Bob hadn't indicted me in 1995 he would have lost the opportunity. Once you're indicted, all you can do is either turn yourself in or work harder. In the end I was already under indictment, I woulda gotten picked up and fucked anyway. They would have taken away the macadamia farm because my indictment was there. So in the end everything worked out.'

Once again, the Navias were packing their bags.

'The three of us left Cancún in a hurry. Wálter went back to Pereira. This time I was really scared. I moved out, went and stayed at a hotel while I sorted some things out and within a week I'd left for Mexico City.'

PART 9
MAGOO IN MEXICO

44

Dinner with Alberto

For Luis, moving from Cancún to the biggest Spanish-speaking metropolis in the world, a city of 20 million people, meant four things: getting a new identity, finding a new apartment, buying a new business and trading in his boardshorts and Hawaiian shirts for something better suiting the weather and his new social circle: a suit and tie.

Fortunately, by the start of 1996 he had more than enough money to buy as many fake passports as he liked. Luis was keeping his millions in offshore accounts plus his usual standbys (safety deposit boxes and real estate), laundering through consulting companies, and still kept at least a quarter of a million in cash at home.

'I had different people doing the passports. I had a guy in the Dominican Republic, I had a lady in Guatemala, I had somebody in Colombia. It's difficult to get really good passports. You can get a fake passport for $1000. You can get one for $500. A decent set will cost you $10,000, but to that you add the bank accounts that go with a good passport, the credit cards, and before you know it you're looking at $50,000 on the low end. I went back to my original roots of being Jewish. I changed my name to Louis Anton Naviansky Bonavia.'[211]

But one Mexican passport wasn't enough. He also splashed out on a set of Guatemalan passports for his family to have for safekeeping. Patricia wanted no part of it.

'Luis tried to make me change my name so many times. We went to Guatemala and he was trying to get me to take a fake passport. I said no. Never. *Neh. Ver.*'

Holed up with their maid in a rented luxury bolthole in the *colonia* of Interlomas, an outlying upmarket neighbourhood ringed by shopping centres, their relationship had hit the skids. Luis hadn't stopped drinking or quit the business, as she'd hoped he would, and the showdown between Reid Constable and Robert Harley in Miami had spooked him enough to start drinking more. While he'd successfully kept his promise to Patricia back in Bogotá not to drink for a year and then given himself licence to have a tipple occasionally, his idea of helping himself long term wasn't to check into rehab or join Alcoholics Anonymous. It was to go on two-day binges every 30 days.

'I would only drink once a month. I decided I might as well limit my fuck-ups to 12 times a year.'

But at least the new legitimate business was promising: Industrias Guantex de México SA de CV, a manufacturer of surgical gloves, household gloves and condoms. His co-partner was a relative of Mexican multibillionaire Carlos Slim Helú.[212] Their business cards had the words 'USA Flex' as a logo, with an American flag in between. An ironic choice of graphic for a man on the run from US justice.

'Unthinkable it's on the card.'

*

In Mexico City Luis met Alberto Sicilia Falcón, a Cuban narco kingpin who, operating as a heroin and marijuana trafficker out of Tijuana in the 1970s with a trusty Great Dane by his side called Skipper, was widely regarded as the first of Mexico's major drug bosses. He's one of the main characters in the first season of the Netflix series *Narcos: Mexico* (in which he is portrayed as a flamboyant homosexual) and James Mills's gargantuan 1986 book on international drug trafficking, *The Underground Empire*. A former CIA-trained, anti-communist operative in Miami by his own reckoning, Sicilia Falcón would go on to bring large amounts of coke into Mexico with Juan Ramón Matta Ballesteros, a Honduran who worked with the Medellín Cartel.

'Alberto was the big boss before Amado Carrillo Fuentes,' says Luis. 'Playing with the CIA is one thing. *Being* the CIA is the only way you can survive. Playing with the CIA you're going to get burnt. And that's what happened to him.'

In real life, Sicilia Falcón wasn't shot in the head as portrayed in *Narcos: Mexico*. Nor was he as open about his sexuality. He went to jail in 1975 and escaped the following year from the Palacio de Lecumberri prison in Mexico City through a tunnel he had personally financed from a property adjoining the jail, decades before El Chapo dreamed up such a thing. But he was arrested days later and sent back to prison. He wrote a book about it in 1979 called *El Túnel de Lecumberri*.

What actually happened to Sicilia Falcón in the 21st century has long remained a mystery and when I spoke to Luis he could not shed any light on the matter, other than they met and had a 'bunch of encounters'. There are some scattered online mentions in the Spanish-language press of Sicilia Falcón being released from prison in 1998, but Luis insists he was introduced to him outside prison in 1996 through a friend, a jetset refugee from the 1970s, Denisse Zavala, the daughter of a very famous Cuban-Mexican film actress.[213] He says their meeting took place at her home in Tecamachalco, Mexico City.

'Denisse knew *everybody*; she knew Alberto back from the days before he went to jail, when he was Alberto Sicilia Falcón, the leader of the Mexican cartels. She had some balls on her. When I needed to travel sometimes with my Mexican passport, she would come with me. She could pull me out of a hot situation. I was concerned about travelling with a Mexican passport so I felt more comfortable going with her. I took her to Bogotá. We travelled through Belize. She loved adventure.'

Luis also alleges Sicilia Falcón's criminal partner when they met was Francisco Sahagún Baca, former head of the much-feared but defunct Division of Investigation for the Prevention of Delinquency (DIPD). Sahagún Baca had been right-hand man to the notorious chief of police in Mexico City, Arturo 'El Negro' Durazo Moreno.

The only problem timeline-wise is Sahagún Baca disappeared in 1989 following his arrest on drug offences in Michoacán state, a mausoleum later being built for him in the city of Sahuayo with the name 'Francisco Sahagún Vaca'. However, it is empty. There was no funeral, nor is there any official record of his death or burial in the civil registry.[214]

'Sahagún Baca was a dangerous character to say the least; a vicious killer. He'd had the free run of Mexico City under Durazo. There were nights that they would go out and shoot the vagrants and the beggars living on the street – like a cleansing of vagrants. I hung out with Francisco and Alberto for the good part of two years. Alberto and I used to meet almost on a daily basis at the Centro Santa Fe shopping centre and have a coffee and Danish.

'There was no publicity that he was released from prison; a big figure like that who escaped. He was the first guy to escape from a Mexican prison – it wasn't El Chapo. Alberto was a big deal in Mexico. He wanted a Colombian connection. I also met him in early 1999 in Chetumal [in Mexico] where I gave him $35,000. He needed it. He was not doing well financially.

'The strange thing is we became good friends and he didn't have too many people he could trust or relate to because of his notoriety in Mexico. His protector was "El Azul": Juan José Esparragoza Moreno.[215] El Azul was the true *consigliere* or ambassador between all the groups; a very powerful man and the smartest operator in that whole Mexico scene.

'Meeting with Alberto, talking to him, hanging out with him, you would *never* think he was nothing but a full-on straight man: a real ladies' man. But I guess he had that fucking wild, crazy touch to him. He did not want to be *known*. We put together a couple of deals. We probably did three trips; that's it. I didn't trust him 100 per cent. It was merchandise that was already in Belize and I renegotiated it. I gave it to his people and they delivered it in Houston, but we only spent a year doing that together.

'The first trip we just sold the coke in Mexico. I wasn't about to risk it crossing the border with him; I didn't know how good his connections were, so we just sold it in Mexico. Later in Chetumal I paid him some money for things we did while I was smuggling in Jamaica. But we made a friendship. Finally I hooked him up with

Sergio Perdomo, an associate of José Orlando Sánchez Cristancho. They handed over $200,000 as an investment for a load.'[216]

*

So what really happened to Alberto Sicilia Falcón?

One of the biggest challenges in writing this book was verifying many of the claims Luis made and his accounts of meetings with people who were either dead or had disappeared. Understandably those criminals who *were* alive weren't going out of their way to lead documented lives, for all sorts of reasons. It is certainly not unheard of in the drug world for traffickers to undergo drastic plastic surgery to evade scrutiny, sometimes with fatal results.[217]

Luis also didn't want me contacting every narco he knew; understandably there were personal-safety issues for both of us if word filtered out that an Australian writer was working on a big-time drug trafficker's memoirs. The whole project was top secret while we were writing it. But Sicilia Falcón presented a particularly unique situation: for someone made so famous by Netflix, it seemed incredible that no one seemed to know whether he was dead or alive. It was one of those rare situations where not even Google could help establish his mortality.

Fortunately I was able to locate a former colleague of his from the 1970s, an American from Albuquerque, New Mexico, called Brian Dennard, and Sicilia Falcón's sister Mercedes (or 'Mercy' for short), who is based in Mexico. It turns out her brother, one of the most legendary but reclusive narcos of all time, died at his home in Mexico City on 24 May 2011 from a stroke.

Luis remembers Sicilia Falcón's house was 'up in the mountains, up in the hills, a wooded area with curving roads behind Santa Fe in the middle of fucking nowhere. He had 16-year-olds as his attendant, gardener, houseboy. I never saw him with any women.' Patricia, who was with Luis, similarly remembers it being 'a little bit like a castle'. During a dinner conversation about the levels of violence in the Bible and the Koran, Sicilia Falcón whipped upstairs and brought down his personal copy of the Koran for the Navias to inspect. He was a rare breed of narco.

Dennard, who got to meet the Medellín Cartel's Pablo Escobar, Carlos Lehder and Jorge Ochoa, says this is true: 'When I first met

Alberto Sicilia Falcón, we talked about Aleksandr Solzhenitsyn all afternoon, played backgammon and talked some more about Roman history and the dictator Sulla.[218] Alberto and I spent more time talking history – Roman, Russian, Greek – than we did about the "monkey business". He was really a brilliant thinker. The house had two pitched roofs, so it looked like one of those old pointed bras like Madonna wore. He called it "The Bra".'

Mercedes Sicilia Falcón also confirms the general location: 'When my brother got out he lived a bit with my ex-husband and me; he lived a bit in the city. Yes, he lived in Contadero, and yes he did have a gardener that was a young guy. He lived for a while on Calle División del Norte in Contadero, and then went further into the mountains.'

Contadero is right behind Sante Fe. It is three kilometres from Centro Santa Fe mall, the biggest in Latin America.

When I told Mercedes that Luis was insisting their meetings happened in the late '90s, she initially responded that her brother was housed in Santa Martha Acatitla prison in Mexico City with his hawk Homero (yes, a *hawk*; I was shown a picture of it behind bars), and she later picked up Sicilia Falcón from the maximum-security Altiplano prison in Almoloya de Juárez, outside the capital, upon his release in 2001.[219] It's the same jail where El Chapo escaped through a tunnel in his cell in 2015.

'I never met Luis or heard my brother speak of him. No one until you, Jesse, has ever contacted me about anything related to my brother's life in or out of prison. Many people have written false things about Alberto; even *Narcos: Mexico* lied. I guess someone that might have met my brother either in jail or out of jail might have invented that he was killed in Tijuana.

'The only real thing *Narcos: Mexico* got right was Skipper the Great Dane, and the fact that my brother was educated. My brother never acted or walked or talked or dressed like a homosexual. I never saw him at home or anywhere kissing or being with men. I did see him with ladies. I picked up Alberto when he was released from Almoloya. I have been really mad at all the crap that's been printed about him and all those shitty people making money out of it.'

Brian Dennard says similarly: 'Alberto was always a bull of a man. The idiotic portrayal of him in *Narcos* is absurd and insulting.

He was a fun guy: smart, intellectual, charismatic and my friend. In a world full of very, *very* bad and dangerous people, he was unique in his intellectualism and cultured persona. There were never any wild parties at his homes. The only thing valid was when in one scene a huge Great Dane walked through. The portrayal of a swishy gay Alberto was ridiculous; though he was bisexual, you would never peg him as gay if you met him.'

But he was eccentric, sometimes conducting meetings while sitting on the toilet.

'He would not use anything but Amino Pon soap.[220] Whenever you came to see him – business or pleasure – he would ask you to bring as many bars as you could bring. It was a fixation of his. Amino Pon smells wonderful and leaves your skin without a soapy residue. Worth every penny. He had a tailor who made him sort of safari outfits; quite a few three-piece suits. He had a barber who came to cut his hair. In his bathroom he had a toilet that was on a very high pedestal, so you were at eye level with him.

'One time when I went to the house in Mexico City, there was a turkey wandering around the yard. Alberto told me that they were going to fatten him up and have him for a feast. About two months later I was back in Mexico City again and we were sitting in his office when the turkey came walking in and jumped up onto his desk. *Gobble gobble.* I asked Alberto, "So what happened to the plan for the big feast?" He said, "Well, he has become a member of the family and quite a good watchdog, plus Skipper gets along with him like a brother, so we have cancelled his execution and given him a name. Meet Arturo."'

*

So could Sicilia Falcón actually have been given leave from jail before 2001?

'Everyone wants to make money out of my brother's name,' says Mercedes. 'The only time Alberto was able to leave jail was in 1985 when our mother died, and that was only with a huge police detail and only for two hours. I ask myself how [Luis's alleged meeting with Alberto] happened if my brother was in jail at that time, and my dad and I saw my brother every day. Alberto had all the green areas redone and taken care of in the jail. He had lots of things done in jail to try to keep it looking nicer.'

I told Luis what Mercedes said, but he was adamant things happened the way he tells it. Making money was certainly not a motivation in him mentioning Sicilia Falcón to me – he was gaining nothing from it; if anything, it was only muddying what had up to that point been a clean, reliable story.

'I'm not lying, Jesse. Everything I tell you is true. *Period*. Either she's covering for him or she never really knew that he was out. For security reasons sometimes it's better not even to tell your family. It's *Mexico*. I was with Sahagún Baca when there was a cemetery stone with his name on it and he was supposed to be dead. I'm telling you I was *with* Alberto Sicilia Falcón.

'As far as I know he wasn't in jail. If he was sneaking in and out of jail, that's a whole different story [*laughs*]. I didn't keep tabs on him that well. It proves the reality of the Mexican system [*laughs*]. There's no fucking way in the world the men I met were imposters. In my business there are no imposters. I respected Alberto. I found him to be a *hell* of a cultured guy, a highly educated man.

'He dressed in grey flannel pants, Oxford button-down shirts, nice sweaters, a pinkie ring, and carried a beautiful gold Dunhill lighter. In that business it's very rare to find a guy like Alberto Sicilia Falcón. He knew the Greek classics. He was a very interesting guy, a hell of a personality, a very good-looking man. A class act.'

But to someone reading this, Luis, wouldn't it give them pause to call your credibility into question?

'I hope they do because they will call the credibility of the Mexican Government into question. Sicilia Falcón was out of prison. There may be a guy serving time for "Luis Navia" in a prison in Mexico who is not Luis Navia. He's being paid $20,000 a year to say he's Luis Navia. Luis Navia's actually out! That's very typical in the Mexican system. I'm not about to make a fool of myself by printing this. I'll go toe to toe with anybody on anything I have ever told you. With all due respect to his sister, I was *with* Sicilia Falcón. Even from the half-crippled way he walked with a cane, there ain't no imposter who could be him. Dying in Mexico is all paperwork.'

Says Mercedes: 'My brother's health was very good. He was healthy and strong. Eight years before he died prostate cancer was detected, which he beat. But before he died frontal-lobe brain cancer was found. He went into surgery and 80 per cent of that cancer was extracted. He had a heart attack three days before his forehead bone was to be rebuilt. Before all that he just enjoyed his life with my dad, my daughter and his six German shepherds and his hawk.'

Did your brother have a cane?

'No, he did not. He only had a very small limp in one foot: the foot that was rebroken several times after all the horrible tortures he went through when he was apprehended; all of that due to the fact that he was loyal and never gave up any names of anyone.[221] He put in almost 20 years in jail just with my parents and me by his side.'

Did he know Sahagún Baca?

'He did know that sonofabitch but not as a friend, not as an associate, not as an acquaintance. He was just the cop in charge of all the instructions, all the tortures, and of everything that was done to him. That's it.'

So Sahagún Baca was actually one of the people involved in torturing your brother?

'Giving orders.'

And was his hawk named after Homer of *The Iliad*? Was your brother into Greek classic literature?

'Yes, he was, and also Greek mythology and Roman. He spoke several languages and learned many of them through books not teachers. My brother was also a great cook and painted.'

*

The truth was I was starting to doubt Luis and it was troubling me greatly, mostly because there was no way I could independently check off some of his claims. This was not the first time in my career I'd had such a crisis of confidence; it's part of the job of being a journalist or biographer. Sometimes a story *is* too good to be true.

Then, not less than 24 hours later, Mercedes contacted me again and said her brother was released in 1994, not 2001: a seven-year difference that made Luis's story totally feasible. It was quite the *volte face* – and left unexplained.

'My brother was released in 1994 after being inside since 1975 and completing his time. He was inside for 19 years.'

I thought you told me he was released in 2001?

'No, I said our *father* passed away in 2001.[222] Our mother passed away in 1985. My father and I picked him up from Almoloya de Juárez prison.'

Sicilia Falcón's sister had also changed her tune about Sahagún Baca.

'It was Florentino Ventura who was the cop in charge of all tortures regarding my brother.[223] Sahagún Baca came after all the tortures my brother went through.'

Okay, so it is possible that Luis met Alberto Sicilia Falcón in 1996–'98 when he said he did, if he were released in 1994?

'Maybe he met my brother afterwards; I just don't know that for a fact. What I do know for a fact is that my brother had nothing to do with anyone or anything related to that lifestyle.'

I read Luis her quote.

'What lifestyle? The narco lifestyle or the homosexual lifestyle?'

So you think Sicilia Falcón could still be alive?

'*Possibly.* In Mexico the limelight will get you fucked. If Denisse Zavala admitted to you that she introduced me to Alberto Sicilia Falcón she'd have *federales* looking at her up the yin-yang. But it could well be that he died of cancer – a journalist would have to check hospital records of the exams Mercedes says he underwent, although he could register in the hospital with a false name. I would say he's dead, but in Mexico you never really know.'

Robert Harley was right: Luis's life really does read like fiction.[224]

45

Airdrops and Raindrops

MEANWHILE LUIS CONTINUED TO bring loads into Cancún but it was getting increasingly complicated. The glory days were over. Alcides Ramón Magaña aka El Metro ('The Subway'), a high-ranking lieutenant of the Juárez Cartel's Amado Carrillo Fuentes, had come in as the owner of *la plaza* or the exclusive smuggling territory. To work in Cancún smugglers now needed official permission from either him or his boss, Carrillo. Both were working with Rasguño.[225]

Metro was a former policeman, like a lot of Mexican drug lords, and once reputedly headed antinarcotics for Mexico's Federal Judicial Police, the PJF or *Policía Judicial Federal*. At the same time he was working as a driver/bodyguard for Carrillo and saved his boss's life on 24 November 1993 after a machine-gun attack by the rival Tijuana Cartel's Arrellano Félix brothers, Ramón and Benjamin, at the Ochoa Bali Hai restaurant at Avenida Insurgentes Sur 1524, Mexico City. Five people died.

Now Carrillo's favourite and a big, bearded man of over 240 pounds (110 kilograms), Metro was running the southeast cell of the cartel from Cancún in cahoots with the corrupt local governor, Mario Ernesto Villanueva Madrid, who received kickbacks in the tens of millions during the 1990s: reputedly $500,000 for every load of cocaine passing through the state of Quintana Roo.

'We were working Cancún, and El Compadre in Reynosa said to cancel operations because Metro had taken over Cancún and he wasn't about to work with Metro; we had to cool off a bit. It was a very volatile situation. The end result when you deal with Metro is that somebody gets hurt. All those trips we did in Cancún, all those airdrops, all those boat deliveries, all that shit, we were doing directly with the *federales*. We worked directly with them and the army; we used to send big gasoline trucks into Cancún and move out all the merchandise in other vehicles and go through the Reynosa–McAllen crossing into Houston. We were working heavily with the Gulf Cartel.'

But an associate of Luis's, a Cuban known only as Sigfredo, didn't follow the Juárez Cartel's script.[226]

'El Compadre had a very good relationship with the *federales*. But when Metro got to Cancún you *had* to work with Metro. El Compadre said, "Listen. I'll do something else but right now Cancún is off the books." I went to El Compadre's daughter's wedding in Monterrey and that's when Sigfredo said, "No, I'm still going to continue working Cancún with my guy in Guadalajara."

'Soon after, Sigfredo went missing. They grabbed him at a deli, forced him into a car, took him somewhere, then tortured him and fucking chopped him into pieces. His head was found somewhere around the beach in Punta Sam and his legs 100 miles away in Chetumal. They fucked him up bad. So we didn't work Cancún. El Compadre was a smart man. He wasn't in the business to have that kind of headache.'

*

With his fondness for hippie clothes and bad case of psoriasis, Pinky Delgado might have been the oddest-looking drug trafficker with the best name in the history of crime, but his sailboats operation to Europe had proven exceptionally lucrative.

A white, blue-eyed Cuban fugitive called Pedro Jiménez aka 'Flaco' (Skinny) had been working for Pinky in England, where he would meet the sailboats filled with cocaine.[227] Flaco, who knew Luis from his time in Cancún, told Luis about the run he was having with the sailboats and in turn offered to introduce him to his European fixer, Nick Fisciatoris aka 'Nick the Fish'.

A Greek and American dual citizen, Nick the Fish was a classic, old-style, pot-bellied mafia figure from New York, but had been living in London since the 1970s. He owned properties in Manhattan, Canada, London and Greece. He was a renowned figure on the British illegal-gambling and horse-racing scene (it's been said he'd spent $50 million on gambling alone), one of the biggest drug wholesalers in the country, and Flaco's point man to the big buyers in England and mainland Europe. He and his pals also lived it up – hookers, fine dinners, all the cocaine it was possible to hoover – sometimes blowing up to $30,000 a night.

Luis was busy enough in Mexico City but the idea of expanding into Europe and making even more money appealed. So he asked Flaco to set up a meeting and Fisciatoris flew out to Cancún to meet Luis, bringing with him a violent British criminal associate straight out of a Guy Ritchie movie, Kenneth Regan, who had a profitable racket selling counterfeit passports. As one British law-enforcement agent later put it: 'Half of the UK's major crime figures were travelling the globe on them.'

Luis: 'Nick the Fish was a very elegant dresser. Not the Italian silk-type look; Oxford or Ivy League. Clean cut, well shaven, smoked a lot. He was one hell of a character. He always had a tremendous wad of cash in his pocket. We all did, but that's one thing I always remembered about Nick: he *always* had a big wad. His middle name might as well have been "Cash". Mobsters don't believe in wallets; they believe in rubber bands. Nick always carried his wad in a rubber band. I never saw him use a credit card. Nick was a classy guy but you did not want to piss him off. He always covered his ass by speaking from payphones; nobody knew where he lived – he was no fool.'

Unlike what is portrayed in *Narcos: Mexico*, business dates between high-level narcos didn't involve sharing a bottle of Scotch. That's a Hollywood cliché.

'In my experience, I went to a lot of meetings in the daytime and never were we drinking Scotch or anything else. In Colombia that was not looked upon favourably. Mexico was a little bit more relaxed but partying was at night after meetings.'

It was a propitious occasion, in any case: Fisciatoris offered to facilitate the right introductions – for a fee. In return, Luis offered to get him cheaper cocaine by cutting out middlemen. They parted ways with a handshake and a mutual commitment to begin planning their first operation together.

*

'The next time I actually worked Cancún was when El Compadre's partner Jesús Aburto, who was working with [the Sinaloa Cartel's] Ignacio "Nacho" Coronel Villareal, told me, "I've got a green light to work through Chetumal. We can bring the merchandise in through Belize."'[228]

A green light meant Metro was getting a financial cut of all the coke moved in his *plaza*. Nacho was giving him 30 per cent. Belize is about 500 kilometres south of Cancún. Chetumal is right on the Belize–Mexico border.

'I said to Jesús, "Man, are you sure? You got all this covered with Metro?"

'"We're covered with Metro. We've got permission, Luis. Everything's cool."

'"Okay, no problem." So I went ahead and gave the signal and had 800 kilos sent to my *recibidores* in Belize. *Perfect.* The fucking trip started out wacko from the start. The Colombians got there with the load. There was so much work going on that there were boats out there all the time. Belize City is a small town; all those offloaders know each other. But the Colombians, *my* Colombians, they gave it to the wrong guy. I was in Chetumal but communicating with my people in Belize. They confirmed that they gave it over but they gave it to "Raindrops".'

Raindrops is the alias of Belizean gangster James Swan.

'I said, "I can't believe this shit. *Fuck*." I got Raindrops' number and called him. At first he didn't want to hand over the merchandise. Imagine that shit. I said, "Listen [*laughs*], let's get one thing straight here. I'm working for a group of people that if you don't hand over the merchandise, you're going to *die* and your whole family's gonna *die*. *Everybody's* gonna die. You're not going to be able to kill any one of us.

We're going to kill all of *you*. That's a fact. It's not something I'm coming up with.

'"Unfortunately, you're not going to die so quick. You're going to have to tell us where the merchandise is. So it's up to you how long you want to live under fucking *tremendous* pain and suffering. It's going to happen within a week. So I'm going to call you tomorrow. You have 24 hours to think about it. I'll call you tomorrow. I'm your friend. Believe me, I don't want to do this. But it's going to happen."

'I called him back the next day and said, "Listen, we'll pay you the pick-up fee. And as a gesture of good faith we're going to give you five extra kilos." Raindrops was like, "Okay, man, it was a hassle, you know. Give me the pick-up fee and 15 kilos." I said, "You got it. Give us the merchandise. The pick-up fee our guy was going to get, it's yours. You did your job. We're going to give you 15 kilos."

'Sure enough, after that he was on me to work with him, he wanted to continue picking up, and Raindrops and my guy in Belize partnered up. I continued working with my main source in Belize and it was the first trip after the Raindrops incident when I personally went to Cancún again to supervise the trip. We had the merchandise and I went to talk to Metro. And that's when it happened, getting put in the fucking crocodile thing.'

46

The Crocodile Thing

CANCÚN WAS NOW GROUND ZERO for coke in Mexico and all the deprivations and excesses of the cartels.

'At night it was the complete underworld. Kilos of cocaine coming in, heads getting chopped; it was a rough scene. Cancún became the number-one port of entry for merchandise in Mexico at that time. Metro was moving tens of thousands of kilos.'

In March 1997 Luis, travelling under one of his many aliases, and Patricia, seven months pregnant with their second child, checked into the CasaMagna Marriott Cancún Resort. He'd told Patricia it was a vacation but it was anything but. Once he got to their room he called a female contact, his liaison with Metro. She didn't answer. But he knew where Metro was likely hanging out with his goons: a hotel he owned.

'So I went over to this hotel in Punta Cancún [the hotel zone] and I order some drinks to see if I can spot Metro or one of his men. And suddenly one of them, this guy called Gil, shows up.'

Gil was Metro's transporter. Shown a photograph by me, Luis believes Gil may be Gilberto Salinas Doria aka 'El Guero Gil', a notorious Mexican narco who worked for Metro and the Juárez Cartel in Playa del Carmen and Reynosa in the mid to late 1990s.[229] He cannot be certain.

'I'd heard he killed some people on the border; a doctor and his family or something.'[230]

Luis explained to Gil he had some merchandise in Belize and was trying to get hold of Metro to talk about it. In truth he wanted to make sure Jesús wasn't lying to him about getting the green light. Metro was busy but Gil suggested they have some drinks, so Luis agreed and they did some coke and began playing pool in the hotel bar.

Over the table, Luis told Gil he'd made arrangements for the Belize coke, some 600 kilos, to be delivered into Metro's *plaza* at Chetumal. One game followed another and for the hell of it their last game was played for money: $250,000 deducted from the cartel's transport retainer if Luis won or 50 kilos 'off the top' of Luis's coke at $5000 a key if Luis lost (about $100,000 wholesale but worth $650,000 in Houston).

Luis managed to lose the game, explained he had a busy schedule the next day and said goodnight. It was 11pm.

*

'Next day I wake up, I had a tennis game at eight in the morning at some nice clay indoor courts. Then I went over to the Café Koba office and I said, "Let me go make a phone call." There was a Pemex gas station in front of Café Koba. Jesús Aburto, who was with me, was getting gas. I go to the payphone and I'm dressed in my tennis outfit, all in white, and suddenly some fucking guy grabbed me by the back, grabbed my hair, because I had long hair, fucking yanked out a piece of my hair, and then hits me. *Boom boom boom*, on the side of the head.'

When he opened his eyes, startled from the blow, Luis saw Metro himself standing over him with two of his *sicarios* by his side. The Subway was unmistakable: fat, full beard, thick black medium-length hair. Jesús was standing by the petrol pump filling up his car, almost oblivious to what was happening.

'What the fuck's going on?' said Luis, spluttering like a man does when he's just been kinghit by Mexican *sicarios* who've come out of nowhere.

'You're working here without permission.'

'What do you mean? Of course we have *permission*. Look, Jesús is right there by the car!'

Luis has total recall of what happened next.

'It happened so fast. They wanted to stick me in their car. Luckily Metro had a [Chevrolet] Tahoe or a [GMC Yukon] Denali, smaller than a [Chevrolet] Suburban, a two-door SUV. If it would have been a four-door I would have been fucked, because they would have thrown me in the car, left, and those two to three minutes were the difference between life and death for me at that point.

'They started trying to put me in the car and I said to myself, "If they put me in that car, I'm dead. I'd rather they shoot me here than they put me in that car." So when they tried to fucking put me in I flipped around, almost did a backflip, I couldn't fucking believe it. Then they hit me in the back with the butt of a fucking AK-47 but my adrenalin was pumping so hard I was still shaking and moving and avoiding getting put in the car.'

Luis had to do some quick thinking. His heart was pounding.

'Let's calm down. Let's fucking calm down here. Look, Jesús is right *there* and he can explain this whole thing. Have Jesús come *here*. We're going to talk this over and if we need to go with you, we'll go with you. The only thing I ask is I ride in the front seat with you, so we can talk.'

'You kidding me, Colombian man?' Metro replied. 'Now you're asking to ride in the front seat. You want to drive too?'

Jesús was told to leave his car at the pump and brought over. Luis got in the front of Metro's SUV, Jesús in the back, with the two *sicarios* beside him, their caps on backwards, the unofficial uniform of hitmen in Mexico. Metro was at the wheel. Luis began pleading for his life.

'Metro, I came here yesterday. I tried to reach out to your lady but I couldn't find her. I went to the hotel and then I ran into Gil. We started drinking, we started snorting, we played a pool game and I lost $250,000.'

'What kind of fucking cockeyed story is that? You expect me to believe that? You're working here without permission. This motherfucker in the back is going around me.'

Luis turned around to Jesús.

'"What the fuck, man? I thought you told me you had this all squared away." I realised then that this motherfucker hadn't squared away shit. He was trying to score one on Metro, slip one in without paying a fee. The guy he was working for was Nacho Coronel – high level, very powerful – so Metro couldn't exactly whack him, but whack me, *yeah*. Right then and there I was a low guy on the totem pole and if they had to blame somebody, they'd blame me. So I said, "Call Gil."'

*

There wasn't any time to waste. Metro had driven to a cement theme park called México Magico on Kukulcan Boulevard, at the entrance of which was a huge, 30-foot-high pink piñata. The nearby lagoons were full of crocodiles.

'Metro used to take people there and throw them in there. That was *known*. We got there and right before we drove off the road to the crocodile enclosure, he kept dialling Gil and I said, "Let me use my phone," and I called Gil a few times and finally he answered and I passed him to Metro.'

The car had stopped right in front of the crocodiles, which were lying in the bright Yucatán sun. Luis was perspiring from the certainty his luck had finally run out.

'I have the Colombian here,' said Metro from the front seat. 'I'm going to throw him to the crocodiles. The only thing that's going to be left of him are these fucking white tennis shoes he's wearing.'

'What the fuck are you talking about, man?' said Gil over the phone.

'The Colombian with the trip in Belize. He's trying to go around us. I'm going to fuck him up.'

'*Noooo*. Don't do that. *Noooo*, man. He owes me $250,000.'

'What?'

'Yeah, last night we were playing pool. He's got to give me 50 kilos in Cancún. That's the deal. Fifty kilos at $5000 a kilo is $250,000.'

Metro turned to Luis, shaking his head in bewilderment.

'So it *is* true,' he said, laughing. 'You're fucking crazier than I am.' There was a pause. His little joke had cut through the tension in the air like Bee Gees on a dancefloor. It meant one thing: Luis would live another day. 'You know, Colombian man, today's your fucking *day*, motherfucker. I'm going to have a drink on you tonight.'

*

When they pulled up to the grand foyer of the CasaMagna and opened the door for Luis to get out, Metro was all smiles.

'Enjoy your evening. *Relaaax*, Colombian man. We'll talk tomorrow. Now I'm going to talk to your fucking partner back here, this piece of shit lying fucking sonofabitch. I'm going to have to call his boss and see what we do with him.'[231]

And he drove off, with Jesús and the two *sicarios* in the back seat. The most terrifying episode of Luis's eventful life had ended, again, with him somehow still breathing. The Magoo of blow had outdone himself.

'There's no words to describe what it's like to get put in a car in Mexico with Mexicans of a cartel that you know kill people every day. Metro was killing people. He was psychotic. He was a psychopath. He *is* a psychopath. He was killing people indiscriminately *every fucking day*. Any tip he got, anybody working, anybody that he *thought* was working, anybody that he *thought that he thought* was working, got whacked. I lost $250,000 playing pool and that's really fucked up. But it saved my life. If I would have gone to bed that night, wouldn't have gone out to the bar and just got up and played tennis, I would have been dead.'

Patricia remembers when he got back to their room at the CasaMagna: 'His face had changed. Really *changed*. He was so afraid; he was in shock. It was a different kind of fear.'

47

Out of Breath

Two months later, on 30 May 1997, Santi, a son, was born at Hospital Angeles in Mexico City. Luis cut the umbilical cord again. Things weren't going well in his marriage with Patricia, but the impending arrival had brought them closer than they had been for a long time: going to the doctor together, buying baby clothes and sharing the excitement of bringing a new life into the world.

The due date had been the 27th and when it didn't happen they went out with friends to the Ochoa Bali Hai, the same restaurant where the Juárez Cartel's Amado Carrillo Fuentes had survived a machine-gun attack by diving under a table. Luis got really drunk.

'I was feeling a little dizzy, probably did a couple of snorts, and I called over the maître d': "Bring me oxygen." He was like, "What do you mean?" So I said it again: "Bring me oxygen." Imagine, you're at a restaurant and you're so drunk you ask for *oxygen*. The restaurant didn't have any oxygen but I was a guy who always got what I wanted.

'So sure enough the maître d' arranged it somehow, called the paramedics, fire rescue, some shit like that, and they brought over to the table one of those little, long green oxygen canisters with two wheels. And I put on my oxygen mask and started to breathe oxygen and continued drinking. Patricia got insulted. Nine months pregnant and she left with a couple of her friends, and I stayed there in the restaurant continuing to party out with my friends and then finally got home. That was the extent of my craziness.'

Says Patricia: 'We were in a really bad situation at that moment. It had been bad for over a year. The only thing that was keeping us together was the fact I was pregnant. I had lost patience with him. I didn't want to be involved in anything to do with him. He travelled a lot and I didn't care. Every time I was happy to see him leave. I was tired. I didn't want him anymore. I'd had enough. I wasn't in love.'

Their relationship, like the out-of-shape Luis himself, had run out of breath.

*

So the last thing Luis's and Patricia's struggling marriage needed was to move all over again, but that's exactly what happened when, with the apartment lease up for renewal, their landlord got suspicious about the bona fides of 'Louis Naviansky'. This time around, Luis's fake passport and birth certificate weren't going to cut it. With Robert Harley on his tail and a single phone call to the US Embassy enough to bring down everything, there weren't a lot of options left. Cancún was all but closed off because of Metro.

'It was really weird. You never know where the heat's going to come from. I really felt the heat from this motherfucker. I had to renew the lease and he knew I was one of the principal owners of Guantex, so I don't know why the fuck that guy got suspicious about me. I was Louis Naviansky, Mexican Jew, but I had no real paperwork to back that up. He knew I was not Mexican. A Mexican knows when you're Mexican and when you're not Mexican. My partner didn't know anything about my narco background, so I couldn't go to him for help. I got a little scared. And I said, "You know what? I better fucking leave."'

It was a wise decision. The USCS had been 'a week away' from nailing him. Contrary to Hollywood movies, not every US fugitive is actively tracked down with singular purpose by a lone federal agent whose every waking moment is spent thinking about nabbing the bad guy. It's simply a matter of using in-country resources (agencies, informants), if they are available, to effect arrests.

'Mexico is not that easy to work in and I got poor support there,' says Harley. 'We were about a week behind when Luis got word that we knew exactly where he was living. I finally got DEA in Mérida or Cancún to get with our people and they had pretty much figured out where exactly he was living in this particular apartment. I think that's the only time we were just about to be hands-on again. Understand that I had other indictments with other people that we were also looking for; so it wasn't like a Tom Hanks film where I'm the only person and I'm following Luis around the globe. It simply is not like that. There's no way I could devote that kind of energy to Luis Navia to the exclusion of all the other responsibilities I had. That's not how it works.'

Says Luis: 'The DEA and US Customs have got all the time in the world. They've got time on their side. They're in no rush to bring me in; I'm already indicted. They're just looking to find out more. These guys get a salary; they couldn't give a flying fuck. If it takes Bob Harley eight more months to pick me up, that's eight more months at $7000 a month. These guys, from the day they start to the day they finish, they're only thinking about their retirement. The biggest thought of a government agent is not catching the bad guy; it's making sure they get the best benefits they can from the government. Time to them is the clock clicking up to retirement.'

*

Luis went down to Colombia that December to see Juanchi about expanding the business, and came back through Panama City. It was while he was in Panama that he got a phone call from Juanchi.

'Listen, before you go back to Mexico, "Fresh" wants to talk to you. Call Fresh.'

It was a name he hadn't heard for years. Fresh, a wiry, dark-skinned black boat captain from San Andrés whose real name was Cordelio Vaceannie James, was one of his transporters from the early 1990s when he was working with Rasguño. He supplied boats and captains from San Andrés to work Cancún and when Rasguño severed his relationship with Luis, Fresh kept the connection. He was living in Panama.

'Using my route they did 44 trips at 1600 kilos a load – that's over 70,000 kilos. He was freaking the fuck out. These guys were working Fresh to the bone. He had to fake a heart attack and go to Panama to stop working with Rasguño. He figured he already had enough money and wanted to work at a slower pace and do his own trips, and get away from the pace and crazy workloads of the big *oficinas*.

'Rasguño Inc. – the Northern Valley Cartel – worked 24/7 all over the world. Fresh must have had $80 million stashed away and he was a *nobody*. I never saw a penny. So he stole from me. He did something he shouldn't have done. He went behind my back with Rasguño. He was always short-changing people.'

Luis got him on the phone.

'Fresh, it's Luis.'

'Ah, Senador, I really need to talk to you. I've got a great connection in Jamaica. We want to start working. We need your source of supply.'

'Right, *okay*, but you owe me. Because of me you met Rasguño. You did 44 fucking trips to Cancún, Fresh. So according to my figures you owe me quite a bit of money. I'm on my way back to Mexico. I'm going to spend Christmas there. If you want we can meet in Panama in two weeks.'

Commissions are another part of the drug business little known to the outside world. If you introduce two people who then go on to work together, you can demand to be remunerated handsomely on each load.

'But they're very difficult to enforce and most of the time they pay a few times and then they just completely forget about you and the two parties continue working and they leave you out of the loop. That's what happened when I took Silvio Bernal and Hernán Prada to see Rasguño. They started working these big loads to Mexico but I never saw a penny. You might get paid once or twice but rarely ever again.

'So unless you were in a really, *really* strong position to make them pay, it was all one big clusterfuck. You could kill them but usually commissions were totally trampled on. In the end, Fresh paid me $1.2 million for the Rasguño trips – around $25,000 per trip for 44 trips – and then he gave me $200,000 to buy merchandise at cost for the first trip we did in Jamaica. The only reason Fresh paid me is he needed me to be a source of supply. I would also take care of the Colombian side of things, which Fresh never really liked handling himself.'

PART 10

CATCH ME IF YOU CAN

48

I Don't Like Cocaine (I Love It)

A MAN ON THE RUN from US Marshals who speaks functional Spanish, desires a Central American climate, and demands a certain level of Latin American creature comforts without having to get around in a moving convoy of armed private security guards has limited options after Colombia and Mexico. Costa Rica? Too many Uncle Sam–loving *gringos*. The Republic of Panama is one place he might end up, and it's where, in March 1998, Luis rented an apartment in the Edificio Miraluz on Calle Ramón H. Jurado in the seaside neighbourhood of Punta Paitilla.

It had been almost ten years since the pockmarked, crooked General Manuel Noriega was captured during the US invasion but Panama was then and remains today a roost for international fugitives. Officially, though, Luis was there for a legitimate reason: to open a Panamanian outlet of his Mexican rubber-gloves business, Guantex International SA. Unofficially, the landlord issue back in Mexico City had him deeply worried and he'd moved for one thing only: moving more cocaine.

'It was a good place for me to start exporting rubber gloves to South America through the Colón Free Trade Zone. I had a legal reason to go there. But after talking to Fresh I had more of a reason to live in Panama.'

Luis couldn't have been closer to temptation, either, his neighbours in the Miraluz building being Fresh and Fresh's light-skinned black cousin from San Andrés, Sonny Bowie, a transporter for the Los Mellizos Cartel in northern Colombia, 'the largest coke organisation at the time – extremely violent, vicious and a lot of heat on them'. Sonny, who practised a voodoo-like religion called Santería and kept a separate room in his apartment for the god Chango, handled logistics for the cartel's ship smuggles through his company, Sea Trade International.[232] Panama was also where Los Mellizos had a law firm, Pérez, Carrera y Asociados, represent their front companies that owned the ships.

*

Fresh's prize contact in Jamaica was the ponytailed and bearded Leebert Ramcharan aka 'The Indian'. Born in 1959, he was of sub-continental Indian origin but a Jamaican citizen: tough, smart, hands-on and in full control of the coke business out of Montego Bay. In 1998, he was unknown. By 2004, Ramcharan had made the list of top-ten drug kingpins under the US Foreign Narcotics Kingpin Designation Act, being named by President George W. Bush. He was personally responsible for moving about 15 tons of coke.[233]

Luis, organising cocaine runs from Colombia to Jamaica, Belize and Mexico with Fresh, as well as getting 'a little piece of the action' with Sonny Bowie, began shuttling between Panama and Jamaica for the better part of the year, living part of the time in Ironshore, Montego Bay. Fresh had a nearby villa just out of town.

'I did about 12 trips with Ramcharan and Fresh. I had my own villa with a butler and maids and all the hookers you could wish for, and a separate villa where I took a girlfriend of mine from San Andrés when she visited.

'Ramcharan basically ran Montego Bay. He had a lot of money and was moving a lot of product. He was the biggest player in Jamaica. He had a house up on the hill that looked like a hotel. He thought he was invincible. He had the finest strip club there, the Flamingo Club on Sugar Mill Road. The Flamingo was in an old sugarcane plantation and it was kind of rustic, but it was really nice and it had a jerk hut in the back with great jerk chicken and jerk lobster.[234]

'Ramcharan was a tough guy, no fucking pussy; he would get

down and dirty. One night at the club there was a fight; he went up to a guy and fucking smashed a bottle right across his fucking head; half his face. He ended up with like 17 stitches in his hand; the other guy ended up with like fucking 35 stitches on his face. He had muscle with him. If they had to put someone down, they put 'em down.

'Jamaicans are a tough group. They are not friendly island bongo players. Jamaicans are mean motherfuckers and that comes from the days of the slave revolts and all that. Most Jamaicans drive around with a machete in their car and they will not hesitate to use it. If there's a problem, they'll get out and have it out with a machete. It is no place to wander off. You just don't take a ride with your girlfriend and "see Jamaica". It's getting better but when I was there people that went to Jamaica stayed in their hotel, all inclusive, and didn't go out.'

*

A long-planned smuggle with his Greek-American contact Nick Fisciatoris had also come to fruition. The cover load was unusual.

'We had a delivery of cactuses to Belize. They'd been imported *from* Holland – they were cultivated there – but we'd changed the paperwork to make it look like they were Mexican cactuses being exported to Holland. We'd spent a lot of time looking for cactuses in Mexico and we could not find them – of course we couldn't find them. Those kinds of cactuses are grown in greenhouses in Holland.

'I remember going to Belize with Fresh when the cactuses arrived and him not wanting to eat at the restaurant at the hotel. He said, "Why don't we just go out the back of the hotel to the dock and we fish for our meal? There's great fish here; parrotfish." I was like, "Are you fucking crazy?" And he went out and actually caught six parrotfish with his fishing line and sinker. And we cooked them in the room. That was something that was so against Luis Navia. I was all about going to the hotel dining room and champagning it. But that's the kind of guy Fresh was.

'In the end the cactuses sat in Belize for about six months. The merchandise was meant to go back to Holland packed in the cactuses. They were ornamental round cactuses that we experimented with – we took out the insides of the cactuses and left them in soil and they could survive for almost a month without completely withering away: half a kilo in each cactus.

'We had that whole situation worked out with Nick over in Holland – he was going to receive it – but Hurricane Mitch came in and just sat on top of Cancún and Belize for I don't know how many days and flooded the warehouse, and all the fucking cactuses died. So then we had to divert the merchandise; it was sitting in Cancún for so long. I said, "Let's just send it to Miami." So we aborted the export operation to Holland and the merchandise was sent to Miami and that's when 350 units got busted by the DEA.'

49

The Separation

WHEN HE WASN'T IN Belize disembowelling Dutch cactuses and packing them with cocaine, or in Jamaica moving thousands of kilos for the Montego Bay mob, Luis was still going down to Colombia from his home base in Panama City. In Bogotá he had an unexpected reunion with Oscar Peláez Monsalve aka Poli, a man he hadn't seen for almost 20 years since he'd left Miami in a hurry.

'I was meeting some Mexicans in Bogotá and I saw Poli at Pepe Cabrera's casino on Avenida Carrera 15 and Calle 98. I found out he was there and I went to see him. He was glad to see me but, overall, he was a very dry guy. Don't think he was overly friendly. We spent time together, we spent a couple of hours talking, and then we hopped in his car. He had two guys with him and his .357 under his thigh. He said, "I'm going to give you a gift" and he went by a club he knew and he picked up two nice chicks and he dropped me off at a hotel. He made sure his hookers gave me a great time. And I didn't see him again. I left the next day.'

Luis also slotted right into Panama life like nothing was up, taking Juliana, now four, to school, coming home at night to have dinner, and doing his husbandly duties in hosting the in-laws who'd come to visit from Colombia. But by now there was no escaping the truth: his marriage to Patricia was in crisis. Guantex International SA existed in name only. It was no more than a cover for Luis's cocaine trafficking. He had no intention to go straight.

Patricia had been unhappy for some time but hadn't let on how she was feeling. Now she was ready to pull the trigger. Leaving a relationship is difficult at the best of times, moreso when your husband is a wanted international felon and running out of people he can turn to, let alone trust. But Luis had run out of excuses for his behaviour.

'Luis promised me that when we went to Mexico City he would start a legal business and stop the cocaine – and he didn't. So one day I found out he was continuing and for the first time he'd started keeping these things from me. I'm not stupid. I was so sad and in that moment I was thinking, "I don't want this."

'I was sure I didn't want that life anymore. I wanted to be a normal person: go to the movies, take care of my husband when he came back from his job. I was really tired of everything. I had two kids. Always something would happen and we'd have to move. I tried to make Luis drop the cocaine, "Let's do something different. Let's go. *Drop* it." We had the coffee business and the latex-gloves business and I thought everything was going to be fine, but after two years of everything being good I realised that he never stopped.

'I always thought that I could make him change; we talked about him retiring many times. So after what happened with Rasguño, when he bought the coffee business in Cancún and the factory in Mexico City to make latex gloves, which was a very good business, I believed that he was retired. I always told him that money wasn't the most important thing, but then I realised that Luis never did it for that; it was the adrenalin.'

He's prepared to concede she has a point.

'That's true. I wasn't hooked on the cocaine business; I was hooked on making a lot of money. I always wanted to retire. But *how* did I want to retire? I always thought big. Patricia thought I was expanding the gloves business immensely in South America through the Colón Free Trade Zone. But when she got to Panama she saw I was still trafficking. The gloves were never sent. She realised I had no intentions to stop drinking or retire. Guantex was a great business but with Leebert Ramcharan we started making millions.'

*

Money wasn't enough for Patricia to stay. It never had been. She just wanted a husband. She stuck out the year and left Panama to spend Christmas and New Year's in Cabo San Lucas, Mexico.

'We went back to Mexico but she stayed and I returned to Panama,' says Luis. 'We did not travel together because I was using a different last name. I was in Panama for about a month and I called her to come down and that's when she said she wanted a separation.'

Patricia remembers it well: 'We were more apart than ever at the end of 1998. We were talking by phone and he said, "I'm not drinking, I'm going to the gym." I'm a very healthy person and I had urged him to go: that it was a good thing for him to do for himself. He told me he was going. But he was fatter than ever when I saw him in Cabo San Lucas. Fat and drinking whisky. When he moved to Panama he also started doing coke again because of the kind of people he was with. I was shocked. "Oh, my God, everything's a lie." In that moment I took the decision. I needed to stop. So I decided to leave him.'

Luis: 'She told me, "No, I've decided to leave you. I'm not going to continue to be a gypsy all my life. I see that you're not going to change. You're going to continue working and drinking, the same lifestyle. I'm through with this life."'

Patricia: 'He was asking me if I wanted to go to Madrid or Barcelona. I said, "No, I don't want to." He said, "But why? You want to separate?" And I said, "Yes." I didn't have the balls to tell him directly. I wanted to say it but I couldn't say it. He said it before I did.

'It was the *drinking*. I think Luis has this recklessness to him because of the drinking. It was a crazy kind of life. You can do anything. You have a lot of money, all the opportunities, beautiful people, the parties. But to survive you have to be someone like me. I never did drugs. I might drink two, three glasses of wine if I go to a dinner, or a little bit of champagne, but that's it. So my head was always clear.

'Luis never fit the profile of a narco. I thought he was going to realise the life was not good for him to continue being in the business, but that was my problem – you think you can change people. You think, "Because he loves me he's going to stop drinking. Because he loves me he's going to stop doing coke." People only change after they decide they want to do it. When you really love and care for someone and they drink and do coke again and again and *again*, you start hating them. I always told him, "You are amazing when you're not drinking and doing coke." We could have been a perfect couple if not for that. I didn't see him for a year after that.'

50

The Postcard

LUIS WAS POLEAXED, BUT only momentarily. For the first half of 1999 he dealt with his existential pain the same way men the world over deal with break-ups.

'Then shit, I went into a depression. I went through a little bit of a hard time there so I hit on this girl, Michelle, who I knew from her working at the Davidoff store. There's a saying in Spanish, *un clavo saca a otro*: one nail takes out another. The best way to recreate your old girlfriend is to get a new girlfriend.'

It was instant lust. Michelle was a Xerox of Luis's estranged wife – just ten years younger. She had the looks of a 1980s swimsuit model – high thighs and slits for eyes – and liked to try out moves from the *Kama Sutra*.

'A girl can have a great body but she doesn't have the sexuality. Michelle was a very hot girl. Sex and exoticness just came out of her pores. She was, *whooah*, one hot situation there. Nicely built, nice ass, nice tits, on the white side with dirty blonde hair and very voluptuous, very sexual. I had to fuck Michelle three times a day. I'd come home and she'd have the room all lit with candles and a beautiful bucket of champagne and roses and she used to give me a super-massage with oils. Michelle was like, "I read this, let's try this." *Whooah*. What the fuck. The body lubricates itself and it's open for this type of sex and, you know, anal sex and front sex, whatever.

'She showed me how to hold off coming. She'd put ice on my balls. I had no Viagra back then; it didn't exist. It was just something in your head. It was crazy but it was beautiful. It's great to experience that. Some men never experience that. It was a fucking trip with her. I didn't have time to be reading no fucking *Kama Sutra* when I was dealing with Nick Fisciatoris, Elias Lemos and fucking freighter loads of cocaine in the daytime.'

*

But he had plenty of time to think about the mistakes he'd made. While they were still together, Patricia had begged Luis to stop taking drugs and drinking and agreed to move to Panama on the condition their relationship would improve. But the night she arrived from Mexico City they'd got their maid to put the kids to bed and gone out to the Davidoff cigar store to smoke with a pair of boisterous Mexicans.

'She gave me a chance. She held up as much as she could. It started to go bad when we were in Mexico already and I was drinking a little too much, and after Santi was born she expected me to settle down a bit and I didn't. Patricia came to live in Panama with the kids and the Mexican maid. But the day I picked her up at the airport I was with these two tall Mexican guys from Guadalajara, with the fucking boots and the big Mexican belt buckles with *toro* and the horns, and we were drinking and snorting and this was the day she arrived. Like nothing changed. I was drinking with two Mexicans I ran dope with. *Hello.* Weren't you supposed to quit?'

Away from the family home, Luis had no problem drinking a bottle of Scotch a night with a friend. He might have had a bottle of Finlandia vodka and a can of Mott's Clamato for the hangover the following evening. He wasn't a faithful husband either.

'I didn't brush it in her face. But Patricia knew that I would go out with Juanchi and when I went to Cartagena and San Andrés, we were fucking partying out. Our informants that we had all over the place said, "Shit, your wife just arrived on a flight." I go, "What?" We had to clear out the apartment, this and that, *ba ba ba*, and we were fucked up, but in the end when she got to the apartment it was just me and Juanchi drinking by ourselves, no hookers, no nothing like that. Still, she wasn't happy about it.'

So you were still partying with prostitutes?

'I partied with hookers for 25 years. *Jesus Christ*. It was like a lifestyle.'

Patricia told me she never found out about the affairs. If Luis had been cheating too, it doesn't particularly bother her.

'I never found out anything, so he was intelligent in that case. If Luis went on a trip and something happened one time with another woman, it's not important. He wouldn't have to tell me. I just don't want to know. The problem is when you have a relationship parallel to your own relationship. I never saw that kind of behaviour in him. I never lost time thinking he went to San Andrés and he fucked somebody. I don't care. I knew he wanted to be only with me.'

When it came to extramarital sex, says Luis, there was a kind of unspoken understanding between them when he was away from home.

'I was always a party animal. That's what fucked me up. I was always unfaithful to girlfriends but only in party mode. I've never been unfaithful to true love. I've been unfaithful to physical *need*. Physical need is like taking a piss. True love is something else. I wish I'd been a different person and wasn't addicted to drinking and snorting. When I didn't drink I was never unfaithful. I wasn't one of those "dry snorters" that snorts coke without drinking. I always drank and *then* I did coke. And then when you do the coke you drink more.

'Some men are just womanisers and get a steady girl on the side and get her an apartment, that kind of situation. I never did that. That's ridiculous. Fucking give your money to another home? Whatever money you have you bring it home. I only got out of whack when I travelled somewhere with my buddies, we were at a hotel and we'd start drinking, snort cocaine, and then you call hookers. It's cheaper to have a hooker. Those fucking lovers that you keep on the side cost you a fortune when they want to go haywire. A hooker doesn't even know what your name is. You're Julio one day, Alex the other, Pepe, fuck knows.'

*

Back at the Miraluz building in Panama after one of his trips, Luis visited Sonny Bowie's apartment. Sonny opened the door and invited him inside. The candles were burning brightly in Sonny's shrine to Chango.

'How are you, Sonny?'

'Everything's fine, Luis. But listen, Senador, while you were gone INTERPOL came and asked for us.'

'INTERPOL? What are you talking about?'

'INTERPOL came to the building. They were asking about you, me and Fresh. They were asking for Luis Navia, American. But don't worry because I've already consulted with Chango.'

Luis was in Panama under his travelling name, Novoa.

'Sonny, I'm out of here. Everything may be cool with Chango but that does not sound good at all to me.'

Luis called his maid over to Sonny's apartment and asked her to pack him an overnight bag.

'I didn't even go back to my apartment. I went to a hotel, registered under another name, I hung out for a few days. Just hearing that comment of Sonny's, I was out of there. I knew he and Fresh were hot. All my life I always fled and avoided and really took seriously any kind of law-enforcement involvement. That was something I didn't fool around with. I left the Miraluz building but I stayed in Panama for a while, renting somewhere else under another name, and kept a very low profile. I had to wrap up certain business with Fresh and that's when I left for about three months to Jamaica. [235] When I came back I went to see Michelle at the cigar store. I asked her, "Do you want to come with me to Europe?" I didn't tell her exactly what was going on. We stayed in Panama for another two weeks, very low key. Then I got my passports and we flew to Madrid via Santo Domingo.'

Before he left there was one last thing to do. Luis had long toyed with the idea of sending Robert Harley a fine silk necktie from Ecuador, and even paid for David Santos, his occasional personal assistant in Panama and Colombia, to pick one up from a men's boutique.

But there was no time for that now. Luis had a picture he'd taken in Cuba in the early 1990s. In it he was seated, dressed up like a yacht captain (complete with white cap), with two men either side of him:

one in the garb of an African dictator and the other an Arab emir. In the background was a 100-foot yacht.

He picked up a pen and began writing on the reverse side. The inscription was brief and deliberately provocative from an international fugitive to a federal agent. Luis signed off with a cheeky nom de plume, a nod to Meyer Lansky.[236]

> Bob
> Dollar for dollar, dictators and Emirs are still the best investments!
> Saludos
> Meyer

And then he walked out the door, leaving instructions for it to be sent when David went to pick up some money in the United States. The thinking behind it was simple enough but diabolically mischievous.

'I wanted Bob to get it with a Miami postmark.'

A couple of weeks later at an office building in Key West, the men and women of the United States Customs Service were turning up for another day's work when a huge laugh reverberated around the office.

'I have a sense of humour,' says Harley. 'I thought it was cheeky and funny. None of this was ever personal. I never took it personal. But I'm surprised we ever found it. I think he just sent it to "US Customs, Key West, Florida".'

51

Burnt Out

GREEK BUSINESSMAN ELIAS LEMOS, the 53-year-old owner of Callisti Maritime, was a friend of Nick Fisciatoris. Like Nick, he spent a bit of time in London, living in Eaton Square, but was based permanently in Milan, where he was staying at the Hotel Manzoni on Via Santo Spirito.

Elias was looking to get into cocaine and had the family money to do it. His billionaire cousin Costas Lemos of Greek shipping company CM Lemos, who died in 1995, had been one of the wealthiest ship magnates in the world. Elias wasn't exactly cut from the same cloth and in 1998 was taken (along with a group of associates) to the High Court of Justice in London to face a claim on the tort of conspiracy by Bankgesellschaft Berlin AG. The judge found against him.

'Elias was a legitimate ship owner who had a tendency towards illegal businesses,' says Luis. 'He was always fooling around with cash. The attractive thing about shipping is the incredible amount of cashflow. At the end of the year there can be losses, you can be working at a loss, but the cashflow is so tremendous that it doesn't matter. The motivation [for any dope smuggler] is the incredible amount of money that you make.'

And because of Sonny Bowie's troubles with INTERPOL and British law enforcement having recently come down on Pinky

Delgado's sailboat operations, Elias had his opening to get started as a partner in a major international drug-smuggling operation.

Jorge García, who'd been promoted to Los Mellizos' head of operations, met Luis in Barranquilla to gauge his interest in taking over shipping responsibilities from Sonny, who had been arrested in Panama and sent back to Colombia. A pot-smoking Colombian-American narco with a nervous tick called 'Willie' had introduced them, and in turn Jorge then met Elias, who was eager to please. The cartel needed ships – and they needed them urgently.

So when Luis arrived with Michelle in Athens from Madrid in September 1999, Luis again using his Mexican passport, Elias was busy looking for vessels to buy. Two Greek hoods – 'Lefty', a friend of Lemos, and 'Greek Peter', a close associate of Nick Fisciatoris – had been entrusted with a sizeable budget to scout for new vessels for Los Mellizos.

'We were definitely planning some big things with them. I was going to bring in new routes with Lefty and Greek Peter, and Los Mellizos were going to buy the ships and supply the merchandise. In Greece it was easy to be a Mexican because nobody knows what a Mexican looks like or talks like. I had just come out of a great winning streak in Jamaica. We were going up in the world. We were doing freighters.'

But Luis was under no illusions about who he was about to work with. The tale of cocaine trafficker Gustavo Salazar Bernal aka 'Macabí' is an example of the dangers faced by anyone who crossed the Mejía Múnera brothers.

Intelligent, capable, industrious, smart and good-looking, Gustavo liked to play tennis at his country club and was involved in the cocaine business. A bona fide criminal but not a murderous one, he owned a boat factory and built fastboats for Los Mellizos, quickly going from nothing to having $20 to $30 million in the bank. Then, says Luis, his whole attitude changed. Gustavo thought he was a bigshot. When there was a discrepancy over 5000 kilos stashed somewhere, Gustavo and the Mejía Múnera brothers had a firm difference of opinion. Gustavo didn't back down.

'Gustavo was never a killer. He was never a true outlaw. That is something you're born with. People make a lot of mistakes. Sure enough, one day Gustavo was waiting to catch a plane, and some guy came up to him and said, "Sir, do you want to get your shoes shined?" He said, "Yeah, might as well. I'm waiting here." So the shoeshine boy bent down, opened up the shoeshine box and whipped out a fucking 9mm Browning with a silencer and just clipped three or four bullets in his head. That was the end of this big shot, Gustavo Salazar Bernal. They make the big mistake of thinking that because they have a lot of money they're big criminals. *No.* You're still the same idiot. On top of that, before they killed Gustavo, they killed his brother Fernando.'[237]

*

The year 1999 would go down as a bad one for ship smuggling in northern Colombia.[238] Starting with a tip-off and crucial lead-up investigations from British intelligence, four 1970s-built vessels – the *Cannes*, the *China Breeze*, the *Castor* and the *Pearl II* – were all busted by British and American forces on the high seas, each carrying significant multi-ton loads of 'merchandise' from the Caribbean Sea to European waters.[239] VAW-125 Tigertails, sophisticated radar planes equipped with Hawkeye technology, were deployed. In total 13,689 kilos (just over 15 tons) were seized and with the *China Breeze* and *Pearl II* alone, there had been 19 arrests in the United States and the Netherlands.

Though there was some dispute over what cartel was responsible for each ship – it was later revealed the DEA and USCS were at odds over the origin of a number of cocaine loads – Los Mellizos were directly linked to at least two of the four. They were heavy blows: the cartel simply didn't have enough ships in reserve to cover all its losses. They'd need to buy new ships outright.

Luis, however, had only minimal knowledge of what was going on with the law-enforcement interest in the Atlantic.

'I didn't know about those ships going down; I didn't know they had lost that many ships. I knew that they'd had some problems [with their ships], I just didn't know specifically which ones. I only knew any of this was going on because of Nick Fisciatoris. We made certain moneys from Nick. Sonny had started to buy a couple of these ships.

While I was in Panama, Sonny used to let us participate in some of his dealings and take us in on some of his profits, and we used to take Sonny in on some of Fresh's and my Jamaica trips. Were we really involved? *No.* Not directly. We made money because Sonny gave us commissions. He was already trying to get away from buying ships in Panama and buying them in Greece and we helped him out with a bit of that.[240] I remember him talking about the *Pearl II*.'

*

Luis, with ships now supplied by Elias Lemos of Callisti Maritime, was promising to get the Mejía Múnera brothers' coke through to the Port of Rotterdam without a hitch.

'When Sonny got arrested and was out of commission, that's when Jorge García came to me to take over. Los Mellizos never knew Jorge came to me. Sonny was hotter than a pistol. What he would do was take his ships from Panama to Suriname to pick up rice – Suriname is an exporter of rice – and from Suriname he would head out to Europe. Los Mellizos already had it down pat, picking up rice in Suriname. But that whole Panama–Suriname pick-up route was burnt out. Suriname was still a good place for smuggling but when that ship left from Panama, even though it was empty, you knew [the DEA] kinda knew it already.'

What Luis brought to the Mellizos organisation was a bold new approach. His innovation in their criminal enterprise was to work the shipping routes in reverse, so as to evade suspicion.

'When we sat to talking, I told them, "Listen, this makes all the sense in the world because that's where we work *backwards*." Come from Greece, go to Brazil, come up that coast, you hit me in Guyana, we never come into this fucking hot Caribbean area. They really liked that.

'So I had no ships coming out of Panama or Colombia or Venezuela. I had ships coming in from Europe down to the Brazil–Venezuela region to drop off goods from Europe and Africa and pick up sugar in Brazil, iron ore and aluminium in Venezuela, then going back out towards Europe. The ships never entered the really hot zone between Panama and the northern coast of Colombia and western Venezuela.

'We would hit and pick up in the eastern Venezuela–Guyana area, which from there in a few hours you are already in the Atlantic. We would hit the ships with the cocaine around 6pm when they were already miles offshore and by midnight they were into the Atlantic. There was *no one* out there.

'We were making $5 million a trip. You don't make that kind of money off legal cargo. Dope business is astronomical. You get it in a suitcase in cash and there's no bullshit about it; it's there. On top of that, the Colombians paid for their ships and we got to *keep* the ships. So we got a free ship and we could have ended up having a bunch of free ships.'

52

Under the Gun

ELIAS AND LUIS HAD a ship: the *Suerte I*. In Spanish, *suerte* means 'luck'. The 7546-ton bulk freighter had been bought in December 1999 at the bargain price of $2 million under its former name the *Aktis*, but it wasn't seaworthy and Elias had called it in to dock in Piraeus, Greece, for $400,000 of urgently needed repairs, much to Luis's annoyance.

As this was Callisti Maritime's maiden joint venture with Los Mellizos, there was a lot riding on its success and no latitude for further fuck-ups. Elias and Luis were charging the cartel $5 million for the voyage plus expenses, but these expenses were blowing out. For almost six months, along with Elias's partner Filippos Makris, the trio had lived at the luxury Four Seasons Astir Palace Hotel in Vouliagmeni, 45 minutes south of Athens, and racked up tens of thousands of dollars in hotel bills, mostly in bar tabs.[241]

Apart from his work commitments during the day, shopping with his Panamanian girlfriend, Michelle, and bracing walks along the coastline, Luis rarely left the hotel and was taking medication to help calm his already frayed nerves over the delays. But for the first time in almost a year he had got to see Juliana and Santi, now aged six and three, who stayed with Patricia at the Astir over Christmas and New Year's. Juliana even became good friends with Elias Lemos's son. Luis took happy snaps of his children clambering over the *Suerte* as it was moored in Piraeus and at the Callisti end-of-year party.

In Luis's initial conception of the *Suerte*'s grand smuggle, the coke would be offloaded from Venezuela to Spain no later than July. The ideal time to hit the Galician coast was actually even earlier: June, when the sun went down at a reasonable hour. This was because by August, people were swimming at beaches until 10pm.

So the whole operation was running months late and encountering conditions that weren't conducive to industrial-scale drug smuggling. After all, when you're trying to keep a low profile without alerting the police, Galician fishing boats are expected to return to shore at certain times of the day, like commercial fishermen on trawlers everywhere. It's important to look normal.

'Fishing boats go out and fishing boats come back,' explains Luis. 'There's travelling *times*. If you're smuggling with a fishing boat, you can't come back at the wrong time. You've gotta play the logistics right. Basically because of the delays we were all under the gun.

'When Elias told me that he was bringing the ship to Greece I thought it was going to be in the country for a month not *six* months. We had planned to be down in Venezuela by March. Bringing the *Suerte* into Piraeus was a big mistake. But once we realised that mistake, we were too far into fixing it and did not have the time to move it.'

*

By 2000 Luis had been working full-time in the cocaine business for 22 years and had made $100 million 'easily', but he'd wasted nearly all of it or had it taken away from him. The bare truth was that he was having cashflow problems yet operating to a different standard of liquidity than most people.

'My situation was very reckless, the lifestyle. The other guys in Colombia would invest their money in land, real estate. I was a man with no solid foundation. Being a fugitive and having no solid ground, you're just all over the place. It eats you up alive. I always had $20,000 in my pocket or in my room for spending and for shopping. I was always going shopping with Michelle and buying things and I was even looking to buy an apartment in Vouliagmeni. I mean, in that business being "broke" is worrying that you only have five to ten million dollars. I had access to a checking account that always had $50,000 to $100,000 available; at least $50,000 that I had direct quick access to.'

Complicating the financial situation further, Willie, who'd become involved with the group after replacing Pedro Jiménez, had audaciously filched a $400,000 introduction fee for setting up Elias Lemos with the cartel's Jorge García.

A Miami-born US citizen with Colombian heritage, Willie came from a wealthy family who lived in Key Biscayne and had known Luis since at least the early 1980s. But that hadn't stopped Willie asking Elias for a commission. The money ended up coming straight out of an $800,000 kitty Los Mellizos had provided to tide him and Luis over for the six months it was going to take to get the smuggle up and running.

'Willie and I were good friends but he was greedy with the $400,000 he took from Elias. It was taken very prematurely. It was a commission on a fucking trip that hadn't happened. This happens sometimes. These fucking idiots meet the Colombian connection, they get friendly and they get fucked.

'Willie convinced Elias to send him $400,000. There was no stipulation anywhere that Willie was supposed to get $400,000 for an introduction, but he pressured Elias so much that Elias gave in. By the time I got to Europe there was already money being transferred for the buying of the *Suerte*, and in one of those transfers Elias gave Willie two transfers of $200,000. I was *extremely* pissed. I was supposed to have $150,000 at least for my expenses when I got to Europe, but the payment of the $400,000 to Willie left us all cash short in Greece.

'Because of that, financially we started off the whole venture depending on Jorge and Los Mellizos for everything – and that's not how it's supposed to be. Then Nick Fisciatoris took another $400,000 from Elias. With that $800,000 that was paid to Willie and Nick we could have made three or four million dollars buying merchandise. We were living great but I wasn't the happiest camper. I just wanted to finish what we were doing with the *Suerte* and go back to Colombia. I knew these big ships were too much of a paper trail.'

*

The protracted delays were also starting to attract the attention of corrupt local cops.

'Some government-connected thugs were hitting up Elias for money because they had suspicions about the *Suerte*. Nick even punched Elias in the face – *boom* – at his cabana at the Astir Palace. One day I saw Filippos Makris with a black eye and he told me that these thugs went to the Callisti Maritime office and brought along some taekwondo guy, who put a kick to the side of his face. I met some of these government dogs and they obviously knew what we were up to. We had to play it down as much as possible and that's when Elias and I thought it best to get out of Athens and go to Milan and stay with his friend Baron Massimo Paonessa.'[242]

Baron Paonessa owned a company with an interest in a granite quarry in Venezuela.

'Massimo had a diplomatic passport from The Vatican. One day we got drunk and he goes into his secret safe room, and inside a safe he whips out like this fucking Masonic outfit from the 1600s, secret-society shit. Massimo had some connections in Venezuela through granite. We were going to start exporting granite from Venezuela and put the granite in the ships with the coke. With Massimo we had also spoken about putting together $50 million and a group of Swiss banks and we were going to make a move to corner the Mexican and Central American coffee market; buy up a lot of the production, a lot of the futures. That would have put a dent in coffee roasters in America that use coffee from the region in their blends.

'We were always scheming. We had big plans. I later found out from law enforcement that they knew about this granite thing and for a while there, when they used to listen in on our phone calls on the Venezuelan end of the smuggle, the numbers were so huge they thought maybe we were referring to the granite, which, in real life, ships in thousands of tons.

'Massimo's wife or his girlfriend was this redhead from Calabria and she was definitely connected to the 'Ndrangheta [the Calabrian mafia], who are really off the wall. They will eat the Sicilians for lunch. They were just starting to get heavily involved in cocaine. Today they control the cocaine coming into Europe. And that's the kind of connections Nick Fisciatoris had and the kind of shit that we were looking at because we were looking at bringing coke into Italy with the 'Ndrangheta. It was a whole different ball game. The 'Ndrangheta is a very closed unit. They are vicious. They give the Russians a run for their money – that's how bad they are.'

*

While in Milan, Luis and Elias also met a Dutch-Indonesian yacht captain and associate of Greek Peter. The captain owned a 40-foot yacht moored in southern Portugal and was planning to rendezvous with the *Suerte* off the Azores, where he would pick up a 500-kilo load for shipment to England.

Luis even went further afield to Paris a few times to have 'another meeting with some other fucking mobster from London about selling more coke . . . that's what we did all day: think about transporting more coke', and stayed at the Hôtel Plaza Athénée on Avenue Montaigne, while Elias went on to London. His hotel bills came to $30,000, paid for by Callisti Maritime.

'I refused to meet with any Colombians in Europe. I avoided London. I never went there. They told me they had cameras in London. I said, "What the fuck am I going to do in a fucking country where you walk into the airport and they've got cameras and eye surveillance. Are you crazy?"'

He didn't do much sightseeing in Paris either.

'Why leave a hotel? The hotel is the best place in any city. You go to any city in the world, why the fuck would you leave the Ritz-Carlton or the Four Seasons? What are they going to show you? You want to see the Louvre? You don't need to go to no museum to see a painting. You can *imagine* a painting. I went into the Louvre once, you know, I walked in, I said, "Yeah, okay, fine, fucking-A, super, dynamite, let's get the fuck out of here. Let's go to a real museum. Let's go to a fucking classic restaurant where they have some kind of recipe from the 1600s or something." *That's* interesting.

'Like New York. For me, the best museums in New York are the fucking Jewish delis. Pretty soon there's not going to be any of them left. In Europe, same thing. We used to go to this restaurant in Paris called Fouquet's.[243] It was right near the Plaza Athénée. The Arc de Triomphe was down the block. I passed by, I looked at it, said, "Yeah, well, this looks really cool," and that's it, *gone [laughs]*. You think I even bought a souvenir? Fuck that shit.

'I went to the Eiffel Tower, and I looked up, I said, "Wow, that's really cool, let's go have some drinks, let's go to the bar, let's spend seven hours in a fucking fancy restaurant drinking champagne." My idea of tourism is to check into a fucking super-incredible hotel, hit the hotel bar and the dining room, and pick an incredible restaurant and knock the hell out of that restaurant every night. 'Cause I don't go to a lot of restaurants. I pick the best one and go there 17 fucking times. Then everybody knows you, everybody knows what you want, where you want to sit, what you drink. I'm very strange in that way.'

When they returned to Athens, Nick Fisciatoris had been busy wheeling and dealing. He'd set up a meeting with the Russian mob. They wanted to buy 50 tons of cocaine, had 'unlimited' demand and would take delivery of the merchandise in Albania. Luis even had the opportunity to buy 15 Russian military submarines through mob connections in Greece, but 'they wanted us to buy all 15 and where the hell are you going to keep 15 submarines?'

53

The Heat

MORE THAN THE DELAY with the departure of the boat or the shortfall in his kitty, what was bothering Luis the most was the attention they were getting.

'Elias really fucked up by bringing the *Suerte* to get fixed in Athens, where *everybody* knew him. He should never have opened up the office there. They all clinged on to him. Greek law enforcement was shaking him down. Nick was shaking him down. The heat we picked up in Greece I blame completely on Elias.

'But, saying that, Nick also brought the heat. Nobody needed to know that Nick was in the mix and somehow or other people put it together that Nick and Elias were together on the *Suerte* deal. And obviously once that was figured out it was quickly figured out that I was the South American connection.

'Elias was not a gangster. He was just someone very well connected in the shipping world that had decided to transport coke. I thought he had everything under control and he was totally okay under the cover of being a legit Greek ship owner. But he was not a natural-born gangster like Nick, or a guy like myself with 20 years of smuggling experience.

'I just wanted to get the *Suerte* out of Piraeus and get the whole trip done, then regroup with some of the other Greeks that Nick introduced me to. Some of them had their own ships and with others we were going to buy ships and work them together, but definitely not in Piraeus.

'I said to Elias, "You should have taken this fucking boat to get fixed in Alexandria, Egypt." Nobody would have even known it was there. We could have told everybody we were still in the process of buying it. It was sitting right there in Piraeus, when everybody in town knew Elias. So we were blown. We were already hot in Greece. It's a shame, that, it's . . .'

He trails off. There's almost misty-eyed whimsy in his voice when Luis thinks about what went wrong.

'I think Elias fucked it up. These guys completely fucked up a good thing.'

*

By the time Luis and Michelle flew into Caracas from Milan in June 2000 and met Jorge García and his fellow Los Mellizos associate Iván de la Vega Cabás, then moved on to Puerto Ordaz, he was walking into a trap.

'I'd already had a couple of close calls in Caracas. We used to keep our planes there, including the Conquest. I didn't want to go back there. So I said to Elias, "This is fucked up. I'm already over here, I've already crossed the fucking puddle, for me to have to cross back, you know, *fuck*. I didn't like travelling. For me, each time you travel under a Mexican passport it's a risk. So, sure enough, I get to Venezuela and these guys were expecting a Greek. Nobody knew I was "The Greek". Nobody knew I was Mexican, nobody in Venezuela knew anything about me except Jorge, but he didn't tell anybody.'

Luis was taking Prozac to help relieve his anxiety.

'You can be taking it and you can be head-deep in shit and you think everything is fine. Willie had warned me: "There seems to be something going on. Stop taking the Prozac. That shit dulls your nerve endings. You need to be sharp, man. I've heard some fucking rumours. I'll keep you posted."'

They got their warning but didn't abort when they had the chance.

'You know it's funny,' Jorge said when he got a moment with Luis. 'We were riding around the other day and there was a car following us.

We stopped the car and we went up to the people in the car. "What the fuck are you doing following us?" It turned out they were some guys from the UN.'

'What? United Nations?'

'Yeah, there's a lot of foreigners here because of the port, the steel; they were guys from the UN.'

'Were they American?

'We don't know. They said they were Canadian.'

'Man, are you sure? What the fuck? That's crazy.'

Days later, Jorge came to Luis again.

'Luis, we found a device on one of our cars. We just hired a taxi and put it in the taxi and told the driver to drive it to Maracaibo.'

'And that's when I said, "I'm out of here. This is very strange." I was having trouble finding my passport and went back to Caracas. But the *Suerte* had come into Puerto Ordaz. I was on another fucking planet.'

PART 11

AN INFILTRATED SITUATION

54

The Phone Call

IT WAS 16 AUGUST 2000 and another stinking hot day in Maracaibo. The only thing worse than being stuck in Venezuelan heat is being stuck in the same heat in handcuffs in the back of a black Suburban outside a police station.

Luis was staring intently at the *gringo* with the skinny white legs and Hawaiian shirt. The door opened and Luis could now see him more clearly. Very handsome, tall and well built, the American had a lean jaw and burry moustache.

Eric J. Kolbinsky was a former investigator and later corporal from the Organized Crime Division (Vice & Narcotics) of the Department of Public Safety in Durham, North Carolina. He'd joined the USCS in 1987 and for his first posting was stationed 'down on the border' in Laredo, Texas, then transferred to Wilmington, North Carolina.

In 1991, Kolbinsky switched again, this time to the DEA in Atlanta, Georgia, as a special agent and first went down to Colombia in 1998. The night before he arrived that November, a fellow DEA agent called Frank Moreno was shot in the chest and killed during an altercation outside a nightclub in the Zona Rosa district of Bogotá. As Kolbinsky remembers: 'The bullet clipped his aorta, exited his back and struck an individual across the street in the head, killing him also.'

Bienvenidos a Colombia. Welcome to Colombia.

Kolbinsky was sent to the DEA Resident Office in Barranquilla in the department of Atlántico. His primary duty was liaison with local antinarcotics police in Santa Marta, 100 kilometres by road to the northeast. He spent a lot of time at the port. The cartels would hide cocaine in loads of bananas or even under bulk carriers carrying La Guajira coal.

'They would attach what we call "parasitic compartments" to the hulls of the ships; like a torpedo tube that they'd weld on to the hull.[244] So divers were always diving these ships prior to them leaving to make sure they weren't full of cocaine. As a rule the DEA very seldom got involved in any sort of enforcement activity. We were always in the background. We had armoured vehicles but we were still restricted where we could travel by road.

'When we went out on operations we were always well prepared; we had tons of cops or military with us. So we weren't shooting out with the bad guys in Colombia – moreso doing jungle ops, where if you get fired on, you fire back in self-defence – but in a regular law-enforcement effort on the streets. We would hang back and advise, that sort of thing. It was still dangerous but not as dangerous maybe as earlier times [with Pablo Escobar]. But where else can a grown man play Cowboys and Indians?'

Luis thought Kolbinsky looked like the Hollywood actor Sam Elliott. He was gentlemanly and mellow in a hippie kind of way: 'He wasn't this redneck motherfucker at all.'

'Hey, Mr Navia, how are you?' Kolbinsky said politely in his gentle Carolinas drawl, as his USCS partner from Houston, Special Agent Vicente M. Garcia, got in the other side of the car. Luis was now sandwiched in the back of the SUV between the full might of American antinarcotics enforcement: DEA and USCS.[245] 'You're being held on suspicion of drug trafficking. We're going to take you back to the United States for a charge Customs has on you for a load you brought into the Keys.'

Luis had spent over a decade running from American authorities, five of them as a fugitive. For him, the United States was a place he could never return.

'I don't know what you're talking about. I'm a Mexican. Luis

Novoa. I want representation from the Mexican consulate. I want a lawyer.'

'Listen, we know you're Mr Luis *Navia*. You're originally from Miami. You're indicted in the Florida Keys. There's no sense in you denying it. We're going to take you back to the US. Let me put you on the phone to someone who knows you.'

Kolbinsky dialled a number on his cell then handed it over. A man's voice came down the line. He too was on his cell. Luis knew immediately who it was. Under American law, Kolbinsky had to hand over his detainee to the agent who'd had him originally indicted, even though the DEA's plan had been to allow Luis to go back to Europe and arrest him there.

'*Er*, hello?'

'Hi, Luis. This is Robert Harley from the Florida Keys. I've been to your mom's house. You know I've been there asking about you. We have an indictment on you.'

'You've got the wrong guy.'

'Luis, *Luis*, listen to me. Your mother lives at Cypress Drive on Key Biscayne. We know who you are. C'mon. *Please*. Cooperate with the gentleman next to you. Make it smoother for yourself. There's no turning back here. Don't talk to anybody down there. Keep your mouth shut. I'll see you in Miami.'

In his gut Luis knew Harley was right. When he handed the phone back, Kolbinsky made the situation plain.

'Well, if you're not Luis Navia, and you're not a US citizen, I can't help you. I'm going to have to turn you back over to the Venezuelans.'

That meant being left with the cop who was threatening to cut him into a thousand pieces. It wasn't much of a choice.

When I asked Kolbinsky to describe how Luis processed being caught once and for all, he laughs drily: 'He was fine but going through some changes. The world was coming down around him at that point.'

55

The Butterfly Effect

FROM THE DEA END, the case against Los Mellizos had originated in Barranquilla, originally a one-man operation, with a so-called 'vetted unit' that was 'working' Iván de la Vega Cabás and the Mejía Múnera brothers. It was run by agents Angelo Meletis and Rick Bendekovic and they were mostly involved in wiretaps, but officially the focus of DEA activity in Colombia was to support local cops in bringing US cases against drug traffickers: whatever work the agency does gets prosecuted in the States.[246]

Vetted units, a kind of special taskforce, were part of the DEA's Vetted Unit Program, initiated in 1996, in which local police officers worked alongside DEA agents stationed overseas in investigative work and intelligence gathering. At the time, there were four such vetted units in Colombia, with over 100 members. Other units had been set up in Bolivia, Peru and Mexico.

But as with the CIA's fraught relationship with the FBI regarding intelligence, there was lack of information sharing and a great deal of rivalry going on between American law enforcement in Colombia, this time between the DEA and USCS.[247]

Senior Special Agent (SSA) Nigel Brooks worked Operation Journey from the USCS Office of Investigations in Houston, while his Spanish-speaking colleague in the investigations unit, Vicente Garcia, was sent down to Venezuela to actively monitor Luis on the ground.[248]

Garcia had previously been the case agent for the prosecution of the crew of the *Cannes* and even boarded the *China Breeze*, before 'we gave it to the DEA, playing nice'.

Brooks was born to a US serviceman father and British mother in Birmingham, England, in 1947, educated in Lydd, Kent, and came to America in 1965. He was drafted into the US Army in 1966, served a tour of duty in Vietnam and started his law-enforcement career in the early '70s with USCS as a sky marshal in Hawaii. He found it was far preferable working with the British, Her Majesty's Customs and Excise (now merged into Her Majesty's Revenue and Customs, HMRC), because it offered better protection for their informant.

'At the time of the *China Breeze*, I was the Acting Resident Agent in Charge [RAC] in Galveston, Texas. Subsequently, I moved to a three-agent group that ran Operation Journey. My partners were Senior Special Agent Denny Lorton and Special Agent Jay Sills.[249] I primarily took the lead because of my relationship with HMCE's National Investigation Service [NIS] and the fact that I was about to retire and was willing to fight for what I believed in. Younger agents could suffer consequences because of the politics involved.

'The NIS was the investigative arm of HMCE. They were roughly equivalent to the DEA but they also investigated other revenue-related crimes in addition to drugs; much like the US Customs Office of Investigations, which investigated drugs, money laundering, export controls, revenue fraud, and so on.

'We worked mostly with HMCE in both Colombia and Venezuela in order to provide complete protection for our source of information inside the organisation. Our relationship with DEA in this investigation was pretty adversarial, the reason being that we had recruited the informant who was inside the organisation, and DEA wanted control of the investigation. We had totally different philosophies of how the investigation should be managed.

'Because the organisation had stopped sending cocaine to the US, and was sending it to Europe, we worked with HMCE to identify and track the load vessels, allowing law enforcement in Europe to identify the receiving groups and make the arrests and seizures there. DEA wanted to be able to just seize the drugs at the source or as soon as they were loaded onto the ships.

'At that time, US Customs, DEA and the FBI had jurisdiction over drug enforcement. However, when it came to foreign investigations, DEA had that remit as they had attaché offices overseas.[250] DEA was incensed that we were running a source on their turf, and under normal circumstances we would not have been able to do so as DEA had primacy. By working with HMCE, we were able to get around that. There were a few occasions where the source's name was revealed to the Colombians, and that was potentially a huge problem due to the fact that at that time there was massive corruption in law enforcement down there . . . to this day I'm still surprised that the [Los Mellizos] organisation never figured out the identity of the source while [the investigation] was ongoing.'

Eric Kolbinsky admits the situation was normal: 'There were always fights about who was in charge.'

Robert Harley agrees but maintains there were no major issues.

'In every agency there are personalities that are difficult. One type of personality is not endemic to DEA or Customs. I tell people that assholes are equally distributed among agencies. It's just a fact. If you have 100 Customs agents, five of them are assholes and nobody can work with them. So if you happen to come into contact with them and that's your only frame of reference, that's what you're going to think about the agency. It's the unfortunate reality of humanity. Nigel Brooks [of Customs] and the others were investigating proactively trying to interdict a load going to Europe and Eric Kolbinsky [of DEA] ran into Luis as a fugitive while looking at other suspects in-country in Venezuela. It was unbelievable. We had an agent down there who actually went *with* the information. They did what needed to be done.'

*

So how had El Senador finally been caught?

Luis's theory about the phone tap in Galerías Mall being triangulated from Europe turned out to be wrong. American federal agents had been in Venezuela for four weeks due to a tip-off from the informant and Luis had been walking around right under their noses – only they hadn't known who he was until his true identity was discovered completely by accident in Puerto Ordaz. Not even their prize snitch had known who Luis was.

'We got a fingerprint off of a glass and that's how we identified Luis,' says Kolbinsky. 'There was a meeting when all of [the cartel] were there and that's when we got a fingerprint. Some unidentified individual showed up in the middle of this meeting. We had no idea that Luis was even supposed to be there. Whatever interception stuff that had taken place over [at the vetted unit] in Colombia, it was not relayed to us that there was anybody else supposed to be at that meeting in Puerto Ordaz.'

Brooks confirms this is true.

'Luis first came to our attention in July 2000 when the final preparations were underway by the organisation for the movement of cocaine to Europe on the *Privilege* and the *Suerte*.[251] He was identified staying at the Hotel InterContinental Guayana in Puerto Ordaz and was using a Mexican passport but with the name Novoa. HMCE and the *Guardia Nacional* got approval from the Venezuelan Government to monitor his phone in his room and through that monitoring determined that he was communicating with Elias Lemos in Italy, and making phone calls to the US, Spain, Greece, Colombia and Mexico.

'Elias was initially intercepted when Luis called him from the hotel in Puerto Ordaz. Much of the time he was being monitored, it appeared he was trying to get some financing. In addition to his interactions with Jorge García and Iván de la Vega, he was also in contact with Jamil Nomani – "Indurain". So I assume that his role was with the European end of the conspiracy. Our intelligence was so good that we knew names of vessels, geographic locations of onloads and offloads, and we were able to identify the exact location of the storage site on the Orinoco.'[252]

Once he had been identified, Luis's subsequent great escape in Venezuela was foiled by the latest high-priced electronic surveillance technology: a Harris Corporation mobile phone–tracing device or digital analyser called a Triggerfish.

'The DEA and US Customs located Luis in Maracaibo,' says Kolbinsky, who knew and worked with Steve Murphy and Javier

Peña, the DEA agents who took down Pablo Escobar and were made famous by *Narcos*. 'We had a Triggerfish, intercepting cell phones. They call it something else now [Stingray]. There's been a couple of generations of improvements since.

'We were sitting up in a hotel room in Maracaibo and we had the number dialled in. It works off the cell signals. Most traffickers knew we could track them by their cells so it made sense Luis was on a payphone. We knew he was in Maracaibo and were monitoring him whenever he and Iván did use their cell phones. We figured out which hotel he was staying in. The Venezuelans reinitiated surveillance at the hotel and followed him to the mall. When I went to the police station to meet him I knew his name already.'

Vicente Garcia, on his first overseas mission, had been following Luis all over Venezuela for close to a month, both on foot and with the Triggerfish, which was the property of the USCS office in Houston. Brooks had sent Garcia to South America with the device because all the other available equipment inside Venezuela was being used on other jobs. Its portability was a key feature.

'From city to city, carrying a large tracking device,' says Garcia. 'My job was just to follow him while I was there, to intercept phone calls. There was a convoy of us: just me and the *Guardia Nacional*. Wherever he went, we surveilled him. We were almost killed twice on the road between Caracas and Puerto Ordaz. There were some cities between that were just horrible places. We stayed at so many holes in the wall; it was crazy [*laughs*]. Navia would be on one floor of a hotel, and I'd be either one floor below or one floor above, almost in the same location he was, so that I could be able to use the Triggerfish. He never saw me.

'Triggerfish was an evolving technology. We had two types of phones: digital, which was barely coming on board, this was 2000; and analogue. The Triggerfish that I had could do analogue with no problem and could do digital limitedly.[253] That was one of the issues: Navia's phone was digital. So I had to be in very close proximity to him in order to be able to pick up traffic from his phone. There were concrete walls in some of these places. It was very difficult to monitor. Today you can get a handheld Triggerfish. Back then mine was the size of a suitcase. So you can imagine: I was dragging a friggin' suitcase with wheels on it all around Venezuela.'

*

Luis's fingerprints were sent through to Robert Harley and the indictment brought against him in March 1995 for cocaine smuggling in the Florida Keys was actioned.

'We had prints on file and it went back to those original arrests in Dade County,' says Harley. 'We had fingerprints from an old Dade County arrest.'

His 25 years in the drug business had come to an end over a pair of minor traffic offences uncovered by Harley's partner Carol Libbey all those years ago, back when, as she drily puts it, Luis was 'young and stupid'.[254]

If ever there is a better advertisement for the benefit of not drinking and driving than Luis Antonio Navia, I don't know what it is.

Says Harley: 'It was critical to proving he was who he was. It was an insignificant moment in his life that really mattered later on. You don't know how the butterfly effect is going to affect you 20 years from now, but it did with Luis. Fingerprints would be the method to confirm who someone is, especially if you're going to expedite their removal. In those days, the arrestee better be a United States citizen or you would have many hoops to jump through to fly them out immediately. This was pre–war on terror days when protocols changed and other nationalities were removed from foreign countries and flown to the US or Gitmo [Guantánamo Bay, Cuba] a bit more often. I was notified very shortly before his arrest, and didn't receive confirmation until he was on his way to Florida.'

*

Vicente Garcia of USCS in Houston was given the task of coordinating the arrest, while awaiting confirmation that arrest warrants had been approved by the US and Venezuelan Governments. Like a Mexican Ray Romano, dressed in jeans and a T-shirt, he blended in easily with the shoppers at Galerías Mall in Maracaibo. A pale *gringo* in 5.11 Tactical shorts and a baseball cap would have given the game away.

'There was a guy following him in the mall, and it was me. He didn't realise I was American. Eric Kolbinsky would stick out like a sore thumb walking around the mall trying to do surveillance: 6'4", blond, blue eyes. I had two *Guardia Nacional* officers with me. They were armed; I wasn't. We're walking and I'm on the phone with my [country] attaché and he's saying, "Don't lose him." And I said, "There are thousands of people in this mall. The only way I won't lose him is if I literally walk with him." And he said, "Walk *with* him." And I said, "Alright, we're going to get into something here." I was *literally* walking behind him.

'And he turned around a couple of times like he wanted to fight with me or something. I stopped, and he just looked at me [*laughs*] and I looked at him. I think he noticed the *Guardias* were a couple of steps behind me as well. He didn't know if he was going to get kidnapped or what at that point. He kept walking and we followed him until we got the okay to make the arrest. The United States cannot do law enforcement in foreign countries. We were there with the *Guardia Nacional* but we didn't do the actual hands-on.'

The man with half a dozen aliases and as many fake passports, 'The Greek', 'El Senador', was busted.

The US Government finally had their man. [255]

56

The Snitch

FATALLY FOR LUIS, THERE was a *sapo*, a snitch or confidential informant, within the Los Mellizos organisation itself and there had been going all the way back to the middle of 1999. He was a Colombian called Tommy Taylor.[256] An unknown second informant inside the cartel, a 'subsource', had facilitated a face-to-face and very risky meeting for Taylor with the Americans.[257] Taylor agreed to testify against the cartel, but only when its leaders had been arrested, extradited and were in the custody of the US Government.

'The whole case came about after the interception and seizure of the *China Breeze*,' says Nigel Brooks. 'We recruited Taylor as a CI from inside the organisation and from that time on had complete inside knowledge of their activities. He was high enough in the organisation that he worked with both Iván de la Vega and Jorge García, and interacted with other members of the organisation from Miguel Mejía Múnera on down. It enabled us to identify all of the main participants including the Mejía Múneras, De La Vega and García. His information was so precise that we had the INMARSAT numbers, cell numbers, onload and offload coordinates, and frequencies and codes used by [Los Mellizos].'[258]

More gallingly, Luis had met the cartel's mole when he arrived in Caracas. After the capture of the *China Breeze*, Taylor (along with the subsource) had been flown from Barranquilla to Houston to provide information on the impending *Pearl II* smuggle to Brooks and his USCS colleagues. They then returned to Colombia and carried on working for the cartel. USCS in turn shared their information with Britain's HMCE but not the DEA, such was the ongoing discord between the two stateside agencies.

'Using Taylor we had run one load into Amsterdam on board the *Pearl II* and had it successfully taken out by the Dutch Prisma team,' continues Brooks.[259] 'We beaconed the ship and monitored the onload off the coast of Venezuela using a British warship, HMS *Marlborough*. Myself and HMCE's drugs liaison officer [DLO] in Miami, Brendan Foreman, were at the command post in Key West at JIATF-East when the onload from the *pangas* took place. *Marlborough* was monitoring from over the horizon using their technical capabilities. The *Pearl II* headed to Africa with a legitimate load, then to Amsterdam where it was searched and the load found. Unfortunately the Dutch were premature and didn't wait for the offload that was to take place over Christmas on the dock.[260]

'This investigation was actually headed by US Customs in Houston with our co-equal partners from HMCE's National Investigation Service and their drugs liaison officers in Colombia and Venezuela. DEA also assisted, but due to the fact they had an extremely poor relationship with Venezuelan law enforcement, all coordination on intelligence was passed from Customs to HMCE and they handled any interaction with the *Guardia Nacional*.

'We worked exclusively with HMCE in Britain and their DLOs in Colombia and Venezuela, mainly because we had the same goal: identify the receiving end and allow the Europeans to take the enforcement action while we provided the intelligence. It was supposed to be strictly an intelligence-run operation with no US law enforcement contemplated.

'The DEA greatly resented the fact that we were running a source in *their* area, and we refused to grant them access; the reason being for the safety and security of Taylor and his family. We just could not allow the possibility of his identity being revealed. Once we identified Víctor and Miguel Mejía Múnera as the leaders of the organisation in early 2000, things became even more contentious with DEA because of the stature of those two.'

'Tommy Taylor was a fucking basehead from Barranquilla,' curses Luis.[261] 'He came from a good family but he was no good. And Iván was the idiot who brought him into the organisation to work in a gopher capacity. He didn't have any routes, *nothing*. He was just a gopher; Iván's assistant. It seems that they caught on to this whole thing and Tommy travelled to the US to see his daughter who was in college or something. They grabbed him at the airport and they shook him up, they scared him, and they flipped him.[262]

'When he came back to Colombia he was already working for the DEA. That's why he didn't know who I was. He didn't know who I was so he could never mention "Luis Navia". He just knew that Iván had a connection in Greece: "The Greek". Little did I know that Tommy had already infiltrated [Los Mellizos] and I walked into an infiltrated situation in Venezuela. When I got arrested and the news came out, a friend of mine that worked for the Mellizos who I'd known for years said, "Shit, it's *El Senador*!" He had no idea I was The Greek either.'

Luis might have got away with his role in the entire Los Mellizos conspiracy had he not handled the glass in Puerto Ordaz. As far as the international authorities were concerned, the figure Taylor spoke of, 'The Greek', was just that: a Greek.

'Navia's name actually never came up either in the Colombian end of the investigation or when they moved to Venezuela,' says Nigel Brooks. 'Taylor never spoke of him, but did identify everyone he was aware of. We used code for people's names and vessels. Vessels were "X" and individuals were "Z". When Luis arrived on the scene he was assigned Z-23, Miguel Mejía Múnera was Z-16, Víctor Mejía Múnera was Z-22, Jorge García was Z-1 and Iván de la Vega was Z-2. The numbers were not assigned in order of rank but assigned as we identified individuals.[263]

'Luis was identified because we were monitoring Jorge's phone and found him at the hotel that way. From that day on, all of his telephone conversations were intercepted . . . basically, *everyone* was screwing the Colombians. The Greeks were screwing them for money to fix their crappy rust buckets; even the Colombians were screwing each other by embezzling. But I guess when you're making hundreds of millions, who cares? We on the other hand had to follow policies and procedures and continually write reams of justification for money for travel, source payments and technical equipment. No wonder no one has yet won the war on drugs.'

As for Luis's suspicions that his hotel room had been broken into by unknown persons, he was right. A redacted intelligence document from the operation confirmed 'the GN [*Guardia Nacional*] gained access to the room and searched [his] luggage', however Brooks says he has no knowledge of Luis's passport being taken.

But why didn't Taylor know Luis's name? The DEA's Eric Kolbinsky has a good idea.

'Iván de la Vega shielded Luis from the others. They didn't need De La Vega if they had direct access to Luis.'

*

In exchange for his cooperation, Tommy Taylor was promised cash and sanctuary for him and his family in the United States, as well as provided with encrypted instant messaging and emails to maintain daily communication with the US and British agencies coordinating Operation Journey until its eventual conclusion.[264]

After the *Pearl II* in Amsterdam became the fourth vessel to be impounded, Taylor provided names, intelligence and phone numbers to tap, then later relayed the coordinates of the cartel's jungle stash sites after seeing them on Jorge García's computer. Intelligence stations were set up in Caracas, Maraicabo, Puerto Ordaz, Upata, Barrancas del Orinoco and Tucupita. With the *Suerte I*, Taylor was leading Luis, Jorge and Iván to their doom.[265]

'We located where all the big stashes were,' says Graham Honey, the supervisor in charge of Operation Journey for the National Investigation Service of Britain's HMCE, which was working closely with the *Guardia Nacional*. 'I can remember the day [our liaison officer in Venezuela] phoned up to say, "We've got it, we've got this big stash," and then they'd move from that one to another one and found even more drugs.'

Using the coordinates provided by their prized informant, American interagency taskforce JIATF-East took satellite images of the Orinoco buildings, docks and *pangas* from space. A meeting between the DEA, HMCE, USCS and Italian, Venezuelan and Colombian parties involved was held at the US Embassy in Caracas in late July to coordinate the takedown, not helped by Venezuelan President Hugo Chávez refusing American drug surveillance planes in the country's airspace.[266] Meanwhile in Italy, the *Raggruppamento Operativo Speciale* (ROS), or Special Operations Group of the Italian *carabinieri*, was working the Albanian angle with the help of anti-mafia public prosecutors in Lecce.

They were in the tiger's mouth but didn't know it.

57

Shitting Match

THE BRITISH, WHO IN Bogotá had their own version of the DEA, known as HMCE, had brought the Americans in on the investigation because they knew they weren't going to get any prosecutions in the UK. The difficulty they had was in proving the individuals involved had committed crimes in their jurisdiction, or establishing a direct nexus to the UK for the drugs being transported into mainland Europe. American antinarcotics agencies, however, had more sweeping powers. And so what would become known as Operation Journey was born.

'My main focus [when I went to Barranquilla in 1996] was on "El Caracol" [The Snail], Alberto Orlandez Gamboa, the head of all the North Coast [Cartel] at the time,' says Rick Bendekovic, former agent advisor to the DEA office in Barranquilla. 'We were able to take him down and he was extradited later.[267] The Brits were working a bunch of cases and included the DEA office in Greece at the time and US Customs in Houston mainly and Miami as well. We used to bring everybody in to certain strategy meetings. That had led to *China Breeze* and the *Pearl II*.[268]

'When we give something an operation name it's to target an organisation. Behind it is going to be, in a perfect world, as best-case scenario, a well-defined organisation at the end of the investigation, or at least it's going to be [a case of] "We suspect these people to be moving stuff" and want to build it into a dismantlement of a criminal organisation. That's what our operation names signify: a *criminal* organisation. The maritime world was complex.

'We were working with the Brits mainly with their technology. A couple of months into it, the Colombians had sunk their teeth into it completely, and it was expanding and it was pretty much all [the DEA] was doing in Barranquilla. Los Mellizos would later become that office's primary objective.'

But both Graham Honey of HMCE and Nigel Brooks of USCS contend there was major infighting between American agencies working the case, not dissimilar to the feud between the CIA and FBI before the Twin Towers attacks on 11 September 2001. The DEA was also resentful of British involvement. Pre-takedown meetings in DC, Galveston, Athens, Barranquilla and Bogotá had laid bare those divisions. Information sharing generally was at best poor and at worse non-existent, with all the problems coming from the DEA's end.

'There was a real shitting match between US Customs and DEA at the time,' says Honey. '[HMCE] always kind of stayed in the background but I like to think we had the lead intelligence all the time this was going on. We were way ahead of what the DEA were doing; we got pissed off with the DEA.'

Brooks agrees: 'We had a massive problem with DEA because they were extremely upset that Customs was running an operation with HMCE in what they considered *their* area: South America. While our strategy was to monitor onloads of cocaine and allow the vessels to head to their destinations, DEA wanted to take the loads as soon as they were received. They wanted *seizures*. The US has been very successful taking out huge loads, but all you get are the transporters and not the organisations receiving it. But we prevailed in our strategy.'[269]

Honey: 'I had the biggest pissing match with Jim Soiles, the DEA attaché in Greece, over the whole thing; we just didn't get on.[270] The DEA took credit for everything but trust me: they had very little to do with it. There were a lot of good guys within the DEA but that whole job we sat with them on a daily basis and they were way off what was going on. The Americans did a huge amount but their problem was they were in conflict with each other a lot of the time and we were trying to dice [sic] between all of the agencies.'

The DEA's Bendekovic concedes this is true: 'We had to stay in our lane. And we did. We put together what we had with what the Colombians had with our joint resources, and once the prohibition of extradition was repealed that was the most valuable tool we had [against the traffickers]. We set up those teams waiting for that repeal of the extradition prohibition. That became the critical tool. Intercepts, informants and all the traditional techniques of gathering evidence and identifying criminal activity, those are the same. They might change in nuance, but it's facing down time in a US jail that really spooked them and really got their attention.'[271]

58

Atlantic Crossing

THE BYZANTINE MACHINATIONS INVOLVED in the seizures of cocaine in the north Atlantic Ocean of 1999–2000 are worth a book on their own and cannot be explained easily, largely because there remain doubts about who owned what merchandise, who owned what ship and who could take credit for bringing it all down.

Gustavo Adolfo Gómez Maya, a narco from the northernmost Colombian department of La Guajira, was arrested for his role with the *Cannes* and the *Castor*, along with his female partner Ivonne María Escaf de Saldarriaga and three other Colombians.

Gómez Maya's client list included Los Mellizos and Beto el Gitano. After the *China Breeze*'s load was initially but wrongfully pinned on Gómez Maya, Iván de la Vega Cabás was subsequently positively identified as being behind the vessel's illicit cargo. Part of the load on the *China Breeze* was intended for Beto.[272]

Says Nigel Brooks of USCS: 'The *Cannes* and the *Castor* was Gómez Maya and *China Breeze* was [Los Mellizos].' But he disputes Gómez Maya was working for Los Mellizos: 'Our source was the person responsible for getting the ships and he told us that Gómez Maya was not affiliated with The Twins.'

For his part the DEA's Rick Bendekovic is adamant '*China Breeze* and *Pearl II* were [Los Mellizos]' and 'there might have been other charges but I know the strongest charges on [the indictment for Beto el Gitano] were the 4000 kilos on the *Castor*'.

Graham Honey of HMCE is not so sure either way: 'There wasn't just one group; there were several groups involved in all these loads. The difficulty with these groups, as we found through the years, is it's an informal arrangement. They all work together, they all did bits together, they may or may not have a part in a load . . . it was always difficult to know exactly who was doing what for who.'

*

What is not in doubt is that the *China Breeze* carried a crewmember working as an informant for the DEA office in Athens, who supplied the source with communications equipment and satellite-tracking devices. Another ship in the conspiracy, the *Regent Rose*, was purposely sunk by the cartel off Cartagena, Colombia, before it could be apprehended.

Says Brooks: 'Sonny Bowie in Panama was purportedly the owner of the *Regent Rose*. Los Mellizos were going to use the vessel to transport a load to Europe, but it was taken offshore and scuttled when they discovered that there was possible law-enforcement interest in it. Sonny had been arrested and was apparently cooperating; the organisation received copies of the debriefs and decided to scuttle the ship.

'Sonny had apparently been jailed in Panama and the organisation had received a copy of a confession by a Panamanian called Wellington Fong concerning previous cocaine smuggling by the *Regent Rose*. Based on this, Los Mellizos decided to make it disappear and use a Greek vessel instead.

'We identified the attorney in Panama [Roque Pérez aka 'Alejandro'] who had handled the paperwork for the purchases of the vessels the organisation was using. DEA approached him, which then led to Los Mellizos taking *Regent Rose* out to sea and sinking it.'[273]

Miami Express, an unmentioned ship linked to Gómez Maya, was captured by Spanish law enforcement in October 1998 carrying just over four tons. The intelligence on it had started with HMCE in Miami. Another vessel, the *Dawn*, had initially been set to go, which would carry a 'parasite' fastboat.

'The boat was to be launched with the cocaine aboard 90 miles from the Portugal–Spain border,' says Brooks. 'The *Dawn* had some serious mechanical problems and was replaced by the Greeks with the *Aktis* [renamed the *Suerte*]. It was on a six-month time charter for $279,000 – which was to be applied as a down payment on the purchase – and Los Mellizos had already invested money in the repairs in Greece. At the end of the time charter, the organisation had agreed to buy the vessel for $1.83 million.'[274]

*

Another enduring mystery of the conspiracy is why the *Suerte* and its sister vessel in Venezuela, the *Privilege*, were never loaded with cocaine. Jorge García and three accomplices were intercepted by the Venezuelan Coast Guard before they could reach the *Suerte* while the *Privilege* left port completely empty, despite some intelligence suggesting it was carrying a five-ton load.

Says Brooks: 'We never did find out if the attempt to intercept was a coincidence or intentional as the agreement with the *Guardia Nacional* was to let the load run . . . I don't think after some reflection that the attempted interception was a coincidence.'[275]

Colombian and Albanian newspapers reported that the *Privilege*, previously the *Misty*, was purchased in Belgium by two Albanians, Arbën Berballa and Aleko Durda, brother of notorious drug trafficker Frederik Durda aka 'Bull'.

Brooks confirms the vessel was bought in Antwerp, left from Ghent, and the original plan of Los Mellizos was 'to offload 500 kilos to a sailboat off Gibraltar, then head to the Adriatic to offload the remaining 5000 [to Italian and Albanian recipients] 20 miles offshore from Albania. The port destination for the *Privilege* was Ravenna, Italy.

'Because Los Mellizos had sources in the Albanian Government, we all agreed that the Italians would handle the Adriatic enforcement and HMCE would monitor the 500-kilo offload off Spain. The number substitution code for this smuggle was "ADRIOTECUN". This code was provided to us in March 2000 long before the actual smuggle. Frederik Durda was identified as being the Albanian controller for the load.[276]

'The *Privilege* was compromised and the organisation found out that there was law-enforcement interest in it while it was in port in

Venezuela. They decided to not use it and it was loaded with cargo. We were fully aware that its use for smuggling cocaine had been abandoned; however we had a huge problem with DEA. Customs was running the source and getting information in real time. So even though we knew it was not loaded, DEA convinced the Spanish that it had been and caused it to be boarded and searched.

'When that happened I received an email from a DEA agent in Barranquilla to the effect that "The Spanish boarded the *Privilege* and found five tons of coke; just thought you'd like to know". We had been advised by HMCE that DEA had encouraged the Spanish to take out the *Privilege* a day before and I personally called the Spanish case agent to advise them exactly where the false compartment was located. Of course, our source was correct – the *Privilege* did not have a load of cocaine.'[277]

*

It is widely believed that Los Mellizos had been tipped off from someone allegedly within or connected to an American agency working on the case, most likely the DEA in Colombia. Víctor Mejía Múnera was reported by Colombian newspaper *El Tiempo* to have called off the load.

Brooks: 'I do not know for sure that Los Mellizos got the information directly from DEA, but our source told us they were aware of law-enforcement interest. When the organisation found out about the law-enforcement interest [in the *Privilege*] it decided to just send it with legal cargo. Our source told us that it would not be used to carry a load, but DEA did not believe us and coordinated with Spanish authorities to have it boarded at sea and taken into the Canary Islands for a search.

'The European end of the *Privilege* and *Suerte* offloads were to be handled by Greek, Italian and Albanian organisations and there was some initial intelligence that payment for the loads was to be in the form of Eastern European arms, which would be transferred to the Colombian paramilitaries. The plan was to allow both vessels to load and proceed to Europe where they would be intercepted by European law enforcement.[278] Unfortunately the loading of the *Suerte* was stopped by premature enforcement action taken by the Venezuelan Navy who intercepted the *pangas*. We still do not know if it was a chance encounter or a deliberate act.

'The subsequent raids on the *finca* [at Doble Uno] and Orinoco location basically ended the operation. And the *Privilege* was boarded by Spanish special forces off the Canary Islands despite the fact that we had advised it was not loaded. Apparently DEA had misrepresented the intelligence to the Spanish who put a great deal of time and effort in unloading the legitimate cargo.'

*

So who were the hapless 'Canadians' from the United Nations who almost got their cover blown while tailing Jorge García in Puerto Ordaz?

No one has owned up, but it's most likely they were DEA agents. Intriguingly, a redacted USCS intelligence document states: 'Z-1 [Jorge] has a source in the GN [*Guardia Nacional*] who is reportedly a lieutenant who has told Z-1 that there are many DEA agents currently staying in Puerto Ordaz [PO] at a hotel there . . . we would suggest that any US personnel in PO keep a very low profile and gradually withdraw in such a way as to raise no suspicion.'

Clearly they weren't inconspicuous enough.

'Given the size of the case and the number of agencies involved, it perhaps was inevitable that it would end prematurely,' laments Brooks, who personally removed a tracking device from the *Suerte* when it was impounded in Galveston. 'Sigma was the HMCE team responsible for technical installations and placing trackers on vessels and vehicles. When it attempted to beacon one of the vehicles the organisation was using [a Ford Explorer] so that Los Mellizos' ranch [at Doble Uno] could be located, a security guard in the parking lot saw it and told Jorge García someone had been under his vehicle. I'm not aware there was any confrontation like Luis has described it.

'The surveillances for the most part were done by a special unit of the *Guardia Nacional* and while US Customs, HMCE and DEA did participate in surveillances I'm pretty sure they teamed up with the GNB. The tracking device was not an active tracker but one that recorded locations and had to be retrieved to download the information, so putting it in a taxi wouldn't have accomplished anything as it was not being actively tracked in real time. That said, there were a number of instances where the organisation saw things, vehicles, and individuals they thought suspicious.'

Graham Titmuss, an investigation officer at HMCE's National Investigation Service in London, who'd been coordinating the case among various HMCE DLOs going back to before it was even called Operation Journey, has no firsthand knowledge of any agents, American or British, pretending to be Canadian.

'At the time of the bust we were not sure where Jorge García was and the DEA were unlikely to know. Despite the DEA claiming all the credit for Operation Journey, it was run by HMCE and US Customs.[279] For my part, Journey became an extension of Operation Jezebel, the first seizure being on the *Pearl II*. Jezebel seizures were from the *Cannes*, *Kobe Queen*, *Goiana*, *China Breeze*, *Castor* and *Svetlana*.[280] But the story of the Canadians seems right. Unfortunately for us the DEA got involved in Venezuela. The DEA were not as covert as we wanted them to be, hence the premature arrests and no drugs being loaded on the *Suerte*.'

His colleague Barry Clarke, a retired HMCE investigation officer who went on to work for Britain's National Crime Agency (NCA), agrees: 'I would put a bet on them being DEA.'[281]

59

Nick the Fish

UNBEKNOWN TO LUIS, NICK FISCIATORIS, his well-dressed, chain-smoking, old-style gangster fixer in Europe, had been on the radar of British intelligence services. He had a close association with Irish cocaine kingpin Brian Wright aka 'The Milkman' (he always delivered) and his lieutenant Kevin Hanley, who were targeted in one of the UK's biggest antinarcotics takedowns, Operation Extend, which commenced in September 1996 and wrapped up in 2007 with the 30-year imprisonment of Wright. This was an operation that focused mainly on Pinky Delgado's operations – the transporting of cocaine from South and Central America to Europe by yacht – but involved law enforcement in the Caribbean, South Africa and Australia.

'Nick Fisciatoris was living in London in the 1990s and featured on a number of major drugs cases,' says Barry Clarke of NCA, one of Britain's most experienced cocaine intelligence agents, having been a member of HMCE/HMRC's operational cocaine team and head of cocaine intelligence.

'Nick lived in New York for years and came to London in the 1970s where he worked the casino circuit. Nick was on the periphery of a number of Branch 3 jobs in the early 1990s when he lived in a flat at the back of Harrods.[282] He was a shadowy figure who was a middleman and broker between UK criminal groups looking for bulk cocaine and suppliers in South America.

'The profits to be made in the early-to-mid-1990s cocaine market were enormous. Many criminal groups looked to cash in at this time. As is always the case, the three things that British organised crime groups – OCGs – struggled with were supply from source, transportation to the UK, and ability to launder huge amounts.

'One British group stood out as the most sophisticated and prolific. They were eventually dismantled and prosecuted but only after an investigation spanning more than ten years. We initially investigated and understood this OCG from a UK perspective, but in time we realised that the wider supply group was international and operated at the highest level.

'Nick's role was undoubtedly well connected – he was known to have travelled to Mexico, Venezuela and Miami during the mid-'90s trying to broker various deals – but he went on to become increasingly unstable and volatile; ultimately a liability. He was well known to HMCE/HMRC at this time as a fixer and broker, but he was never truly understood. We now know that he attempted to broker numerous importations into the UK from South America and Holland. He dealt with the Navia group, but it was Brian Wright that was the real power in London as he had the finance and status.

'The supply chain above and below Luis was working with some of the UK's biggest traffickers and criminals; albeit they probably weren't aware of each other on a day-to-day basis. They, like us, law enforcement, were involved in groundbreaking business.'

*

When Operation Extend blew up Pinky Delgado's sailboat racket in 1998/'99 and Brian Wright's right-hand man Kevin Hanley was arrested, Wright fled to the Turkish Republic of Northern Cyprus – which had no extradition.[283] Fisciatoris had been close to Wright but they were now estranged. Another associate, Kenneth Regan, who had 'corrupt access at Heathrow airport' and had come with Fisciatoris to Cancún to meet Luis in 1996, was also arrested and convicted for heroin trafficking in 1998. He subsequently turned supergrass for the British authorities.[284]

As for Pinky, he'd long disappeared into South America along with his gopher Flaco, the man who introduced Luis to Fisciatoris, and Flaco's replacement, Willie. Of Luis's direct acquaintances, only fellow Miamian Alex DeCubas got nailed in the Extend investigation but nearly two dozen people went down for combined jail terms of over 200 years. The *Suerte* disaster would be Nick Fisciatoris's last hurrah.

'In all honesty, we didn't establish the link between the Journey suppliers and Extend suppliers until long after the arrests, and only when the supply chain started to cooperate in the United States,' says Clarke. 'All we initially knew was that Pinky [Delgado] and Mario [Alex DeCubas] were the nicknames of the suppliers. Pinky had the contacts – in reality the "contract" – in the UK to move bulk cocaine every year. This was primarily to Brian Wright and Kevin Hanley, but with Nick Fisciatoris making the introductions and taking a brokering role. So Nick was linked to both investigations. I was aware of Operation Journey but I wasn't one of the officers leading the case.

'In the aftermath of Operation Extend, when we arrested many of his associates, Nick left the UK. I met him a short time after in Athens – DEA Athens informed me that Nick had turned up at their office and wanted to talk. I met him twice over two days, but he didn't say much that we didn't already know. He was clearly attempting to gauge how much evidence we had against him. He didn't mention Operation Journey and I couldn't push him as I was also very conscious of future criminal proceedings.

'Nick was really interesting to talk to; a fascinating character from another age. The British criminals viewed him as unstable, demanding and as a liability. He was often referred to as "the lunatic". He was an old-style criminal, very engaging and funny in a sinister way: straight out of a film set. Nick provided me with some background and filled in some blanks but he wasn't inclined to give us the whole story. In reality we never had enough evidence to charge him so he slipped away. We heard no more of Nick after that. I last saw him circa 2001, and he was in his 60s then so likely he is dead by now.'[285]

60

Clear and Present Danger

A FTER HIS TALKING TO in the Suburban from Eric Kolbinsky, Luis slept on a chair at the police station. The next day Luis, Iván de la Vega Cabás and Michelle Arias were flown by helicopter to a military base in the foothills of Caracas.

The cavalry was there to escort them. There were around 150 Venezuelan soldiers at the airfield when they left, aboard ten army helicopters. They'd come to Maracaibo from the capital specifically for the transfer. Iván was also headed for an American jail, an indictment being obtained by the United States Department of Justice five days before his capture in Maracaibo, charging him with conspiracy to import cocaine.[286]

The short journey gave Luis some time to think. Would he try to stay in Venezuela and get a lawyer? The process of formal extradition potentially would give Luis and Iván another year in the country, where they would cool their heels in jail. The other option was simply bribing someone. Luis had tried to bribe the Colombian cop with $500,000, an offer to which he gave momentary consideration, but he said his hands were tied.

When Luis offered a million, he was told the Americans were already involved and there was nothing they could do: 'There's no money deal here. It's far beyond that.'

The security situation on the ground was tense, with fears expressed

Los Mellizos could ambush their convoy with rocket launchers like something out of *Clear and Present Danger* and assassinate Luis, Iván, Michelle and everyone else before they cooperated.

In Caracas, trucks loaded up with confiscated cocaine from Operation Journey thundered through the gates of the military base. So he could have one last night with his girlfriend, Luis paid $200 to an army captain in exchange for a barracks room with an air conditioner.

Even under interrogation and scared for her life, Michelle held the line on Luis's cover story: that he was a Mexican businessman called Novoa.[287] Feeling remorseful, he gave her a thin, 22-carat gold tie-link chain as a parting gift. Luis also sent a soldier to buy him a new button-down shirt and clean khakis, as he knew sooner or later he was going to be photographed.

'I didn't want to look like a fucking bum. If I was going back to America I was going back in style.'

*

Luis got to make a phone call to Patricia in Mexico. The guard who let him use the telephone had a gun on him.

'It must have been two o'clock in the afternoon. I looked around and I said to myself, "I could yank this gun and shoot this mother-fucker and make a run for it." But I knew I wouldn't get far because it was a mountainous area with difficult terrain and I wasn't in the best shape. I wasn't going to last long, especially with Kolbinsky's long legs.'

When the phone was answered, his estranged wife wasn't home.

'The maid picked up the call. Juliana was at school. Patricia wasn't there. The only one that was there was Santi.'

It was a poignant moment: the international felon being caught at last and not being able to tell his own son what was happening. All Santi could say was, 'Oh, *Papá*.' Tears welled up in Luis's eyes.

'It wasn't like I could have a conversation with him. He was three years old. When I spoke to him it was "*Googoo, gaga, Papá*." I didn't tell him anything. My family didn't know what I was doing in Venezuela. It broke my heart, thinking I might not see my son for 25, 30 years. I told him I loved him very much and that I hoped to see him soon. And that's when I decided I had to get out of this mess as soon as I could.'

*

Night had fallen in Caracas and a light-grey USCS Lockheed P-3 Orion was on the runway being readied for the three-hour trip to Florida, its red, green and white lights glowing in the darkness. Eric Kolbinsky and Vicente Garcia would accompany the two arrestees on the flight over.

Luis was ordered to make a final call to Los Mellizos in Puerto Ordaz, to pretend he was still in Maracaibo and 'to let them know we were not under arrest'. The man he spoke to on the other end of the line was Wilmer Joiro, a *sicario* from a violent family in the Alta Guajira and the right-hand man of Jorge García. Wilmer wasn't at all convinced by the ruse and would have already known Jorge had disappeared into the wilderness.[288] It didn't wash. When Luis got a moment alone with Iván, he suggested they pay the *Guardia Nacional* to escape.

'Listen, Iván, what we gotta do is get put in jail here in Venezuela, get $2 million, pay these guys off and get the fuck out of here and go back to Colombia. With two million bucks they'll let us go. We can fight this.'

'Are you fucking crazy, man?' Iván replied, totally incredulous at what he was hearing. 'You know what's going to happen to us when this thing comes down and the Mellizos find out we've been arrested? The first thing they're going to do is have us killed in jail. They're the ones that are going to kill us.'

'Iván, *Iván*, what the fuck are you talking about? We've been working for these guys, made them money.'

'Who do you think you're working for, Luis? If we stay in Caracas we're dead.'[289]

That was when the penny dropped. A man can watch only so many friends die and survive only so many kidnappings in the cocaine business before he realises the game is up. This time Mr Magoo had struck out for good.

'Now *that's* when I said, "Listen, I'm Luis Navia and I'm ready to go back to the United States. And fuck this shit."'[290]

Luis's former wife Patricia Manterola, daughter Juliana Navia and Luis at the beach in Cancún, Mexico, 1994. Says Luis: 'Cancún was fun and games by daytime, but by night thousands and thousands of kilos were coming in.' *Courtesy of Luis Navia*

USCS Special Agent Robert Harley (INSET): 'Attempts were made [to capture Luis in Mexico], but I always felt they were a day late and a dollar short, each time.' *Courtesy of Robert Harley*

Luis and son Santi in Mexico, circa 1997/'98.
Courtesy of Luis Navia

Luis and Juliana in Guatemala, 1998.
Courtesy of Luis Navia

The Houston conference for the seizure of the M/V *Cannes*, along with the impounded four tons of cocaine. This was a watershed moment in what would become the 12-nation Operation Journey. USCS Commissioner Raymond Kelly is in the dark suit.
Courtesy of Vicente Garcia

The M/V *Cannes*.
Courtesy of Vicente Garcia

A screen grab of a USCS PowerPoint presentation showing the four main targets in the takedown of Los Mellizos (The Twins).
Courtesy of Nigel Brooks

❖ Miguel Mejia

❖ Victor Mejia

❖ Ivan De La Vega

❖ Jorge Garcia

Some of the cocaine found on board the M/V *China Breeze*.
Courtesy of Vicente Garcia

The cheeky picture postcard Luis sent to Robert Harley while on the run in Panama. *Courtesy of Luis Navia*

Luis, Juliana, Santi and Luis's girlfriend Michelle Arias in Caracas, Venezuela, right before the takedown. *Courtesy of Luis Navia*

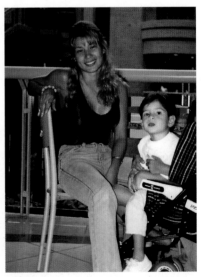

Michelle and Santi. *Courtesy of Luis Navia*

DEA Special Agent Eric J. Kolbinsky (SECOND FROM RIGHT) and USCS Special Agent Vicente M. Garcia (SECOND FROM LEFT) in Venezuela in 2000 with unidentified members of the Colombian National Police and Venezuela's *Guardia Nacional* prior to leaving Caracas on a plane for Maracaibo to arrest Luis. Both Kolbinsky and Garcia followed Luis through Venezuela prior to his arrest. *Courtesy of Eric Kolbinsky*

Kolbinsky at a cocaine lab in the Sierra Nevada de Santa Marta, Colombia, with a seized kilo. *Courtesy of Eric Kolbinsky*

A satellite view of the enormous Orinoco Delta, the location of jungle stash sites for an estimated 25 tons of cocaine. Says Luis: 'The Orinoco Delta, that is *huge*. It makes the Everglades look like a little fucking backyard.' *Planet Observer/Universal Images Group via Getty Images*

Guardia Nacional officers with part of the seized Los Mellizos cocaine in Puerto Ordaz, Venezuela. At the time it was the South American country's biggest ever coke bust. Operation Journey officially netted 22,489 kilograms or almost 25 tons. *Associated Press*

The photograph that marked the end of Luis's 25 years in the cocaine business. Says Luis: 'This was taken by Kapinsky [Eric Kolbinsky] before we left the military barracks in Caracas where I was being held with Michelle Arias and Iván de la Vega.' *Courtesy of Nigel Brooks*

A Colombian reward poster for Los Mellizos: drug lords and twin brothers Miguel and Víctor Mejía Múnera. *Associated Press*

Luis and alleged Jamaican drug trafficker Richard 'Storyteller' Morrison at Federal Correctional Institution, Coleman, Florida. While sharing a cell with Luis at the Federal Detention Center in Miami, Morrison would wake early each morning to tie his running shoes. Says Luis: 'He said to me, "You've gotta be *strapped*." He called tying his shoelaces being strapped. You never know when you're gonna have to fight. How are you going to fight somebody in a pair of fucking slippers?'
Courtesy of Luis Navia

Luis playing the drums for his prison rock band, Prizm.
Courtesy of Luis Navia

A post-release Luis enjoying being a dad again with a young Santi.
Courtesy of Luis Navia

Luis by the beach in Islamorada, Florida, November 2019.
Courtesy of Jesse Fink

The old devils. Luis and fellow cocaine smuggler Jorge 'El Gordito' Cabrera, Islamorada, Florida, November 2019. In 1995 El Gordito was famously photographed in Miami with Vice President Al Gore and at the White House with Hillary Rodham Clinton.
Courtesy of Jesse Fink

Eric Kolbinsky, Robert Harley and Luis Navia meeting together for the first time, St. Petersburg, Florida, November 2019. Luis bought Harley the tie as a gift. *Courtesy of Jesse Fink*

Luis and the man he affectionately calls 'Bob'. *Courtesy of Jesse Fink*

PART 12
SOWING THE SEEDS OF LOVE

61

The Business Deal

AT 3AM ON 19 AUGUST 2000 Luis was taken for processing at USCS. At 5am he was taken to the Federal Detention Center (FDC) in Downtown Miami. The FDC, run by the Federal Bureau of Prisons (BOP), is a faintly Stalinist, featureless grey prison building where 1300 prisoners of all descriptions and offence levels are held awaiting trial, sentencing or to appear in court as witnesses: rapists, murderers, gang members, cartel figures, heroin addicts.

After changing into green jumpsuits, Luis and Iván de la Vega Cabás were put in general population with other prisoners on separate floors. Luis was given a government-appointed attorney who spoke to him in Spanish like a low-class Cuban, *cubanaso*, and he listened quietly downstairs in the interview room as his case file was being read out on not one but two cocaine-trafficking indictments: the original March 1995 indictment from the Florida Keys and new charges for his role in the *Suerte* smuggle. When it was over Luis spoke in English.

'What am I looking at here?' he said, shifting in his seat.

'*Un pingal de años.*'[291] A shitload of years.

Luis couldn't believe what he was hearing.

'When the lawyer said that, I said to myself, "I've definitely got to get rid of this motherfucker."'

*

It was high time to start interviewing different attorneys. Luis was on the same floor as legendary 'cocaine cowboy' Willy Falcón, who was back in the clink after beating serious drug-trafficking charges four years earlier.

'We were both on the tenth floor. He hadn't gone to trial yet as it took a long time for him to go to trial. At first they were both together, him and Sal Magluta.'[292]

The first lawyer Luis met he didn't like. Then Falcón recommended one of his defence attorneys, John Bergendahl, who agreed to sit down with him. What follows is Luis's recollection of their conversation.

'Luis, I could charge you $250,000 right now and take your case, but I've got to be honest with you. There's not much I can do for you. Your '95 indictment is 4600 kilos, there's confiscated merchandise, I know for a fact there's a few people from that old indictment who are still sitting in jail that would *love* to testify against you to get their time off.

'Plus, if we fight these guys, they'll bring in this Operation Journey indictment and make it into a formal indictment and there's 25,000 kilos of dope confiscated. Your co-defendant, he's going to testify against you. You don't have a chance. They're going to nail you. You could be looking at a possible life sentence here.'

'What do you mean "life sentence"? I didn't kill nobody.'

'You don't understand. Your level is way up there. Right now you're at level 43.'

Level 43 is the highest offence level under the *United States Federal Sentencing Guidelines*. In other words: life.

'Wait a minute. I told these people I'm willing to do ten years.'

'*Ten* years?'

'Yes. I'm willing to give them all my money, do ten years and that's it.'

'*No, no, no.* You don't understand. You're going to have to give them the money, cooperate totally, completely do everything they ask you to do plus more, and *then* you'll get ten years – and that's being extremely lucky.'

'What?'

'Yes. If you do cooperate the first time around, I doubt that you'll get something less than 14 [years]; you'll get 14 to 17 and that's with a great attorney with a great plea deal. And we could work something out like that, but you have no other choice. You need to cooperate. That's what Colombians do. Colombians treat this as a business. This ain't no mafia, this ain't no blood pact. You get caught, you cooperate, it's a *business deal*.

'Right now you are going to make the most important business deal of your life. That's why the US dollar says "In God We Trust". The only part where they mention God is on the dollar. To them, religion and dollars, it's the same thing. You've got to be sharp, you've got to be on your feet. If you've ever been sharp, this is the time to be sharp. There's no fucking up here.'

'*Wow*. Okay.'

*

When he got back to general population, Luis told Willy what had happened with Bergendahl. Willy suggested Luis get an attorney who specialised in deals; Bergendahl's own style was to fight cases.

'Willy was the first one who took me aside and said, "Listen, you better call yourself an attorney that specialises in doing plea deals. I do *not* suggest you take this to trial." And it was either him or someone else in the unit that recommended I hire Ruben Oliva to cut me a plea deal.

'So I called Ruben. He came across the right way. He's Cuban. I never wanted a Cuban attorney; I always wanted to go with a Jewish attorney – I always said to myself *Jewish* attorneys, *Jewish* accountants and *Jewish* doctors – and I had already given $35,000 to another attorney who was kind enough to return it. And Ruben charged me I think it was $100,000, and that was the most Ruben had ever charged in his life.'[293]

62

The Roadmap

SEVEN DAYS INTO HIS confinement at FDC, in the early evening of 26 August, Luis was eating dinner at a four-man table with 100 other prisoners in the common area. There was a bank of televisions at the front of the room showing the nightly news. A prisoner at his table finished chewing a mouthful and turned to Luis.

'Hey, isn't that you on TV?'

'I was like, "*What?*" I look up and go, "What the fuck?" A CNN special report comes on, all about Operation Journey. They fucking showed me and Iván getting off the plane in handcuffs, a map of Venezuela with arrows of ships going everywhere – three arrows to the US, three arrows to Mexico, four arrows to Spain, three arrows to Italy – and 25 tons of cocaine confiscated in Venezuela. *Major* drug bust. Everybody on the fucking floor turned around and looked at me. I hadn't even realised it.'

USCS Commissioner Raymond Kelly was addressing a roomful of journalists and photographers at a press conference in Washington, DC, flanked by DEA Deputy Commissioner Julio Mercado, Rear Admiral David S. Belz representing JIATF-East, and other men in suits. There was no mention made of the Mejía Múnera brothers, Jorge García, Sonny Bowie, Nick Fisciatoris, Willie, Elias Lemos, or anyone else involved in the conspiracy. Instead, bumbling Iván was being cast as the supervillain in charge of his own cartel, 'the De La

Vega group', with Luis his lieutenant.[294] Kelly described it as 'one of the most complex networks we have ever seen'.

'We wiped out a sprawling organisation whose tentacles reached around the world. Massive amounts of cocaine will be kept off the streets of Europe and America. And thanks to this global law-enforcement effort, we now have a powerful new blueprint for fighting the international drug trade.'[295]

For anyone watching at home, the import was clear: this was a historic takedown of one of the world's biggest ever cocaine-smuggling operations, right up there with the dismantling of the Medellín and Cali cartels. But for Patricia and Luis's family, it was the first time they'd heard he'd been arrested.

The following day, 27 August, Luis's 45th birthday, Operation Journey hit the papers.[296] His downfall was global headline news.

Reputed head of drug ring taken to US after
arrest
The New York Times

12-nation effort breaks up Colombian drug
operation
The Washington Post

Major drugs cartel smashed
BBC News

$1bn haul of cocaine seized in 12-nation operation
The Independent

US deals blow to cocaine trade as 25 tonnes
seized
The Guardian

Luis's newfound celebrity at the FDC also caused quite a stir. Within half an hour a Special Operations Response Team (SORT), colloquially known as the 'Goon Squad', came and put him and Iván in solitary in the Special Housing Unit (SHU). They had to switch from green to orange jumpsuits.

'The Bureau of Prisons is a totally different entity to DEA, FBI, US Customs. FBI doesn't tell them more than they need to know. "This is a criminal. We picked him up on a drug bust, *ba ba ba*." BOP has its own rules and regulations. Their duty is to keep the prisoner *alive*. They don't get paid for dead bodies in custody. They have their own internal security team, Special Investigative Services, and they have to figure out if you're gang related, which cartel you belong to, and not to put you on a floor with another member of a rival cartel.

'So SIS put us in the SHU right away for 90 days because we were high-profile prisoners. We got separated right away. I was on one side and Iván was on the other. I couldn't see him. They wanted to find out everything about us and our affiliations before putting us back in general population. I had a five-man custody detail. Every time they moved me, five guys were assigned to me. Not moved me from floor to floor, but just to get some sunshine.

'Solitary was a relief because you get time for yourself. And I looked out my window and I saw the Hard Rock Cafe, bayside, the backside of Biscayne Bay, and I said, "Well, look at this, man. I come back to Miami and I got a penthouse." I was in the penthouse. It was the top floor and I was alone. The SHU is great when you're alone because you've got your own little apartment.

'When you've got to share it with somebody, well, then you've got to shit in front of somebody. You've got no privacy. But when you're alone in the SHU? *Fuck*, man, you start doing your push-ups, you set yourself. You get your breakfast, you eat, you relax, take a nap, then you do some push-ups, then you do lunch, then you ask the guard to let you out and go to the library for two hours and type letters to your girlfriends, shit like that. Then you come back, take another nap, do some more push-ups, then it's dinner, and you go to bed at nine o'clock and wake up at six. It's a routine. I got a little depressed but I was more concerned about getting out.'

*

It was upstairs in an attorney–client interview room at SHU that Luis came face-to-face with Robert Harley, the man who'd been looking for him for nigh on a decade. Ruben Oliva of Miami law firm Rojas

334

& Oliva, PA was representing Luis. There was no ceremony. No speeches. They all shook hands and got down to business.

'Bob was a gentleman. He looked like a small version of Robert Redford. Short, stocky, blond guy.'

So Eric Kolbinsky looked like Sam Elliott and Harley looked like Robert Redford and you'd had them both on your tail?

'*Exactly*. And I'm Dustin Hoffman.'

Laughs Harley: 'As long as you're not, you know, Hannibal Lecter, I am professional, civil and polite. This is what polite society demands of people. I didn't meet the plane from Venezuela because its arrival was sooner than my ability to drive to Miami from the Keys.

'Luis was a character from the first moment we met. He was joking from, like, minute one. He wanted coffee and we got him coffee. He was very much himself. He was not a wiseguy. He was literate, a thinker, he listened, he processed what was being said to him, and he asked relevant and intelligent questions. So I was like, "He's *not* what you picture a major narco trafficker to be." Luis is just not that person. It's an interesting thing. I don't think it's easy to put these people into a box. It's just not that simple. Not at that level.

'I had a very frank and adult conversation with Luis and I laid out a roadmap for him and told him, "You've got huge life choices ahead of you. You can die an old man in prison or you can be honest from day one and do what you can to salvage the rest of your life." Basically convincing him he needed to get on board right away. The choice was up to him.'

Luis could see he had a shot at freedom; he wasn't going to blow it.

'I remember Bob saying something like, "After this is over I just want you to relax and sell hot dogs on Key Biscayne. But whatever you do, do *not* lie to me." I realised I had one more opportunity. That I could actually get out of there. When you're in that situation and they tell you, "You have life choices to make," they're giving you an opportunity to have a *life*. If I had been a violent offender that scenario would have never happened. Bob would have never come to me on those terms. To these people violence makes all the difference in the world. They're in the drug business. They understand the drug business. They have a badge to be violent; we don't. When you shoot back, you've got a problem.'

63

Closed Doors

B Y NOW OPERATION JOURNEY was all over the nightly bulletins in Colombia and Mexico, but Patricia had found out early. A Colombian friend of hers in Mexico City knocked on her door unannounced at about 8pm on the evening of 26 August 2000 and asked her to come to his car. They then drove a short distance and picked up another Colombian friend, parked in a side street, and turned off the engine.

'Patricia, we're pretty sure Luis has been taken by the DEA. We think he's now in the United States.'

Still, she was shocked when she turned on the TV a couple of hours later and saw the footage from Fort Lauderdale airport of Luis being escorted off the tarmac.

'The newsreader was the father of a friend of my daughter,' says Patricia. 'I was like, "Oh, my God." Even from a distance I knew it was Luis. I was just happy they didn't read out his name.'

*

The next day, the fallout on the Navia family was swift and devastating.

Luis's nephew Andrés Blanco: 'My grandmother woke me up with a newspaper in hand, screaming, "Read this and tell me it's not true!" But she also kept a paper bag full of cash that was always kept in her locked closet, which was called Fort Knox, where she kept anything valuable.

She had electronic shutters installed when my grandfather died. It was a literal period of darkness after the news came out about my uncle, because she kept the windows closed for weeks. She just hid away. She didn't want to see anyone. I think my mother, my grandmother and my brother Martin and I probably took the brunt of that.'[297]

Laura: 'It was horrible. My mother was hurt, ashamed of her son, and very upset. She locked herself up in her home and did not want to see anyone. She fell into a deep depression. She rolled down all the electric hurricane shutters and stayed in the dark. Friends would come to visit to check up on her, and she refused to answer. Simple tasks like going out to the market were incredibly difficult for her. She was too ashamed to be seen. There was a very severe and noticeable deterioration in her mental and physical health that started with Luis's arrest and imprisonment. At the same time, it brought her some peace, knowing that he was safe in prison. At least she knew where he was, and she could visit him.'

Andrés: 'When my uncle was arrested, a lot of things clicked for me. Looking back, I do remember feeling watched at our hotel in Caracas. We were at the pool and you know when you feel eyes are on you? I'm a relatively perceptive individual and I just remember being like, "That woman over there has been watching us." Later we found out all the phones were bugged.

'My uncle's saving grace was being arrested. He may not have been killed by anyone, but he was going to kill himself the way that he was doing drugs, drinking, smoking and being overweight. He was going to have a heart attack; die on the toilet. It was very embarrassing for my grandmother. I think that was the point of the beginning of a decline for my grandmother physically and mentally. I think that's when we started to see the first signs of Alzheimer's. Her cognitive skills suffered.'

Luis: 'My mother was shocked and she closed her doors to the world. She was a little embarrassed, I guess, but she knew I wasn't exactly on the right track. She and my sister both *knew* what I did. I was an adult. That was what I chose to do. They didn't know the specifics of the cartels I worked with, but they knew I wasn't an accountant in Bogotá.'

For Laura, especially, life was about to change dramatically.

Laura: 'The pressure from Luis's arrest was not easy to handle. It was a hard situation to explain to my children, family and friends, even though it was in the newspapers and on TV – how do you face that? It brought shame to us all. Even though Luis was away from us for many years, we considered him the head of the household since my father passed away. We had old-fashioned views of the "man in charge". My children always argue this and insist I am – they adamantly say that I am – but I don't see myself this way. They are very protective of me.

'To say my plate was full is an understatement. When I look back, it was a challenging time. I was working and carried the responsibility of not only raising my two teenage sons [as a single woman] but caring for my ageing mother as well. When in the midst of it, you do what you need to do to keep the boys in school and to keep life as normal as possible. Andrés and Martin were the source of my strength.'

Andrés: 'For my mother it was difficult because everything came down on her. There were attorney's bills to pay. She was the glue that kind of held everything together. The strength she showed during that period is astounding.'

Luis: 'It was very hard on Laura when I was in jail. Nobody helped her. Just like nobody helped Patricia. Laura also got cancer: she lost a kidney. So I've been surrounded by great women on both sides. She's a hero to me. She tells her kids, "Listen, your uncle's not perfect. But your uncle's your uncle, he's my brother, and he's been very good to all of us. So even though he's not perfect, *please*, respect him." She allows no disrespect and no bullshit.'

Laura: 'It's nice to hear my brother say that. He and I were brought up to be very close. Our parents always taught us we were one. This is how it still is; we are very different but unconditional with one another. I do not agree with the life he chose to lead. Many times, I did mention this to him, and he would always say he would quit the business soon. That being said, Luis is very loyal. Loyalty is important, and I taught this to my children. Family is family, and we need to be there for one another.'

*

At FDC, Luis was hardly to see his family over the coming months, but they came to visit him when they could: his mother María, sister Laura, nephews Andrés and Martin.

Laura: 'It was very difficult; I was in tears. Just thinking about it now I choke up. Those were incredibly difficult times. While it was good to see Luis, the circumstances were awful.'

Luis's estranged wife didn't have a visa to enter the United States and Juliana and Santi knew absolutely nothing about what had happened to their father.

Patricia: 'They thought he couldn't come to Mexico because he didn't have a visa. But he called all the time.'

Luis: 'The kids were small and going to school and had other things on their mind. I said to my family, "Listen, this is my problem, this is my time, I need to live in here, I don't need to be reminded of how nice life is on the outside." You're in *prison*. I knew people who had their family come visit them every fucking weekend. Who the fuck wants to put their family through that fucking torture? There was no life on the outside for me. I didn't want contact. I was happy in my prison. I was doing my own time. I don't need to see people. My world is the inside.'

Andrés: 'To watch my grandmother begin to deteriorate like she did and the struggles my mother had to go through to keep it all in order, we were the ones constantly visiting my uncle in prison. And when he needed money or something, the call came to us. My uncle tried to shield Patricia as much as possible from his time in prison. I don't think they ever visited him so they never saw the ugly side of it all. They never really confronted the fact he was in prison.'[298]

Patricia: 'Luis was always worried about his mother and sister. He's the kind of person who takes care of everybody. He always supported his mother and his sister and his nephews. The good thing for him is they weren't living in Colombia; they were living in Miami. My father found out the truth [about Luis] when everything was in the news. My mother is three years older than Luis. I think she always knew but she never told me anything. She came to visit us in Bogotá when Juliana was born, in Cancún a few times and in Panama. She cared about him, and I know she was worried about it.'

*

A couple of months into solitary, Luis felt confident enough to phone Patricia and ask her to travel from Mexico City to Colombia to talk with the heads of the cartels and, he says, 'recover monies owed to me'. He had no one else to turn to.

'I wanted to see where they stood. If they'd said, "Don't say anything, we'll cover your expenses but just hang in there," I would have hung in there.'

'He wanted money to pay the lawyers,' says Patricia. 'He wanted to know how they could help him. I think in that moment Luis wasn't okay [mentally]. He was desperate. He was crazy to send me down there. If I had told them he was thinking of cooperating with the US Government, they would have killed me right away.'

But she agreed to go. For a week, Patricia, showing a loyalty to Luis that probably wasn't deserved, shuttled between Cali, Pereira, Armenia and Bogotá attempting to get an audience with drug lords and paramilitary leaders.

'It was very difficult. I was crazy. *Imagine*. I don't know what I was thinking, really. I was worried about Luis but we were in it together when everything happened. Luis asked me to do it. Nobody wanted to do it. Not even Laura. I didn't think too much about it. I wasn't scared; maybe I should have been [*laughs*]. If someone asked me to do it again, maybe I wouldn't do it. They could have killed me if they'd wanted: "disappear" me. But I never felt like something was going to happen because Luis wasn't that kind of guy.'

Luis 'Miki' Ramírez, Francisco 'Juanchi' Moya, Hernán 'Papito' Prada Cortés, Fernando 'Marulo' Marulanda and others from Luis's two decades in the business in Colombia were all on her checklist.

'I tried to reach people. Everybody was afraid of meeting me. Nobody wanted to meet; maybe they thought I was with the [DEA], but I wasn't. I just wanted to do the right thing in that moment. Nothing worked, nobody showed.'

But word did get through to her eventually from an intermediary that she, Luis and the kids were safe; no one was in danger, whatever Luis chose to do going forward. Their message was simple: Luis should look out for himself and do what he needed to do to get back with his family. A couple of million that was owed to him, however, wouldn't be paid. No money would be forthcoming for lawyers' bills or anything else. Luis would just have to bear the financial and legal brunt of what was coming to him.

That still left the boss of all bosses at that time in Colombia: Luis Hernando Gómez Bustamante aka Rasguño. It was his word that mattered most and he was the only cartel leader whose blessing Luis felt was absolutely critical. For Patricia, he wasn't an easy man to find, embroiled in an intra-cartel war with North Valley rival Diego León Montoya Sánchez aka 'Don Diego'.

'I spoke with the *comandante* of a paramilitary group and he connected me to "Ras" when I was in Cali; I spoke to Rasguño on [two-way] radio.'

Their conversation was brief over the crackling audio line but she got the assurance she was looking for from a man who had held her own husband to ransom.

'Don't worry, Patricia. Everything's okay between me and Luis.'

64

Rule 35

THE MAN LUIS BELIEVES he owes his freedom to today was the man who hunted him down all those years: Robert Harley. The key issue was defining the word *leadership*.

'The guy who held the key to my liberty, to my freedom, was Bob. Was I a leader in a "leadership role"? *Leadership role* is really fucked up because your base offence level is 38 for the amount of cocaine. Anything over 150 kilos is base level 38: 150 kilos is *nothing*. For the US Government, a kilo is an immense amount of drugs. Then they add on two points for a manager role. Then they add three points for leadership, which is an extra ten years. So when you get to level 43, you're looking at life. In our business, you're looking at fucking mega years.'

Says Harley: 'This was the source of a lot of discussion. For the duration of my investigation of Luis, I believed him to be in a leadership role. Some of the attorneys from what was then called the 959 Group out of DC, which was the special prosecutions unit, still saw him [in] a leadership role.[299] But once the in-depth debriefing started to take place and we were able to verify what his activities were, it was very clear he was a broker; he was not the leader of an organisation. There were several layers above him.

'So are we going to charge a boat captain [for] leadership in an organisation that has 14 levels above him? No, we don't. Well, then why do we charge the broker in Colombia as a leader if he has three,

342

four, five levels above him? This was my argument. It was literally a discussion about what does that term mean.

'Everybody who sat through all the debriefings, and you were able to then put that together with, say, murders that took place of people above or around Luis, you realised that he did not have the capacity to control the fate of anyone. So if you can't control other persons' fate, then how are you a leader? You are a worker. You're *part* of the organisation. He did have "enhancements" for his role. He just was not the leader of an organisation. He wasn't a cartel person. He was an opportunist from Key Biscayne, Florida.'

*

Negotiations went on for a year. Harley had never heard of the mysterious narco The Doc, the reason Luis left the United States in the first place, back in 1988.

'I never saw an indictment out of Tucson. The original prosecutor out of Miami, Pat Sullivan, and another one called Guy Lewis who originally indicted the case, had to deal with the 959 Group. One day these guys showed up after Luis had been brought in and we were starting to debrief him, and I had an altercation with one of them, a *major* discussion in the hallway about them showing up at the 11th-and-a-half hour and telling us how to conduct an investigation.[300] There may have been an indictment out of Tucson and the 959 Group never said anything to me or to Luis.'

Luis was in the FDC for a total of 13 months, three of those in solitary.[301] Situated right in the heart of Miami, it was a 'very accessible place for government agents', so he spent most of his time in interview rooms. One of the people who went to meet him was Barry Clarke of Britain's HMCE.

'I met Luis in Downtown Miami while we were trying to track down the suppliers of the Operation Extend cocaine ring in the UK and he was cooperating as part of the wider Journey case. He had not been on our radar during Extend. We knew that Brian Wright and Nick Fisciatoris had met with people in Paris, Mexico, Venezuela and elsewhere, but not who. Luis had some knowledge of those suppliers and confirmed some details for me – he was a very astute operator.'

He also shared a cell with Richard 'Storyteller' Morrison, an alleged Jamaican drug trafficker who refused to cooperate with the US Government and would wake up early each morning to immediately tie the laces on his tennis shoes so he was prepared in case of a fight.[302]

'We shared a two-man room. A certain bond is created when you room with somebody for months and months. He said to me, "You've gotta be *strapped*." He called tying his shoelaces being strapped. You never know when you're gonna have to fight. How are you going to fight somebody in a pair of fucking slippers? He built a great physique in prison.'

The debriefings dragged on for over a year and Luis wasn't at all confident of being able to convince Harley he wasn't a leader or organiser for the Keys indictment, especially taking into account the *Suerte* bust: the buying of the ships, the elaborate planning of the routes.

'I *was* an organiser. But in my case, those three [sentencing] points meant that instead of seeing my daughter when she was nine and my son when he was six, she would have been 19 and he would have been 16. I would have missed all their years growing up. I was looking at 20 years, possibly 25 or 27 – if not life. If you have two indictments, your sentencing guidelines go through the roof. My big thing was to get out in time so that I could spend time with them and I was with them during their teenage years.'

Some creative thinking was required. Luis's eureka moment was using Francisco Moya – Juanchi – the first name mentioned in the March 1995 indictment (Luis's was second) to his advantage. Luis went to Harley figuring he was going to get slugged hard only on the Florida Keys rap, because he was going to plead guilty to a technicality on the *Suerte* indictment. When a defendant pleads guilty to charges on a US federal indictment, they are prosecuted with what's called an 'information' instead. Put simply, it's a lesser rap.

'I said, "Bob, I will admit to you that all of my life I've been in a leadership role. But on this one [Keys] indictment, Bob, I wasn't. I would not lie to you. I can't afford to lie to you. This was Juanchi's deal. I never wanted to work with these motherfucking Cubans from the Keys; I didn't know these fucking idiots. One day I met them in

San Andrés; they knew my name because Juanchi gave them my name. I had just met them. Juanchi was the organiser on *this* indictment. So on this particular case that I am being nailed on, I was not an organiser. That's the truth.'

Harley didn't say anything.

'He let me sweat it right out.'

*

A couple of days later, Luis got a visit at the FDC from Ruben Oliva. What follows is Luis's recounting of the conversation.

'I got the best news I'd ever want to give you. Bob's going to take off "organiser": the leadership role.'

'I go, "Oh, my God. *Ooowhooah*." That's like if they would have told me, "You're free." I was brought in on one indictment, my first offence. And for being my first offence I got a reduction. In the end they never counted that Venezuela thing as a second offence. It was a one-count information.[303] I supplied information, the indictment's there, but they don't hit you with the full load of the indictment. My guidelines were only based on the Keys case – on one indictment, that's it.'

Says Harley: 'I'm not too sure, it would have been after his extradition to the US, but the [Journey] indictment was dismissed presumably due to his cooperation on the Journey case. As Luis started to cooperate all I did was put in the effort to corroborate what he had to say, verify that he wasn't screwing the government, and then when I got things that I thought were pretty critical I got them to other agents, agencies and prosecutors that I thought would use it to Luis's benefit.

'Most of my own efforts preceded Luis's indictment and arrest, and he cooperated immediately. But in the long run it's really about successful prosecutions for the government. I was honest and frank with him and I gave him the opportunity. I think he saw an opportunity and seized it. He's always been an opportunist. I pretty much made sure Luis got a fair shake. I testified on his behalf for Rule 35. I helped him get ingratiated with agents I thought could use what he had in his brain to help him reduce his sentence. He was on board, fully.'

Ruben Oliva was beaming. According to Luis, his attorney told him: 'So now we can go before the judge and we're looking at 11 years, but with a "5k1" it's nine years and then we can work on the Rule 35. You can be out of here in five years.'

*

What saved Luis from copping a full sentence for the Keys indictment was Section 5k1.1 of the *United States Federal Sentencing Guidelines* (aka a '5k motion' or 5k1, which applies before sentencing) and Rule 35(b) of the *Federal Rules of Criminal Procedure* (which applies after sentencing). In other words: cooperation. Under Rule 35, a term of imprisonment may be reduced 'if the defendant, after sentencing, provided substantial assistance in investigating or prosecuting another person'.

On 30 November 2000 Luis pleaded guilty to conspiracy to import five kilograms or more of cocaine (Docket No. 95-10007-CR-KING) and guilty to conspiracy to possess with intent to distribute five kilograms or more of cocaine on board a vessel subject to US jurisdiction (Docket No. 00-6308-CR-KING). The latter charge carried a maximum term of life and the amount of cocaine involved over the two indictments was 9375.5 kilograms or just over ten tons.[304]

But in exchange for his cooperation, pleading guilty early and accepting criminal responsibility for his conduct, he effectively went in front of the judge on 6 July 2001 as a one-time offender. Luis says the *Suerte* indictment did not count towards his sentence.[305]

'I was caught at the perfect time,' is how he explains it. 'It was the perfect moment. Timing was everything. The government needed cooperation from us. My original sentence was 11 years, and with my 5k1 – reduction before sentencing for the cooperation you've done up to the moment – I got sentenced to nine, *boom*, and then from nine is when you start working on your Rule 35. My Rule 35 gave me a reduction of four years. Why do you think Colombians that traffic such tremendous amounts of coke and kill so many people get out in seven years? Because they do Rule 35. They *all* cut deals. Cocaine is a *business*. Because it's a business at all times, you cut the best deal possible for yourself.

'I was Ruben Oliva's first major case. People were amazed what Ruben did for me, but I got my time off because I was a lot of help and because I was never a violent person. I did five years because I killed nobody. Did I ever order anybody to get killed? *No.* If I'd killed an American citizen I'd still be in jail. If I'd been suspected of killing Colombians, I would probably have done five more.'

The court also granted his request to undergo a drug/alcohol treatment program, which got him a year off his sentence.

'That's why you ask for that. They put you in a separate dorm and you go through the drug/alcohol treatment, which is just bullshit; you go to these classes and they talk about all this shit. Taking on Ruben Oliva was the best thing I did. Nobody could believe the great deal he got for me, and as a result he started getting all the major Colombian drug dealers as clients. Today he's probably the top cooperation lawyer in the country. He'll charge millions for a plea agreement like nothing.'

Things would turn out well for Harley too. Just over a week later, he married his longtime sweetheart Mary at the Hotel Bellagio in Las Vegas. Carol Libbey attended. His father, Robert Sr, was his best man.

65

The Typewriter Room

O N 25 August 2001 Colombia's DIJIN, the *Dirección Central de Policiá Judicial e Inteligencia* or Central Directorate of the Judicial Police and Intelligence, launched a raid on two Bogotá apartments owned by Víctor and Miguel Mejía Múnera and used sledgehammers to uncover $35 million in cash that had been hidden behind interior wall cavities, the biggest such discovery in the world at the time.[306] The action came just days after the arrest of The Twins' accountant, Félix 'La Mica' Chitiva. It was the crowning moment of *Operación Horizonte*, a Colombian offshoot of Operation Journey. The money, wrapped in plastic, was stored in $100,000 bundles of $100, $50 and $20 bills. It took eight days to count.

The Mejía Múneras were nowhere to be found, having fled into the jungles of the interior. But soon news would emerge they'd bought for $2 million a paramilitary franchise called *Bloque Vencedores de Arauca* (Arauca Victors Bloc) from paramilitary leader Carlos Castaño Gil. Changing into army fatigues allowed them to smuggle even more cocaine, because being classified as paramilitary commanders rather than actively hunted down as drug lords gave the brothers better protection of their smuggling routes. The reason: the Colombian Government at the time was actively seeking an armistice with paramilitary groups it was fighting in northwest central Colombia, which would culminate in the Justice and Peace

Law (Law 975) of 2005. Bogotá newspaper *El Tiempo* declared the Mejía Múneras had 'mocked the government' by becoming *paras*.

Castaño's ACCU group and The Twins' bloc would be absorbed into another group called United Self-Defenders of Colombia (AUC), a murderous front for drug trafficking that was branded a Foreign Terrorist Organisation by the US Government.[307] After the paramilitaries in the jungles eventually 'demobilised' in their tens of thousands (a large number but not all of them), surrendering arms and confessing to war crimes in exchange for drastically reduced sentences and suitably comfortable 'jails' in which to serve their time, The Twins decided they didn't want to go into custody as part of the deal. They started another criminal enterprise, Los Nevados, and became fugitives.

So it wasn't long before the Mejía Múneras had a $5 million bounty put on their heads by the DOS. In 2004, The Twins were indicted for narcotics trafficking in Washington, DC and in 2007 they were named among the Most Wanted Drug Traffickers by the DOJ and Colombia's Most Wanted by DIJIN. That same year, they were declared Specially Designated Narcotics Traffickers by the USDT.

In 2008, Víctor was killed in a shootout with national police at a ranch over 200 kilometres north of Medellín, while Miguel was captured days later hiding in a secret compartment in a tractor-trailer and extradited from Colombia to the US the following year as a Consolidated Priority Organizational Target of the Organized Crime Drug Enforcement Task Force. He was indicted for multi-ton cocaine loads between 1994 and 2004 and sentenced to 14 years' jail by a New York court in 2016.[308]

*

Before dawn on 5 September 2001, Luis was sent in an air-conditioned bus along with other inmates for the 430-kilometre journey from the FDC to low-security Federal Correctional Institution (FCI), Coleman, outside Orlando.[309] It was the luxury express and Luis went out of the way to avoid the alternative.

'If you're a problem inmate and they want to fuck with you bad, they put you on something called "diesel therapy". That means they put you on a bus from Miami to Seattle, and you hit every fucking county jail there is in between. And that's the worst. Because you have to wake up at three in the morning, the bus takes off at five, you're in a bus all day, then the next day the same thing. That breaks a lot of people.

'You want to do your thing, *boom boom*, and then get assigned to your prison, your home. What prison you go to depends first on your level of security, where you have your family and where you request to go. That's if you're a nice guy and you cooperate. But if you fight the government and say, "Fuck you," and they give you 35 fucking years, you get shipped away wherever they want and they'll ship you to a penitentiary. The inmates own that place; the guards don't. In a US penitentiary you're going into *their* house. A guy that's doing life, what the fuck does he care? You look at him the wrong way, he'll fucking take his fork and put it in your fucking eyeball.'

*

As Luis's fellow prisoners were not the most dangerous felons in America, there was a low risk of being stabbed with a fork in the eyeball or being murdered while asleep in his two- or three-man cell or 'cube'. Was he ever worried about being the victim of a cartel revenge-killing while inside?

'No, *never*. They're not that stupid. You're dealing with smart men here. The cartels have killed a lot of people but they aren't killing Americans or committing more crimes in America to make their situation worse.'

Instead, over the next 108 months he concentrated on his rehabilitation.

'I would sit and type debriefings for hours and send it all to Ruben Oliva. I worked it myself. No attorney can work it for you. You've got to work your case yourself. I was totally dedicated to working on my time reduction.'

Some letters were even written in freehand, in Luis's neat handwriting. He signed each one 'A. Newman'. *A new man.*

'I *was* a new man. Information is knowledge and knowledge is money in this business. And that's why every day I used to rent the typewriter room at Coleman and from two to four I used to write my whole history and send it to Eric Kolbinsky and other agents. I worked hard at what I was doing. That was my job. Ruben did a great job because I did a great job for him. I was constantly sending memos. I sent him 100 to 150 memos to forward to the agents. I was building my whole Rule 35. I was working diligently every day, *typing*, *typing*, *typing*. It was like writing a book.'

He also got visits from the DEA and other agencies.

'It was more historical information that Luis was providing to us,' says DEA agent Eric Kolbinsky. 'Who he had done loads for, how much, when it was, that sort of stuff.'

But again there were no visits from his family, owing to their longstanding visa and passport problems from a decade of being on the run. Juliana and Santi still didn't know Luis was in jail, though he'd write letters and paint pictures for them. But his former Honduran lover from the Navia Gallery in LA, Daniela Villareal, visited often, six to eight times.

'For a year she would fly in from California and stay at a local hotel. For three days at a time she would come in every day at 8am and leave at four. No sex, no nothing. Visiting rights at Coleman is you sit at a table and buy snacks and you talk and you eat. She used to spend three days with me. Everybody there would be freaking out at this fucking beautiful six-foot-tall girl. I'm extremely grateful to her for doing that.'

*

So the obvious question is why, for all the time he was in jail, Luis's family didn't visit him and Patricia couldn't simply fly the 2000 kilometres from Mexico City to Miami. It wasn't like the Navias weren't thinking of him: they wrote him letters and he'd call them whenever he could.

In Mexico, it's a legal requirement that both parents accompany a minor and sign the application for a child's passport before an official. Prior to Luis's arrest in Venezuela, Santi Navia, who was born in Mexico City and was only a toddler, had an expired Mexican passport. Patricia tried to renew it without Luis, who was in Spain at the time, but she needed Luis's authorisation to be able to travel overseas with Santi. Her idea was that Luis could go to the Mexican consulate in Spain and sign a form giving her permission to travel with Santi alone (another legal requirement), but Luis, then in the midst of planning for the *Suerte* smuggle, only had fake passports on him in names that most clearly weren't Navia.

Of course, it was suicide to present a fake passport to a consular official, no matter how well it was made, especially so if Luis and Santi had different surnames on their documents. So Patricia asked a lawyer in Mexico if she could take Santi abroad with a Colombian passport (which he had through her Colombian nationality), but was informed that because her and Luis's son, then only three, was born in Mexico she needed to have him travel on a Mexican one. The former couple was in a bind. So Luis came up with a plan.

Patricia: 'I was told the person I had to see worked in the passport office and you gave them money. I didn't know it was a fake passport; I swear. They gave me the passport; everything appeared exactly as it should.[310] I travelled to Europe with the kids. Santi went to Spain, then he went to Venezuela. We entered Mexico with that passport. Time passed and after everything that happened with Luis in Venezuela, we were supposed to come to the United States to see him in jail.

'So when I went to the American embassy in Mexico City to get Santi's visa for the US – Juliana and I already had our visas – I was really confident about what Luis had told me: that Santi's passport had been issued by people who worked in the passport office. I never thought I was doing anything really wrong. But the Americans called me over and said, "You have a false passport." I said, "That's not possible." Then they found out Luis's name and they asked me why Luis was in jail. I was like, "Oh, my God." I thought everything that was happening had to do with him, but no: it was all because of the passport. None of it was my fault. But maybe I was stupid to follow the orders of my husband.'

Luis: 'They wanted to put Patricia in jail. That was one scary fucking moment. She had to stay in the US Embassy and I had to call Ruben Oliva. He had to pull all these strings, call [prosecutor] Pat Sullivan, and Pat had to call the embassy down there and tell them to keep the Mexicans out of it; that I was of valuable interest to the US Government. They didn't hand her over. Thank God my kids were young. In the end they took her visa, my daughter's visa and they never gave Santi his.'

66

God Exists

WHEN HE WENT INSIDE, Patricia moved to Argentina briefly with the kids to be with her Italian boyfriend, but they broke up and she went back to Mexico City. She was single for a year before she met Ignacio Bargueño, a broker for an investment bank. He was dark featured, handsome, blue eyed, square jawed, moustachioed and permatanned: every inch the total nightmare for any prisoner pining for his estranged wife behind bars.

But by now Luis had accepted everything was over between him and the woman he loved. He was happy that Patricia was with a good man. All he was concentrating on was surviving prison. His old cellmate at the FDC, Richard 'Storyteller' Morrison, would join him at Coleman but be housed in a separate unit. The experience proved much less stressful than Luis expected. Instead of *Escape from Alcatraz* it was more like the garlic-cutting scene in *GoodFellas*: certain luxuries could be had for a price but friendships came free. He hung out with Colombian and Cuban drug smugglers and had a right royal time.

'It was a little scary at first but I thought it was going to be much worse. Prison was the thing I feared most in life but I had the best, *best* time. I know that throughout my years in prison – the worst thing that I thought could possibly happen to me – I had somebody who helped me make those probably the best years. God exists. There's something out there bigger than you that actually cares for you, for whatever reason, and is by your side, helping you out and making these really bad times bearable and good.

'I had great friends all around me. We were fucking cracking up and cracking jokes all the time. I used to sweep the area in front of my unit and got $5.60 a month or something like that. I paid $100 for a bottom bunk. I had a commissary account with $400 a month.[311] A lot of people don't have a hundred bucks in prison; a lot of people don't receive a penny. Fifty bucks is a lot of money in prison. Four hundred was a lot; sometimes you couldn't spend it. A lot of people use their money because they don't want to eat the prison food. That wasn't my experience. I always found the prison food to be good.

'We didn't run the place; it was a federal prison. But whenever they had chicken, we'd buy up all the chicken and have chicken *paella*. We had any kind of food. We never brought in liquor, we never brought in lobster, we never did that; we weren't *ridiculous*. We knew we were in prison. I didn't need to eat a lobster. I've eaten 29,000 lobsters in my life. But I adapted very well and we lived very well. The only thing is we couldn't go nowhere and we weren't getting laid.

'The only person I had sex with while I was in prison was myself. Sex is overrated. You get horny and shit, you start looking at these prison guards. Some of them were nice. I kept notebooks. They all have portraits of naked ladies Scotch Taped onto them. But *fuck*, it gets wild in there. I saw a lot of Puerto Ricans. They tend to be degenerates. They don't care what they fuck. They'll fuck anything.'

For recreation, he played drums in a prison band called Prizm. Finally, after 25 years, his musical career had taken off – it was just behind bars.

'Like the prism of, you know, a triangle, the prism, Pink Floyd.[312] We played rock 'n' roll: Pearl Jam, Bush, Nirvana. I also played for the church choir and the country band. We had great instruments. The feds finance great instruments. I had fucking Pearl drums.'

The only real discomfort he encountered was asleep in his bunk. Luis was having nightmares. He'd often scream in his sleep and have to be woken up by fellow prisoners.

'They would tell me it was happening because of what I'd done in my life and it was like my demons coming back to haunt me, now that

I was away from it all. I don't know [*laughs*]; I don't remember. They thought it was because of the people who had been killed or tortured [during my time as a drug trafficker]. These people didn't really know me, but they figured, "This guy's freaking out and he was in the drug cartels and it's a withdrawal symptom from his past." Again, I don't know. I don't have that much time to be thinking about that shit. I was thinking of how I was going to make a living after I got out.'

*

Luis walked out of prison on 27 July 2005 on supervised release for a term of four years, under which he was forbidden from possessing a controlled substance or any firearms and had to submit to drug tests. He never did the in-jail drug/alcohol program, being released before he was due to start. His conditions were he could not commit another crime, associate with anyone involved in criminal activity or engage in informant or special-agent work without the permission of a court.

Between his conviction and release, September 11 had reshaped the focus of American law enforcement from drugs to terrorism and seen USCS merge with the Immigration and Naturalization Service (INS) and Federal Protective Service (FPS) to become United States Immigration and Customs Enforcement (ICE), under the aegis of the newly formed Department of Homeland Security (DHS).

'Before I knew it, five years were over. They went by quick. When you're sitting in prison, you think, "Fuck, five more years," but you keep yourself busy every day. I never had a sickness, never had a fight, never was picked on, never had issues with any other group, was always in a very good mood, never suffered from depression, always had my case going in the right direction. I was playing drums, I had a reading routine, I was in great health, I exercised a lot, I was in a right frame of mind, had no distractions, I was very *focused*.

'I had to be at my best with my dealings with the US Government, which isn't exactly a pushover; believe me, they're not nice guys. They don't give you any freebies. If you don't earn it, you won't get it. A guy called Randy Richardson picked me up. He worked for Bob Harley down in US Customs in Key West and since Bob was my arresting agent he sent Randy. That's not normal. The warden was freaking out.

They sent an ICE guy to pick me up? I was very fortunate. They could have made me sign deportation papers.'

Though he'd been conferred citizenship through his parents in 1968, Luis had never got around to claiming the official paperwork to prove it – a naturalisation certificate. He'd simply let it lapse, not thinking it would ever become a major issue, and it had become just that.

'Usually when they release you [from jail] into the world, if you can't prove American citizenship either they send you to a detention centre to be deported, or if you're a Cuban – they can't send you back to Cuba – they make you sign deportation papers.[313] That means that when the US opens relations with Cuba [which happened under President Barack Obama], they can send you back. The BOP didn't make me sign that because they thought Randy was there to take me to a detention centre. He wasn't and he didn't think about it. They didn't think he was going to take me to a Best Western and get me a room [*laughs*] so my sister could pick me up the next day. He also gave me a tour of Tampa on the way.'

As she had always been, through thick and thin, Laura was by her brother's side.

'My sons and I picked up Luis in Tampa, and we were so happy to see him.'

Luis can still remember the day she pulled into the car park: 'The first song I heard on the radio when I was driving with my sister and nephews down to Miami was "Sowing the Seeds of Love".'

Laura: 'I was not pleased with his hotel bill. Somehow he had managed to rack up $700 in phone calls in 24 hours.'

It was just another one of Luis's great escapes; perhaps the greatest in all the adventures of the drug world's Mr Magoo.

PART 13
FLICK OF THE SWITCH

67

Everything Kills People

FOR A 68-TON COCAINE conspiracy (of which 25 were seized), Luis serving only five years in jail on charges that could have put him away for life seems outrageous – even if he cooperated. After all, the man transported at least 200 tons of cocaine over the course of his drug-trafficking career.

I ask Robert Harley if critics of these plea deals and light sentences handed out to drug traffickers are justified.

'They're missing the entire point of our criminal justice system. One, if the objective of our criminal justice system is to punish and rehabilitate people, then I'm here to tell you that we've been a success with respect to Luis Navia personally. Two, you cannot buy dope with the Pope. This is my rule. There's no way to make successful big cases with John Q. Citizen.

'The US Government *has* to get in bed with people like Luis Navia to dismantle global organisations. The only way you do that is with a carrot or a stick. So the carrot is we won't use the stick. And that is how you make successful cases. I couldn't tell you exactly how many individual cases, arrests and successful prosecutions Luis's cooperation resulted in, but the value to the US Government in the efficiency of investigations *far* outweighs any need collectively for society to have punished him for a longer period of time. In my world, that's a success story.

'So, in the balance, when you assign value to one direction or the other – either strict punishment or cooperation and doing Rule 35–type work – there's no way around it. There's a cost to incarcerating people and there's a cost to doing unproductive investigations with no information. In the big picture the US Government came out ahead in both respects.

'We punished Luis, incarcerated him, rehabilitated him, put him back out, and we netted *many* successful investigations because of the deal we made with him. It's a cost-benefit approach to jurisprudence. But I know a lot of people resent the fact that he was out in five years.'

Even Luis concedes he was fortunate.

'The criminal justice system is the criminal cooperation system, at least when it comes to the war on drugs.'

*

One of the first things Luis wanted to do when he got out was go down to Mexico City.

'I wanted to reunite with my kids and make it in the real world. I wasn't scared of going back to prison. I was scared of losing what I love most – my kids and family. Before, I had sacrificed them for the business.'

But to do that, he needed a real passport, not one of the seven fakes he'd used while on the run. Throughout his years as a drug smuggler, when using a real passport, Cuban issued, he'd travelled as a resident of the United States with a re-entry permit. So though he was raised and educated in the United States, was granted citizenship in 1968 through his parents, and had an American accent, as far as the BOP and ICE was concerned he was Cuban. He had insufficient American documentation.[314]

'Mary Kramer, my immigration attorney, told me to go to the passport office and show my parents' naturalisation certificates and some other paperwork I had, and give them the whole spiel on how I came to America in 1960. I only had photocopies. My alien registration card had a picture of me when I was five years old and the lady behind the counter said, "Yes, that looks like you," stamped the form and told me to take a seat. "You'll have your passport shortly."

I just happened to hook up with the person that looked at all of my paperwork and accepted what I said. Nobody could believe it. Ruben Oliva told me, "That's America! Today was the day your planets aligned again. Hold on to that passport, Luis, and don't you ever lose it, because you'll never get another one that easily."'

Luis, out of prison clothes and in his new garb of aviators and khakis, met his family in the lobby of a hotel in Zona Rosa.

'It was beautiful,' he says, with nostalgia. 'Patricia brought Santi and Juliana to the hotel and of course I was at a group of payphones at the side of the lobby in front of the gift shop. As usual I was working the payphones. It was an incredible moment, very emotional, a lot of happiness. Santi was kind of lost because he would talk to me on the phone but he had never really seen me. I had always told my kids that I was working out my immigration issues to be able to travel to Mexico, and their immigration issues to be able to travel to the US. So he'd been very small the last time we saw each other. Juliana was very happy too but she was more wary of me.'

For Santi it was effectively the first time he'd met his father: 'When we parted I was three, so I didn't have much of a memory of him. I grew up without him there but I knew he was *somewhere*. I was excited. I'd only found out he was coming the day before, so there was no preparation. I was wearing my school uniform. And I saw him and he looked just like the pictures I'd seen. I'd only really seen him in pictures since I was a baby. "Shit, that's *him*." We walked up to each other and hugged. It was a great feeling. I was very happy. My mom left and then we went up to his hotel room and I had to do some homework and he was helping [*laughs*].'

Patricia: 'They were happy but Juliana was a little bit weird. It wasn't easy for Juliana and Santi. They grew up not having a normal attachment to their father. I never knew when they were going to be reunited again. With Luis gone, Ignacio had become the father of my kids. Juliana would say to him: "You're going to walk me down the aisle when I get married." But I never let them forget their real father. I always put a photo of him next to their beds. They needed to know that they had a father; that he was a good person; that he loved them.

'I always spoke highly of Luis. In Latin America, when people get divorced things can get nasty. But I think you always have to be civilised. So it wasn't like they saw him last week and they were speaking to him again today. When kids don't see their father for such a long time it's natural there is going to be stilted conversation.'

Juliana: 'When my mom first told me he was coming, at first I was like, "*What?* What do you mean?" I started crying. It was like this ball of emotion that came over me. I just didn't believe it. I was crying but I also didn't know how to feel. I would talk to him on the phone, but it's not the same. I always had an *idea* of my dad because Ignacio was my father figure. So for me he was this person that would call me on the phone or I'd get cards from him.

'When we finally met at the hotel I was standoffish because this was someone I was supposed to know and have a connection with and I didn't feel like that. I could see how excited he was to see me and he was very happy and loving, but I just didn't have that connection. It had fallen away. I had become used to my father being this faraway figure and I was okay with it. It wasn't something that was missing.'

*

Luis stayed in Mexico City a week, using a taxi from his hotel to drive Santi and Juliana to school and taking them out to dinner and tenpin bowling. If the kids pressed him on why he'd been gone so long, he just stuck to the story: he'd been having 'immigration problems'.

Juliana: 'I felt wary of him. I didn't really understand why immigration problems could be so big for my dad not to be with us. I have memories of me when I was little getting into a fight with my mom, and I would just cry and want my dad to be there. I would sometimes pretend to be calling him on the phone. "I'm on the phone with my dad!" And obviously I wasn't. It was really hard.

'I remember this one time I was in third grade and it was Father's Day. And even though I had Ignacio [as a stepfather] it wasn't the same. And there was this song they made us memorise about your dad – 'Hoy Tengo Que Decirte Papá' ['Today I Have to Tell You Dad'] – and I'd just *cry, cry, cry, cry.* I would sing it, hold my tears back, then just go to the bathroom and cry. I also had a book in first grade that they gave us – this big, thick book, a Father's Day gift, 100 blank pages – but I didn't have anyone to give it to. So every Saturday or Sunday when I was feeling really sad, I'd think about my dad and write him letters.'

Understandably, given everything she had been through, Patricia also had mixed feelings of her own seeing Luis just turn up after being away so long.

'I looked at him and my first thought was, "Oh, my God. He's become shorter." [*Laughs*] You know when people take a pill and it makes them shrink? He looked so old: short and old. That was my first impression. That's the *truth*. "I can't believe I was married to him. He's so fat and so old." [*Laughs*] In that moment it was different. When a man is young, at 30, 35, 40, 42, 43, they look the same; you're not going to see much difference. Luis wasn't like that anymore.'

*

Reintegrating into Miami society was easier than Luis expected. His family stuck by him and no friends walked away from him for his drug past; as he tells it, it was an open secret that he worked in the drug trade.

'Everyone knew me from what I was before; they all knew what I was into. I came back and I was the same guy I've always been. The business never changed me.'

His family's travel ban was eventually overturned through the US embassy in Mexico City and ICE, and Santi came to Miami for Christmas in 2008, with Juliana following shortly thereafter. Luis would play them Neil Young's 'Cinnamon Girl' and 'Ohio' in the car. That same year both his children received US citizenship. For the next three years, Luis was just a regular single dad in Miami raising two small kids – except he was also making up for lost time. Unlike everyone else, they still knew nothing of his narco past.

'When they went to live with him in Miami, he cooked for them and he treated them like they were babies,' laughs Patricia. 'Sometimes he treats Santi like a baby; he forgot he's not a baby. He's very protective of them.'

Luis: 'I took them to school every morning. They did their first communion. I signed them up to do catechism. Took them to rowing

practice. Took my son to karate and all the karate championships.
I was really into it with him. I'd cook dinner for them every night,
make them breakfast, make their school lunch. They lived with me.
Patricia gave me that. It gave her a little time to have her relationship
with Ignacio.'

Clearly your children mean everything to you, Luis. So you can't
avoid this: What would you say to someone who had lost a child
to cocaine? (In 2019 the son of one of Luis's cousins had overdosed
on cocaine cut with fentanyl, which had rattled him and made him
deeply uncomfortable when he attended the funeral.)

'I am sincerely sorry; I am. But the reality is you could have lost
them to an automobile accident, you could have lost them to an
overdose of Xanax, you could have lost them to a bad vaccine. In my
opinion, alcohol is worse than cocaine. What are we supposed to tell
the parents of a kid who loses his life because he was drinking? Go sue
Johnnie Walker Black?'[315]

Do you feel remorse?

'Not completely. I don't feel any remorse for trafficking cocaine.
I did something illegal not something *immoral*. Look at the people
who smuggled pot and now it's legal. Legality has nothing to do with
morality. I don't swallow that for a fucking minute. Slavery was legal.
Today, people pay their workers $5 an hour or less. They're worse
than anybody. I would have been immoral if I'd tortured people,
stolen from people, killed people to steal from them, been a liar,
brought some Albanian girls as hookers on a ship that was coming
back empty from transporting a load to Europe. I didn't do any of
that. I consumed my own product. I *believed* in my product.

'Where I feel remorse is for the pain I caused my family and those
families that have suffered from or lost a loved one to cocaine abuse.
I should have studied, become a professional and not gotten involved
in that business. So my answer is how can you feel complete remorse
if you did that for 25 years? I was totally convinced that it was my
business and it was a good business and we were providing a product
that society *wants*.

'It's an entertainment product. Did Joseph Kennedy feel any
remorse for the victims of overdosing on alcohol?[316] *No*. Do the

cell-phone companies feel any remorse because some motherfucker got cancer of the brain from using a cell phone? *No.* Do the pharmaceutical companies feel remorse because they put out a drug called OxyContin and half the nation got hooked on fucking heroin because of that? *No.* It's a *product.* God put the coca plant on this earth. It's just that some fucking degenerate white man went to Peru and made it into a powder and put it up his nose, when it was never intended to be used that way. *Everything* kills people.'[317]

68

Team America

'WHEN I GOT OUT OF PRISON, my family still lived in Mexico and I could have gone back to Mexico or Bolivia or Ecuador and with what I knew about how the system, DEA and other agencies work, and their limitations, I could have lived in Bolivia and done small loads to Europe – where even if my connection there got caught, there would be little chance of Europeans coming for me in Bolivia.[318]

'Europeans are not proactive like Americans in going after people overseas. Also American prosecutors are not taking cases where the dope does not end up in the United States. Working big and being part of the largest multinational smuggling operation with Los Mellizos brought the heat and problem to me. So knowing that, if I'd wanted to get back into the business I would have established some kind of legal business and worked small: 30 kilos every 90 days to Europe or Eastern Europe and net for myself $300,000 every 90 days. Exporting it and making it into another country is easy. It's the selling that has become a little difficult. But I didn't want that – my drug days were over.'

*

Over the following years Luis went down to Colombia and Panama dozens of times and quite judiciously won't reveal exactly what business he was involved in, or his precise role in the war on drugs beyond his Rule 35 efforts. The information remains strictly classified.

But he has cogent words of advice for any ex-narco contemplating going over to the other side.

'Undercover work, what they call joining "Team America", is effectively drug dealing with a licence.[319] If things go well a source can make a lot of money; you're rocking 'n' rolling. You're back in the drug business; you're a drug dealer again, at a high level. You're not an informant in Miami, dealing grams – you're dealing with major loads and shit like that. But don't think the DEA sets you up and you're covered with beautiful IDs.

'You don't have a badge. It's your responsibility to report if you see anything of interest. They just throw you out there. You've got to work that shit yourself. They do jack shit. You live or die. A drug dealer knows what he's in for. It's crazy out there. I think the drug business is a great business. It's a moneymaking business – but with big money comes big risks. The problem is there are too many informants and your life expectancy is very short. If you want to be in the drug business you're playing with fire. When I started in cocaine there were not nearly the amount of informants out there, and the DEA did not have the kind of information they have today: all of which they have gathered over the course of the last 30 years. It's not the same game from when I was involved; if you're in the drug business now, chances are you'll get burned.'

Depending on who pays the bill, good money can be made being a so-called 'asset' – the rewards are lucrative, in the millions – but payment is often held up by bureaucracy and paperwork. It is believed, however, that the DEA caps payments to informants at $250,000.[320] The really big money for ex-narcos is working privately on Rule 35s for cartel leaders already in prison.

'There's a lot of money on the table. If you're well hooked up, you can do it. It's the exception, not the norm. If you wait for the DEA to pay you you're fucking dead in the ground. They might ask an informant to go out there to be a drug dealer, but they don't finance him like a drug dealer. With Rule 35s, money can be made from another angle. It's the guy in jail who pays. Informants get a retainer and they go to work. But it's not as easy as it sounds. To keep it legal you need the defendant's [case] agent and prosecutor to approve this "third-party cooperation". This approval is becoming tougher to get from prosecutors. It largely hinges on defendants with money being able to effectively "buy" their freedom.

'When it is approved, sometimes the guy in jail has the information and they need feet on the ground: a sharp person to carry through the operation and be a liaison between DEA agents and the operation itself. The informant has to work hand in hand with the DEA and a lot of people simply don't get on with agents. So the informant has to have their trust. The guy in jail will hire a person who knows the business and won't get agents pissed off or double deal. It's legal but it's a grey area; the best thing is not to do it.

'Team America work is the other side of the coin. Supposedly one is legal and one is not. It's a business. You're still working for the same dollar. An informant has got to be able to flick that switch. When they go completely to the other side, it's a complete 180; but they're still at the same side. Personally, I can be Mexican, Colombian, cop, narco, bad guy, good guy, [American] Indian, cowboy. It's all the same shit to me. I've been in this business 45 years: 25 one way, 20 the other.'

Luis agrees the DEA is more prepared to risk the lives of ex-narcos and civilian Colombians and Mexicans in the war on drugs than its agents in the field. A lawyer representing major cartel figures in Miami told me: 'The American criminal justice system runs on informants. That's what it relies on.'

'Why risk the life of an agent when the DEA can just risk the life of somebody that's not an agent?' says Luis. 'Government agents don't risk their lives. Nobody's going to kill them. Colombian cartels know exactly who works for the DEA, ICE or FBI. They've got all that information, they've got all their data, but they're not going to kill one of them because if they do kill an American the DEA is going to go after them immediately. So that's going to put an end to your business.

'The cartels let DEA agents exist. They know what clubs they go to, they've got hookers working that fuck 'em. Agents have got it made in the shade. They get double pay when they're in Colombia. They live like kings down there. They're white guys with great moustaches; they're getting laid left and right. They carry a gun and a badge and they have a great time. And *everyone* knows they're a DEA agent.

'I'd tell any Colombian who's considering going to the other side, "You better know what you're doing being an informant because you're definitely disposable if you're not American." The DEA can't go around losing the life of an American. That's a major fuck-up and a major career block. That's why they'd rather use Colombians. Most of these confidential informants or CIs are Colombian.

'There have been meetings where the Colombian [CI] thinks he's signed up when he's not really signed up. It's really a no-lose situation for the agency. It's tricky. A lot of these Colombians are doing it so they can get their visa, but the DEA is right upfront with them: they don't guarantee anything. If you do something spectacular, yeah, they'll put in for some money and a visa but in the meantime it's a case of "See what you can do". They send them out there and they have to come up with *something*.

'You can't have a source who's a *gringo*, who's an American citizen, and because of your recklessness he gets killed. Then you've got a problem. Then you've got a *career* problem. That's why when a DEA source goes down there [to South America] they have to be very careful. A DEA agent can't just tell them, "Hey, go down to Colombia and get fucking killed." That agent will be doing paperwork for the next ten years and they'll be doing it out of somewhere like Bumfuck, Utah.'

69

Smoke and Mirrors

IT WASN'T UNTIL 2009 when Juliana was 15 and Santi 12 that they found out about what Luis did for a living between 1978 and 2000. He and Patricia, who a year later with Ignacio was given a permanent residency visa to join her children in Miami, had been putting it off for as long as possible.

'We were afraid because they didn't grow up in that kind of [narco] life; they went to an American school in Mexico City,' says Patricia. 'I'd always told them not to smoke, not to do drugs, and being their father Luis was so worried to tell them; like *crazy worried* about what they were going to think of him.'

Says Luis: 'I told them because there's no reason why a father shouldn't see their kids for five, six years. You just don't fucking disappear for six years. I was truthful with them. I didn't want them to think that their dad didn't visit them because their dad was out partying in Europe and not thinking of them.

'So I sat them both down and said, "Listen, I have to be truthful with you guys because I don't want you to think I never loved you or I put you on a second level or you were second to anything. The reason I didn't see you for six years is that I was in jail. I couldn't visit you because I *couldn't* visit you. I went to prison for a situation that you can google my name and find out. It was a mistake I made in life.

'"When I was younger I got involved in some illegal business and in the end because of some business dealings in Greece, they finally caught me and I went away. That's why I didn't see you. I love you both most in life. I couldn't see you because physically I was in jail and could not get out. The only thing I ever thought about while I was in jail was you guys."'

As a 12-year-old boy, Santi absorbed the news reasonably well – there's some coolness cachet having a cartel figure as a father, even though he never let anyone know about it – but Juliana didn't receive it kindly.

Juliana: 'I never told any of my friends or anything. In Miami I knew a couple of people whose parents used to be in the cartels, but it wasn't something that we talked about. I did know this one boy whose father actually knew my father – he was part of the Cali Cartel – and he would always brag about how his dad was in the cartel, how he was in prison in Orlando, and this was before I found out about my dad. I always thought it was super-weird that he would talk about that.

'Somehow jail came up with Dad. I was like, "You weren't there for us." I would get really mad when Dad would reprimand me because in my mind I always had that idea he didn't have the *right* to reprimand me and my brother because he didn't raise us. In my mind the only person who could yell at Santi and me was my mom. And then my dad exploded: "I wasn't there for you not because I didn't want to be there for you but because I *couldn't* be there for you. I was in jail!"

'I stopped and I stared and I was like, "Oh, my God." I was shocked. It was a big, *big* change for me to come to Miami to live with my father, someone I didn't really know; I was 15. I was going through all sorts of changes. Deep inside of me, and I still feel this way, I kind of resented my dad for not being there my whole life. And it's not his fault. But me finding out that jail was the reason he wasn't there for me kind of put a small dent in our relationship at first. Then, as time went by, finding out he went to jail made me understand more why he hadn't been there; it made things better. Not that I approve of what he did because I don't. But it kind of gave me peace in a sense because I knew the real reason.'

Patricia: 'Juliana needed time to understand. In the beginning, she wasn't okay. There was distance between her and Luis and she was judging him in some ways. I told her, "A lot of people make mistakes; we all make mistakes. You need time to recover from this but your father paid a price. He loves his liberty." Now, because she took the time to know him, I think finally she can be okay with her father. Luis is a great father; an amazing father. He missed a lot of their childhood and I think that makes him really sad, mostly because he missed Santi growing up.'

Luis's nephew Andrés is one family member who isn't totally convinced Luis and Patricia played it right.

'I always thought it was very weird that his children were shielded from this, relatively significantly, up until they moved to the US and then things were kind of explained.'

But Luis is unapologetic: 'That's what you do. How are you going to tell a six-year-old kid you're in jail? Why would you tell them that? What benefit is that going to bring? I'm the one who knows when they're ready and they were ready at the right time.'

So what lesson do you think you passed on to your kids?

'They've *seen* it. You don't become a drug trafficker nowadays. Today is not the right time for drug trafficking. That era is over. Part of the reason I did what I did was timing. Everything in life is timing. I happened to be in a situation where all the dots connected perfectly. I became a drug trafficker at the highest level because I started at the highest level with Bia Gálvez and the Medellín Cartel: suitcases full of millions of dollars. It's a money game. If Bia had been dealing grams I would never have continued in the drug business. I could make more money selling life insurance. I wasn't living in a fucked-up apartment in Hialeah full of cockroaches. I never had to go out and sell grams in Liberty City [a working-class neighbourhood in Miami with a high concentration of African Americans]. I was hit, like, *boom*. Studio 54. Learjets. That's why I got into it. I'm not ashamed of what I did.

'So yeah, I wasn't a doctor or a lawyer; my kids accept that. We now have a great relationship. They think I'm a gifted person in the sense that I can play both worlds: the legal business world and the other thing. And while I was in the other thing I still maintained a very straight persona and image. They admire me in the sense of, "There's nothing you can tell my dad that he hasn't seen or hasn't done."'

Juliana: 'I know Dad loves me and I love him. I feel I judged Dad harshly at the beginning and even now I feel like I'm kind of harsh on him just because sometimes I don't like the attitude he takes. Yeah, he has some things to be proud of but I don't like the fact he flaunts [his cartel associations]. It bothers me that he's flaunting something like that. He loves the rush. He's very easygoing. I admire a lot of the traits that my dad has. He did an amazing job with me and my brother; especially with me back then. I could be a big pain and he had all the patience in the world. We have very similar personalities. It was just nice to see myself in my dad.

'When I think that he missed mine and Santi's childhood it makes me really sad. My dad is the best dad in the world. For everything he's gone through and we've gone through [as a family], he could have easily forgotten about us and not cared. I think it's something super-respectable and admirable that the first thing he did when he got out [of jail] was to get his papers in order to come to see us in Mexico and bring me and my brother to Miami. He always put his family first; he always did it for his family. Yeah, he made a lot of mistakes. But he always had our best interests at heart. And I think that's everything that my dad does: he does it with the interests of my brother and me at heart.

'I think what my dad needs to get from this whole experience [of writing the book] is to get his drinking under control, because I feel a lot of the mistakes that happened in his life could have been avoided if he wasn't drinking. I see a pattern over and over that is affecting his life: whether it's Mom and Isabelle or me and my brother. He needs to get healthier. I also know I need to be nicer to him and not to be so judgemental. I'm very proud of him. Nobody's had the life that he's had. It's an unbelievable life and he should be proud of it. I just feel he thinks of those people that ran the cartels as role models or as heroes. But they're not. And I feel that's something that he needs to realise.'

*

Luis, what do you think Juliana and Santi would say is your best quality as a father?

'That I'm always thinking of them, that I do everything for them, that I think of them first, and I struggle to make it better in life to give them a better life, and to show them that hard work and discipline goes a long way. I make every effort for them to have a good education so they can become professionals and I would never, *ever* tell them to get into the drug business. I've always been good to my kids, I've always been good to their mother, and I've always been good to everybody around me in the drug business. Yes, it was illegal but I've always been very honest in my illegal business – unlike a lot of people who are very dishonest in their legal business.'

When you were a drug trafficker do you think you failed them as a father?

'*Yes*. The minute Juliana was born, that's it; I should have quit. Thank God nothing happened but I put everybody in danger by being in that business. I should have bought a couple of McDonald's franchises and laid back. Patricia would have been completely supportive if we'd done that. She never knew about my excessive spending. She never had control over the money. I should have said, "Sweetheart, stash it all. Don't let me spend." But I didn't have a game plan or a life plan. That's what I tell Juliana and Santi: "You've got to have a life plan." The cocaine business is all a bunch of smoke and mirrors. In the end you're going to get super-fucked. It's not a totally bad business, it's just high risk; I have a lot of nostalgia for it.'

70

The Forbidden Apple

FOR A MAN WHO ESCAPED DEATH so many times, life after jail was not so kind to Luis and he suffered a string of personal tragedies and hardships.

Patricia's and Ignacio's move to Miami to be with Luis, Juliana and Santi saw them have a son, Sebastián, a year later.[321] But Sebastián was only two when Ignacio, aged 50, suddenly and unexpectedly passed away. The circumstances cannot be divulged.

'He was an excellent man,' says Luis. 'I was so fortunate to have him in my life. What hurt me so much about Ignacio dying was that my kids lost a great, *great* father. He was a killer-looking guy. He should have been in fucking Mexican soap operas. He was the opposite of me. I'm social havoc. I pray to Ignacio every night. I've cried for Ignacio more than I have for my dad.'

At time of writing, Sebastián was nine and Luis had taken the small boy under his wing. Fully bilingual, he's a bright, intelligent, even brilliant child; and Luis dotes on him.

Says Patricia: 'Luis has a very special relationship with Sebastián. I think it's because of all the time Luis missed with Santi. He didn't see Santi from the age of three through to nine. I don't see him as a father. For Sebastián, his father figure is Santi. But Luis is very special to Sebastián, for sure. Sebastián loves him.'

Luis, however, sees himself as a father to Sebastián 'without a doubt'.

Who's right? I don't know, though Patricia is best placed to say. But on a personal level it's very touching to witness this veteran tough-guy narco be so fond of and clearly disarmed by a child who is not even of his own blood. It says a lot about Luis's character and his goodness that he regards it as his moral duty to be the boy's guardian when his real father, Ignacio, cannot be here.

When I had dinner with the Navia family at Patricia's home in Brickell, Luis spent a lot of time with Sebastián talking about mathematics and aliens. Patricia's new husband, David Donald, a rock musician, was away on tour.[322] The evening was totally normal, apart from a social call midway through from one of Luis's old cartel friends in Colombia: one of the big bosses who'd done his time and was now a free man. It was akin to getting a call from Tony Soprano. When Luis answered his cell phone in Spanish, his voice changed. It became much deeper, more *macho*. He left the room to continue the conversation. His past – as much as he was trying to escape it – was still very much a part of his life. It would always be with him.

'I consider Sebastián my son. In the first week in catechism when he was seven, we asked him, "What do you think, God and all this?" and he goes, "Oh, it's all fake news. It's all different dogma presented in different ways just to take money from the different groups. Religion is a business. It's all fake news."

'Sebastián's lived experiences that you and I have never lived. He's seen things. His soul has been opened to dimensions we don't know. His father died unexpectedly and he understood that at age six. And when you understand things like that, your mind starts to try to find answers elsewhere; places where you and I have never had to go to, thankfully – maybe unthankfully. Maybe if more people suffered more intense situations, then they wouldn't be such idiots and such morons.'

So why was it okay for him to find out about his dad's death so early and your kids not to find out you were in jail?

'You couldn't hide Ignacio's death because there was a mass, the parents and everybody – it's obvious. My kids were in Mexico. They had no reason to know. They spoke to me every day. Sebastián never spoke to his dad again. You can't say, "Your dad's on vacation."

In that kind of situation you've got to break out because there ain't no coming back. *Remember* – I was coming back.'

*

In 2017, Luis's mother, María, died aged 95. As with the death of his father, Luis Sr, it left him with some conflicted feelings, though there had always been great love between them.

'She was the one who brought us up. I'm not going to say she was a bad mother. But her style maybe wasn't the kind of style I needed to make me into a more formed and disciplined individual. My mother was not that disciplined. She never worked. A lot of mothers that had a rich husband, like she did, always wanted to go out and do something on their own. She wasn't like that. Is it good or is it bad? I can't say. It is what it is. But maybe that wasn't the best type of mother a person like me needed.

'My mother knew what I was doing; it was *obvious* what I was doing because I was living in Bogotá. She used to go see me down there because she was my mother; she loved me unconditionally. She knew I had some illegal moneys coming in, yeah, but also she felt I was involved in legal business. She didn't want to realise the whole picture and I gave her no reason to realise it; to her I was a very respectable legal businessman that had a lot of money, though she worried she would one day get a phone call that I was dead. She'd tell me, "This is not the type of thing to do forever, just get out. Get out while you're ahead." But I didn't listen to anybody.'

So when you look back on your life, who do you feel loved you the most?

'Laura. My sister has always had an unconditional love for me, in good or bad, you know [*pauses*]. It was only the two of us siblings. She's always been there for me, even at my lowest. *Totally*. I love her two sons, my nephews, Martin and Andrés, as if they were my own. She and my mother never saw the nastiness of the business.'

Laura: 'We never knew the reality, the true extent, of Luis's business. We were in la-la land when it came to this. Honestly, we were somewhat stupid. After what I know now, I look back and am disgusted. The writing was on the wall, but I guess we didn't want to admit the truth to ourselves. Luis's past business and life is not an easy subject for me. It brought my family so much pain and anguish that I have asked my brother on numerous occasions not to bring up the past. He is lucky to be able to start a new life.'

Andrés: 'My uncle's eccentric. He tends to put his foot in his mouth, speaks before he thinks, says things to be outrageous, likes to push buttons. When you have an argument with Luis, come at him with the truth and expect to have a discussion about it, he'll fly off the rails and you'll have a fight. But within an hour or two he's calling to apologise. He's got a very good heart but the maturity of a 25-year-old – maybe less [*laughs*]. My mother, Laura, is probably the complete opposite. More measured; a more sensitive personality. They couldn't be more different in that regard. They're probably polar opposites. My mother took care of my grandmother right up until the very end. My grandmother didn't want to be put in a home and my mother made sure that wish was honoured and took care of her with the help of some nurses. She was with her every single day.'

Laura: 'Luis is outgoing, loud, and speaks his mind; quite an extrovert. He's ever the life of the party; an anything-goes kind of person which in the right setting can be a lot of fun. In spite of his boisterousness and mischievousness, he's always a noble person. He's very loyal and is a good friend. Luis is more like my mother, whereas I am more like my father. I'm a quiet, reserved individual.

'I want to say that Luis and I had the same upbringing; however, being a woman at that time, I was held to a very different standard. There were different expectations at the time. Luis was given opportunities I was not given. Had I had the chance to go to Georgetown instead of him, I know I would have made the most of that incredibly privileged situation, which he squandered to party. Luis got away with things I would never have.'

*

Luis's relationship with Isabelle Meneses came about when she threw him a party on leaving jail in 2005. They'd known each other for decades, meeting the first time as teenagers, and she has never made any secret of her disapproval of Luis's criminal career. She never knew Luis when he was a cocaine trafficker but opened her heart to him when he came out of prison. She was totally against him doing this book and was the only person in his inner circle apart from his nephew Martin who would not be interviewed.

'I fell in love with Isabelle the day I met her,' says Luis. 'She was like the girl your mother tells you is the kind of girl you should marry: beautiful, very intelligent. She says the biggest crime I committed was not getting out of the drug business the day I had my first child: exposing my kids to that shit.'

Luis now has a strained relationship with Isabelle's family because of his drinking and has 'said a couple of things that insulted the whole family and I really fucked up'. On one occasion she straight up called him a 'functioning psychopath'. He's *persona non grata* at Meneses family events.

As he puts it pithily: 'I ate the forbidden apple, which was bringing up my past in front of her family.'

*

Throughout the writing of *Pure Narco* I couldn't help but think Luis retained lingering feelings for Patricia – not necessarily romantic, but a deeper, loving attachment. It would be understandable, given what she did for him as a wife and continues to do as a presence in his life. The regret he feels for what he put her through must be hard to live with sometimes.

Their daughter, Juliana, regards her as a hero: 'I think my mom did an amazing job by always keeping my dad's image in my brother and me. I always had a picture of my dad on my nightstand and we had photo albums of him. Any time I would bring him up or ask about him, she was always there to tell me stories about him. She would *never* avoid the topic. I don't know anyone else who would do that for their kids with their dad being in that situation. I could understand if my mom didn't want to talk about it. But she did. She didn't want us growing up thinking we didn't have a dad, even though he wasn't there. He was always there in my mind. If it wasn't for her I feel that it wouldn't have been as easy as it was for my brother and I to go back into a relationship with him.'

Pure Narco

Pure Narco

Luis agrees: 'Patricia did such an incredible job with the kids. She was the key – not just in the way she handled them but always speaking good about their dad. I'm sure she went through some really tough times, and in the toughest moments is when she proved how amazing she is. She continues to be beyond amazing. There's not enough I can say about the quality of woman that Patricia is. I've been blessed to have her as the mother of my kids.'

Do you still love her, Luis?

'Yes, in the true sense of the word. She is the mother of my kids and I realise that I've been very fortunate and blessed to have her in my life, but we could not live together as man and wife. But I probably love her more now than ever before.'

Patricia: 'You don't stop loving people but you start loving them differently. I love Luis, of course. I care about him, of course. But I also love his girlfriend. She's amazing. Isabelle's the best person in the world for him. I tell him, "You have to take care of her," if they have a fight or something. "If you break up with her, I'm going with her." I'd take her side, not his.'

71

There Is No War

PART OF HELPING THE US GOVERNMENT fight the war on drugs, of course, is testifying against your former associates. For decades it's been an accepted part of the cocaine business that when American law enforcement is circling, or a cartel has already been brought down, negotiation and counternegotiation in and out of the courtroom is all part of the game.[323] Luis has been called up as a witness in some major cases that went to trial.

'I spoke the truth. The government let me go under the condition that I would help them in the future and I kept my word to them. They respect that. When I testified against a former associate – I won't name him – I told the court he was my friend, that he was always a gentleman. I could have sat anywhere in the courtroom and I went and sat right behind him and we spoke. He turned to me and said, "I appreciate that you've been truthful."

'With another associate I looked at him straight in the face and I testified, right then and there. He stole a trip from me and I assumed a million-dollar debt; most of the debt was my profit. I've always been very truthful in court. In that case, that individual got what he deserved. It's over, buddy. Wake up. Smell the coffee.

'While I was in the business I was under the threat of death every day of my life. If you lost a load, we're going to kill you. If you don't pay us, we're going to kill you. So, okay, kill me now for testifying.

I'm not scared of dying for being involved. I've been under the "You're gonna die" cloud for 20 fucking years: the cloud of death, torture and possible fucking life imprisonment. So what's more "You're gonna die" cloud? That's how I look at it. If you're scared of dying, then don't get involved in this business. What the fuck's wrong with you? You're not joining a fucking convent. You're joining a drug cartel.

'The cartels are winning forever and ever. There is no war. It's *nothing*. It's all a big joke. It's a big pay cheque for the people in the DEA. They are not stopping drugs at all. The only way to stop the drug trade is when cocaine in South America is more expensive than cocaine in North America. To me, the DEA is a private enterprise involved in drugs but with permission to do so. The DEA is the fourth cartel and they are as powerful as they are because of the information they have. They could never get this far with good old-fashioned police work. *Impossible*.

'The DEA's perfect scenario is to grab a guy who thinks he's hot, a boss, and they offer him leniency, no jail time, citizenship, if he cooperates, so they can catch a bunch of people. What they want to do is look at the networks working inside their country. For example, find a guy in Colombia who's sending shit to Mexico. Tell him you have a G2.[324] [The DEA will] put up the plane, they'll put up *everything*.

'You [the informant] go down there, the Colombian guy puts up the 2000 kilos to put on that G2, they'll fly it over to Mexico (they've got their own pilots), then they'll work the local contacts and work the case for three or four months, and all those phone numbers they get – Joe calling Bill and Bill calling Peter – before you know it, they've got tremendous intel on the [drug-trafficking] network going on in their country.

'The only way to do that is through true infiltration. Police work is very difficult. Starting from scratch and being a policeman? *No*. You've got to have a guy who's an ex-drug dealer who knows somebody that knows somebody that knows somebody that *connects* you. And then you've got to watch out. You can't paint it too fucking pretty because then everybody will know it's a set-up. That's the only way police agencies work. It's the only way they're going to have big arrests and be able to justify a pay cheque. That they end up doing some damage? *Yes*.

They put away whoever is working at the time. But soon enough somebody else comes in and takes their place [*laughs*]. It's a no-brainer.

'America will never win the war on drugs. This is all *bullshit*. The drug business is growing because of simple economics. I remember when people used to send 100 kilos of cocaine like it was some incredible thing. The Mexican loads today are 20,000 kilos at a shot. When I started, the Medellín Cartel was at its peak. When I ended, the Medellín Cartel was nowhere, it was dead. Five fucking cartels – Medellín, Cali, Northern Valley, Coast, FARC – went down the drain. The Mexican cartels took off like fucking bats out of hell.

'The Colombians now are working to India, Sri Lanka, China, Europe, Australia. It's harder to get cocaine from Colombia to China than Colombia to Miami, obviously, but the amount of money coming into Colombia is still *unbelievable*. The profits are through the roof. The Colombians left the US market to the Mexicans – they send the Mexicans the coke but they let the Mexicans handle distribution. It's incredible what's coming into the US. I'm not saying there aren't Colombian groups working the US – they're doing it through the Caribbean: Haiti, the Dominican Republic – but today it's all about globalisation. Everything is about distribution and consumption and getting it to the end user, as it always has been. The business will never end. It will *never* end. People will never stop doing drugs. Cocaine is a nasty drug but it's a great business. It will be around forever.'

*

I ask Luis what he'd do if he were in charge of American drug policy and what he'd do to end the war on drugs. Interdiction or interception of drugs from source to the street doesn't seem to be working. Nothing does. In 2016, the US Government spent $4.7 billion on interdiction efforts in Central America – nearly 20 per cent of the total federal budget for drug control.

'The key is education. Education can lower the numbers of people consuming drugs, but there has to be better educational programs so people avoid becoming addicted to alcohol and hard drugs in the first place. We have had educational programs in place for 30 years now but consumption of drugs is still growing.

'We have a country of 300 million. You can't do here what you do in a country of 30 million; those lower population numbers are manageable on a social level. Lower population and fewer drug users means drug-rehabilitation programs are easier to implement. So there has to be a change in mentality here in the United States. We need to try to make the whole sequence a lot less violent in all aspects. To get a better hold of and control on the tremendous violence that is associated with the transport, distribution and selling of cocaine, you need to decriminalise.

'Now I could take the dollar figure that it would cost to buy all the coca leaf [in South America], and buy all the coca leaf there for a lot less money than it takes to run the DEA. You take $3 billion, buy up all the coca leaves in Colombia and Peru, and burn it. That's *it*. There's no cocaine for anybody. There's no cocaine this year, motherfucker. Do it through the Department of Agriculture, so you're not buying cocaine, the powder; you're buying the leaf, an agricultural product.

'I told this to the US Government in a debriefing. It's like when United Fruit used to corner the fucking banana market. They used to buy up *all* the bananas in Central America so there were no bananas for anybody to export. The price of bananas would shoot up. The US Government makes the public believe you get rid of drugs by burning confiscated drugs. *No*. You get rid of drugs by buying it at the farm level *and* burning it.

'But can you imagine what would happen if there was no cocaine? The reaction from dealers in the urban cities when you tell them they've no crack or coke to sell? What do you think? They're just going to go and take a job at 7-Eleven? They're gonna go apeshit. And then they're gonna run into the suburbs, kidnap your wife, steal your car, put a hot iron in your baby's back, take your jewellery, and then you have a crime wave that's shooting out of the urban centres into the suburbs. The DEA lose their jobs and their pay cheques and their pensions, and have to switch from their laidback cushy jobs to becoming city cops, so they don't want to hear about that. They told me: "Shut up and don't you ever say that again." And they know it's true.

'So it all gets back to education. You have to educate people *not* to snort cocaine. The solution is going to be all through education.

There's no violent solution to this. So buying up all the coca leaves doesn't solve shit, it just creates another problem. But it would solve most of the problem of cocaine supply. America could have the most educated country in the world but we have a country full of morons, where eighth graders don't even know how to do math. American college kids binge drink. You ever seen a Korean, Hindu or a Pakistani go to college here and binge drink? No, they're binge studying.'

72

Crossing the Line

W HEN I ASKED ROBERT HARLEY where he ranked Luis in the
company of famous American cocaine traffickers Max
Mermelstein, George Jung and Barry Seal, he replied: 'He's right in
the middle of that range of people. We're talking 100-plus loads of
750 to 1000 kilos apiece. Maybe more. And I mean *real* loads, that's
500-plus [kilos each time]. That's a lot of product.'[325]

Where does Luis rank himself in their company?

'We were all up there as far as amounts of cocaine.[326] They were
the first ones who went to Medellín and met with Pablo Escobar. I was
there for many years and met all these major players also, including
Pablo. The difference is they got caught early. And then of course
they become famous. Barry Seal, he got caught real quick, started
working for the US Government, he got killed and *then* he became
famous.

'Seal did his thing, though I probably handled more merchandise
than he did. The thing is, I've always been black or white. I never
worked for the DEA when I was smuggling. I never worked for *any*
law-enforcement agency when I was smuggling. When I was a drug
smuggler, I was a drug *smuggler*. For 25 years I never got caught and
flipped and went down there [to South America] working for the DEA,
like Seal did. Seal got popped three years into his working endeavour.
That's when he started going down there for the DEA.

'I wasn't caught until Operation Journey. I had a very long run. Most people don't have that run. I look at Willy Falcón and Sal Magluta. They started in 1978 and were arrested in 1991. I went from 1978 all the way to 2000 without being caught. I never killed anybody, I never carried a gun; I didn't need to. I was backed by the most vicious, feared people in the business. With that kind of firepower behind you, you don't need to carry a gun. The only time I ever held a gun was with Mario; it fucking misfired. I always maintained my sense of humour, and I remained independent.'

Would he name himself, Mermelstein, Jung and Seal as America's most successful cocaine traffickers?

'No, because we all got caught. Or we're dead. The most successful cocaine traffickers are the ones we've never heard about. People in Colombia, Peru, Miami, Maryland or New York, who smuggle drugs and they make $10 million and they buy a car dealership and make $50 million from the car dealership. Nobody knows what they did, and they have a beautiful life. That's the most successful kind of drug smuggler. Silvio Bernal, who I took to see Rasguño, has worked since 1975 and to this date has never been indicted and is worth at least a billion. You've got to be a fool to do what I did.

'Everybody in Colombia was shocked when the bombs started going off in the 1980s and the problems began with Pablo. The whole business started getting bad connotations. Up to then, in Miami, everybody wanted to hang out with the cocaine dealers. Even after the cocaine-cowboy massacre in Dadeland, still, *fuck*, The Mutiny was going full blast. Everybody wanted you to be at their parties: high society, film stars, *everybody* – cocaine dealers were movie stars. We were the life of the party. In Colombia, we got invited to the best parties. Then, when the shit started getting violent with Pablo, it was "Keep away". Attitudes towards us changed and now nobody wants to be associated with a drug dealer or a smuggler.

'The word narco has been trashed. Remaining true to the narco business is not being a killer; it's trafficking cocaine. In Colombia in the early 1980s, before all this shit started to happen, narcos were accepted in society. Narcos were just "colourful" people who were invited to society parties and it was always great to have the narco come. You not only brought the good dope with you but your interesting character too. That's when nobody knew about the violence. There was always violence, a hit is a hit, but it was kept in the background and conducted in a more civilised way. Cutting off the heads of ten or 15 people, that's taking it to another level. Narcos were not killers, like today. Basically they were just rich guys doing a business that nobody really knew about; it was a new business and there was even a song written about it: 'Cómo Lo Hacen' by Frankie Ruiz. The lyrics go: *Cómo lo hacen? Yo no sé. Cuál es el negocio?* "How do they do it? I don't know. What's the business?"[327]

'And now, because of all that violence, because nobody stayed a true narco, everybody started to get weird and violent, fucking kidnapping and cutting heads, nobody wants to have nothing to do or be associated in any way with the word narco. You're no longer a pure narco; you crossed the line. They started to fuck it up years ago. If you want to be a part of a criminal element in society, keep it professional. If they'd just kept it on a business level, narco wouldn't be so terrible now. Nobody wants to be close to a narco today. We're bombarded with so much negative media on the word narco, but if you can see a positive side to it, then that would be me.'

PART 14
THE BELLY OF THE BEAST

73

Stockholm Syndrome

MAKING HUNDREDS OF MILLIONS in the drug trade isn't all it's cracked up to be, according to Luis, who still uses valet parking at his apartment building when he can just as easily park himself; old habits die hard. You see, when you get that rich, chances are you'll be kidnapped or killed.

'It's a great idea to make $100 million in the drug business but the best idea is to get out. We were just so caught up in who we thought we were: that we were untouchable, that we were these amazing businessmen handling huge amounts of money, juggling the cartels on one side with trying to do legal stuff on the other, that we lost sense of reality. If you make $100 million and stay in [the drug business], you're staying in an element that is totally murderous, conniving, thieving. You're dealing with people that will cut your head off, will kidnap you; you're in a very violent criminal environment. And if you do have $100 million and it's stashed away, believe me, there are people that will try to take it from you.

'Maybe getting involved in cocaine was my own way to rebel for being so mad at myself for not actually having become the person I knew I was given every opportunity to become. I've always been mad at myself for that. So by taking it to these extremes, that was my way to rebalance my life as much as possible and expunge that inner disapproval of myself. It was my way to slap society in the face and show them that I was making huge amounts of money by not being a doctor or dentist or lawyer or traditional businessman. I loved that. And while I was active in that business for all those years, I was proud of my business and I loved my business. I was very happy being in that business. To me it was the best business in the world. I never thought of the moral aspects of it.

'But after so many years of being inside this crazy, socially unacceptable, off-the-wall business I was then affected with a sort of Stockholm Syndrome where you start relating to your captors. And I hate myself for being so reckless with money. So when I look back, the biggest thing that I got out of all that, staying in the business for so many years, was being *alive*.

'If you have $100 million, even $10 million, you should get the hell out of Dodge. A lot of money can bring you a lot of problems. More money, more criminal mentality. More money, more criminal activities. More money, more criminal elements surrounding you at all times.

'The problem originates with mindset. If you say, "I'm going to get into the business and when I make $5 million I'm out," if you get out there's no problem. It's when you stay in and betray your original plan and say, "Just a few more trips and then I'm out," *that's* when you slowly start changing your mindset, lose focus and become out of touch with reality.

'If people know that you have $100 million and you're not a badass sonofabitch with badass genes who won't saw them to death, they will come after your money. They will eat you alive. Maybe that was my saving grace: that I never had that much at one time that people wanted to go after me, or that I was always working for someone who had more. Even if people *thought* I had that much – and many did – I always continued working for people that had a lot more than I did and were verified cut-your-head-off types. That's why people never really came after me: because of the people I worked for.

'If I'm honest with myself, I failed at the business. My cocaine days were a failure. As a drug trafficker I was very much a success because I smuggled in a lot of trips and I lost very little. But I got into the business to become a very rich man, a billionaire, and I played it wrong. My only failure was as a money saver; I don't have $100 million. I was a lousy administrator. I made the biggest mistake ever: not separating the lifestyle and the drugs and the partying from the business.

'In the cocaine business it's very hard to have partners. There are few people that you can really trust. I was always concerned with getting caught so I felt a partner could be a liability. He gets caught he knows everything about you. So it was very hard to do everything I was doing by myself, not get caught, keep a family, stay alive, make money and expand the business.

'Although I'm a believer in God, money was the ultimate. My goal in life was always to have lots of money. Money is my driving force. It always has been and there's a direct correlation between money and happiness in my life. When I have no money, I am a very unhappy character. When I have money, I am very happy. But money's very cheap, you know, in the sense it's something you can count. That's how cheap it is. How can you count your family's life or the life of a loved one? There's no counting that. How do you count love? When you can count something, it's a very cheap commodity.

'So the best thing that happened to me was getting arrested. Because since I didn't do the right thing for myself, someone else did it for me. My life was going nowhere. In the end I lost 90 per cent of my money but I've been blessed in other ways. My family loves me, they accept me, they cradle me. Nobody I know has that. I'm still paying for past mistakes – but always thankful that each day I learn and I'm healthy.

'A friend of mine in Miami is being deported to Colombia. He's sitting in an immigration detention centre in Louisiana. He was here working with the government; he was signed up with the DEA. He's got an awful situation on his hands with his family, with his deportation. If he gets deported it's a death sentence.[328] If you work with the law and you're not an American citizen, they can turn on you tomorrow morning, just turn their face and say, "We never met you. Leave the country." And that's it: you're *fucked*. If you're Colombian, you should only be an informant if you're willing to lose it all and you don't know how to do anything else. This guy produced so many cases for these people. No one from the government has gone to bat for him and he's in a fucking jam.

'So yeah, I have to work for a living and wake up at six and deal with construction workers – they're a more hardcore group than the drug cartels – but I have good health to do it; that's a blessing. I keep my day job because consulting for the government has a very limited upside. It's a business that if I concentrate on, it will work. I can build it up to be something good.'

74

Collateral Damage

LUIS HAS A NEW APPRECIATION of the country that naturalised him.

'I feel American but not 100 per cent 'cause I'm not. I'm a mix of different cultures. I'm very Colombian and I'm very much American and I'm a little bit Cuban. But my heart is between the US and Colombia.'

Society has been incredibly generous to you given the death and destruction you dealt in by trafficking cocaine.

'I was incredibly generous to law enforcement. I didn't get anything for free. My aid to law enforcement merited my discount in time, because my testimony and the incredible amount of information I provided in the end benefited society; if you think removing criminals from the street is a benefit to society, I helped do that. But I don't think my testimony dented the supply of cocaine in the world at all, and I don't think El Chapo's capture will dent the supply of cocaine in the world at all.'

*

Somewhat surprisingly, the conviction and sentencing of El Chapo in 2019 actually irritated Luis. He never met El Chapo, but he did do 'a few trips in the mid-1980s with a Colombian whose main guy was El Chapo; however, no one knew him by that name. In the early days they called him 'El Rápido', The Fast One, because everybody used to take a long time and he came up with his tunnels and he was handing merchandise over in four days. El Tío would take 30 to 45 days. You'd send it to Mexico with El Chapo and in *four* days it would be in LA.'

So what annoys you about his sentence?

'They talk so much about El Chapo and how bad he was and, yes, obviously in that business you have to be bad, but he was from complete poverty, no shoes, dirt floor. He came from a very poor family in Badiraguato, Sinaloa, and he was in a situation in which he had to do what he had to do to get ahead in that area: marijuana and eventually poppies were being grown and he was surrounded by people who were in that business. He was a sharp guy and he succeeded in that business. He had no education. It's a rough business and it's a rough world. He had to do what he did. It was his only way out.'

But he chose to be a killer, Luis.

'When you get to that level you have to be, just like when you get to be president you have to order drone attacks on innocent people. It's kill or get killed and you know it. The world is full of violence. I loved doing what I did. I treated cocaine as a product that needed to be moved, just like coffee. My business model was getting contraband from point A to point B and, yes, that contraband created collateral damage – sad, bad, *whatever* – but that was my business model: transport and logistics and trading a bit.[329]

'I stuck to what I felt very comfortable with; I never got really involved in any other part of the business, even the money-laundering side. So killing, *no*. It takes a special soul to do that. I was not that guy. You should never, *ever* change who you are. You should never let anything change your true self. Circumstances change a lot of things about us, but there are some lines you don't cross.

'I got into it for the money and, yes, I did a lot of drugs, yes I know some people got whacked, but I never crossed *that* line. I was never a bad guy. I never tried to become a bad guy and I won't pretend to be. If I'd become a bad guy I would have been dead, *immediately*. These people smell if you're scared. They're wild animals. They never sensed fear in me because I stayed *myself*. I was nuts, of course. It's not normal for a kid with a good background to get into the cocaine business and for that business not to change them. But I just remained who I was. I always kept that very clear in my mind. That's what saved me.[330]

'Don't get me wrong. If somebody got killed, somebody got killed. It's not like I went apeshit over it, but it was never in me to approve it and that was not me or my business model or my life model. I saw a lot of it – not with my own eyes – but I *knew* a lot of it. I knew it was going on. People get killed every day. People overdose. The military will go in and kill a lot of innocent people. Even the US Government – to kill one Taliban leader they drone a fucking place and they kill 40 or 50 innocent people. That's a known fucking *fact*.

'The government is working with snitches all the time.[331] They risk the snitches. They put 'em out there. They know they're gonna get whacked. Some of them do, some of them don't, I can't generalise like that. But the government is just another side of the same coin. They've just got a badge. My business model was not to kill; my business model was to export cocaine. Killing was collateral damage. It was not the core of my business model to go out and kill other human beings like it is when you're part of the military.

'Who I really detest are the politicians that go to school, go to the Ivy League colleges, take classes in public policy and ethics, educated men who know the difference between right and wrong, and yet they're elected into office to serve the people and they are corrupt. That's the worst crime of all: educated people doing bad to the people that elected them. I just did bad to myself.

'I'm an educated man who got into a business that I shouldn't have gotten into or I should have gotten out a lot sooner. I'm not going to get into the part about how the drugs harmed other people: that's a whole different thing. But I should have seen the difference. The real big punishments should go to educated people who know the difference between right and wrong that are caught betraying the public's confidence and who are corrupt. There's a lot of money out there that could be put to a lot of good use in the public sector and it's siphoned off to corrupt politicians. They are the worst criminals.

'I crossed a line when I began killing myself by indulging in the product. Cocaine is a bad motherfucking drug; it's dangerous and completely destructive to yourself and your family. By getting involved in my own product I killed the essence of my business, which was making money. If I hadn't consumed the product and not been drinking and not been partying, I could have turned $15 million into billions. I only harmed my family and myself through the worst weapons: drugs. They will make you suffer for a lot longer than any gun wound or gunshot will.

'So it's a big moral thing there. It's what happened to me. That's how I failed. I would never say to anybody, "Do cocaine." I've never seen a guy that smokes pot come home and beat up his wife. Alcohol is a whole different scene, a very dangerous and nasty drug, and when you mix it with cocaine it's total destruction.'

75

The Heaven Part of Hell

O N 28 MARCH 2018, Luis went to a reading by the American crime author T.J. English at Books & Books in Coral Gables for his book about the Cuban mob, *The Corporation*. Luis had always been fascinated by 'The Cocaine Wars', Carl Hiaasen's 1979 *Rolling Stone* article that had spooked Oscar Peláez Monsalve to leave the United States so abruptly, and had only recently learned that Poli had died since their brief meeting in Pepe Cabrera's Bogotá casino.

Luis was feeling nostalgic for his cocaine days and the quiet, impassive killer who had been his guide and teacher. The well-known gun of Medellín hadn't been quick enough pulling out his trusty .357 Magnum during an attempted carjacking outside a bank. Poli had clocked the gunman on the passenger side, where his girlfriend was sitting. He just hadn't seen the second killer behind him. He'd been shot dead at almost point-blank range.

In 'The Cocaine Wars', Hiaasen had interviewed a group of Dade County detectives and one of them was Roberto Diaz. Luis was sure Roberto and Poli would have known each other from the cocaine cowboys era.[332]

'Jesus, it's a war,' one of the cops had told Hiaasen. 'The Colombians have got the money, they've got the mobility, they've got the manpower. It's unbelievable. If the Cubans want to hit you, they'll take you out to the Everglades, shoot you in the back of the head and dump you there.

Not these assholes. They like shooting people in public, in the busiest shopping centre in Miami. They don't give a shit.'

So, after the reading was over, Luis got talking with some retired detectives from New York and Miami, told them he wanted to contact Diaz for this book, and they promised they'd put the two in touch. A few days later, Luis's phone rang. It was Diaz.

'Hey Luis, I got your number from my buddies. How can I help you?'

'Well, Roberto, I think we may know someone in common. His name is Oscar Peláez.'

There was a long silence on the other end of the phone.

'Oscar *Peláez*? Luis, how do you know Oscar Peláez? What exactly did you do for him?'

'I was his chauffeur. I used to secure the apartments where he went to sleep at nights. "Poli" they used to call him.'

By now Luis was convinced Diaz thought he was a Colombian hitman – with good reason. If you drove for Poli, you also knew how to use a gun.

'Luis, when you were with Poli did you ever hear the name "El Colorado"?'

'Yes.'

'How did you hear of El Colorado?'

'Well, I knew Poli wanted to kill him.'

'Do you know who El Colorado was?'

'No, I have no idea who he was.'

'Luis, *Luis*. I'm El Colorado. We raided one of Poli's apartments after a tip-off.'

Instantly, Luis had a flashback: Poli had been looking for El Colorado to whack him and had brought people from Colombia over to do the job. Luis just didn't know who El Colorado was or why exactly the two men had been at war. Now, to his horror, he was speaking to the target of his own boss's assassination plan and had implicated himself through being his employee.

Suddenly everything he'd long suspected had become very clear. Poli wanted to kill El Colorado solely because of the raid on his apartment: being held and photographed, the confiscating of photo albums, the roughing up of Poli's family. It wasn't a case of a dirty Miami cop stealing merchandise. Diaz's raid had been a personal affront to Poli. He was out for *vengarse* – revenge.

'Shit, Roberto . . . I knew he had a hit on El Colorado. But I really didn't know El Colorado was *you*. Yeah, I was Poli's chauffeur but I was also working as a salesman for New England Mutual Life Insurance.'

'Poli had a hit on me, Luis. I can't say the Dade County police department had a hit on Poli, because a police department doesn't put hits on people, but if we would have run into him, we would have gunned it out right then and there because we knew who he was; we knew what kind of character we were dealing with. And you were Poli's *chauffeur*?'

'Yeah, that's right.'

'In other words you were driving a fucking hearse, Luis. You would have been right in the middle of a fucking gun battle. You would have been dead. Nobody would have walked out of there alive.'

When he ended the call, Luis was rattled. He phoned his lawyer, Ruben Oliva, immediately.

'I asked him if I could possibly have some trouble from that association: like an attempted murder charge. Usually in that business, when you're a chauffeur you're very good at the wheel and you're also a hitman if you need to be. I was driving a fucking time bomb. Ruben said not to worry, nothing's happened: "Poli's dead. There's no gun, there's no victim."'

A few weeks later Luis met Diaz at his office and took a photo of Poli from Diaz's collection on the condition he never showed anyone. On seeing the famous Dade County cop in the flesh for the first time, Luis knew he was talking to the one and the same El Colorado.

'He looked Irish: red, freckly, tall, strong. Roberto's a tough dude. I was looking at a guy that my boss was going to kill. He didn't want to show me pictures of Poli. All these years had passed, I'd told him Poli was dead, and he was still hesitant to let me take a picture. I had to give him my word that I knew Poli was dead. He thought it could have been a vendetta after many years; and I'd walk in there and shoot him. He still thinks Poli's *alive*; that's how much of a cop he is.

Roberto knew what he was dealing with. He knew he was dealing with the devil himself.'

*

To this day Roberto Diaz remains haunted by his time on the frontline of the cocaine wars. He and his team were the real *Miami Vice*. He was happy to talk for *Pure Narco* but against the wishes of his wife, who wanted no part of it – understandably.

Luis and I sat down with the former detective at Cayo Esquivel, a seafood restaurant in Miami. Diaz had retired in March 1985 at the age of 32 and become a private investigator. He looked like a beefed-up Chuck Norris: neatly combed blond-red hair, a short-cropped grey beard flecked with red whiskers, icy blue eyes. Solidly built and standing six feet tall, at 67 he still looked formidable, with a big chest, big hands and forearms like small torpedos.

A resident of Westchester in the western part of Miami, a Donald Trump–voting Republican and a Christian, Diaz drinks but has never smoked and never touched drugs. He was born in Cienfuegos, Cuba, his parents of French-Swiss and northern Spanish stock.

'I'm the only Cuban guy with red hair,' he jokes. 'When the Dadeland shooting happened none of the police departments down here were ready for what came afterwards. I had a Colombian source that told me that there were two Colombian groups warring in Dade County. The source told me that one group had a truck and that they had made it bulletproof. The source told me that the two groups were armed with machine guns and hand grenades. I believed my source and wrote a memo to my captain with what the source told me. I was told that the source was full of shit. No one at the time had any idea that the Colombians were capable of having these weapons.

'Sure enough, the day of Dadeland, I was off [duty] and got a call from my sergeant telling me to come in because of the shootout at Dadeland. They had found the abandoned "war wagon" nearby. From then on it was one homicide after another, oftentimes multiple homicides. No one was prepared for what the Colombians did. One detective from homicide, Mike McDonald, who has since died, was on his way home driving on the Florida Turnpike when two speeding cars went by him, one on either side of his car, with guys hanging out the window firing MAC-10s at each other. He was caught in the middle of this and he's got a little .38 calibre revolver. Hits were being done in the open, in shopping-centre parking lots, at intersections. Bodies dumped on the side of the road.

'The same Colombian source gave me the info on Oscar Peláez. It must have been good [intelligence] and the source must have said that Poli was a big player for homicide to have initiated an investigation on him. We went after him and got him and his family at his house. They were all brought into our office and interviewed. The same source later contacted me and told me that Poli had put a hit on me. I guess Poli was pissed because we disrupted his operation or style of living. I notified my command staff verbally and by memo, but again, none of them took it seriously. I certainly did but no special watch order or protective detail was assigned to me.

'The Anglo mentality was that these Colombians were just a bunch of yahoos. The command staff didn't think these people were as well organised as they were. They knew the firepower they were using but, typical of the time back then, the command staff just didn't do much by way of arming us with adequate firepower. It was me, myself and I – that was it. I obviously took it very seriously knowing what these guys could do.

'Life went on, we kept investigating, Colombians and Cubans kept getting killed. We were spread so thin that we didn't have time to concentrate on one particular person. We were not prepared for these types of investigations. Our focus was investigating homicides; it was a whirlwind of stuff happening and we were trying to catch up. We were outgunned and outmanned. We were *way* behind the eight ball: guys with a six-shot versus guys with a MAC-10. So the tactic was just to make life miserable for these pricks, harass the shit out of these people, and try to put a stop to the killings.'

*

Diaz doesn't deny roughing up Poli.

'There could have been a couple slaps upside the head. *Bam bam*. It was to put the fear of God in him. "We know who you are.

We're going to fuck you over, you miserable piece of shit. You think you rule the streets here? Get the fuck back to Colombia, you fucking Indian." We brought his whole family into the homicide office. The Colombians were very on the move; they kept different stash houses. They were no fools. They were *prepared*.

'I don't know how many people Oscar Peláez killed or had killed but, from what Luis has told me, he was a real bad guy. During the time we investigated Poli, as far as I can recall, none of us knew how bad he was or that he was feared by any of the other Colombians. One Colombian, Conrado Valencia Zalgado aka "El Loco Martel", was extremely dangerous and violent. I had his photo and when we showed them to witnesses – the few we could find – they would flinch and knew who he was and how violent he was.

'We were constantly working. I remember guys sleeping at the desks in the homicide office, working countless hours, going home to shower, flopping in bed, and being called two to three hours later because there had been another drug-related homicide. So when I was given Luis's phone number all these years later and I spoke with him I was suspicious. But he was very forthcoming and honest.

'Luis is a very non-typical narco. He's really a rare species; he's not a lowlife. He has class and pedigree – unlike the Cubans who came in the Mariel boatlift who were bad motherfuckers. He reminds me of these little coral fish who live among poisonous coral. And if any other fish touches that coral they get poisoned. But these little fish are immune from any of that poison. Luis lived among these killers, these heavy hitters, and he had some scary times. He was able to survive that; not a lot of people can do that.

'When Luis verified that Oscar Peláez had put a hit on me, it blew my mind. I kind of flashbacked to when the source told me that Poli had put a hit on me. I was hesitant to meet with Luis because of this, but, again, he was very open with me so I accepted meeting him. I was not aware that Poli called me El Colorado. My friends used that nickname for me and some still do.

'The *Rolling Stone* article didn't change the way we did our investigations. I just remember that all cops in general were frustrated with all the crap that was going on. We just kept doing our jobs.

But I was surprised that Luis said it caused Poli to leave Miami. Go figure that the power of the pen caused him to leave town. Luis told me that Poli was killed by some street thugs in Colombia when he was ambushed in an apparent attempted robbery. [*Pauses*] I hope so.'

Luis's memory of the stone-cold killer remains untainted, even with the knowledge of how close he came himself to being killed in a shootout with Dade County police.

'I feel bad about working as a driver for Poli, because if he'd killed Roberto, I would have burned in some kind of fucking hell. It's a miracle Roberto's alive. His saint should be Carl Hiaasen because if it weren't for that article in *Rolling Stone* Poli would have never left and Roberto would very possibly now be dead. This is, like, *Pulp Fiction* shit [*laughs*], let me tell you. I now love them both. But in my book, Poli's no psychopath. And I will fucking defend him and his honour. Nobody can tell me differently. If he's in hell, it must be the heaven part of hell.

'I knew who he was but there was something about him that touched me. He's been a big influence on my life. I loved Poli. I cry sometimes. I get really sentimental; I've shed tears for him. I still haven't met anyone that matches him – in terms of the way he lived his life. Every time I hear the Elton John song "Ballad of a Well-Known Gun", it reminds me of Poli.[333] He was black and white. There was no fucking grey area there. He was one of a kind.'

76

Crooked Road

L UIS SPEAKS OF BEING afflicted with Stockholm Syndrome in relation to his time in the cartels yet it could also apply to his unusual relationship with American law enforcement. Seeing the Danny DeVito–like Cuban-American walking alongside the nearly 200 centimetre–tall Southerner Eric Kolbinsky, you would never think one had put handcuffs on the other 20 years ago.

The two men are now good mates. They bonded after Luis got out of jail and the pair began working together on a bunch of historical drug cases that ended in successful prosecutions. Like Robert Harley, Kolbinsky lives in St. Petersburg, Florida, and is happily married to Lorena, the sister of Carolina Gómez, a former Miss Colombia and Miss Universe runner-up. She's 20 years younger than he is and, like her sibling, very beautiful. He jokes that 'the agents who went down to Colombia always came back with a Colombian wife, even the married ones'.

Luis and I drove four hours from Miami to St. Petersburg to see Kolbinsky and spent an evening bar-crawling downtown. Michael Diorio, a retired agent for the Department of Homeland Security, also joined us.

'It's not like I have a lot of friends; it's not like I *knew* a lot of people,' admits Luis. 'Eric's my friend; one of my very few friends.'

At a celebration in Miami for Kolbinsky's retirement and

65th birthday in 2017, Luis turned up. He walked into a crowded room of law-enforcement officers of every shade and hue.

'DEA, FBI, ICE, policemen – they were *all* cops. I felt like one of them. When I was there, they went around and asked everyone what relationship they had with Eric, and when they got to me, I was the last guy. I told them, "Eric and I were in the same business. I was a smuggler and he was a cop. We were both in the drug business."'

To this day Kolbinsky doesn't go anywhere without a firearm and is fully badged up, even when walking with his and Lorena's toy Pomeranian. When he heard the news that Luis was publishing his life story, he was thrilled.

'I think it's great. I think it's awesome. He's a character. Luis rolled with most of the major players back in the day. He really is lucky to be alive, in the sense that it's not a job you normally retire from: most people end up dead or in federal prison for the rest of their lives. He got lucky. Luis just spent a few years inside and lived. He never screwed anybody over. I guess he was an honest dope transporter.'

The fan club is mutual, even if Luis steadfastly refuses to pronounce Eric's surname correctly. Invariably it leaves his mouth as 'Kapinsky', is stored in his phone as such, and he doesn't seem to care when you correct him on it. It's become a sort of running joke.

'Kapinsky's a slim, good-looking guy. He's got more pussy than any drug dealer I've ever met. He partied out more than I did. It's a miracle his dick is still on his fucking body.'

'Ever since I arrested him I've been babysitting this guy,' Kolbinsky joked wrily as we watched Luis stagger out of yet another bar in what locals call 'St. Pete'. At one point during the night, Luis, emboldened by alcohol, had got up on an empty stage where a band had set up their equipment, sat down at the drum kit and started bashing out a solo. One of the band members had to step in and take the drumsticks away from him. 'He lives in the past. It never leaves these [narco] guys.'

Their unusual friendship, I believe, speaks volumes about Luis's character. In some ways he is a model example of prisoner rehabilitation. But in the eyes of many he will always be a criminal – including, it should be said, Luis's own. That is fair enough. He may talk up his non-violence as a factor that separated him from other narcos, but the fact is inescapable: he chose bad over good. That, arguably, was his worst crime of all. Fifteen years after he'd got out of jail, I often got the sense he didn't quite know what he truly was at heart: law-abiding American citizen or South American *bandido*. There's an inner struggle of sorts going on and it's being played out every day. In one unguarded moment, Luis admitted as much.

'That's the hard part – finding out who my true self is. Still having trouble figuring that one out. To tell you the truth I'm a little scared of myself. I'm scared of what I'm capable of.'

It was this man I felt great fondness for; stripped of all his bluster and artifice and just laying it down as real as he could. The man concerned only with making money and talking up his cartel pals I never related to or cared for. It was a welcome sign that for Luis's storied criminal past he was just like the rest of us: still searching for meaning and purpose and now coping with a life where his every whim wasn't accommodated. He'd lived in a complete bubble for most of his life: a self-confessed spoiled child of rich Cubans who'd seamlessly evolved into a spendthrift American cocaine trafficker. Until now, the true value of money had never really hit home. Now he was facing hard reality. The narco fantasy was well and truly over.

*

Luis also remains on good terms with the man who brought him down, Robert Harley, though it's clear to me over lunch at Dr. BBQ in St. Petersburg that their relationship can never be much more than jailer and prisoner. They might have been buddies in another life and under different circumstances, but they made moral choices that sent them on separate paths, and their sense of right and wrong runs deep and in opposite directions.

After putting off retirement, Harley is now employed by the DHS's Homeland Security Investigations division (HSI) and doubles as a supervisor in the Department of Justice's Office of Professional Responsibility (OPR) or internal affairs unit, which investigates attorneys employed by the DOJ. His official title is Resident Agent in Charge, ICE, OPR, Tampa.

He and Kolbinsky have just physically met for the first time and the two men have an easy rapport typical of agents serving the same government master. But, by contrast, there's an air of hesitancy and caution about Harley when he's around Luis. From where I'm sitting this seems totally understandable, not least because of the fact Harley is still an active agent and there are rules and protocols to follow when meeting ex-convicts (though Luis does do his best to break the ice by buying Harley a tie adorned with Texas state flags on it for old times' sake, which he is very happy to receive). Defining their friendship depends on which of the pair you ask.

'Every once in a while I'd meet Luis at Cracker Barrel in Florida City and have a cup of coffee, whatever, just to talk,' says Harley. 'People would call me, agents from other agencies and ICE, and say, "What's the deal with *him*?" and I would tell them the back story.'

Luis: 'Bob is straighter than Eric but we have a great friendship. He's a career guy, sharp. I've met his wife. A federal agent does not normally come around with his wife and introduce you to his wife; you being an ex-cartel guy. They do that because they trust you. These guys put away a lot of people in jail.'

'That's true,' replies Harley. 'I am straight. I am honest, frank and fair. But the job doesn't define me. I'm a career person. Over 33 years you start to judge character and Luis is an opportunist. He benefited from making bad choices and doing criminal activity but at the root of his person, is he an evil person? Some people do things for the money and the thrill, but it doesn't make them an evil person. It makes them a *criminal*. Some people are evil people but not all evil people are criminals. Luis does not pose a threat to me or anybody else. He's not that kind of person.'

Would you call yours a friendship?

'That would be a little odd. I'm not sure about a friendship. It's an odd relationship and I think this is why: I was always honest and I never made it personal. I was not mean or rude or arrogant. I just laid it out, matter of fact. I think a good person doing bad things responds to that type of relationship, if you follow my logic.'

Why did Luis do it?

'It's adrenalin, purely. This is all about the art of the deal and being on the edge of all that craziness. He enjoyed the thrill of it all and a little bit of the risk and the excitement, and let's face it: the money, the women, the drugs. He enjoyed all the carnal pleasures of being in that business.'

His nephew Andrés Blanco thinks Luis romanticises his life. Would you agree?

'I do think Luis romanticises his life too, but I think, in fairness, *everyone* does. That is the coping mechanism for the average human. The dysfunctional human is the one that focuses on all their negativity in their life and drives themselves into depression. The rest of us rationalise our bad behaviour so we can move forward. It's absolutely true; this book is a way for Luis to, I don't know [*pauses*]. . . put a good spin on a kind of dark life.

'Everyone finds a road to personal redemption. I think Luis saved his life. He has a sense of humour as a defence mechanism for himself – and it works. Was he violent? *No*. The people that he worked with? Yeah, *absolutely*. Do you impute the violence to him, though, as a member of the organisation? If you don't pull the trigger, what is your culpability? I don't know. These are big questions with no answers from me.

'Luis is not threatening; he's unassuming and self-deprecating. He's not dumb and he's inoffensive for the most part. He comes across as a joker and a businessman. Somebody you'd be willing to conduct a business transaction with. And I think that has served him well. That's the only reason he's alive. But he's not innocent by any means. These were bad moral choices by him. It wasn't like he woke up one day and said, "You know what [*laughs*], I'm going to be a drug smuggler." The road's a lot more crooked than that. I ended up where I am because of a sequence of events. But I very well could have been somebody different. And I came from a good family in South Florida with a great education. So what does that mean?

'I'm not a moralist; I don't do the job because of the morality of it all. I'm not an ultra-conservative. I am a *pragmatic* person. This is what the law is. This is what I was hired to do. It's a contract relationship between me and my employer. I never passed a value judgement on the people that we were chasing unless they committed what I considered to be the "personal crimes". If you rape somebody, if you beat up somebody, if you shoot somebody, if you kidnap them, if you threaten them, to me that changes the nature of the crime. And I've absolutely met people that I thought were just faulty human beings that were bad for society. Luis is not like that. These are people that commit crimes of opportunity.

'It's about *greed*. It's not because they make these moral decisions. It's exciting. There's a risk factor involved. There's a risk–reward relationship that they can't get away from. I've seen Luis probably a half-dozen to a dozen times; texted and talked to him by telephone dozens of times, maybe as much as a hundred times. And that's an accurate account of the relationship.'

*

Harley did send Luis a kind text the day after their lunch of ribs and tacos in St. Petersburg. It wasn't just a courtesy thank-you note but a word of advice. Luis wasn't selling hot dogs on Key Biscayne like the still-active ICE agent had once hoped – he was yelling at guys called José all day on a speakerphone from the driver's seat of his car. It was time for a change; a re-evaluation or reloading. It was a plea: *don't sweat the small stuff.*

'When I think about your life, Luis, I really believe things came together in such a way to allow you a giant second chance. It was your intellect and effort, to be sure, but don't discount the gift of karma you've been given. Life is good and you're here and healthy. Enjoy it whenever possible.'

Of course, Harley was right. It struck a chord with the rehabilitated narco. There was a moment on the roadtrip when I felt I saw a side of Luis I had never seen before. We were coming through a tollbooth on the Everglades Parkway and he handed over a ten-dollar note to a chinless, moustachioed collector wearing a Florida Turnpike Hawaiian-style shirt. The collector's nametag said 'HARVEY'. Harvey took the money, diligently counted out the change for the $3.25 toll and cheerfully said, 'Have a great day,' to Luis.

Harvey, who appeared to be a simple man, did his stultifyingly boring job day in, day out in a tiny, cramped box surrounded by a swamp full of crocodiles in the middle of nowhere. When we pulled away from the booth, I turned to Luis and said, 'You know, mate, your life could be a lot worse. You could be sitting collecting coins in a tollbooth in the Everglades like Harvey.'

The look on Luis's face was hard to describe, but one of realisation, peace and acceptance. The truth had finally hit him in the unlikeliest of places. After we got back to Miami, Luis called me to ask if we could hit some yoga classes together before I left to fly home to Australia. Maybe there was more to his life than making money, after all.

77

On the Hook

THE BIG MYSTERY IS how much money Luis still has: onshore and offshore. He surely has money *somewhere*: his kids went to good private schools, his ex-wife is living more than comfortably, and he admits 'I've always lived well' and 'Whenever I'm short three or four thousand dollars, three or four thousand dollars appears'; but, reasonably enough, he wouldn't tell me how much he'd managed to *keep* from his drug days or where he kept it.

'It's not very good to share that information. I don't want to get into that. Nobody had to sell nothin'. It's an *unanswered answered* question. But my late brother-in-law, Vicente, lent me money and helped me out a lot.'[334]

Equally I asked him several times to give me an accurate figure of how much he'd *made* over the course of his criminal career – he'd quoted me anywhere from $80 million to $120 million – but he couldn't settle on one number.

'I don't think he knows; I don't think we know,' says Robert Harley. 'Here's the problem. In his job, the job Luis had in the operation, he was on the hook in both directions. He's on the hook to get the product and if the product is lost he's the one that's on the hook for paying the bill, because the owners of the product rarely go without being paid. So he might have made millions of dollars but it also cost him millions of dollars, because there were plenty of loads that were

413

taken *off*. Just the ones in the Keys I can think of, off the top of my head there's at least seven or eight that were taken off and maybe there were a dozen that were successful. So what really is the profit margin in that? I'm not sure.

'And you have to picture that the finances in those days were a little different to today. You were still talking about having to get cash collected from all the distribution points, consolidated and smuggled back out and into Panama, Colombia or Venezuela. So even if you have a successful load, you're still not going to get 100 per cent payoff – and you're going to use it to downpay for the next one anyway. Luis made millions but, in the end, I don't know. I don't believe he has any money stashed anywhere. I truly believe that. I'm not saying it's impossible but I never saw that kind of money trail.'

Either way, I couldn't help but feel maybe Luis, El Senador, had got away with the greatest smuggle of his career. Are his millions hidden away or is he really what he says he is: just a hardworking regular guy who gets up at 6.30 in the morning and comes home at night exhausted to unwind on his deck with a few grapefruit vodkas? Is he both? Is he less Mr Magoo and more Keyser Söze from *The Usual Suspects*? Only he knows.

I was curious to know if his views about money had changed at all, now that he had his family around him, safe and well. He'd had incredible wealth and blown it. He'd led an exciting life and been imprisoned. He'd completed a full circle from civilian life to criminal life and then back to civilian life again. What does being 'rich' now mean to him with the benefit of hindsight? Had he actually realised there was another path to happiness and contentment?

'You should have at least $2 million stashed away earning interest and have some sort of ongoing concern returning $20,000 a month. With that, $2 million in a bank account and no mortgage on your home, you're good to go. You don't need $50 million. Some people don't need money and are very bohemian. Some people think living in a hammock under a tree is very nice and comfortable. I don't. I need to live in a nice place. I don't know; different strokes for different folks. But I'm a rich man in that I have my kids, I have my family, I know people that did a little time in jail and they managed to keep

$20 million, but they've lost family members to cartel violence. I'm very rich and very fortunate for what I have.

'The US Government did me a favour by picking me up because I was so far gone and into Neverland that I would have never gotten out on my own. I was living in the belly of the beast. I would tell anybody if you have the opportunity: *go to school*. The moral of my story is to get an education; there's a lot of money to be made legally. It might not be as fun or so fucking adrenalin-driven as cocaine, but it's a very tough world out there in this business and if you have half a brain you have *options*. Take the education option. You're going to make more money by going to school and becoming a professional, working at it, and putting your heart into it. I put my heart into it *and* I risked my life for what I did. So risk your life for what you're going to do, motherfucker, and you will be very successful in today's world because intelligence and hard work are rewarded.'

*

Luis Antonio Navia spent his life trying to escape responsibility, escape mundanity, escape his father's expectations, escape reality. He did that through criminal enterprise, alcohol, drugs, hedonism, sex and the pursuit of material wealth via legitimate and mostly illegitimate means.

The beast makes us all believe that to be happy we constantly have to have *more*. But the more successful he was as a drug trafficker, the more dangerous the job became. Even when materially he had everything he'd always wanted, he was never satisfied and his health suffered as a result. Luis didn't see it then, but he was creating his own prison. The beast had swallowed him up. There was no way out, whichever way he turned. A man can spend his life on the run from the law but he cannot evade hard truths about himself.

Luis's goal in life was to make hundreds of millions of dollars, ostensibly as a way of filling the vast shadow left by his father and masking his own feelings of inadequacy for not finishing university or making it as a businessman in the real world, yet it was something he could never achieve. He made the money but he couldn't fill the shadow. That's because a criminal life cannot deliver a man prestige and dignity; the accumulation of money itself cannot either. But a regular job, his devotion to his two children and his ex-wife's child, and his uncommon willingness to confront the demons he still lives with have all delivered Luis humanity, humility and honour that are beyond price. He has now filled the shadow. His is ultimately a true redemption story.

Being on the run with no endpoint is no life at all. It was time to come in. It was time to own his mistakes and take responsibility for them. It was time to cut the most important business deal of his life. The person who held the key to his own freedom wasn't Robert Harley, Eric Kolbinsky or anyone else in American, British or European law enforcement. It was Luis. He'd held that key all along, only this time he finally believed it, backed himself and went for it.

Luis's 25-year adventure as a narco came to a close because the choice facing him was clear: certain death in Colombia or going back to the United States and facing up to all the things he'd spent his life running away from. In the end, ironically, federal prison in Coleman and a humdrum construction job became sweet freedom from an illusion he'd sold himself: that a selfish life can be lived without consequences. It took Luis losing everything – his money, his reputation and, most of all, his liberty – to escape the beast.

Boom.

EPILOGUE

The Icepick

A TYPICAL DAY ON A construction site in Miami, Fort Lauderdale or the Florida Keys is a far cry from Luis's 1980s cocaine heyday. His Miami is not the art-directed neon cityscape of Michael Mann, but traffic jams on the interstate, industrial lots, print shops, hardware stores, and a cast of tough-looking Cubans and Dominicans who aren't doing their jobs properly – all of which boils his blood.

He's perpetually on the phone, whether in his car or out of it, worries constantly, and has a major texting problem behind the wheel. Many times I had to yell out 'LUIS!' to stop him running up the back of a car while he was checking Google Maps or asking Siri to dial the number of a contractor. To meet him, you would have no idea he'd been a multimillionaire hundreds of times over. He acts, looks and talks like a stand-up, normal Hispanic American, but has an endearing habit of charming cashiers when he pays a bill. After having dinner with me and Santi one night, he left the restaurant, walked two blocks to a Mexican *paleta* store, then returned with a coconut ice cream for the young girl who had served him. He retains an easy charm around women. It all betrays his past. El Senador ain't dead yet.

'I wake up at seven in the morning and meet some welder in the hot sun and get under a fucking pool deck that's 100 degrees down there, and fucking make it through a manhole to show this motherfucker where he has to clamp a piece of steel to, so that he can weld a railing on the outside. Or go to a building and have to go up seven or eight flights of stairs, because there's no elevator yet to see the conditions on the eighth floor to see where we're going to anchor a louvre.'

It might be a comedown, and honestly it probably is, but from where he's been Luis is just glad he's alive, free, has his marbles and kneecaps and is still able to walk. He's an unlikely embodiment of the American dream. Civilian life, however, still took some getting used to. As we were wrapping up work on the book Luis called me from Miami International Airport while checking in for a business flight to the Caribbean. After years of smuggling coke through airports around the United States, he'd finally been detained by Transportation Security Administration agents.

'I put my briefcase through the TSA check and everything was fine but then got to the gate and reached into the side pocket of my briefcase to get my boarding pass, felt something and it was a fucking icepick. I was going to throw it away but I figured the right thing to do was hand it in, because I'd already passed security. If I'd thrown it in the garbage somebody could have picked it up or cameras would have caught me throwing it away. The TSA chief, the assistant TSA chief, six TSA agents, Miami police and everybody came on the scene when I handed it in. Everybody and their mother took pictures of my driver's licence and my passport.'

'That's a murder weapon, sir,' said one of the cops. 'Have you ever seen the movie *Basic Instinct* with Sharon Stone?'

'I don't remember seeing it but I'm sure I'll watch it when I get back home.'

It had been a stressful situation and they eventually allowed Luis to board. But doing the right thing hadn't panned out quite as he'd expected.

'I'll soon find out if I get put on some kind of terror watchlist. In the computer I'll forever be the guy that tried to sneak an icepick past security at Miami airport, even though I voluntarily handed it in. Lesson learned. Always check your bag before you travel in case you have a murder weapon inside. In the old days if I'd found an icepick in my bag I would have just thrown it in the garbage, wiped it clean of fingerprints and walked away. So I guess I am reformed.'

Months later, a warning notice duly arrived from the Department of Homeland Security, letting Luis know he'd violated title 49, Code of Federal Regulations (CFR), section 1540.111(a) of the Transport Security Regulations. He wasn't criminally sanctioned but had been temporarily barred from going through the quick line at the airport. When Luis texted Robert Harley about it, concerned about the ramifications, he got the reply: 'You've been on a lot worse lists.' It was a slap on the wrist, even though it was the US Government that had failed to detect his banned item.

'My whole life has been a security checkpoint walking through with an icepick in my briefcase. Burning the candle at both ends until one day, *bingo*.'

The question, though, needs to be asked: Why'd you have the icepick in the first place?

'Miami welders are a rough crowd.'

Narco Nicknames

El **Azul** The Blue One
El **Búho** The Owl
El **Caballo** The Horse
El **Caracol** The Snail
El **Chapo** Shorty
El **Chino** The Chinaman
Chupeta Lollipop
El **Cochiloco** The Crazy Pig
El **Compadre** The Godparent
Cuñado Brother-in-Law
El **Diablo** The Devil
El **Enano** The Dwarf
Flaco Skinny
Gitano Gypsy
El **Gordo/El Gordito** The Fat One
    or Fatty
El **Halcón** The Hawk
El **Hombre Del Overol** The Overall
    Man
La **Madrina** The Godmother

El **Mejicano/El Mexicano**
    The Mexican
El **Metro** The Subway
La **Mica** The Monkey (The Female
    Monkey)
El **Mocho** The Amputee
El **Mono/La Mona** Blondie
El **Negro** Blackie
El **Padrino** The Godfather
Patemuro Wall Kicker
El **Patrón** The Boss
El **Poli** The Cop
El **Príncipe** The Prince
El **Rápido** The Fast One
Rasguño Scratch
El **Senador** The Senator
El **Señor de los Cielos** The Lord of
    the Skies
El **Tigre** The Tiger
El **Tío** The Uncle

Characters

Not all the people mentioned in the book are listed here but these are the main ones. Typically, Spanish surnames are double-barrelled, but not all. The father's surname (patronym) comes first, then the mother's (matronym). In the book proper, characters with Spanish surnames are generally first referenced by the patronym, eg: Pablo Escobar. Here we have listed both names where known or relevant. Aliases or nicknames, common among drug traffickers, are also used where known and some characters are only known by their aliases or nicknames. Pseudonyms are noted. – JF & LN

The capos (cartel bosses and major cartel figures)

B

Alberto Barrera aka 'Paco' Colombian. Independent transporter reputedly beheaded by the Medellín Cartel in the mid-1980s.

Griselda Blanco Restrepo aka 'La Madrina' (The Godmother) Colombian. Major trafficker for the Medellín Cartel. Arrested in 1985 in California. Sentenced to three concurrent 20-year sentences in 1986 but released in 2005. Killed in 2012.

C

José Antonio Cabrera Sarmiento aka 'Pepe' Colombian. Major trafficker for the Medellín Cartel. Arrested in 1985. Sentenced to 30 years' jail in 1986. Believed to have been released in the 1990s for his cooperation in the trial of Panamanian dictator General Manuel Noriega. Now deceased.

Rafael Caro Quintero aka 'El Príncipe' (The Prince) Mexican. Guadalajara Cartel leader. Arrested in 1985 for the murder of DEA agent Kiki Camarena, he was sentenced to 40 years' jail but released in 2013 on a legal technicality. An arrest warrant was reissued but he remains on the run in Mexico and in the top ten of the FBI's Most Wanted Fugitives.

Carlos Castaño Gil Colombian. Paramilitary leader and member of Los Pepes. Assassinated by his brother José Vicente Castaño Gil in 2004. Vicente is believed to have died in 2007.

Pablo Correa Arroyave Colombian. Major trafficker and partner of Pablo Escobar in the Medellín Cartel. Killed by Escobar in 1986.

E

Claudio Endo aka 'Mono Endo' Colombian. Major drug lord affiliated with the Cali Cartel. Killed in 1994.

Pablo Emilio Escobar Gaviria aka 'El Patrón' (The Boss) or 'El Padrino' (The Godfather) Colombian. Most notorious narco in history and boss of the Medellín Cartel. Killed in 1993.

G

Luis Fernando Galeano Berrio aka 'El Negro' (Blackie) Colombian. Major trafficker and partner of Pablo Escobar in the Medellín Cartel. Killed by Escobar in 1992.

Luis Hernando Gómez Bustamante aka 'Rasguño' (Scratch) or 'Ras' Colombian. Leader of the North Valley Cartel. He was first indicted in the Southern District of Virginia in 1997 and offered a surrender deal by the DEA at the Cartagena Hilton in December 1999. He rejected it because he refused to become an informant. Arrested in Cuba in 2004 after travelling on a fake Mexican passport, he was extradited to Colombia in 2007, then extradited to the United States in 2007. He was sentenced to 30 years' jail in 2013 for trafficking 550 tons of cocaine, among other charges. Believed to be currently imprisoned at the FDC in New York.

Gustavo Adolfo Gómez Maya Colombian. Major trafficker who worked as a transporter for different cartels. Extradited in 2001 and sentenced to nearly 14 years' jail in 2002.

Joaquín Archivaldo Guzmán Loera aka 'El Chapo' (Shorty) Mexican. Sinaloa Cartel leader who can safely claim to be the most famous narco since Pablo Escobar. After a decade of being a fugitive in Mexico, he was arrested in 2014, escaped prison in 2015, was recaptured in 2016, extradited to the United States in 2017, and sentenced to life in prison plus 30 years in 2019.

H

Arcángel de Jesús Henao Montoya aka 'El Mocho' (The Amputee) Colombian. North Valley Cartel leader and brother of Orlando Henao Montoya. Arrested in and extradited to the US from Panama in 2004, he was sentenced to nearly nine years' jail and released in 2012.

Orlando Henao Montoya aka 'El Hombre Del Overol' (The Overall Man) Colombian. Original head of the North Valley Cartel. Killed in prison in 1998.

M

Fernando Vicente Marulanda Trujillo aka 'Marulo' Colombian. Major trafficker and boss of the Pereira Cartel. Extradited to the US in 2010. Sentenced to 17 years' jail in 2013 for drug trafficking and money laundering.

Miguel Ángel Melchor Mejía Múnera aka 'Pablo Mejía' Colombian. Head of Los Mellizos Cartel with brother Víctor. Named in FBI's Most Wanted Drug

Traffickers in 2004. Captured in 2008, extradited to the United States in 2009 and sentenced to 14 years' jail in 2016.

Víctor Manuel Mejía Múnera aka 'Chespirito', 'Sebastián' or 'Pablo Arauca' Colombian. Head of Los Mellizos Cartel with brother Miguel. Named in FBI's Most Wanted Drug Traffickers in 2004. Killed by the PNC in 2008.

Gerardo Moncada Cuartas aka 'Quico' (Kiko) Colombian. Major trafficker and partner of Fernando Galeano in the Medellín Cartel. Killed by Pablo Escobar in 1992.

O

Fabio Ochoa Vásquez aka 'Fabito' Colombian. Major trafficker and one of the five main heads of the Medellín Cartel and the youngest of the Ochoa brothers. Arrested in 1999, he was extradited to the US two years later. In 2003, he was sentenced to 30 years' jail.

P

Oscar Peláez Monsalve aka 'El Poli' (The Cop) Colombian. Independent distributor aligned with the Medellín Cartel. Now deceased. Not to be confused with Colonel Oscar Peláez, former chief of the investigative branch of the PNC.

Carlos Octavio Piedrahíta Tabares Colombian. Major transporter for the Medellín Cartel. Killed in 1988.

Hernán Prada Cortés aka 'Papito' Colombian. Major trafficker for various groups including the Medellín Cartel. Arrested in Colombia in 2004, extradited to the United States in 2006 and sentenced to 28.5 years' jail in 2009.

R

Leebert Ramcharan aka 'The Indian' Indian-Jamaican. Major Caribbean drug lord. Arrested in Jamaica in 2004, extradited to the United States in 2007 and sentenced to 37 years' jail in 2008.

Luis Enrique Ramírez Murillo aka 'Miki' (Micky or Mickey) Colombian. One of the biggest Medellín Cartel figures of the 1980s and '90s, he turned against Pablo Escobar and became one of the driving forces of Los Pepes. Jailed for various offences, he is now walking free and lives in Bogotá.

Alcides Ramón Magaña aka 'El Metro' (The Subway) Mexican. Major drug lord and lieutenant of Amado Carrillo Fuentes in the Juárez Cartel. Arrested in 2001, he was caught alone in Villahermosa, Tabasco, by Mexico's Special Operations Airborne Group (GAFES), the same unit that caught Rafael Caro Quintero. He'd shed 20 kilograms and shaved off his moustache to try to slip the dragnet. Sentenced to 47 years' jail in 2007.

José Gonzalo Rodríguez Gacha aka 'El Mejicano' or 'El Mexicano' (The Mexican) Colombian. Major trafficker and one of the five main heads of the Medellín Cartel. Killed in 1989.

S

Orlando Sabogal Zuluaga aka 'El Mono' or 'Mono Sabogal' Colombian. Right-hand man for Rasguño in the North Valley Cartel. Arrested in Spain and extradited to the United States in 2006, sentenced to six years' jail in 2010. Died of colon cancer in 2020.

José Orlando Sánchez Cristancho aka 'El Hombre Del Overol' (The Overall Man) Colombian. North Valley Cartel leader and former right-hand man of the Cali Cartel's Rodríguez Orejuela brothers. Shares a nickname with Orlando Henao Montoya, but he is the 'fake' Overall Man and Henao is the 'real' one. Arrested in 2001 on money-laundering charges, he was extradited to the United States in 2001 and was jailed until 2006, whereupon he returned to Colombia. However he was re-extradited to the US in 2017, on bank fraud and money-laundering charges, making him the first Colombian drug trafficker to be extradited twice. Sentenced to eight years' jail in 2018.

Alberto Sicilia Falcón Cuban. Major drug lord and pioneer of cocaine trafficking in Mexico. Sent to jail in 1975, he escaped but was caught days later. Released from prison in 1994 and died in 2011 in Mexico City, according to his sister, Mercedes.

U

Jairo Iván Urdinola Grajales aka 'El Enano' (The Dwarf) Colombian. Major drug lord and leader of the Cali and North Valley cartels. Killed in prison in 2002.

V

Edgar Guillermo Vallejo Guarin aka 'Beto el Gitano' (Beto the Gypsy) Colombian. Major trafficker and silent partner of Hernán Prada Cortés. Arrested in Spain in 2008 and jailed in the United States. Released early and returned to Colombia where he survived an assassination attempt in August 2019.

José Vallejo Lopera aka 'El Mono' or 'Mono Lopera' Colombian. Major trafficker and partner of Fernando Marulanda of the Pereira Cartel. Killed by Pablo Escobar in the mid-1980s.

Z

Camilo Zapata aka 'El Halcón' (The Hawk) Colombian. Trafficker affiliated with the Pereira Cartel. Now has interests in cattle ranching and farms and lives in Medellín, Colombia. Pseudonym and fake nickname.

Other narcos (low- to mid-level cocaine traffickers and/or cartel figures)

B

Sonny Bowie Colombian. Transporter for Los Mellizos Cartel. Briefly jailed in Colombia and rumoured to have died of cancer.

C

Félix Antonio Chitiva Carrasquilla aka 'La Mica' (The Monkey or The Female Monkey) Colombian. Accountant for Los Mellizos and former trafficker for the Medellín Cartel. Arrested in 2001, extradited to the United States in 2002 and sentenced to 30 years' jail. Released in 2008.

D

Alex DeCubas aka 'Coco' or 'Mario' Cuban-American. Major trafficker. Arrested in Colombia in 2003. He was sentenced to 30 years' jail but was released in 2012.

Iván de la Vega Cabás Colombian. Low-level operative of Los Mellizos and based in Venezuela at the time of Operation Journey. Arrested in 2000, sentenced to just shy of 20 years' jail (reduced to 10.5 years) in FCI Loretto, Pennsylvania, and released for deportation in 2009. Now lives in Barranquilla, Colombia. Suffered a heart attack in 2019 and believed to have survived.

Lester Delgado Cabrera aka 'Pinky' Cuban. Major trafficker. Never caught. Whereabouts unknown but believed to be in Brazil.

'The Doc' American. Major trafficker. Based in Tucson, Arizona. Real name, whereabouts and fate unknown.

F

Nick Fisciatoris aka 'Nick the Fish' Greek-American. Fixer and major drug wholesaler based in Europe. Believed to have died in 2012.

Eduardo Fonseca aka 'El Compadre' (The Godparent) Mexican. Luis's *recibidor* in Reynosa, Tamaulipas, Mexico. Whereabouts and fate unknown. Pseudonym. Real nickname.

Diego Forero Cuban-American. Transporter for Luis in the 1980s. Pseudonym.

G

Bia Gálvez aka 'La Mona' Aruban. Distributor for the Medellín Cartel. Pseudonym. Real nickname but she doesn't like it.

Jorge Enrique García Molinares aka 'Cuñado' (Brother-in-Law) Colombian. High-ranking transportation chief in the Los Mellizos Cartel and superior to Iván de la Vega Cabás. Reported directly to the Mejía Múnera brothers. Escaped the Orinoco Delta with the help of indigenous people, was arrested in Spain in 2002 and became a key informant for Spanish judge Baltasar Garzón. Believed to be walking free in Europe. Whereabouts unknown.

Gordon Gray aka 'Goo' American. Bush pilot for Luis in Colombia and Mexico. Pseudonym and fake nickname.

J

Cordelio Rodolfo Vaceannie James aka 'Fresh' Colombian. San Andrés–based trafficker. Killed in 2018.

'Joel' Colombian. Right-hand man of Poli. Killed in 1980 in a cartel-related revenge assassination. Real name unknown.

K

Angelos Kanakis Greek. Chairman of Callisti Maritime. Sentenced to seven years' jail in 2000 and fined €50,000. Whereabouts and fate unknown.

L

Elias Lemos Greek. Shipping magnate, owner of Callisti Maritime. Sentenced to 18 years' jail in 2000 and fined €250,000. Lost an appeal against his sentence in 2011. Whereabouts and fate unknown.

Brian Livingston American. Cocaine dealer. Believed to have died of cancer in jail in 1992.

M

Filippos Makris Greek. Ship owner and shareholder of shipping company J. Lemos. Sentenced to seven years' jail in 2000 and fined €50,000. Whereabouts unknown.

Joseph Martino aka 'Joey' Italian-American. Mobster in the Lucchese crime family. Killed in 1988.

Javier Mercado Cuban-American. Major trafficker and partner of Bernardo Palomeque and Francisco Moya. Killed while airdropping at Dog Rocks, The Bahamas, in 1990. Pseudonym.

Francisco Moya aka 'Juanchi' Colombian. Major trafficker and partner of Bernardo Palomeque and Javier Mercado. Sentenced to seven-and-a-half years' jail in the Netherlands and the United States for cocaine trafficking and was released in 2017. Turned his hand to farming tilapia and now lives in Santa Marta, Colombia. Pseudonym and fake nickname.

N

Evangelista Navas Villabona aka 'Mario' Colombian. Enforcer/*sicario* for Poli. Died of natural causes in prison, date unknown.

Jamil Nomani aka 'Indurain' Bangladeshi-Colombian. Recruiter of shipping crews for Los Mellizos. He was married to a Colombian and lived in Colombia. Whereabouts and fate unknown.

P

Bernardo Palomeque Cuban-American. Major trafficker and partner of Francisco Moya and Javier Mercado. Never jailed, he lives in Miami. Pseudonym.

S

Adler Berriman (Barry) Seal American. Former TWA pilot and smuggler for the Medellín Cartel. Murdered by the cartel in 1986.

T

Tommy Taylor Colombian. The snitch inside Los Mellizos. Believed to be living under witness protection in the United States. Pseudonym.

'El Tío' (The Uncle) Mexican. Luis's *recibidor* in Tijuana, Baja California, Mexico. Real name, whereabouts and fate unknown.

W

'Willie' Colombian-American cocaine trafficker. Never apprehended. Whereabouts and fate unknown. Real nickname. Not to be confused with Willy Falcón.

Characters

Brian Wright aka 'The Milkman' Irish. Major trafficker and associate of Nick Fisciatoris. Arrested in Spain in 2005, he was sentenced to 30 years' jail in 2007. Released in 2020.

US and UK law-enforcement agents

B

Rick Bendekovic American. DEA agent in Colombia and former DEA country attaché to Spain. Now retired.

Nigel Brooks British-American. USCS agent in Houston, Texas. Now retired.

C

Barry Clarke Briton. HMCE (later NCA) officer. Now retired.

D

Roberto Diaz Cuban-American. Dade County Public Safety Department (later Metro-Dade Police Department) detective. Now retired. Pseudonym.

G

Vicente Garcia American of Mexican descent. USCS agent in Houston, Texas. Now retired.

H

Robert Harley American. USCS (later ICE) agent in Key West, Florida. Still on active duty.

Graham Honey Briton. HMCE officer. Now retired.

K

Eric Kolbinsky American. DEA agent in Colombia. Now retired.

L

Carol Libbey American. USCS agent in Miami. Now retired.

T

Graham Titmuss Briton. HMCE officer. Now retired.

Historical figures

B

Fulgencio Batista y Zaldívar Cuban. Former president of Cuba. Overthrown by Fidel Castro in 1959. Exiled from Cuba in 1960, he died in Marbella, Spain, in 1973.

C

Fidel Alejandro Castro Ruz Cuban. Former prime minister and president of Cuba. Died in 2016.

Hugo Chávez Venezuelan. Former president of Venezuela. Died in 2013.

G

Luis Carlos Galán Sarmiento Colombian. Former presidential candidate in Colombia. Assassinated in 1989.

César Gaviria Colombian. Former president of Colombia.

Ernesto 'Che' Guevara Argentinean. Cuban revolutionary. Executed in La Higuera, Bolivia, in 1967.

L

Meyer Lansky American. New York mobster. Died in 1983.

Julio Lobo y Olavarria Venezuelan-Cuban. Sugar magnate. Friend of Luis Navia Sr. Exiled from Cuba in 1960, he died in Madrid in 1983.

N

Richard Nixon American. Former President of the United States and neighbour of Luis Navia Sr. Died in 1994.

R

Charles 'Bebe' Rebozo Cuban-American. Richard Nixon's best friend and neighbour. Friend of Luis Navia Sr. Died in 1998.

Julius E. Rosengard American. Lawyer and gambling representative in Cuba for mobster Meyer Lansky. Friend of Luis Navia Sr. Died in 1974.

T

Santo Trafficante Jr Italian-American. Florida mobster. Died in 1987.

Luis Navia's family members, important business associates, friends or girlfriends

A

Michelle Arias Panamanian. Luis's former girlfriend in Europe and Venezuela from 1999 to 2000. Lives in Panama City. Pseudonym.

B

Sebastián Bargueño Manterola American. Second son of Patricia Manterola. Half-brother to Juliana and Santi Navia. Lives in Miami. Pseudonym.

Andrés Blanco American. Luis's nephew. Son of Laura Blanco and Vicente Blanco. Brother of Martin. Pseudonym.

Laura Blanco (née Navia) Cuban-American. Luis's sister. She divorced her late husband Vicente and now works as an executive for a major government authority. Lives in Miami. Pseudonym.

Martin Blanco American. Luis's nephew. Son of Laura Blanco and Vicente Blanco. Brother of Andrés. Pseudonym.

Vicente Blanco Colombian. Luis's brother-in-law. Died in 2017. Pseudonym.

María S. Bonavia Cuban. Luis's mother. Died in 2017.

Katie Brooklyn American. Luis's former girlfriend in early 1980s Miami. She hasn't touched a drug of any form since 1986 and now lives a quiet life running a pottery studio in Vermont. Pseudonym.

C

Reid Constable American. Luis's former corporate attorney. Lives in Sarasota, Florida. Pseudonym.

Lisa Cushing American. Luis's girlfriend when he first went down to Colombia to live permanently. Died in a plane crash in the early 1990s.

K

Gerald (Gerry) Kane American. Part-owner of Lobo-Kane with Luis. Died in 1985.

L

Mike Laburd Trinidadian-Canadian. Businessman who allegedly engineered the Lobo-Kane sugar scam. Whereabouts unknown. Pseudonym.

M

Patricia Manterola Colombian. Luis's ex-wife. Widow to defacto partner Ignacio Bargueño who died in 2013, aged 50. Now remarried. Lives in Miami. Pseudonym.

Isabelle Meneses Ecuadorian-American. Luis's girlfriend after being released from prison. They were estranged at time of completing the book. Lives in Miami. Pseudonym.

N

Juliana Navia Colombian-American. Luis's daughter. Lives in Miami. Pseudonym.

Santi Navia Mexican-American. Luis's son. Lives in Miami. Pseudonym.

Luis Navia y Cuscó Cuban. Luis's father. Died in 1982.

O

Ruben Oliva Cuban-American. Luis's defence attorney.

Acronyms

959 Group Field-enforcement group of the DEA's Special Operations Division
AB *Armada Bolivariana de Venezuela* (Bolivarian Navy of Venezuela)
AE *Armada Española* (Spanish Navy)
ACCU *Autodefensas Campesinas de Córdoba y Urabá* (Peasant Self-Defence
   Forces of Córdoba and Urabá or Peasant Self-Defenders of Córdoba and
   Urabá)
AGC *Autodefensas Gaitanistas de Colombia* (Gaitanista Self-Defence Forces
   of Colombia)
AUC *Autodefensas Unidas de Colombia* (United Self-Defence Forces of
   Colombia or United Self-Defenders of Colombia)
AWAC Airborne early warning and control system
ATF Bureau of Alcohol, Tobacco, Firearms and Explosives
BACRIM *bandas criminales* (criminal bands)
CIA Central Intelligence Agency
CFR Code of Federal Regulations
CI Confidential informant. Also called asset or confidential source (CS). In UK
   agency parlance, may be referred to as 'sensitive intelligence'; in Colombian
   drug lingo, *sapo*; pejoratively, snitch
CNN Cable News Network
CNP *Cuerpo Nacional de Policía* (National Police Corps), Spain
BANDES *Banco de Desarrollo Económico y Social* (Bank for Economic and
   Social Development), Cuba
BLOC Blue Lightning Operations Center (part of USCS)
BOP Federal Bureau of Prisons *see also* **SIS**
DC District of Columbia
DEA Drug Enforcement Administration
DHS United States Department of Homeland Security
DICI *see* **DIJIN**
DIJIN *Dirección Central de Policiá Judicial e Inteligencia* (Central Directorate
   of the Judicial Police and Intelligence), Colombia
DIPD *División de Investigación Para la Prevención de la Delincuencia*
   (Division of Investigation for the Prevention of Delinquency), Mexico.
   Sometimes referred to as *Dirección* (Directorate)

DLO drugs liaison officer (Her Majesty's Customs and Excise, UK)

DOJ United States Department of Justice

DOS United States Department of State

DUI Driving under the influence

FARC *Fuerzas Armadas Revolucionarias de Colombia – Ejército del Pueblo*
   (Revolutionary Armed Forces of Colombia – People's Army)

FBI Federal Bureau of Investigation

FCC Federal Communications Commission

FCC Federal Correctional Complex

FCI Federal Correctional Institution

FDC Federal Detention Center

FIU Florida International University

FLETC Federal Law Enforcement Training Center

FPS United States Federal Protective Service

FWS United States Fish and Wildlife Service

GCHQ Government Communications Headquarters, UK

GNB *Guardia Nacional de Venezuela* or *Guardia Nacional Bolivariana*
   (Bolivarian National Guard of Venezuela or Venezuelan National Guard)

HMCE Her Majesty's Customs and Excise, UK

HMRC *see* **HMCE**

HSI Homeland Security Investigations division of DHS

ICE United States Immigration and Customs Enforcement

INMARSAT International Maritime Satellite Organisation

INS United States Immigration and Naturalization Service

INTERPOL International Criminal Police Organisation. Also abbreviated as
   ICPO-INTERPOL

IRS Inland Revenue Service

JIATF-East Joint Interagency Task Force – East. Now absorbed into
   JIATF-South

Los Pepes A Colombian vigilante group formed by prominent narcos to
   terrorise Pablo Escobar and his associates. Stands for People Persecuted by
   Pablo Escobar. In Spanish, *Perseguidos por Pablo Escobar*

MDLEA Maritime Drug Law Enforcement Act

MIDAS Miami Investigative Drug Asset Seizure Group (part of USCS)

NCA National Crime Agency, UK (formerly **SOCA**)

NCNB North Carolina National Bank

NDDS Narcotics and Dangerous Drugs Section of the DOJ

NIS National Investigation Service (HMCE)

NOAA National Oceanic and Atmospheric Administration

OCDETF Organized Crime Drug Enforcement Task Force

OCG Organised crime group

OPR Office of Professional Responsibility of DOJ

PA Professional Association

PD Police Department

PLC *Partido Liberal Colombiano* (Colombian Liberal Party)

PNC *Policía Nacional de Colombia* (Colombian National Police)

PJF *Policía Judicial Federal* (Federal Judicial Police), Mexico
RAC Resident Agent in Charge
ROS *Raggruppamento Operativo Speciale* (Special Operations Group), Italy
SHIT Special Homicide Investigation Team (SHIT Squad)
SHU Special Housing Unit (Federal Bureau of Prisons)
SIS Special Investigative Services *see also* **BOP**
SNO Statement of No Objection
SOCA Serious Organised Crime Agency *see also* **NCA**
SOD Special Operations Division of DEA
SORT Special Operations Response Team
SOS Source of supply
SA Special Agent; also *Sociedad Anónima* (Anonymous Company), equivalent to Inc. or Ltd.
SA de CV *Sociedad Anónima Capital Variable*. Equivalent to Inc. or Ltd. in Mexico
SSA Senior Special Agent
SVA *Servicio de Vigilancia Aduanera* (Customs Surveillance Service), Spain
SWAT Special Weapons and Tactics
TAMPA *Transportes Aéreos Mercantiles Panamericanos* (Pan-American Mercantile Air Transport). Later became known as Avianca Cargo
TSA Transportation Security Administration
UM University of Miami
UN United Nations
UNODC United Nations Office on Drugs and Crime
USCG United States Coast Guard
USCS United States Customs Service
USDA United States Department of Agriculture
USDT United States Department of the Treasury
USMS United States Marshals Service
USN United States Navy
USS United States Ship
WITSEC United States Federal Witness Protection Program (Witness Security Program]
WMJX 96X FM
WHYI Y100 FM

Gazetteer

Bolívar Department of Colombia
Bogotá Capital city of Colombia
Boyacá Department of Colombia
Brickell Neighbourhood and financial district adjoining Downtown Miami
Brickell Key Man-made residential island in Brickell
Bucaramanga City in Colombia
Buenaventura Port city in Colombia

C

Caldas Department of Colombia
Cali City in Colombia
Canary Islands (Islas Canarias) Archipelago in the Atlantic Ocean off the coast of northwest Africa. Autonomous community of Spain
Cancún City in Mexico
Cape Sable Cape in the Everglades National Park. Southernmost point of the continental United States
Cape Verde Island country located off the west coast of Africa. Portuguese speaking
Caquetá Department of Colombia
Caracas Capital city of Venezuela
Cartagena City in Colombia
Cartago City in Colombia
Cauca River River in Colombia. In Spanish, *Río Cauca*
César Department of Colombia
Chetumal City in Mexico
Ciénaga Town in Colombia
Ciudad Juárez Border city in Chihuahua, Mexico. South of Texas. Base of the Juárez Cartel
Coconut Grove Neighbourhood in central Miami
Colón Free Trade Zone A free port at the entrance of the Panama Canal
Contadero *Colonia* of Mexico City
Coral Gables City in Miami-Dade County, south of Miami
Cordillera de la Costa Mountain range in Caracas
Córdoba Department of Colombia
Costa Rica Country in Central America. Spanish speaking
Costa Caribe, La (The Caribbean Coast or the Coast) Caribbean coast of northern Colombia. Shortened to *La Costa*
Curaçao Island country in the Caribbean off the coast of Venezuela. An autonomous country of the Kingdom of the Netherlands, along with the Netherlands, Aruba and Sint Maarten. Dutch and Creole speaking

D

Dade County County in Florida encompassing Miami. In 1997 it changed its name to Miami-Dade County
Dadeland Commercial district of Kendall suburb in Miami
Delta Amacuro State of Venezuela

Democratic Republic of São Tomé and Príncipe Twin-island country located off the coast of west Africa. Portuguese speaking

Dog Rocks Reef in The Bahamas

Downtown Miami The central business district of Miami

E

El Águila Town in Valle del Cauca, Colombia

El Dovio Town in Valle del Cauca, Colombia

Envigado Town outside Medellín, Colombia. Location of Pablo Escobar's *La Catedral*

Essequibo *see* **Guayana Esequiba**

Essequibo River River in Guyana. In Spanish, *Río Esequibo*

Everglades, The Region of tropical wetlands in southern Florida

Everglades National Park National park in southern Florida. Constitutes 20 per cent of the entire Everglades

F

Facatativá City in Colombia

Florida Keys Archipelago in southern Florida

Fortaleza City in northeastern Brazil

Fort Lauderdale City in Florida

Fundación Town in Colombia

G

Galicia Autonomous region of northwest Spain

Galveston City in Texas

Georgetown Neighbourhood of Washington, DC. Location of Georgetown University

Grenada Country in the Caribbean. English speaking

Grove Isle Man-made residential island in Miami

Guadalajara City in Mexico

Guantánamo Bay Location of US naval base and detention camp in Cuba. Known as 'Gitmo'

Guatemala City Capital city of Guatemala. In Spanish, *Ciudad de Guatemala*

Guayana City Port city in Venezuela. In Spanish, *Ciudad Guayana*

Guayana Esequiba Region of western Guyana claimed by Venezuela

Guayaquil Capital city of Ecuador

Guaymas City in Mexico

Guyana Country in northeast South America, formerly known as British Guiana. English speaking

H

Haiti Country in the Caribbean. French and Creole speaking

Havana Capital city of Cuba

Hialeah City in Miami-Dade County, Florida

Hollywood City in Florida, between Miami and Fort Lauderdale

Houston City in Texas
Hyannis Port Town in Massachussetts

I

Interlomas *Colonia* of Mexico City
Ironshore Suburb of Montego Bay, Jamaica

J

Jacksonville City in Florida

K

Kendall Suburb of Miami
Key Biscayne Island town in Miami
Key West Island city in the Florida Keys, Florida
Keys, The *see* **Florida Keys**

L

La Guajira Department of Colombia
Lake Harbor Town in Florida
La Peñita de Jaltemba Beach town in Mexico
Lecce City in the Apulia region, Italy
Leticia City in Colombia
Liberty City Neighbourhood in central Miami
Little Darby Island Island in The Bahamas
Little Havana Neighbourhood west of Downtown Miami
Los Olivos *Barrio* of Medellín. Location of Pablo Escobar's death
Los Rosales Upmarket *barrio* of Bogotá

M

McAllen Border city in Texas. North of Tamaulipas
Magdalena Department of Colombia
Magdalena Medio Antioquia A sub-region of the department of Antioquia in Colombia
Maicao Town in Colombia near the border with Venezuela
Maiquetía Port city in Venezuela. Location of Simón Bolívar International Airport, servicing Caracas
Manaus City on the Amazon River in Brazil
Maracaibo City in Venezuela. Location of Luis's arrest
Marathon City in Florida
Mariel Port town west of Havana
Mariusa National Park National park in Venezuela's Orinoco Delta. In Spanish, *Parque Nacional Mariusa*. Also *Parque Nacional Delta del Orinoco*
Mashta Island Neighbourhood in Key Biscayne
Medellín City in Colombia
Melbourne City in Florida
Mérida Capital city of Yucatán in Mexico

Mexico City Capital city of Mexico. In Spanish, *Ciudad de México*
Miami Beach Oceanside neighbourhood in central Miami
Miami-Dade County *see* **Dade County**
Miami River River that runs through Downtown Miami
Michoacán State in Mexico
Montego Bay City in Jamaica
Montería City in Colombia
Monterrey City in Mexico
Moore Haven City in Florida

N

Naples City in Florida
New Orleans City in Louisiana
Norte de Santander Department of Colombia
Northern Cyprus *see* **Turkish Republic of Northern Cyprus**

O

Okeechobee City in Florida
Orinoco Delta A large, flat region of tributaries at the mouth of the Orinoco
River
Orinoco River River in Colombia and Venezuela. In Spanish, *Río Orinoco*
Orlando City in Florida

P

Palomino Town in Colombia
Panama Country in Central America. Spanish speaking
Panama City Capital city of Panama. Not to be confused with Panama City,
Florida
Pereira City in Colombia
Piraeus Port city in Greece
Playa del Carmen Resort town in Mexico
Polanco Upmarket neighbourhood of Mexico City
Pompano Beach City north of Fort Lauderdale
Port of Rotterdam Port in the Netherlands and the largest in Europe
Puerto Ordaz Town in Venezuela, part of Guayana City
Puerto Rico Island territory of the United States, located in the Caribbean
Puerto Vallarta Resort town in Mexico
Punta Paitilla Neighbourhood of Panama City
Punta Sam Residential community in Cancún

Q

Quantico Town in Virginia. Location of the headquarters of the FBI Academy
Quintana Roo State in Mexico

R

Raleigh City in North Carolina

Represa del Sisga Dam northeast of Bogotá
Reynosa Border city in Tamaulipas, Mexico. South of Texas
Risaralda Department in Colombia

S

Sahuayo City in Mexico
St. Petersburg City in Florida
San Andrés (Isla de San Andrés) Island off the coast of Nicaragua. Part of the
    Colombian department of Archipelago of San Andrés, Providencia and
    Santa Catalina
San Nicolas City in Aruba
Santa Fe *Colonia* of Mexico City
Santander Department of Colombia
Santa Marta City in Colombia
Santo Domingo Capital city of Dominican Republic
Sierra Nevada de Santa Marta Mountain range in northeastern Colombia
Sierra Parima Mountain range in northern Brazil and southern Venezuela
Sierra de Perijá Mountain range in northern Colombia and western Venezuela
Sinaloa State in Mexico
South Beach Oceanside neighbourhood in central Miami, just south of Miami
    Beach
Star Island Man-made residential island in Miami
Sucre Department of Colombia
Suriname Country in northeastern South America, formerly known as
    Surinam. Dutch speaking
Tabasco State in Mexico

T

Tallahassee City in Florida
Tamaulipas State in Mexico
Tampa City in Florida
Tecamachalco *Colonia* in Mexico City. Shortened from Lomas
    de Tecamachalco
Tijuana Border city in Baja California, Mexico. South of California
Tolú Resort town in Colombia
Trinidad and Tobago Twin-island country in the Caribbean, close to
    Venezuela. English speaking
Tucupita City in Delta Amacuro in Venezuela's Orinoco Delta
Turkish Republic of Northern Cyprus An internationally unrecognised state in
    Europe and considered part of the Republic of Cyprus. Recognised only by
    Turkey
Turnberry Isle A residential resort in North Miami. Now the JW Marriott
    Turnberry Resort & Spa

U

Upata City in Venezuela
Urabá A sub-region of the department of Antioquia in Colombia

US Virgin Islands Island archipelago territory of the United States, located in the Caribbean. Officially named Virgin Islands of the United States. The main islands are Saint Croix, Saint John and Saint Thomas. Previously known as the Danish West Indies

V

Valencia City in Venezuela
Valle del Cauca Department of Colombia
Valledupar City in Colombia
Vedado Upmarket neighbourhood in Havana
Venetian Islands Chain of six man-made residential islands in Miami
Vouliagmeni Upmarket seaside suburb of Athens, Greece

Z

Zulia State in Venezuela

Operation Journey: By the Numbers

Vessels captured
Name: M/V *Cannes*
Flag: Panama
Seized: 14 January 1999, off
    Jamaica
Cocaine haul: 3803 kilos

Name: M/V *China Breeze*
Flag: Panama
Seized: 27 May 1999, off
    Puerto Rico
Cocaine haul: 3880 kilos

Name: M/V *Castor*
Flag: Panama
Seized: 31 May 1999, off Venezuela
Cocaine haul: 4000 kilos

Name: M/V *Pearl II*
Flag: Panama
Seized: 23 December 1999, in
    Amsterdam
Cocaine haul: 2006 kilos

Name: M/V *Suerte I*
Flag: Malta
Seized: 17 August 2000, off Grenada
Cocaine haul on ship: none
Cocaine haul on land in Venezuela:
    8800 kilos

Name: M/V *Privilege*
Flag: São Tomé and Príncipe
Seized: 31 August 2000, off Canary
    Islands (Spain)
Cocaine haul: none
Total official cocaine seizure:
    22,489 kilos (24.78 US tons)

Arrests by vessel
China Breeze: 5 (United States)
Pearl II: 14 (The Netherlands)
Suerte I: 13 (Venezuela), 2 (Italy),
    1 (France), 8 (Greece)
Total arrests: 43

Nations involved
Albania
Belgium
Colombia
France
Greece
Italy
The Netherlands
Panama
Spain
United Kingdom
United States
Venezuela

Glossary

A

Acuatizar To ditch or land a plane on water
Aeropuertos clandestinos Clandestine airports or illegal runways
Anillo de seguridad Security ring
Arepa A kind of flatbread made of corn flour, water and salt. Popular in
    Colombia and Venezuela
Asset Confidential informant or source, often handsomely paid
Assistant US Attorney Federal prosecutor representing the US Attorney
Avenida Avenue

B

Bahía Bay
Bandido Bandit or outlaw
Barrio Neighbourhood (Colombia). *See also* **Colonia**
Base *see* **Freebase**
Based out Stoned on base
Basuco A variant of base
Bisturí Scalpel
Blanco White
Bloque Bloc or unit
Blow Cocaine
Broker Law-enforcement slang for go-between or middleman in a cocaine deal
Bump Snort drugs, usually cocaine. *See also* **Toot**
Burnt out or **burnt** Past its usefulness; fucked; 'this guy's burnt'
Bush pilot Pilot of small planes who is skilled in landing on illegal runways or
    airports in remote areas

C

Calle Street
Cajitas azules Blue boxes. Refers to cocaine packages owned by the Medellín
    Cartel, Colombia

441

Caleta A residence used for storing cocaine. Alternately used as a term for a secret compartment in a room that is designed to facilitate a quick escape. *See also* **Stash house**

Caletero Minder of a stash house. *See also Caleta* and **Stash house**

Camiseta Literally, shirt. Cuban slang for 'wife beater' singlet

Campesino Peasant

Capo Drug lord

Carabinieri Military police (Italy)

Carriel A kind of 'man bag' used in Antioquia, Colombia. Worn on the side with a shoulder strap, buckle and closed cover

Caterpillar Brand of marine diesel engine

Cell phone Mobile phone

Cigarette or **cigarette boat** *see* **Go-fast boat**

Ciudad City

Clean No drugs on board

Cocaine cowboys Catch-all term used to describe drug traffickers of the late 1970s/early '80s period in Miami when drug-related violence between Cubans and Colombians and among Colombians themselves was at its peak. Also used as the title of a well-known documentary on the subject

Colonia Neighbourhood (Mexico). *See also Barrio*

Comandante Commander (paramilitary)

Compadre Godfather, godparent, co-father

Consigliere Italian mafia term for advisor or right-hand man

Contador Accountant

Contrabandista Smuggler

Coronado Literally 'crowned' but in drug-trafficking parlance means to get cocaine to its destination and get paid

Crack Cocaine mixed with water and baking soda or ammonia and heated until a mass forms that hardens when dried. Commonly smoked

Croqueta Croquette

Cubanaso Low-class Cuban

Cubano Cuban

Cube Prison unit or cell

Cut Adulterate pure cocaine with an additive to increase profitability

Cuida carga On-board controller or guard of cocaine load

D

Debriefing Post-mortem of actions or decisions made during a particular law-enforcement event or operation. Can also refer to a verbal or written record of a cooperating witness or defendant

Delegación Borough (Mexico)

Department Political subdivision in Colombia, of which there are 32

District Attorney Chief prosecutor at state or county level

Dope Can be used to refer to any kind of drugs including cocaine but commonly marijuana

Doper Another word for *Narco*

E

Eduardoño A Colombian boat ideal for smuggling. *See also* **Open fisherman** and *Panga*

Eight ball Eighth of an ounce or 3.5 grams of cocaine

Enhancement An increase in punishment in a criminal penalty

Escolta Escort or bodyguard. *See also* *Guardaespalda*

F

Fastboat see **Go-fast boat**

Feds US federal agents

Federales A 'Spanglish' word for Mexican federal police or other federal agencies

Finca Ranch or farm

5k1 or **5k motion** Refers to section 5k1.1 of the *United States Federal Sentencing Guidelines*, which allows for a reduction in a custodial sentence for cooperation prior to sentencing

Flipped Became an informant

Freebase Similar to crack but purer and more dangerous to make. Cocaine typically mixed with water, ammonia and ether

G

Gitano Gypsy

Go-fast boat A narrow, multi-engine-powered, V-shaped boat designed for fast speeds on open water. *See also* **Fastboat**

Gordito see Gordo

Gordo Fat

Grand jury A body under the US federal legal system that must approve an indictment before it is initiated against a person

Green light Permission to move drugs through an area on payment of a commission

Gringo Foreigner or American

Guardaespalda Bodyguard. *See also Escolta*

Guero Fair-haired, white or blonde in Mexican Spanish

H

Heat Police or DEA attention

Hot In danger or peril

Hotter than a pistol Under surveillance

I

Indictment A formal charging document in the US federal legal system that requires grand-jury approval before being initiated against a person. It essentially means there is enough evidence to proceed to trial

Indian Indigenous South American

Information A formal charging document in the US federal legal system that does not require grand-jury approval but will go to a magistrate or other judicial officer before being initiated against a person

J

Jai alai Pronounced 'hi lie'. An indoor sport of Basque origin popular in Miami in the 1970s and 1980s

K

Key Kilogram (kilo) of cocaine; also a reef or low island, as in Key Biscayne or Brickell Key (synonymous with cay or *cayo* in Spanish)

Key Rat Person who grew up in Key Biscayne

Kicker Passenger whose job is to throw cocaine out of a plane over a designated airdrop spot

Kitchen Cocaine processing facility or coca-paste refinery

L

La Catedral Pablo Escobar's tailor-made prison in Envigado, 'The Cathedral'

Lam *see* **On the lam**

Lavador Money launderer

Level 43 The maximum offence level of the *United States Federal Sentencing Guidelines*

Load Consignment of cocaine for delivery by boat or plane

Loco Crazy

M

Macho Masculine

Mafia An organised crime group with strict hierarchy and codes

Mariachis Group of musicians playing mariachi music from Mexico

Marielitos Immigrants from Mariel, Cuba, in the Mariel Boatlift. Also referred to as 'Mariel Cubans'

Marimberos Marijuana smugglers. Typically refers to smugglers from northern Colombia (La Guajira, Barranquilla, Santa Marta) but can also refer to Cuban smugglers in Miami

Mellizos Twins

Merchandise Cocaine

Mestizo Mixed race

Miranda rights (Miranda warning) Verbal notification by law enforcement of one's legal rights, such as the right to remain silent

Mothership Main vessel in maritime smuggling operation

Mona Blonde or fair-haired (feminine, Colombia)

Mono Blond or fair-haired (masculine, Colombia)

Mule A low-level cocaine courier

N

Narc DEA agent or any counternarcotics law-enforcement official. Not to be confused with *Narco* or *Narcotraficante*

Narco or *Narcotraficante* Drug trafficker. *See also* **Doper**

Narcotráfico Drug traffic

Negro Black

Glossary

O

Oficina Office. In drug-trafficking lingo, it refers to the central office, day-to-day operational headquarters, or enforcement and collection arm of a cartel. Most commonly they act as SOS (source of supply) for transporters

On the lam American slang for flight from justice or arrest

Open fisherman Another name for a centre-console fishing boat with an open-deck layout. *See also* **Eduardoño** and ***Panga***

P

Padrino Godfather

Paella A slow-cooked rice dish of Spanish origin commonly made with meat, beans, seafood and vegetables

Paisa A native of the northwest of Colombia (Antioquia and other departments)

Paleta A kind of Mexican ice cream on a stick, like a popsicle

Panga Outboard-powered fishing boat. *See also* **Open fisherman** and ***Eduardoño***

Paras Paramilitaries

Patrón Boss

Pinga Cuban slang for 'dick'

Pista de ciclismo Cycling track

Playa Beach

Plaza Exclusive smuggling zone or territory

Popped Killed

Pot Marijuana

Puta Bitch or whore

Q

Queso Cheese

R

Recibidor Receiver of merchandise

Repartidor Distributor for wholesaler of merchandise

Represa Dam

Represalias Retaliation

Rola The feminine for a native of Bogotá (masculine, ***Rolo***)

Routes Tried-and-tested aerial or nautical pathways for drug smuggling

Rule 35 Refers to Rule 35(b) of the *Federal Rules of Criminal Procedure* under which a jail sentence can be slashed 'if the defendant, after sentencing, provided substantial assistance in investigating or prosecuting another person'

S

Sagrado Sacred or holy

Sapo Literally frog or toad. Snitch or informant

Secuestradores Kidnappers

Screwy Not right

Sicario Hitman
Snitch Informant
Spook Spy
Stash house A residence used for storing cocaine. *See also* ***Caleta***
Suerte Luck

T

Takedown Final stage of operation
Taken off An unsuccessful load that has to be paid for. As in 'taken off' expected profit
Team America DEA slang for source or informant (as in 'he joined Team America')
Thai stick Cannabis plant (leaves, buds) twisted into a compact, cigar-like cylinder for smoking
Third-party cooperation Euphemism for an informant privately hired by an inmate to help get a reduction in sentence. *See also* **Rule 35**
Toot Snort drugs, usually cocaine. *See also* **Bump**
Toro Bull
Trip *see* **Load**

U

Unit see **Key**
US Attorney Chief federal prosecutor

V

Vengarse Revenge

W

Weight Large amount of cocaine
Whacked Killed
Wiseguy Mobster or member of the mafia
Working DEA slang for building a case against someone or an organisation

Criminal Organisations

The following are drug cartels and mafia groups Luis worked for, was connected to or supplied directly or indirectly between 1978 and 2000. Names of individuals mentioned were active during this period. – JF & LN

Colombia
Medellín Cartel (*El Cártel de Medellín*)
Leadership: Pablo Escobar, Ochoa family, José Gonzalo Rodríguez Gacha
Notable figures: Carlos Enrique Lehder Rivas, Luis Fernando Galeano Berrio, Gerardo Moncada Cuartas, José Rafael Abello Silva, José Antonio Cabrera Sarmiento, Pablo Correa Arroyave, Diego Murillo Bejarano

Cali Cartel (*El Cártel de Cali*)
Leadership: Rodríguez Orejuela brothers, José Santacruz Londoño, Francisco Hélmer Herrera Buitrago
Notable figures: Victor Patiño Fomeque, Juan Carlos Ramírez Abadía, Claudio Endo

North Valley Cartel (*El Cártel del Norte del Valle*)
Leadership: Orlando Henao Montoya, Luis Hernando Gómez Bustamante, Diego León Montoya Sánchez, Wilber Alirio Varela Fajardo
Notable figures: Juan Carlos Ramírez Abadía, Jairo Iván Urdinola Grajales, Carlos Alberto Rentería Mantilla, Arcángel de Jesús Henao Montoya

North Coast Cartel or Coast Cartel (*El Cártel de la Costa/El Cártel de la Costa Atlántica*)
Leadership: Dávila family (Santa Marta), Nasser family (Barranquilla), José Rafael Abello Silva (Santa Marta), Alberto Orlández Gamboa (Barranquilla)

Pereira Cartel (*El Cártel de Pereira*)
Leadership: Fernando Marulanda, José Vallejo Lopera, Carlos Arturo Patiño Restrepo

The Twins Cartel (*El Cártel de Los Mellizos*)
Leadership: Mejía Múnera brothers

Mexico
Juárez Cartel (*El Cártel de Juárez*)
Leadership: Amado Carrillo Fuentes

Gulf Cartel (*El Cártel del Golfo*)
Leadership: Juan García Abrego, Osiel Cárdenas Guillén

Tijuana Cartel (*El Cártel de Tijuana)*
Leadership: Arrellano Félix family

Guadalajara Cartel (*El Cártel de Guadalajara*)
Leadership: Rafael Caro Quintero, Miguel Ángel Félix Gallardo, Ernesto
    Fonseca Carrillo

United States
Lucchese crime family in Florida (La Cosa Nostra or Sicilian mafia)

Italy
'Ndrangheta or Calabrian mafia

Jamaica
Leebert Ramcharan organisation

Albania
Durda brothers organisation

United Kingdom
Brian Wright organisation

Spain
José Ramón Prado Bugallo aka 'Sito Miñanco' organisation

Acknowledgements

Jesse Fink

Thank you first and foremost to the law-enforcement agents involved in Operation Journey, Luis Navia's capture in Venezuela, and the ongoing fight against international cocaine trafficking who agreed to be interviewed for *Pure Narco*. This book could not have been written without the benefit of their collective experience in the frontline of the war on drugs.

My thanks to active ICE agent Robert Harley; retired USCS agents Carol Libbey, Vicente Garcia and Nigel Brooks; retired HMCE agents Barry Clarke, Graham Honey and Graham Titmuss; retired Metro-Dade Police Department detective Roberto Diaz; and retired DEA agents Eric Kolbinsky and Rick Bendekovic.

Eric, especially, was incredibly generous to both Luis and me during our time together in Miami and St. Petersburg, Florida, read a rough early draft and kindly agreed to write the foreword. You're a legend, 'Kapinsky'.

Roberto vetted the chapters on Poli and the cocaine cowboys era while Vicente, Nigel, the two Grahams and Barry took the time to carefully check the chapters on Operation Journey for accuracy, for which I'm hugely appreciative. Nigel also went beyond the call of duty, not only in reading a full draft but supplying images and background information on Operation Journey, including redacted intelligence documents, redacted emails from Tommy Taylor, and his own written summary of the takedown. I can't thank you enough, Nigel.

Thanks to Luis's family – Patricia Manterola, Santi Navia, Juliana Navia, Sebastián Bargueño Manterola, Laura Blanco and Andrés Blanco – for answering my phone calls as well as your kindness, hospitality and generosity during my stay in Miami.

My thanks also to Katie Brooklyn, Bia Gálvez, Richard Booth, Brian Dennard, Mercedes Sicilia Falcón, Gary Noesner, Peter Walsh, and all our pseudonymous and anonymous sources in and out of the cocaine trade.

It would be remiss of me not to mention our stellar support team at Penguin Random House Australia: Alison Urquhart, Patrick Mangan, Justin Ractliffe, Alex Ross, Bonny Maddah, Benjamin Fairclough, Louise Ryan, Emily Hindle, Lucy Ballantyne, Alice Richardson and Nerrilee Weir. It was Ali who originally commissioned *Pure Narco*. This is our third outing together and she has been the single biggest champion of my writing career. I look forward to us publishing more books.

In the UK, thanks to Kelly Ellis and Ciara Lloyd at John Blake Publishing. In the US, thanks to mapmaker Alicia Freile at Tango Media.

Lastly, a note of gratitude to Luis. His is a complex, confronting and oftentimes unsympathetic story but I believe he is a good man at heart, despite his character flaws and myriad mistakes. We're all imperfect. It takes a true *bandido* to own up to it publicly. I tip my hat to you, my friend.

Luis Navia

Patricia, you have been a blessing in my life from day one and raised three of the most incredible kids: Juliana, Santi and Sebastián. I love the four of you.

Laura, you are the most amazing sister a brother could wish for and I am blessed to have Andrés and Martin as my nephews.

CL, thank you from the bottom of my heart for the wonderful gift you gave me that came at the right moment; 2005 was a great year! V for victory and love!

Luis Emilio González Chávez, thank you for your loyalty and friendship over the years.

Ruben Oliva, thank you for your total support and guidance during the most important negotiation of my life.

And to Jesse Fink, thank you for piecing together this 25-year (make that 45-year) rollercoaster ride.

Bibliography

Articles (Print and Online)
Longer pieces from *The Washington Post* and *Omni Magazine* were especially useful in reconstructing the Amtrak siege in Chapter 6. – JF & LN

'A 14 años de cárcel fue condenado alias El Mellizo en Estados Unidos',
    no byline, *W Radio Colombia*, Bogotá (Colombia), 7 January 2016
'The afterlife of Pablo Escobar', Jon Lee Anderson, *The New Yorker*, New
    York, 26 February 2018
'Alleged drug baron held in Florida', Lenny Savino and Wanda J. DeMarzo,
    The Miami Herald, Miami, 27 August 2000
'A poco más de 20 años, aún queda la duda sobre la muerte de Amado Carrillo,
    el "Señor de los Cielos", líder del Cártel de Juárez', no byline, *Vanguardia*,
    Saltillo (Mexico), 4 September 2018
'Arbitron to reissue Miami survey in wake of 96X diary tampering', Marc
    Kirkeby, *Record World*, Vol. 35, No. 1626, New York, 2 September 1978
'Art market: painting withdrawn from sale after artist declares it a fake', Dalya
    Alberge, *The Independent*, London, 19 May 1993
'Asesinado Juan Manuel Gaviria Vásquez, testigo "estrella" de E.U. contra clan
    de Los Mellizos', no byline, *El Tiempo*, Bogotá (Colombia), 28 July 2009
'Así destrozó la vida y la honra a muchos inocentes el prevaricador Garzón',
    no byline, intereconomia.com, Madrid, 19 February 2012
'The avalanche of cocaine hitting Europe', no byline, *Spiegel Online*, Hamburg
    (Germany), 9 November 2019
'The avenger: in Colombia, a father has taken on a drug baron with a vicious
    reputation to get justice for the brutal killing of his son – and so far dad
    is winning', Douglas Farah, *The Washington Post*, Washington, DC,
    26 March 1996
'BACRIM in Venezuela', no byline, insightcrime.org, Washington, DC, 7 April
    2015
'Baltasar G. tras Castaño', no byline, *El Tiempo*, Bogotá (Colombia),
    6 February 2004
'Bartell to tighten control', Ray Herbeck Jr, *Billboard*, New York, 18 February
    1978

'The bell tolls for him', Sean Rowe, *Miami New Times*, Miami, 31 July 1997

'Big smuggler of cocaine is arrested, Mexico says', Tim Weiner, *The New York Times*, New York, 14 June 2001

'Billions of dollars of cocaine are smuggled into the US by sea every year, and the Coast Guard says it can only stop one-quarter of it', Christopher Woody, *Business Insider Australia*, Sydney (Australia), 20 November 2018

'Bizarre plea fails to cut prison term', no byline, *The South Florida Sun-Sentinel*, Deerfield Beach (FL), 16 Jan 2002

'Brazil's cocaine trade leaves widespread violence in its wake', Anabel Hernández, *Deutsche Welle*, Bonn (Germany), 27 August 2019

'Capturan en Tabasco al *capo* Alcides Ramón Magaña', Jesús Aranda, *La Jornada*, Mexico City (Mexico), 14 June 2001

'Capturan hombre de confianza de "Los Mellizos"', no byline, *El País*, Cali (Colombia), 3 January 2005

'Car bombs in Colombia kill 25, injure 150', Douglas Farah, *The Washington Post*, Washington, DC, 13 May 1990

'Charles "Bebe" Rebozo, 85, dies', Richard Pearson, *The Washington Post*, Washington, DC, 10 May 1998

'Clear and present danger', Simon Carr, *The Independent*, London, 25 November 1998

'Coast Guard seizes record amount of cocaine', Associated Press, *The Arizona Daily Sun*, Flagstaff (AZ), 13 May 2001

'"Cocaine cowboy" deported to Dominican Republic after his bid to stay in US fails', Jay Weaver, *The Miami Herald*, Miami, 19 November 2018

'Cocaine cowboys', Jack Anderson, *The Washington Post*, Washington, DC, 22 June 1980

'Cocaine in Germany: the "South American tsunami"', Volkmar Kabisch, Jan Lukas Strozyk and Benedikt Strunz, dw.com, Bonn (Germany), 28 December 2018

'A cocaine story', Alfred Peza, *AIM*, Tirana (Albania), 15 March 2001

'Cocaine surge to Europe fuelled by new gangs, violence: report', Axel Bugge, reuters.com, London, 14 December 2018

'The cocaine wars', Carl Hiaasen, *Rolling Stone*, New York, 20 September 1979

'Colombia arrests 10,000 after slaying', Associated Press, *The New York Times*, New York, 21 August 1989

'Colombia capo may be first ever extradited to United States, twice', Victoria Dittmar, insightcrime.org, Washington, DC, 7 March 2018

'Colombia captures head of drug traffickers', Xinhua News Agency, Woodside (NY), 1 March 2006

'Colombia commemorates 30 years without Luis Carlos Galán as questions remain', Adriaan Alsema, *Colombia Reports*, Medellín (Colombia), 18 August 2019

'Colombian criminal arrest reminder of dissolved cartel's influence', Leonardo Goi, insightcrime.org, Washington, DC, 28 March 2017

'Colombian drug smuggler gets 30 years in prison', United Press International, *The Orlando Sentinel*, Orlando (FL), 8 October 1986

'Colombia elites and organised crime: "Don Berna"', Jeremy McDermott, insightcrime.org, Washington, DC, 9 August 2016

'Colombia-led multinational operation seizes 94.2 tonnes of cocaine in 105-day period', Helen Murphy and Luis Jaime Acosta (Peter Cooney, editor), reuters.com, London, 30 April 2019

'Colombian police capture reputed drug lord', Reuters, *The Christian Science Monitor*, Boston (MA), 29 April 1992

'Colombian police seize $35 million/US-raided raid finds bags of cash in walls of two Bogotá apartments', John Otis, *The Houston Chronicle*, Houston (TX), 26 August 2001

'Colombian, 31, gets life in Amtrak siege case', United Press International, *The New York Times*, New York, 29 February 1984

'Colombia's drug trade', no byline, *Colombia Reports*, Medellín (Colombia), 26 June 2019

'Columbia [sic] drug lords vie for cocaine trade control', Bernd Debusmann, *The Globe and Mail*, Toronto (Canada), 2 August 1988

'Convicted cocaine smuggler posed with Mrs. Clinton, Gore', Terry Frieden, CNN, Atlanta (GA), 23 October 1996

'Cops puzzled over drug submarine', Andrew Selsky (Associated Press), *The Washington Post*, Washington, DC, 30 September 2000

'Corruption in Venezuela has created a cocaine superhighway to the US', Nick Paton Walsh, Natalie Gallón and Diana Castrillon, CNN, Atlanta (GA), 17 April 2019

'Court sentences Jamaican drug boss to 37 years', no byline, reuters.com, London, 24 May 2008

'Cuban sugar-wolf', Drew Pearson, *The Panama American*, Panama City (Panama), 23 April 1956

'Customs: more cocaine seized on ship in Philadelphia than estimated', Associated Press, WITF, Harrisburg (PA), 27 June 2019

'DEA feels better about Venezuela after raid succeeds – the 16 arrests and seizure of 10 tons of cocaine eased fears that the country would not co-operate with US agents', Associated Press, *The Orlando Sentinel*, Orlando (FL), 26 August 2000

'Decomisan en Venezuela más de cinco toneladas de cocaína', Reuters, *El Mundo*, Madrid, 21 August 2000

'Desperado at twilight – book chronicles life of Lauderdale's Jon Roberts', Chauncey Mabe, *The South Florida Sun-Sentinel*, Deerfield Beach (FL), 1 January 2012

'Drug arrest removes big shipper, agents say', Lenny Savino, Knight Ridder Tribune News Service, *Sunday Star-News*, Wilmington (NC), 27 August 2000

'Drug barons like Howard Marks always claim to be Mr Nice. Don't fall for it', Tom Wainwright, *The Guardian*, London, 13 April 2016

'Drugs bust hits 32 countries in one swoop, Customs and intelligence forces unite to arrest thousands in Caribbean', Christina Lamb and Jeremy McDermott, *The Sunday Telegraph*, London, 26 November 2000

'El desayuno está a bordo', Jorge A. Rodríguez, *El País*, Cali (Colombia), 12 September 2000

'El lujoso apartamento que enfrenta a dos narcos', no byline, *El Tiempo*, Bogotá (Colombia), 28 June 2015

'El ocaso de un oscuro personaje: Arturo Durazo, el implacable', Carlos Álvarez, *La Prensa*, Mexico City (Mexico), 30 November 2018

'Escobar: 17 años de historia del criminal', no byline, *El Tiempo*, Bogotá (Colombia), 2 December 1993

'Esta es la confesión que Rasguño hará en E.U. [US]', no byline, *El Tiempo*, Bogotá (Colombia), 22 March 2007

'Eureka jury names drug "kingpin"', no byline, *San Francisco Examiner*, San Francisco (CA), 2 April 1986

'Ex contador de "Los Mellizos" dice que en Ralito delinquían sin control alguno', Asdrubal Guerra, *W Radio Colombia*, Bogotá (Colombia), 16 June 2008

'Fact and fiction in the war on drugs', Prospero, *The Economist*, London, 1 September 2016

'Family fights in court over Cuban sugar mills', José de Cordoba, *The Wall Street Journal*, New York, 4 April 1999

'$5,000 found in train compartment', no byline, *The Washington Post*, Washington, DC, 13 October 1982

'Former KXGO owner indicted in Humboldt cocaine-ring case', Peter Sibley, *Times-Standard*, Eureka (CA), 2 April 1986

'4-year fight in Florida "just can't stop drugs"', Joel Brinkley, *The New York Times*, New York, 4 September 1986

'Gang boss linked to Colombian drug lords: US documents tie Quebec Hells Angels leader to cocaine traffickers', George Kalogerakis, *The Vancouver Sun*, Vancouver (Canada), 3 May 2002

'Gjykata spanjolle: "Kolumbiani, ortaku dhe furnitori i Frederik Durdës', Habjon Hasani, arkivalajmeve.com, Tirana (Albania), 1 May 2008

'Glades co-op directors are re-elected', no byline, *The Clewiston News*, Clewiston (FL), 17 December 1964

'Godfather for hire', Yudhijit Bhattacharjee, *The New Yorker*, New York, 30 July 2018

'Granja venezolana escondía operación masiva de contrabando de cocaína', Associated Press, *Critica*, Panama City (Panama), 28 August 2000

'Guilty plea in sugar fraud case', United Press International, *The Town Talk*, Alexandria (LA), 2 August 1985

'Guilty: The Milkman – international cocaine smuggler who always delivered', Ian Cobain, *The Guardian*, London, 3 April 2007

'"Head of the snake" cut off: global drug boss arrested', Knight Ridder Newspapers, *Deseret News*, Salt Lake City (UT), 27 August 2000

'Historia de "narcoficción"', Jorge A. Rodríguez, *El País*, Madrid, 25 September 2000

'Home-grown coca plagues Colombia: toxic cocaine byproduct spreads addiction to young', Michael Isikoff, *The Washington Post*, Washington, DC, 9 January 1989

'Honduras elites and organised crime: Juan Ramón Matta Ballesteros', Steven Dudley, insightcrime.org, Washington, DC, 9 April 2016

'How dealing cocaine in Colombia led to mortgage fraud in Aventura', David J. Neal, *The Miami Herald*, Miami, 1 October 2018

'How drug lords make billions smuggling gold to Miami for your jewelry and phones', Jay Weaver, Nicholas Nehamas and Kyra Gurney, *The Miami Herald*, Miami, 16 January 2018

'Imprisoned drug trafficker's dad, son plead guilty', Ann W. O'Neill, *The South Florida Sun-Sentinel*, Deerfield Beach (FL), 6 June 2003

'An incursion into Venezuela, straight out of Hollywood', Julie Turkewitz and Frances Robles, *The New York Times*, New York, 7 May 2020

'Indictments charge sugar-export scam', Associated Press, *The Orlando Sentinel*, Orlando (FL), 22 June 1985

'In brief', no byline, *Broadcasting Magazine*, New York, 2 August 1976

'Interpol's Mexican chief kills two, commits suicide', UPI Archives, United Press International, Washington, DC, 18 September 1988

'Interview: Jorge Ochoa' (transcript from 'Drug Wars' series), *Frontline*, pbs.org, Medellín (Colombia), 2000

'Interview: Juan David Ochoa' (transcript from 'Drug Wars' series), *Frontline*, pbs.org, Medellín (Colombia), 2000

'Is this the new Medellín Cartel?', Adriaan Alsema, *Colombia Reports*, Medellín (Colombia), 5 June 2019

'Italy: international drugs bust highlights Albania's role' (original source: Agenzia Nazionale Stampa Associata, Rome, in Italian), *BBC Monitoring European*, London, 10 February 2001

'José "El Mono" Abello regresó a Santa Marta y ya fue objeto de un atentado que presagia otra guerra', no byline, *El Tiempo*, Bogotá (Colombia), 3 September 2008

'Julio Lobo: el millonario a quien el Che le propuso dirigir la industria azucarera en Cuba', no byline, cibercuba.com, Havana (Cuba), 11 November 2018

'Jury finds Noriega guilty on 8 of 10 counts, Noriega guilty on 8 counts', Richard Cole/Associated Press, *The Morning Call*, Allentown (PA), 10 April 1992

'Jury sentences convicted Navas to life in prison', United Press International, *Technician*, Raleigh (NC), 29 February 1984

'La generación de la mafia', no byline, *El Tiempo*, Bogotá (Colombia), 9 September 2001

'La policía abandonará esta semana el registro del "Privilege" si no halla droga', Jorge A. Rodríguez, *El País*, Madrid, 12 September 2000

'Las gambetas de "Micky"', no byline, *El Espectador*, Bogotá (Colombia), 18 October 2008

'La tumba vacía de Sahagún Baca, primo de Martha, y los cárteles de Michoacán', Francisco Javier Larios Gaxiola, elregio.com, Monterrey (Mexico), 15 July 2018

'Long day's journey into fright', Ronald K. Siegel, *Omni Magazine*, Vol. 11, No. 3, New York, December 1988

'Los carteles de la coca', no byline, *Semana*, Bogotá (Colombia), 16 March 1987

'Los celos enfermizos del "Mellizo"', no byline, *Semana*, Bogotá (Colombia), 1 February 2014

'Los errores en la protección al informante que delató a "Los Mellizos"', no byline, *El Tiempo*, Bogotá (Colombia), 28 January 2016

'"Los Mellizos", el mayor clan del narcotráfico desde Pablo Escobar', no byline, *La Razón*, Madrid, 13 February 2004

'Los narcogemelos', no byline, *Semana*, Bogotá (Colombia), 1 October 2001

'"Los Nevados", el nuevo cartel de "Los Mellizos" Mejía Múnera que declaró guerra al estado', no byline, *El Tiempo*, Bogotá (Colombia), 15 December 2007

'Major drugs cartel smashed', no byline, *BBC News*, London, 27 August 2000

'Marijuana and meth are getting more popular in America, but cocaine has declined', Carolyn Wilke, *Science News*, Washington, DC, 23 August 2019

'Mexico arrests accused drug cartel kingpin', Chris Kraul, *The Los Angeles Times*, Los Angeles, 14 June 2001

'México: duro golpe al narcotráfico', María Elena Navas, *BBC Mundo*, London, 13 June 2001

'Mexico's Interpol chief dead in suspicious "suicide"', no byline, *Executive Intelligence Review*, Vol. 15, No. 9, Washington, DC, 30 September 1988

'The Mexican poppy eradication campaign', Peter B. Bensinger (administrator), *Drug Enforcement*, Drug Enforcement Administration (United States Department of Justice), Washington, DC, February 1977

'Miki Ramírez: de delator a capo del narcotráfico', no byline, *El Tiempo*, Bogotá (Colombia), 4 July 1996

'Mob figure's slaying surfaces after six years', Gail Epstein and Amy Alexander, *The Miami Herald*, Miami, 1994 (exact date unknown; from clipping)

'Navas believed to be cocaine importer', no byline, UPI Archives, United Press International, Washington, DC, 14 October 1982

'Navas is convicted: sentencing set today', *Wilson Daily Times*, Wilson (NC), 28 February 1984

'Noriega found guilty on eight of 10 counts', *Tulsa World*, Tulsa (OK), 10 April 1992

'Norte del Valle Cartel', no byline, insightcrime.org, Washington, DC, 17 November 2015

'Notorious drugs baron dubbed "top, top man" who smuggled £5million worth of cocaine into Britain hidden in watermelons is jailed for more than 17 years', Harriet Arkell, *The Daily Mail*, London, 3 October 2014

'Officials: mobsters', Warren Richey, *The Fort Lauderdale Sun-Sentinel*, Deerfield Beach (FL), 19 August 1994

'Officials seize $35 million in drug money', Associated Press, *Times-News*, Twin Falls (ID), 26 August 2001

'$1bn haul of cocaine seized in 12-nation operation', Jan McGirk, *The Independent*, London, 27 August 2000

'Opposition leader upsets Colombia's plantation owners with science: sugar kills more people than cocaine', Adriaan Alsema, *Colombia Reports*, Medellín (Colombia), 11 June 2019

'Over 50 tonnes of cocaine seized at Antwerp's port in 2018', Oscar Schneider, *The Brussels Times*, Brussels (Belgium), 11 January 2019

'Pablo Escobar: ¿qué escribía en sus libretas?', no byline, *La Prensa*, Lima (Peru), 2 December 2016

'Pair get life terms in murder', Henry Fitzgerald, *The Fort Lauderdale Sun-Sentinel*, Deerfield Beach (FL), 23 January 1997

'Personality spotlight: Pablo Escobar Gaviria: Colombian cocaine king', UPI Archives, United Press International, Washington, DC, 20 June 1991

'Police officer, member of the cartel' (in Greek: 'Αστυνομικός, μέλος του καρτέλ'), no byline, *Ta Nea*, Athens (Greece), 28 August 2000

'Reputed head of drug ring taken to U.S. after arrest', John H. Cushman Jr, *The New York Times*, New York, 27 August 2000

'Revelará Rasguño nexos con narcotraficantes mexicanos', Notimex (news agency), *La Jornada*, Mexico City (Mexico), 20 July 2007

'Security concerns mount as drug smuggler's trial nears', David Gibson, *The Fort Lauderdale Sun-Sentinel*, Deerfield Beach (FL), 30 November 1986

'Sentencia de 47 años de prisión a Ramón Alcides Magaña [sic], "El Metro"', no byline, *Proceso*, Mexico City (Mexico), 21 June 2007

'Sicarios acaban con la vida de Cordelio Vaceannie', no byline, *Semanario El Extra de San Andrés*, San Andrés (Colombia), 5 February 2018

'Sicarios intentaron matar a excapo del narcotráfico "Beto el Gitano"', no byline, *El Tiempo*, Bogotá (Colombia), 16 August 2019

'The siege, the gunman and the FBI negotiator', Phil McCombs, *The Washington Post*, Washington, DC, 16 October 1982

'The sleaze connection', Guy Gugliotta, *The Washington Post*, Washington, DC, 22 September 1991

'A Spanish-speaking gunman holding two young children hostage told. . .', Craig Webb, UPI Archives, United Press International, Washington, DC, 10 October 1982

'Sugar concern admits fraud', Associated Press, *Asbury Park Press*, Asbury Park (NJ), 3 August 1985

'Sugar smuggling is under investigation – dealers are accused of evading US import quotas', Anthony M. DeStefano, *The Wall Street Journal*, New York, 21 June 1985

'Suspect's detention extended', Ellis Berger, *The South Florida Sun-Sentinel*, Deerfield Beach (FL), 29 August 2000

'13 firms linked to major fraud in sugar trade', Mary Thornton, *The Washington Post*, Washington, DC, 22 June 1985

'There's no business like drug business', Nicholas Pileggi, *New York Magazine*, New York, 13 December 1982

'Thomas Leroy Wolfe', no byline, *The Oklahoman*, Oklahama City (OK), 2 November 1985

'Trafficker's guilty plea ends lengthy drug case', Larry Lebowitz, *The Miami Herald*, Miami, 17 June 2003

'Trafficker sentenced to 20 years in prison', Ann W. O'Neill, *The South Florida Sun-Sentinel*, Deerfield Beach (FL), 23 July 2003

Bibliography

'Traffickers-turned-"paras" find way to foil extradition', Gerardo Reyes and Steven Dudley, *The Miami Herald*, Miami, 8 September 2006

'Train gunman yields child, then gives up, with 2 dead', Associated Press, *The New York Times*, New York, 12 October 1982

'12-nation effort breaks up Colombian drug operation', Rick Weiss, *The Washington Post*, Washington, DC, 27 August 2000

'23 plead guilty in sugar scam', Kevin McGill, Associated Press, New York, 11 July 1985

'Two from ship's crew charged in $1 billion cocaine bust at Port of Philadelphia', Virginia Streva, *PhillyVoice*, Philadelphia (PA), 19 June 2019

'200 years for cocaine gang', Paul Cheston, *The Evening Standard*, London, 14 June 2002

'Two sugar companies owned by Lobo family are declared bankrupt: Olavarria & Co., Galban Lobo Co. say $25 million lien precludes possibility of settling debts', no byline, *The Wall Street Journal*, New York, 17 November 1966

'Un mese appostati sull'Orinoco il carico era nascosto sott'acqua', Daniele Mastrogiacomo, *La Repubblica*, Rome, 10 February 2001

'USCG sets new record for cocaine seizures', Richard R. Burgess, *Sea Power*, Vol. 42, No. 11, Washington, DC, November 1999

'US court condemns Colombia drug trafficker "Rasguño" to 30 years', Taran Volckhausen, *Colombia Reports*, Medellín (Colombia), 3 December 2013

'US deals blow to cocaine trade as 25 tonnes seized', Jane Martinson, *The Guardian*, London, 28 August 2000

'US unloads record bust of 20 tons of cocaine', Adam Tanner, reuters.com, London, 24 April 2007

'Venezuela raid nets 5 tonnes of cocaine', Gabriella Gamini, *The Times*, London, 22 August 2000

'Venezuela: Chávez backs international anti-drugs push', *Oxford Analytica Daily Brief Service*, Oxford (UK), 28 September 2000

'Venezuela: National Guard confiscates two more tons of cocaine' (original source: *El Nacional*, Caracas, in Spanish), no byline, *BBC Monitoring Americas*, London, 24 August 2000

'Venezuela: police seize five tons of cocaine in international operation' (original source: *El Nacional*, Caracas, in Spanish), no byline, *BBC Monitoring Americas*, London, 20 August 2000

'Venezuelan raids net record cocaine haul', Alex Bellos, *The Guardian*, London, 26 August 2000

'The voice of reason', Sierra Bellows, *Virginia Magazine*, Charlottesville (VA), Winter 2010

'VAW-125's Tigertails', Troy Miller, *Wings of Gold*, Vol. 28, No. 4, Falls Church (VA), Winter 2003

'War on drugs has helped cocaine traffickers conquer swathes of Central America, study suggests', Harry Cockburn, *The Independent*, London, 1 April 2019

'Women in law enforcement', no byline, ice.gov, United States Department of Homeland Security, Washington, DC, 3 October 2018

Pure Narco

'The world's deadliest criminals: Colombian cocaine cartels', no byline, *The Miami Herald*, Miami, 8 February 1987

'Young Amtrak hostage taken to foster home', UPI Archives, United Press International, Washington, DC, 14 October 1982

Books

The following titles between them provided interesting background into the sugar and/or cocaine trades, the DEA and the war on drugs, the American mafia and Colombian cartels, pre-revolutionary Cuba and Latin America, and other aspects of Luis's story. Some personal recommendations: Enrique Cirules's book *The Mafia in Havana* is an essential resource for background on the mob in Cuba; William C. Rempel's *At the Devil's Table* is the go-to book on the Cali Cartel (and formed the basis for season three of *Narcos*); while Peter Walsh's *Drug War* is an excellent primer on the British law-enforcement aspect to Operation Journey. – JF & LN

A Brief History of Cocaine (Second Edition), Steven B. Karch, CRC Press, Boca Raton (FL), 2006

American Desperado: My Life as a Cocaine Cowboy, Jon Roberts and Evan Wright, Crown Publishers, New York, 2011

The Art of Doing: How Superachievers Do What They Do and How They Do It So Well, Camille Sweeney and Josh Gosfeld, Plume, New York, 2013

At the Devil's Table: The Untold Story of the Insider Who Brought Down the Cali Cartel, William C. Rempel, Random House, New York, 2011

Big Deal: The Politics of the Illicit Drug Business, Anthony Henman, Roger Lewis and Tim Malyon with Betsy Ettore and Lee O'Bryan, Pluto Press, Sydney (Australia), 1985

The Bullet or the Bribe: Taking Down Colombia's Cali Drug Cartel, Ron Chepesiuk, Praeger Publishers, Westport (CT), 2003

The Cocaine Wars: Murder, Money, Corruption and the World's Most Valuable Commodity, Paul Eddy and Sara Walden with Hugo Sabogal, Century, London, 1988

Colombia's Narcotics Nightmare: How the Drug Trade Destroyed Peace, James D. Henderson, McFarland & Company, Inc. Publishers, Jefferson (NC), 2015

Dangerous Liaisons: Organized Crime and Political Finance in Latin America and Beyond, Kevin Casas-Zamora, Brookings Institution Press, Washington, DC, 2013

The Dark Art: My Undercover Life in Global Narco-terrorism, Edward Follis and Douglas Century, Gotham Books, New York, 2014

DEA: The War Against Drugs, Jessica de Grazia, BBC Books, London, 1991

Down by the River: Drugs, Money, Murder and Family, Charles Bowden, Simon & Schuster, New York, 2002

Drug War: The Secret History, Peter Walsh, Milo Books, Preston (UK), 2018

El Túnel de Lecumberri, Alberto Sicilia Falcón, Compañía General de Ediciones, Mexico City (Mexico), 1979

460

Bibliography

Full Circle: The Remarkable True Story of Two All-American Wrestling Teammates Pitted Against Each Other in the War on Drugs and Then Reunited as Coaches, Chuck Malkus and Jerry Langton, Simon & Schuster, New York, 2018

Gang Land: From Footsoldiers to Kingpins, The Search for Mr Big, Tony Thompson, Hodder & Stoughton, London, 2010

Gangsters of Miami: True Tales of Mobsters, Gamblers, Hitmen, Con Men and Gangbangers from the Magic City, Ron Chepesiuk, Barricade Books, Fort Lee (NJ), 2010

Hotel Scarface: Where Cocaine Cowboys Partied and Plotted to Control Miami, Roben Farzad, New American Library, New York, 2017

Hunting LeRoux: The Inside Story of the DEA Takedown of a Criminal Genius and His Empire, Elaine Shannon, William Morrow, New York, 2019

The Infiltrator: My Secret Life Inside the Dirty Banks Behind Pablo Escobar's Medellín Cartel, Robert Mazur, Back Bay Books, New York, 2009

Inside Central America: Its People, Politics and History, Clifford Krauss, Summit Books, New York, 1991

Killing Pablo: The Hunt for the World's Greatest Outlaw, Mark Bowden, Atlantic Monthly Press, New York, 2001

Los Jinetes de la Cocaína, Fabio Castillo, Equipo Nizkor, Bogotá (Colombia), 1987

Loving Pablo, Hating Escobar: The Shocking True Story of the Notorious Drug Lord from the Woman Who Knew Him Best, Virginia Vallejo (translated by Megan McDowell), Canongate Books, Edinburgh, 2018

The Mafia in Havana: A Caribbean Mob Story, Enrique Cirules, Ocean Press, Melbourne, Australia, 2010

Miami Babylon: Crime, Wealth and Power, A Dispatch from the Beach, Gerald Posner, Simon & Schuster, New York, 2009

Narcoland: The Mexican Drug Lords and Their Godfathers, Anabel Hernández (translated by Iain Bruce with Lorna Scott Fox), Verso, London, 2013

Pablo Escobar: My Father, Juan Pablo Escobar (translated by Andrea Rosenberg), Ebury Press, London, 2016

The Politics of Drug Violence: Criminals, Cops and Politicians in Colombia and Mexico, Angélica Durán-Martínez, Oxford University Press, New York, 2018

Raising Cane in the 'Glades: The Global Sugar Trade and the Transformation of Florida, Gail M. Hollander, University of Chicago Press, Chicago (IL), 2009

Richard M. Nixon (*The American Presidents* series), Elizabeth Drew, Times Books, New York, 2007

Stalling for Time: My Life as an FBI Hostage Negotiator, Gary Noesner, Random House, New York, 2018

The Sugar King of Havana: The Rise and Fall of Julio Lobo, Cuba's Last Tycoon, John Paul Rathbone, Penguin Books, New York, 2010

The Takedown: A Suburban Mom, a Coal Miner's Son, and the Unlikely Demise of Colombia's Brutal Norte Valle [sic] *Cartel*, Jeffrey Robinson, St Martin's Press, New York, 2011

The Underground Empire: Where Crime and Governments Embrace, James Mills, Doubleday & Co., New York, 1986

Wiseguy: Life in a Mafia Family, Nicholas Pileggi, Simon & Schuster, New York, 1985

Documentaries

Cocaine Cowboys, Billy Corben (director) and Albert Spellman (producer), Rakontur, Miami (FL), 2006

Declassified: Untold Stories of American Spies (Episode 305: 'The Norte Valle [sic] Cartel'), Domini Hofmann (executive producer and director), CNN, Atlanta (GA), 2019

The Godfather of Cocaine, William Cran (writer, director and producer), *Frontline*, PBS, Boston (MA), 1995

The Invisibles, Sherry Fynbo (executive producer), Beyond Entertainment, Sydney (Australia), 2020

Pin Kings, Jon Fish (producer), Brett Forrest (writer) and Victor Vitarelli (executive producer), *Sports Illustrated*, New York, 2016

The True Story of Killing Pablo, David Keane (director and executive producer), History Channel (A&E Networks), New York, 2002

Documents, Research Papers & Monographs

'American gambling activities in Cuba anti-racketeering', confidential memo sent to FBI director from Legat, Cuba, United States Government, Washington, DC, 25 June 1958

'America's habit: drug abuse, drug trafficking, and organized crime', Irving R. Kaufman (chairman), report by the President's commission on organised crime to the President and the Attorney General, Washington DC, 1986

'Auto de procesamiento', Juzgado Central de Instruccion Numero Cinco Audencia Nacional Madrid, Sumario 7/03, Contra la Salud Publica, Administracion de Justicia, Madrid, 5 February 2004

'The Cali Cartel: the new kings of cocaine', drug intelligence report, Drug Enforcement Administration (United States Department of Justice), Washington, DC, November 1994

'Colombian drug trafficker sentenced to 40 years in prison', United States Immigration and Customs Enforcement press release, Washington, DC, 24 April 2012

'Colombian paramilitary leader extradited to the United States to face US drug charges', United States Department of Justice Office of Public Affairs press release, Washington, DC, 4 March 2009

'Colombia: the shape of trafficking to come?', no byline, *International Narcotics Review*, DCI (Director of Central Intelligence) Crime and Narcotics Center, Central Intelligence Agency, Langley (VA), June–July 1995

'Confidential informant communications', Nigel Brooks, redacted emails from Tommy Taylor, United States Customs Service, Washington, DC, 2000

'Confidential: Operation Journey update as of 6/6/00', Nigel Brooks, redacted intelligence document, United States Customs Service, Washington, DC, 2000

'DEA Congressional Testimony: statement by Thomas A. Constantine, administrator, Drug Enforcement Administration before the Senate Foreign Relations Committee, Subcommittee on the Western Hemisphere, Peace Corps, Narcotics and Terrorism regarding international organized crime syndicates and their impact on the United States', Drug Enforcement Administration (United States Department of Justice), Washington, DC, 26 February 1998

'Domestic implications of illicit Colombian drug production and trafficking', Richard B. Craig, *Journal of Interamerican Studies and World Affairs*, Center for Latin American Studies at the University of Miami, Vol. 25, No. 3, Miami, August 1983

'Drug control: DEA's strategies and operations in the 1990s', report to congressional requesters, Norman J. Rabkin (editor), United States General Accounting Office, Washington, DC, July 1999

'The Drug Enforcement Administration's international operations (redacted)', audit report 07-19, Office of the Inspector General, United States Department of Justice, Washington, DC, February 2007

'Ecuador prosecutes landmark money laundering case', unclassified diplomatic cable, United States Embassy, Quito (Ecuador), Public Library of US Diplomacy, wikileaks.org, no headquarters, 3 March 2008

'The FCC's broadcast news distortion rules: regulation by drooping eyelid', Chad Raphael, *Communication Law and Policy*, Vol. 6, No. 3, Mahwah (NJ), Summer 2001

'Former Miami-Dade County resident sentenced to more than 8 years in prison for bank fraud and money laundering schemes', Drug Enforcement Administration press release, Kevin W. Carter, Special Agent in Charge, Drug Enforcement Administration (United States Department of Justice), Miami, 27 September 2018

'FY 2017 performance budget congressional submission', Drug Enforcement Administration (United States Department of Justice), Washington, DC, 2017

'Head of drugs gang convicted', HMRC news release issued by The Government News Network, London, 2 April 2007

'A history and analysis of the Federal Communications Commission's response to radio broadcast hoaxes', Justin Levine, *Federal Communications Law Journal*, Vol. 52, Washington, DC, 2000

'Human rights in Mexico: a policy of impunity', Ellen L. Lutz, Americas Watch Committee (Human Rights Watch), New York, June 1990

'Impact of the South Florida Task Force on drug interdiction in the Gulf Coast area: hearing before the subcommittee on security and terrorism of the committee on the judiciary United States Senate', 98th Congress, first session on the scope of the drug problems in Alabama and other Gulf states, Mobile (AL), 28 October 1983

'The interface between extradition and asylum', Sibylle Kapferer, Legal and Protection Policy Research Series, Protection Policy and Legal Advice Section, Department of International Protection, United Nations High Commissioner for Refugees, Geneva (Switzerland), November 2003

'International extradition and the Medellín cocaine cartel: surgical removal of Colombian cocaine traffickers for trial in the United States', Steven Y. Otera, *Loyola of Los Angeles International and Comparative Law Review*, Vol. 13, No. 4, Los Angeles, 1991

'Juárez Cartel leader sentenced in Manhattan Federal Court to 27 years in prison for importing more than 200 tons of cocaine into United States', United States Attorney's Office press release, United States Attorney Southern District of New York, United States Department of Justice, Washington, DC, 2 December 2009

'Judgment, between Bankgesellschaft Berlin AG et al. and Elias Dimitris Lemos et al.', The Hon. Mr Justice Creswell, High Court of Justice, Queen's Bench Division, Commercial Court, 1996 Folio 1681, Royal Courts of Justice, London, 22 January 1998

'Leadership protection in drug-trafficking networks', David C. Hofmann and Owen Gallupe, *Global Crime*, Vol. 16, No. 2, London, 2015

'Life of a cell: managerial practice and strategy in Colombian cocaine distribution in the United States', Joseph R. Fuentes, dissertation thesis, City University of New York, New York, 1998

'Maritime security report', Office of Ports and Domestic Shipping, United States Department of Transportation (Maritime Administration), Washington, DC, November 2000

'Mi historia en prisión', Iván de la Vega Cabás, self-published, Barranquilla (Colombia), 19 May 2010

'Nicolás Maduro Moros and 14 current and former Venezuelan officials charged with narco-terrorism, corruption, drug trafficking and other criminal charges', United States Department of Justice press release, Office of Public Affairs, United States Department of Justice, Washington, DC, 26 March 2020

'Mafia & Co: the criminal networks in Mexico, Brazil and Colombia', Juan Carlos Garzón (translated by Kathy Ogle), Woodrow Wilson International Center for Scholars Latin American Program, Washington, DC, June 2008

'Muy señores nuestros', letter by Julio Lobo announcing the appointment of Luis Navia Sr as vice-president of Galbán Lobo Trading Company SA, Havana (Cuba), 11 March 1957

'The narco threat to US security: Venezuela's criminal regime fuels regional instability', Ambassador Roger F. Noriega (Retired), statement before the Senate Caucus on International Narcotics Control US Counternarcotics Strategy, Washington, DC, 11 June 2019

'Navia draft debrief', Barry Clarke, notes of interview with Luis Navia, Her Majesty's Customs and Excise, Miami, 2001/'02

Bibliography

'Nota de prensa sobre la "Operación Ostra"', Ministerio del Interior press release, Ministerio del Interior, Madrid, 15 September 2000

'Operation Journey', briefing presentation transcript, William Ledwith, chief, International Operations Drug Enforcement Administration and Jeffrey Casey, executive director, Office of Investigations, United States Customs Service, Washington, DC, undated (circa August–September 2000)

'Operation Journey: a blueprint for the future, Special Agent in Charge, Houston, Texas', Nigel Brooks, Microsoft PowerPoint presentation, United States Customs Service, Washington, DC, 2000

'Origins of Operation Journey', Nigel Brooks, typewritten summary of Operation Journey, private document, Houston (TX), 2002

'The regression of a country', Camilo Castellanos, *El Embrujo*, Colombian Platform for Human Rights, Democracy and Development, Bogotá (Colombia), November 2009

'Re: M/V *Suerte I*, attention: Mohamed', fax to Coastal Maritime Inc. (Colombia) from Angelos Kanakis of Callisti Maritime Inc., Piraeus (Greece), 2 May 2000

'The speed of light', print advertisement for Michelob Light Racing Team, Anheuser-Busch, St. Louis (MO), 1980

'Structure of international drug trafficking organizations: hearings before the permanent subcommittee on investigations of the committee on governmental affairs United States Senate', 101st Congress, first session, Washington, DC, 12–13 September 1989

'Treasury targets Colombian drug traffickers', United States Department of the Treasury Office of Foreign Assets Control (OFAC) press release, Washington, DC, 30 August 2007

'United States of America v. [redacted]', Criminal Docket for Case [redacted], United States District Judge James Lawrence King, United States District Court, Southern District of Florida, Key West Division, Key West (FL), 3 March 1995

'United States of America v. Iván de la Vega Cabás', Judgment in a Criminal Case, Case Number: 1:00-6274-CR-HUCK, United States District Judge Paul C. Huck, United States District Court, Southern District of Florida, Miami Division, Miami, 18 January 2002

'United States of America v. Iván de la Vega Cabás', Amended Judgment in a Criminal Case, Case Number: 00-CR-6274-PCH, United States District Judge Paul C. Huck, United States District Court, Southern District of Florida, Miami Division, Miami, 26 February 2008

'United States of America v. Luis Navia', Judgment in a Criminal Case, Case Number: 00-6308-CR-KING, United States District Judge James Lawrence King, United States District Court, Southern District of Florida, Miami Division, Miami, 19 July 2001

'United States of America v. Luis Navia', Unopposed Motion to Transfer and Consolidate This Action to Lower Number Case, Case Number: 00-6308-CR-DIMITROULEAS, United States District Judge William P. Dimitrouleas, United States District Court, Southern District of Florida, Fort Lauderdale Division, Fort Lauderdale (FL), 27 October 2000

'United States of America v. Néstor Suerte', Memorandum and Order, Criminal Number: 00-0659, United States District Judge Kenneth M. Hoyt, United States District Court, Southern District of Texas, Houston Division, Houston (TX), 4 June 2001

'U.S. Drug Enforcement Agency and counterparts from other nations announce developments in large anti-drug operation', rush transcript, CNN, Atlanta (GA), 26 August 2000

'U.S. officials say they have stopped major Colombian cocaine network', rush transcript, CNN, Atlanta (GA), 26 August 2000

'White House fact sheet: cooperation between the United States and Colombia on counter-drug programs', The White House, Washington, DC, 30 August 2000

Motion Pictures/Streaming Series

Inside the Real Narcos, Stuart Cabb and Will Daws (executive producers), Channel 4, United Kingdom, 2018

Loving Pablo (aka *Escobar*), Fernando León de Aranoa (writer and director, based on the book *Loving Pablo, Hating Escobar* by Virginia Vallejo) and Javier Bardem, et al. (producers), Pinguin Films/Dean Nichols Productions/Millennium Films, et al., Spain, 2017

Pablo Escobar: El Patrón del Mal, Carlos Moreno and Laura Mora Ortega (creators), Caracol Televisión, Colombia, 2012

Narcos, Chris Brancato, Carlo Bernard and Doug Miro (executive producers), Gaumont International Television, United States/Colombia, 2015

Narcos: Mexico, Chris Brancato, Carlo Bernard and Doug Miro (executive producers), Gaumont International Television, United States/Mexico, 2018

Televised News Reports/Online Videos

'A billion dollars' worth of cocaine seized', *CTV News*, CTV Television, Scarborough (Canada), 26 August 2000

'Cocaine: why the cartels are winning', *The Economist*, YouTube, London, 23 August 2018

'Colombian police kill major drug trafficker in raid on ranch', AP Archive, YouTube, London, 21 July 2015

'USA: Colombian drug ring: arrests', Associated Press Television News and United States Customs Service Video, Story Number 192665, AP Archive, London, 26 August 2000

'World's largest drug bust in Mexico', AP Archive, YouTube, London, 22 July 2015

Bibliography

Websites

archives.gov

bop.gov

cbrayton.wordpress.com

colombiareports.com

courtlistener.com

dea.gov

derechos.org

directnews.gr

drug.addictionblog.org

elregio.com

extradicion.com.co

familytreenow.com

fas.org

fiscalia.gov.co

forbes.com

formatchange.com

fredmitchelluncensored.com

govinfo.gov

hndm.unam.mx

ice.gov

inmatereleases.org

insightcrime.org

interpol.int

jaimemontilla.com

justice.gov

knightcenter.utexas.edu

law.cornell.edu

marinetraffic.com

medellinabrazasuhistoria.com

medellinliving.com

mercado.com.pa

murderpedia.org

narconews.com

newspaperarchive.com

ncjrs.gov

offshoreleaks.icij.org

opencorporates.com

pbs.org

pepes.exposed

planespotters.net

proyectopabloescobar.com

racingsportscars.com

reuters.com

sanctionedlist.com

saltwatersportsman.com

shipspotting.com

sortedbybirthdate.com

state.gov

treasury.gov

sudnews.it

sunshineskies.com

tovima.gr

tni.org

tradewindsnews.com

travel.state.gov

ufdc.ufl.edu

unodc.org

wikileaks.org

wired-gov.net

zougla.gr

Endnotes

1   Debriefing is a law-enforcement term that refers to a review or rundown of actions taken during a particular event or operation, such as the takedown of a criminal conspiracy.

2   A full list of all the Spanish words used in the book and their meanings, as well as drug-trafficking slang, can be found in Glossary. Diacritics or accent marks are frequently used but familiar geographic names such as Mexico and Mexico City are spelled without accents.

3   It was no fault of Wright, who evidently spent a great deal of time trying to verify the claims his subject was making and apparently even cautioned Roberts not to include his war tales in the book.

4   Perhaps wisely, Luis has made a general habit of shying away from all forms of social media but he did once join Facebook. 'The only friend I had was "Popeye",' he laughs, referring to Pablo Escobar's chief *sicario*, the late Jhon Jairo Velásquez Vásquez. Popeye died of cancer in February 2020.

5   As 'Louis Navia'.

6   US tons. A metric ton is 1000 kilos. A US ton is 907.185 kilos.

7   Luis changed his plea after initially pleading not guilty. 'You plead not guilty to everything,' he jokes. 'That lasts for about a month.'

8   Isabelle Meneses is a pseudonym. All the members of Luis's family and inner circle have been given false names for their protection, apart from his deceased parents. All pseudonyms used in the book are indicated.

9   A lifelong partyer and Scotch drinker, in recent years he has observed a rule of not drinking alcohol during the 40 days of Lent.

10 Mr Magoo was a cartoon character voiced by actor Jim Backus for 40 years. The myopic, elderly Magoo got into calamitous situations but always managed to come out on top through dumb luck; perhaps why Luis identifies with him so much.

11 An eerily prescient joke, given the COVID-19 pandemic in 2020.

12 The kidnapping, brutal torture and murder of DEA agent Enrique 'Kiki' Camarena Salazar by the Guadalajara Cartel in 1985 bears out that statement. Camarena's story formed the basis for the first season of *Narcos: Mexico*.

13 In Spanish, *mono* is literally 'monkey', but in Colombian Spanish it is used to refer to Caucasians or a white person with light hair. The feminine is *mona*.

14   Since 2003, ICE has been part of the United States Department of Homeland Security (DHS).

15   Ignacio Bargueño is a pseudonym.

16   In reality, though, it's probably best known around the world for being used in the title of an Enya album. Sadly Venezuela, physically a very beautiful country, is not a destination visited by many tourists and its economy has now all but collapsed. It is not just a failed state but a narco state. Former US diplomat Roger F. Noriega used the very term in testimony to the Senate Caucus on International Narcotics Control in Washington, DC in June 2019. A CNN report earlier the same year revealed 240 tons of cocaine was crossing the border every year from Colombia to be transported north. In March 2020, Venezuela's president, Nicolás Maduro Moros, was indicted by the United States on charges including narco-terrorism and cocaine trafficking. A $15 million reward was offered for information leading to his arrest and/or conviction. A coup attempt by US mercenaries was foiled two months later.

17   The *Post* gave it the full treatment: raids on 'snake-infested bunkers' filled to the brim with cocaine as 'monkeys looked on from the trees'.

18   A key is drug slang for a kilo. The figure of 68 tons was based on estimates that informants provided to the DEA. European cocaine prices in 2000 fluctuated depending on where the drug was sold, but these were the prices contained in an official USCS PowerPoint presentation. According to data from the United Nations Office on Drugs and Crime (UNODC), a gram was worth $138 on the street in Finland, but $33 in the Netherlands. At December 2019 prices a kilo of cocaine in Colombia would cost $1000 and fetch $70,000 on the street in Europe.

19   It was made up of separate settlements/processing facilities Pascualandia, Coquilandia, Villa Coca, Tranquilandia I, Tranquilandia II and Tranquilandia III.

20   In the calendar year 2017, the Federal Criminal Police Office of Germany announced that 639 tons was confiscated globally (similar figures were recorded in 2018 and 2019). An accumulated 41 tons was seized at the port of Antwerp in Belgium in 2017, 50 tons in 2018.

21   A description used by USCS in a PowerPoint presentation to describe De La Vega's role in the maritime transportation organisation.

22   What Luis calls 'Northern Valley' is commonly called North Valley Cartel. *El Cártel de la Costa* operated out of the Colombian cities of Santa Marta and Barranquilla, as well the Dutch protectorate of Aruba.

23   Drug slang for kilograms.

24   In fairness to Mermelstein, who as part of WITSEC died in 2008 while living under an assumed name in Kentucky, his second wife was Colombian: Cristina Jaramillo.

25   The Cartel of the Suns (*El Cártel de los Soles*), a group that emerged from inside the ranks of the Venezuelan military during the presidencies of Hugo Chávez and Nicolás Maduro Moros, is now allegedly one of the most powerful cocaine cartels in the world. Says Luis: 'They are fucking exporting more shit out of Venezuela into northern Africa and Central America than ever before.' The Cartel of the Suns was named in the US indictment against Maduro in March 2020.

26   It has also been claimed that Brazil is the world's second biggest consumer of cocaine, after the United States, with 1.46 million users. A gram of coke in Brazil costs six to ten times less than it does in the US.

27 Bikers remain heavily involved in cocaine distribution.

28 Perhaps an underestimate. At the time of Luis's arrest the average salary for a DEA special agent was roughly $100,000.

29 Colombians also call Medellín the 'City of Eternal Spring'.

30 Explains Luis: 'I always use a Jewish name. All my fake Gmail accounts are under Jewish names.'

31 An alternate spelling seen in news reports is Kalisti.

32 Other departments where Los Mellizos had influence were Antioquia, Magdalena, La Guajira, César, Santander, Norte de Santander, Boyacá and Caldas.

33 Chitiva, from Barranquilla, turned against Escobar as the Medellín Cartel crumbled. He is tall and dark with black straight hair, bushy black eyebrows and long arms. La Mica, which means 'The Monkey' but in the feminine, was a nickname Chitiva picked up in high school: 'You look like a female monkey.'

34 Luis's *modus operandi* was to keep his true identity secret, even though Víctor had met Luis at Luis's Bogotá apartment in 1993 and knew his real name. Víctor had wanted to send cocaine to Cancún, Mexico. 'There was a reason for that. I was already a fugitive. I did not want the heat travelling across to me in Venezuela.'

35 A pseudonym.

36 Says a former girlfriend: 'Luis was never someone you looked at and thought, "*Wow*, what a good-looking guy!" But there was something about him. He was very confident and flirtatious and funny and sweet. He was a very elegant gentleman, very suave, and knew how to treat a lady: with much respect and attention.'

37 Galicia in Spain's northwest has long been a hot spot for the smuggling of contraband in Europe.

38 A pseudonym.

39 The fake passports were Dominican, Colombian, Panamanian, Mexican, Guatemalan and Venezuelan, including some doubles.

40 All pseudonyms.

41 Juliana, born in Colombia, was given a visa for 72 hours. Santi had no problem: he was born in Mexico.

42 Luis believes they met.

43 A Greek report claimed it was $200,000.

44 Oddly, the fact that the boat and captain shared the same name was completely coincidental. Single-name Hispanic aliases are *de rigueur* in the Latin American drug trade, even for Bangladeshis. Jorge García had another story to Luis's: Nomani was 'Indian' (subcontinental) and the Filipinos were recruited by Nomani's brother in the Philippines. Former USCS senior special agent Nigel Brooks confirms Nomani was Indurain's real name. He is referred to as 'Nomadi' in Spanish court documents.

45 In 2002, as part of extradition proceedings against Hells Angels member Guy Lepage from Quebec to Florida, it was revealed by a confidential informant or CI to the DEA that Los Mellizos had been sending tons of cocaine to Quebec. The Hells Angels would send trucks filled with cash to Miami as payment. Lepage was mentioned in Spanish court documents.

46 Los Mellizos had already delivered a substantial amount of 'weight' under the radar into Europe (one report claimed ten tons a week in the US and Europe).

47   Explains Luis: 'The *oficina* is a main office for each cartel that handles SOS [source of supply]. They would give me the merchandise in Colombia and I would use my different routes to place the merchandise in the States. So the *oficina* acts as headquarters for day-to-day operations as well as debt collections, keeps track of merchandise in different countries as well as merchandise en route, and also keep tabs on representatives they have in different countries distributing the merchandise. They have an accounting department, a collections department, a transport department. Some outfits are bigger than others. In all my years I always dealt directly with the head person of a particular *oficina*. My *oficina* always worked different routes at the same time.'

      The most famous *oficina* is Medellín's La Oficina de Envigado, which after the death of Pablo Escobar became a cartel in its own right under Diego Fernando Murillo Bejarano aka 'Don Berna', doling out cocaine as well as assassinations. A lawyer representing a roster of cartel bosses who spoke on condition of anonymity says it was effectively 'the accounts receivable department of the Medellín Cartel. It controlled all of the street gangs; whole neighbourhoods.' In 2019 there were reports out of Colombia that La Oficina de Envigado has combined forces with paramilitary group *Autodefensas Gaitanistas de Colombia* (AGC or Gaitanista Self-Defence Forces of Colombia) aka *Clan de Golfo* (Gulf Clan) aka Los Urabeños, along with the Santa Marta–based Pachenca gang and *Clan del Oriente* (Clan of the East) from Magdalena Medio Antioquia to form a new super-cartel. Says Luis: 'La Oficina de Envigado existed while Pablo was around. But that was always a collections office as well as a hit office.'

48   Not as far-fetched as it might seem. Historically, coca plantations have been successful in Formosa (Taiwan), the island of Java in the Dutch East Indies (Indonesia), Okinawa in Japan, and Ceylon (Sri Lanka).

49   The amount impounded altogether on the ground in Venezuela is unclear. A number of reports claimed five-and-a-half tons in plastic barrels were found on an island in the delta. The coke was apparently hidden under a camouflage tarpaulin on a platform built above mangrove roots. Another report said two tons were confiscated in a separate raid in Barrancas del Orinoco. Another report said two-and-a-half tons was found on the abandoned farm in two pits. A collective figure of ten tons was also given. Luis estimates that of the 25 tons amassed at the fishing camps 15 were seized in the raid.

50   Other *guardaespaldas* (bodyguards) and *sicarios* (hitmen) were 'Gardel', 'Nando', 'El Tío', 'Popeye' (no relation to Pablo Escobar's henchman Popeye), 'Tuso', 'Chino' and 'Dinastía'. All were named in Spanish court documents.

51   Not technically true. Mobile phones are triangulated not landlines. Triangulation is a technique by which one can determine a mobile phone's location by measuring the strength of its signal from the nearest mobile-phone tower, drawing a coverage radius from that tower, and then measuring the strength of its signal from second and third mobile-phone towers, again drawing a coverage radius around each of the towers. Where the three radial circles intersect pinpoints the location of the phone.

52   An identical copy was later recovered from Iván de la Vega Cabás.

53   The boat's captain, Néstor Suerte, was convicted in the United States after Malta, where *Suerte I* was registered, waived its jurisdiction over the vessel and consented to its boarding and searching, as well as the application of

American law under the Maritime Drug Law Enforcement Act (MDLEA). This is done by issuing a Statement of No Objection (SNO). Suerte contested that the US had no jurisdiction over him to bring him to trial. A trial court agreed but it was overturned on appeal. Suerte then pleaded guilty and received a sentence of time served. The Filipino crew was repatriated to the Philippines.

54 Who 'they' were is unclear, though a BBC report quoting *El Nacional* newspaper in Venezuela said 'those arrested [in Operation Journey] were transferred to the Counternarcotics Command's [*Comando Antidrogas*'s] headquarters where they are being questioned in the presence of the officials of the Prosecutor-General's Office so that a case could be opened against them and they could be placed under the orders of the appropriate courts'.

55 His biographer, John Paul Rathbone, estimates it would be equivalent to $5 billion today.

56 Luis Sr was a supporter of Batista; Luis believes his father and the dictator knew each other. Batista's daughter Marta María Batista Fernández was a friend of Luis's sister Laura when they both lived in Miami, meeting at Miami-Dade College.

57 He gave them back to Rosengard when he fled Cuba in 1960 to protect the jewels. Luis says his father's plan was never to emigrate to America permanently: 'We thought we were going back.'

58 It is an irony not lost on Luis that Nixon created the DEA by Executive Order in 1973.

59 The company filed for bankruptcy in 1966 over tax debts.

60 The mill eventually closed down in 1977.

61 Fidel Castro went to the same school in Havana before it was moved to Miami after the revolution.

62 Claudia Betancourt is a pseudonym. Omar, another pseudonym, had a drug- and people-smuggler friend, real name Julian Brown, whose family owned the Compleat Angler Hotel in North Bimini, where Ernest Hemingway stayed from 1935 to 1937 and wrote *To Have and Have Not.* 'The Browns ran Bimini for *years,*' says Luis. 'They were smuggling pot way back in 1971, '72, '73. Julian was in jail in the US in '75. Unheard of; back then, that was an incredible crime. He was Omar's best friend. The hotel burned down in 2006, with Julian inside. Julian tried to save the merchandise they had stashed up in the roof; coke not pot. He died in the fire.' A second brother, Frank, was electrocuted in 1970. A third brother, Ossie, was beaten to death with a lead pipe during a home invasion in 1996. A fourth brother, Spence, died on the Browns' boat, the *Alma B,* after it capsized off South Bimini in 2000. The patriarch of the family, Captain Harcourt Neville Brown, died of natural causes in 1997.

63 A pseudonym.

64 Andy later married Marivi Lorido, a friend of Luis's sister, Laura. Luis sold his new car, an Audi Fox, to Andy's brother, René, a jai alai player who got caught up in a match-fixing scandal in 1979. Clau, Luis's girlfriend, was a good friend of Marivi. Technically, Luis was still living at home with his parents but using the rental property as his animal house.

65 It's worth pointing out that Bia has a conflicting story to Luis's about how he found out she was a dealer: 'That life for me is finished. I'm a very private person. I don't talk much about my past. I have lived a fulfilling life. I enjoyed

it very much. But I never used a gun in my whole life and I never menaced anybody.' Luis is adamant his version is the truth and as he described. It was the only thing they disagreed on during the writing of this book. Says Bia: 'Luis's story about the Learjet and the emeralds is not true. What I said to him was that I sold emeralds and that's why I travelled to San Francisco. I used to take Learjets to carry money. He never saw an emerald or the other stuff.'

66   Colombian magazine *Semana* effectively said as much in 1987: *Es la organización criminal más peligrosa del mundo.* 'It is the most dangerous criminal organisation in the world.'

67   Roland and Andreina are pseudonyms.

68   Fabio Ochoa, along with Pablo Escobar and Fabio's distributor in Miami, Rafael Cardona Salazar, is said to have ordered the assassination of Barry Seal.

69   Manolo Varoni, Peter Sharwood, Marcos Geithner and David Patten are all pseudonyms.

70   Pepe (a common Spanish nickname for José) also had a business relationship with a Miami pilot called Jack DeVoe, who ran a small fleet of Piper Navajos under the name DeVoe Airlines from Miami to a constellation of smaller cities in Florida and Alabama: Key West, Orlando, Melbourne, Jacksonville, Fort Lauderdale and Tallahassee. It called itself 'The On-Time Airline' and it proved to be just that for Cabrera. The US Government later calculated that DeVoe had done over 100 smuggling runs from Colombia via Little Darby Island in The Bahamas to Florida, transporting three-and-a-half tons in wing fuel tanks and using eight to ten contract pilots. DeVoe made millions each month. He was arrested and sent to jail for 30 years in 1984, his airline shut down altogether.

       As for Cabrera, after he was sentenced to 30 years in prison in 1986 for trafficking more than eight tons of cocaine, he was named 'one of the top five cocaine smugglers in the world' by a Florida state prosecutor and among the 'world's deadliest criminals' by *The Miami Herald*. More convictions on trafficking and racketeering charges followed. He eventually cut a deal with the US Government to testify against Panamanian dictator General Manuel Noriega and was released from jail early, as well as being granted immunity from further prosecution and being allowed to keep part of his fortune. He is now deceased.

71   In the documentary *Cocaine Cowboys* Jon Roberts claimed Rafael Cardona Salazar aka 'Rafa' or 'Rafico' 'really controlled almost every kilo of coke that came into this country through the people from Medellín' and 'there was nobody higher than him for the Medellín Cartel in this country'. Luis says the claim is 'a bit exaggerated – but *yes*; at that point Rafa was the cartel's main guy, the high-level point man, in the United States representing the Medellín Cartel: Pablo and the Ochoas. This was the early '80s to approximately '84. But there were associates of Medellín – Pepe Cabrera, for example – who didn't give their complete load to Rafa to distribute.' Cardona was murdered in Medellín in 1987.

72   In 1989 a US Senate subcommittee, the Permanent Subcommittee on Investigations, declared as much: 'What is commonly referred to as the Medellín Cartel is actually made up of approximately 200 individual trafficking groups which ally themselves in order to coordinate different phases of cocaine production, transportation and distribution.' Joseph R. Fuentes's excellent 1998 doctoral dissertation thesis, 'Life of a cell', defines

a cartel in Colombian practice as being 'a geographically closed area in which are grouped a loose federation or coalition of major drug-trafficking organisations that have formed alliances for the self-serving purpose of reducing the risky nature of the business in which they participate'.

73 Quico is the standardised spelling for Moncada's nickname in Colombia, but Kiko is also an accepted variant.

74 Leticia is located on the border with Brazil and Peru. Porras died in 2010.

75 Says Luis: 'Jorge is a very smart man; very charismatic; great people skills. To be able to handle Pablo and The Mexican, the Cali Cartel, the Castaño brothers and everybody else that followed, you can imagine what sort of organisational ability and intelligence Jorge has. That ability to handle people is an art form.'

76 A doctor friend of Luis, who shall remain nameless, makes an interesting observation: 'Escobar and the other violent narcos needed to believe in the delusion that they were *bandidos* – kind of like Robin Hoods that were helping the poor – in order to assuage their malignantly narcissistic egos. Luis is, at his essence, a very good person with high morals and many regrets now; there's a good degree of shame and guilt there – the opposite of the psychopathic serial killers with whom he associated for so many years. It's like the excitement and the fact that one could die at any second became an even more powerful drug than money or cocaine for these guys.'

77 During a 15 December 1989 shootout with Colombian police in a banana grove outside Tolú, on the Caribbean coast south of Cartagena, The Mexican, aged 42, his son Freddy Rodríguez Celades, 17, and their bodyguards were cut to pieces by AH-6 Little Bird light attack military helicopters equipped with miniguns. Its recreation was one of the best scenes in *Narcos*. Almost exactly four years later, Escobar himself, 44, would be slain in another shootout with Colombian police.

78 Randall Ghotbi is a pseudonym.

79 Lopez, the one and same from the radio scam, is now deceased.

80 A pseudonym.

81 A pseudonym.

82 Says Bia: 'Luis came to water my plants at the apartment, so that was the way he found out what I did [dealing cocaine]. Poli came to my place and told him about [me dealing]. I never wanted Luis to get involved in anything. I got pissed off with Poli about that and he apologised.' Replies Luis: 'I don't remember Poli coming to the apartment and telling me that. If I was in Bia's apartment watering the plants and Poli came over and I opened the door for him, believe me: that meant I already knew she was involved with cocaine. How could I have been partying with Poli and all that and not know anything?'

83 Some reports claimed three assassins were involved.

84 It was later revealed to be a hit connected to Griselda Blanco's organisation. Two gunmen, both Colombians, were identified.

85 *Rola* is a slang term for a woman from Bogotá.

86 Slang for snorting.

87 A statement that would seemingly contradict a claim in Roben Farzad's book about The Mutiny, *Hotel Scarface*, that anybody who was anybody in the cocaine scene in Miami went to the hotel.

88 The Omni Hotel is now the Hilton Miami Downtown.

89   The Ingram Military Armament Corporation-10.

90   *Paisa* is a term for people from the northwest of Colombia, particularly Medellín.

91   *Loco*, meaning crazy in Spanish, was one of Luis's many nicknames, because of 'my demeanor in general – funny, off-the-wall comments, drinking, partying'. Another was 'La Luisa' because of his long hair. 'Not very many people from Colombia and in the business had long hair; it was just me and Fabito Ochoa.'

92   As one DEA agent puts it: 'South Florida is the gateway to South America, and all the shenanigans that go on in South America are just as prevalent there. It's the fraud capital of the United States in terms of different scams and credit card business, and there's always issues with corrupt cops down there. Miami is a sunny city full of shady people. Everybody's working a fucking angle.'

93   Being Cuban also had its advantages, especially after the release of *Scarface* in December 1983. Says Luis: 'A lot of Miami started getting developed with dope money. But up until *Scarface* Americans didn't know much about Cubans. For all they knew Cubans were *¿Qué Pasa, USA?*, the [PBS-produced bilingual] TV show with Rocky Echevarría [aka Steven Bauer] who did the movie *Scarface*. That's the reason Andy Garcia went to LA to become a movie star – because of the success that Rocky was having – and then he surpassed Rocky. Americans thought Cubans were working in hotels or superintendents of buildings. Now they were fucking cool, dangerous, another type of level; like the equivalent of Don Corleone but Cuban. So it elevated Cubans to a position of intrigue. You went to San Francisco and said, "I'm a Cuban from Miami," that was like saying, "I'm a gangster."'

94   Says Luis: 'When he was racing for [B&J Racing] Bernardo drove a Mustang and Javier drove a Corvette. We went to the first [sports car] Grand Prix of Miami in 1983.'

95   Diego Forero, Leif Bowden, Terry Wozniak, Roger Lisko, Brett Spiegel, Bernardo Palomeque, Javier Mercado and Francisco Moya are all pseudonyms. B&J Racing is also a fake name.

96   Octavio Piedrahíta was later indicted for money laundering in Florida and was behind a massive 1762-kilo cocaine seizure in 1982 in Miami. It has been claimed that Piedrahíta organised the 30 April 1984 assassination of Colombian politician Rodrigo Lara Bonilla but the Ochoa brothers have blamed Pablo Escobar. In 1983 Bonilla, then Minister of Justice, accused Escobar, a member of the movement *Renovación Liberal* (Liberal Renewal) who harboured ambitions of becoming president of Colombia, of being a drug trafficker. Bonilla was also behind the raid on Tranquilandia in March 1984. Piedrahíta was assassinated in 1988.

97   Says Luis: 'Mesa was killed, I believe, in Miami around 1983, '84.'

98   Luis had several apartments in Miami during this time: Biscayne and 21st, Venetian Islands, The Palace on Brickell Avenue.

99   Ippolito, who died in 2006, was a well-known New Jersey mob identity and southern California restaurateur who raced speedboats. He was mentioned in a 1980 ad for Michelob Light Racing Team. He was probably most famous for his friendships with Caan and Simpson, and in the 1980s and '90s served separate jail terms for marijuana and cocaine trafficking.

100   Helios and Catalina are pseudonyms.

101   Says Luis: 'The Colombians later began delivering with drop-off cars. They would just drop off a car at a parking lot, hand you the keys, you'd go get the car, do your thing and return the car the next day.'

102 Ironically, in the mid-1980s the truck was eventually busted carrying a load of 60 kilos but Diego managed to slip away from the police and escaped. Says Luis: 'The truck was parked outside a restaurant and some kind of freak situation happened and a police dog smelled the coke or something and suddenly the truck was surrounded by cops and hauled away. A dog just happened to smell what was inside the truck. It was not that Diego was being followed. He saw the commotion and the truck being hauled away, all from a distance; that's why he was never arrested. Later I heard that they now use the truck in police presentations to show how drugs are being hidden in vehicles.'

103 According to Luis, sampling your own product wasn't regarded highly among the higher echelons of the cartels: 'Most of those high-level guys, if they did [snort], they did it very privately. On the Coast [in Colombia] there was more snorting among the high-level guys. There's more of a party atmosphere there; people are more happy-go-lucky. Pablo Escobar didn't really like it. He'd have a beer; he'd smoke. He loved to smoke pot. A couple of his hitmen would get really high. Even Popeye talked about it. The Mexican, I believe, didn't snort coke.'

104 A pseudonym.

105 Says Luis: 'It's essentially the same thing as crack; although we used a propane torch, which gives a very clean burn, and pure base. As opposed to crack, which when it gets to the street is not as pure and is usually smoked in a smaller pipe with a simple everyday lighter.' Freebase is commonly made with cocaine, water, ammonia and ether. Crack is commonly made with cocaine, water and baking soda or ammonia.

106 The reason he and Katie are still alive is that they were smoking quality coke, even if it were mixed with other things. In Colombia, what's also called *basuco* ('Colombian crack') is much lower quality: typically crude or low-grade coca paste mixed with gasoline, kerosene, solvents, sulphuric acid, brick dust, and other additives/chemicals. It's cheap on the street, highly addictive and frequently lethal.

107 Luis believes Brian Livingston died of colon cancer in prison. There is a report from northern California's *Times-Standard* on 2 April 1986 of a William Brian Livingston, 38 (described as 'one of Humboldt County's biggest cocaine dealers'), being indicted by a federal grand jury in Eureka (CA) for 'managing a large-scale cocaine ring' at Fieldbrook, 465 kilometres north of San Francisco on the Pacific coast. He had surrendered to authorities in San Francisco after a three-year investigation by the FBI. The article states Livingston, then employed by Record Plant Recording Studios in Los Angeles, had 'distributed a total of at least 88 pounds [40 kilos] of cocaine in Hawaii, San Francisco, Las Vegas, West Palm Beach [FL] and Humboldt and Sonoma counties' with sales totalling $2 million and 'most of the cocaine [coming] from Florida'. Assistant US Attorney Peter Robinson is quoted: 'I am confident [Livingston] is the largest cocaine dealer prosecuted in Humboldt County.' Another report published the same day in *San Francisco Examiner* says Livingston 'operated from 1976 to 1983'. This individual would appear to be the one and the same Brian Livingston Luis knew and worked with and he believes it is, confirming Livingston's Record Plant employment and Humboldt County residence, though it cannot be verified with 100 per cent certainty. A death record for Sonoma County, north of San Francisco, lists one William Brian Livingston as passing away on 26 October 1992 with a birth date of 14 June 1947. So this person would have been 38 in April 1986: the same age as the William Brian Livingston indicted in Humboldt County for cocaine trafficking.

Endnotes

108   Now the Hotel Kabuki in Japantown at 1625 Post Street, San Francisco.

109   According to Ronald K. Siegel in a 1988 piece for *Omni* magazine, Mario
was doing coke in the carriage and the sound of him sniffing was recorded
64 times on tape. Siegel, a psychopharmacologist, recreated the incident for
the judge, complete with artificial heat, a legal cocaine substitute, chemicals
(putrescine, cadaverine) designed to replicate María's decaying corpse,
and sounds from audio tapes of the siege. He concluded: 'Under the right
conditions any brain will hallucinate.' Siegel died in 2019.

110   It was also revealed Mario had married a woman called Estella in a New
York correctional facility. Marriage records indicate he married a 'Soledad E.
Bonilla Nocua'. Estella too was sentenced on cocaine-related charges in 1976,
but escaped from prison in West Virginia in 1977. The couple had two sons,
Freddie, then 13, and Angelo, 11. Luis believes Mario died in jail and this was
confirmed by former FBI Crisis Negotiation Unit head Gary Noesner, who
told me, 'Mario died in prison from a stomach [aortic] aneurysm. Not sure
what year.'

111   Sometimes spelled 'Micky' or 'Mickey'.

112   Pablo Escobar's former mistress, the journalist and author Virginia Vallejo,
has called them 'the kings of marijuana'. In August 2019 Camilo Dávila
Jimeno was caught in Mexico and extradited to the United States for cocaine
trafficking. His brothers Juan Manuel, Raúl and Pedro are considered the
major hitters in the family, along with their cousin Eduardo.

113   His group was called *Autodefensas Campesinas de Córdoba y Urabá* (Peasant
Self-Defence Forces of Córdoba and Urabá or ACCU).

114   'The time of the violence' or 'The Violence'. It was a catastrophic civil war
that lasted from 1948 to 1958. Over 200,000 people were killed.

115   Pastrana served as president of Colombia from 1998 to 2002.

116   FARC announced a unilateral ceasefire in 2015 and, two years later, as part
of a peace accord with the Colombian Government, handed over its weapons.
It has re-emerged as a political party, *Fuerza Alternativa Revolucionaria del
Común* (Common Alternative Revolutionary Force).

117   Grouper-on-human attacks are not unknown in the diving scene, especially by
Atlantic goliath groupers, though there are no known reports of humans being
killed by groupers. More likely the five poor souls were eaten by sharks or they
died from their injuries or drowning, though it's a good story.

118   The name Camilo Zapata and the alias El Halcón are both fictional but the
man is very real.

119   Paco is a common nickname for Francisco, but Luis says Barrera's first name
was Alberto.

120   By 1986, cocaine smuggling in Florida had actually *increased* and George D.
Heavey, a regional commissioner of USCS, would concede in *The New York
Times*, 'We're overwhelmed. It's like fighting the Chinese Army.'

121   Greg Lazzara and Pino Fatone are pseudonyms.

122   Both Caro Quintero and El Cochiloco are featured characters in *Narcos:
Mexico*. El Cochiloco was killed by the Cali Cartel in 1991.

123   However, The Doc did contact Luis when Caro Quintero was arrested in
Costa Rica to see if something could be done for him. The date of the arrest
was 4 April 1985. Caro Quintero was subsequently extradited to Mexico for
his involvement in the murder of DEA agent Kiki Camarena. Today he is on
the run. See Characters for details.

124 El Tío is not to be confused with Teodoro García Simental of the Tijuana and Sinaloa cartels. He also has the nickname 'El Teo', but it is spelled differently.

125 Gordon 'Goo' Gray and Alejandro Álvarez are both pseudonyms.

126 Matta Ballesteros aka 'El Negro' is another character featured in *Narcos: Mexico*. After being kidnapped by Honduran forces and US Marshals in 1988 while on a morning jog in Tegucigalpa, he was flown to the Dominican Republic and renditioned to the United States. Matta Ballesteros's removal caused riots in Tegucigalpa, and five people were killed. He was convicted of the kidnapping of Kiki Camarena as well as drug trafficking and remains in prison.

127 The MU-2 was manufactured by Mitsubishi between 1963 and 1986.

128 In the 2012 Colombian soap opera *Pablo Escobar: El Patrón del Mal*, Correa is shown being accidentally shot by two of Escobar's *sicarios* while tied to a chair. Says Luis: 'All I know is he was killed because of the differences he had with Pablo. He wasn't the only one that Pablo killed. [Hugo] Hernán Valencia was killed and I remember Alonso Cárdenas, a brother-in-law of the Ochoas, was killed. That was kind of the start of the "Everybody that worked big had to pay Pablo" era. It was almost the beginning of the [Medellín] collections office, which later became La Oficina de Envigado.' Valencia was shown being killed in the same episode of *Pablo Escobar: El Patrón del Mal*.

129 A third Pablo, José Pablo Correa Ramos, the former president of football club Deportivo Independiente Medellín, was assassinated in 1986.

130 According to the late Popeye, Escobar only used the notebooks to write down the names of the people he wanted assassinated.

131 Kevin's was Escobar's favourite nightclub.

132 Javier Peña, the DEA agent whose pursuit of Escobar formed the story for the first two seasons of *Narcos*, estimates he was responsible for over 10,000 murders.

133 Francisco Hélmer Herrera Buitrago aka 'Pacho' was a homosexual narco and one of the heads of the Cali Cartel, but probably best known outside Colombia as one of the main characters in *Narcos*. He is played brilliantly by Argentinean actor Alberto Ammann. Herrera also appears in *Narcos: Mexico*. According to William C. Rempel's book *At the Devil's Table*, Herrera's feud with Escobar started when Herrera refused to hand over a Colombian man Escobar wanted killed. The targeted man had murdered an associate of Escobar's friends over a love triangle gone wrong in New York and sought Herrera's protection.

134 A pseudonym.

135 There are also reports that the duty was much higher: $12 to $15 per 100 pounds.

136 The company's name has been changed.

137 Both pseudonyms.

138 Says Luis: 'You can buy the *assets* of a business – and *not* the business. In this case that was not permitted because the banks wanted somebody to buy the business and be responsible for the debts of the business; when you just buy the assets you are not responsible for any debts or obligations of the business.'

139 Defunct and since merged with other banks. Now trading as Bank of America.

140 After Kane's death, Lobo and his lawyers discovered the scam while going through company records. Said Lobo: 'I found drawback papers of questionable accuracy were being furnished in connection with a Canadian

export [of sugar] and that other documents ostensibly exporting sugar to the Caribbean were totally fraudulent.'

141 It's estimated $5 million was swindled by Lobo-Kane.

142 Eduardo Fonseca is a pseudonym. In English *compadre* is usually taken to mean friend but in Spanish can also mean godfather, godparent or co-father. As Luis explains: '*Padrino* literally means "godfather". But in Mexico *compadre* is used a lot more than in other parts of Latin America and it is usual in Mexico that two very close friends or associates call each other *compadre* as a term of endearment, which was the case with El Compadre. When I met him, the person that introduced us called him *compadre* – so I started calling him El Compadre – and later I was godfather at his daughter's wedding – *padrino de boda* (best man) – so then we were actually *compadres*.'

143 In Colombia, Marulo was also well known for dispossessing local farmers of their land through threats and intimidation.

144 Booth concedes he was there but strangely denies throwing money down a chute. He also claims, somewhat bizarrely, he didn't know what Luis did for a living: 'I never saw or heard of his business dealings because it could only hurt my reputation and career. I was shielded from that. One time Luis had fallen asleep and woke up. I was still going. He gave me, like, $10,000 and told me keep the party going while he left to conduct his business.'

145 Feathering means to pitch or angle the outer blades of the propellers so that they lie flat with the slipstream. Unfeathering means to regain normal pitch. When blades are feathered the plane can't be propelled forward. The blades need to have pitch for the plane to move.

146 Writing in *New York* magazine in 1982, Nicholas Pileggi reported that illegal drugs had gross sales of $79 billion in 1980. Or in the words of US Attorney General William French Smith: 'About equal to the combined profits of America's 500 largest industrial corporations.' It was the biggest industry in New York.

147 In 1993, Accetturo was convicted of racketeering and sentenced to 20 years' jail but got out in 2002. He's now in witness protection.

148 Halcón managed to get out of the business and is living to this day. Says Luis: 'He's living in Medellín off the fat of the land. He made a lot of money.'

149 The going price was $16,000 a key. Says Luis: 'The market was flooded. It was the '80s: everybody was bringing shit in.'

150 One report had Joey being bludgeoned. Another said he was suffocated with a cushion.

151 Four men were implicated in Joey's murder: Cassone, Oscar (also known as Irving) Schwartz, Fabio Decristofaro and Joseph Marino. In 1996 a group of Lucchese crime family wiseguys including Cassone, Marino, Frank Suppa and Anthony Accetturo, already in jail and wanting to secure a reduction on their sentences, testified against Schwartz and Decristofaro. The pair was sentenced to life in jail. Says Luis: 'Schwartz and Decristofaro were the ones who actually hit him over the head and clubbed him to death.'

152 Says Luis: 'Joey Ippolito was always being hooked, having to pay off a bunch of fat slobs up in New York that had nothing to do with what he was doing but expected payment. I've seen Anthony Accetturo Jr come and slap Joey Ipp's ex-partner, Eddie Trotta, at the restaurant Tiberio in Bal Harbour because he expected Joey's ex-partner to pay him for just being Anthony Accetturo's son.'

153 Annette Soudry and Billy Basto are pseudonyms.

154 A Botero fake of 'The Dancers' valued at $500,000 was withdrawn from a Christie's sale in 1993 after the artist called it a 'very vulgar copy'.

155 Reid Constable and Daniela Villareal are pseudonyms.

156 The actual quote (from 1986) was *Preferimos una tumba en Colombia a un calabozo en Estados Unidos* or 'We prefer a grave in Colombia to a jail in the United States.' Escobar and other narcos formed a terrorist group called Los Extraditables ('The Extraditables') to wage war on the Colombian Government over the issue of extradition. Extradition was first signed into Colombian law in 1979, instated in 1983, repealed in 1987, reinstated by presidential decree in 1989, repealed again in 1991, then reinstated permanently in 1997, but the treaty was declared invalid in 1998 by Colombia's constitutional court. Where the law currently stands is open to debate. A Miami lawyer told me: 'Officially there's no extradition. Unofficially there is. It's called "administrative extradition".'

157 According to Luis, Cushing died in a twin-engine plane crash in the Rockies of Colorado during a snow-skiing holiday circa 1991. No newspaper reports are available to verify this claim.

158 Says Luis: 'The *paras* later killed Juanchito. The shootout was at his farm. He was with a longtime friend and associate called "Mata Tigre". They died with arms in hand.'

159 Escobar *sicario* Popeye, who said 'the most successful' of all his 257 killings was Galán in the Channel 4 series *Inside the Real Narcos*, also claimed politician and former justice minister Alberto Santofimio Botero was allegedly behind it, along with José Gonzalo Rodríguez Gacha aka The Mexican. (Other rumoured participants have included elements within the Colombian military and intelligence services and the *paras*.) Santofimio was sentenced to 24 years' jail in relation to the assassination of Galán in 2007 but released a year later, then had his sentence reinstated in 2011. He was placed under house arrest in 2017. Says Luis: 'Santofimio was the one who got Pablo involved in politics and he was the root of all the problems that came afterwards. If Pablo had stayed out of politics I think things would've been different.'

160 Ceiling is an aviation term that refers to the height measured from the earth's surface to the base of the lowest cloud layer. Generally it means low cloud and a lot of fog. A low ceiling is highly problematic on illegal runways or *aeropuertos clandestinos* (clandestine airports), which are usually made of dirt, because of lack of illumination or lack of a clear approach from dwellings or uncleared vegetation.

161 Says Luis: 'Moñón ran Ciénaga – he had absolute power in that area and had large expanses of banana land, the big cash export crop.' His full name was Carlos Manuel Dangond (sometimes seen spelled as Dangon) Noguera. He died in 1991.

162 During a typical drug-smuggling run, a light aircraft legally enters a country's airspace, lands at a legitimate airstrip, lodges a flight plan with the local civil aviation authority, then stops at an illegal airstrip and picks up merchandise. The smuggler then replaces the assigned call letters (registration marks) on the plane – indicating the plane's country of origin (such as Venezuela, prefix YV) – with whatever a paid-off air-traffic control official tells the smuggler to replace it with (Colombia's prefix is HJ or HK). The official then reports the

plane is travelling to a false destination. The drugs get delivered, unloaded and the correct call letters are put back on the plane on its return to its country of origin. Some planes, though, do not work with any air-traffic control at all and fly in totally illegally.

163 There were two World Cup qualifiers in Barranquilla in 1989: the first on 20 August, two days after the murder of Galán, which was Colombia vs Ecuador. The second was 17 September, Colombia vs Paraguay.

164 Shrugs Luis: 'Where are bodyguards when you really need them? I almost get killed by a guy at a fruit stand with a machete but can survive the cartels.'

165 Both pseudonyms.

166 Two car bombs went off in Bogotá on 12 May 1990, killing 19 people, following on from hundreds of bombings throughout Colombia in 1989. Six people were killed in another car bomb in Cali. Probably the worst of all of Escobar's atrocities was the bombing of Avianca Flight 203 on 27 November 1989, killing 107 people in the air and three on the ground in the mountains outside Bogotá. Luis Galán's replacement and later Colombian president, César Gaviria, had been scheduled to be on board but didn't catch the flight from the capital to Cali.

167 For $5000 Luis had a Colombian-made passport that said he was born in Santa Marta: 'It was a very well-made passport. Five thousand dollars in Colombia back then was a shitload of money.' He also had a national identification card that was made to look like it had been notarised in 1968 when he was 13. 'That was a super-good one.'

168 The same Patemuro threatened to kill former Assistant US Attorney Bonnie Klapper during her prosecution of the Norte del Valle Cartel. In 2012 he was sentenced to 40 years' jail in the United States and ordered to pay a $5 million fine. The name Patemuro is a unique one. Says Luis: '*Pate* could refer to "kick" (*patear*) and *muro* to "wall". I do not know the origins of the nickname but the closest thing to the meaning would be "wall kicker", or maybe he played soccer and he had a very powerful kick. All these rich guys in Colombia had soccer fields on their farms and they were all soccer aficionados.'

169 Luis was mostly using a kind of open fisherman boat called an *Eduardoño*, which is named after the company that makes them: Eduardoño SA.

170 Rasguño gave an interview to Bogotá newspaper *El Tiempo* in 2007 in which he said he knew Escobar 'a little. But later we became enemies, because the guy was nuts. I did not go to Medellín to go after him, but I did take take two trucks with dynamite from him and two helicopters that were going up to Cali carrying weapons. I also used to call the cops and report cars. They almost did me in [sic] in Cartago on his orders. It was a police major from Cartago . . . when Escobar died I went to the Coast and said, "No more." But there are so many expenses that you have to go back. Maintaining your bodyguards and that deluxe lifestyle – which is not a good life at all – is very expensive.'

171 A criminal favour with no benefit involved.

172 The real reason was the discovery on one of Galeano's properties of a stash of over $20 million that had been withheld from Escobar and gone mouldy. In Robert Mazur's *The Infiltrator*, he writes: 'Moncada had hidden a mountain of money in a Medellín home to evade Escobar's efforts to finance a war against the Colombian Government and its efforts to establish an extradition treaty with the US.'

173 This was according to Escobar's chief *sicario*, Popeye. A 2017 film made about Escobar, *Loving Pablo*, depicted the two men being butchered with

a chainsaw. Mazur claims both men were hung upside down by their feet and tortured with blowtorches.

174 A 1987 non-government organisation report published in Colombia described *mariachis* thus: *la debilidad de casi todos los narcotraficantes*. The weakness of almost all drug traffickers.

175 William C. Rempel's book *At the Devil's Table* details a plot by the Cali Cartel to aerially bomb *La Catedral* while Escobar was inside, using MK-82 bombs sourced in El Salvador. It was foiled at the last minute but might explain the haste with which Escobar fled the prison.

176 The website Pepes Project (pepes.exposed) has released thousands of pages of previously classified documents concerning Los Pepes. Whether American law-enforcement agencies were also involved in these extra-judicidial killings is not proven, but it is widely believed to be true. Carlos Castaño Gil claimed before he died in 2004 that 'Los Pepes worked with the tacit cooperation of the US Government. The Colombian authorities did not oppose us either.' Another excellent website, Medellín Abraza Su Historia (medellinabrazasuhistoria. com), details that victims of Los Pepes included 'Alba Lía Londoño, music teacher of Manuela Escobar, the drug lord's daughter; Nubia Jiménez, nanny of Escobar's children; Alicia Vásquez, general services employee of one of his properties; and Juan Carlos Herrera, a minor who was a friend of [Escobar's son] Juan Pablo Escobar.'

177 A declassified 1995 CIA report stated that with the fall of Medellín and Cali 'Ramírez may be best positioned in Medellín to benefit from the fall of the Cali kingpins'. He ended up getting an amnesty for his Los Pepes crimes from the Colombian Government, but served jail time for creating paramilitaries in 1997 and money laundering in 2013.

178 It's just over 700 kilometres west-northwest of Cartagena.

179 Cortés is sometimes spelled Cortéz in news reports. Silvio Bernal is a pseudonym for a trafficker who has flown under the radar of law-enforcement authorities. Just to confuse things, 'El Hombre Del Overol' (The Overall Man) is a nickname Cristancho shared with Orlando Henao Montoya, the big boss of the North Valley Cartel. Cristancho is known as 'the fake Overol', Henao 'the real Overol'. According to folklore, Henao wanted to confuse authorities and ordered Cristancho take his nickname too. However, Luis disputes this: 'Cristancho was definitely part of the Cali group but never a power player. He was made out to be more [important] than he was. He was always devious and played both sides. It was never a pre-planned strategy between him and Orlando; I don't believe he and Orlando ever had that great a personal relationship.'

180 The pseudonymous Bernal, an associate of the Ochoa brothers of the Medellín Cartel, was also allegedly a money launderer but was never indicted or arrested. Arturo Beltrán Leyva was killed by Mexican special forces in 2009. His brothers are Carlos, Alfredo and Héctor. The Beltrán Leyva Cartel is a splinter group of the Sinaloa Cartel.

181 Pablo Escobar had a copy of a US indictment against Urdinola while 'imprisoned' at *La Catedral*.

182 During the writing of *Pure Narco*, the authors met El Gordito in Islamorada, where he is a wealthy landowner. He has plans to write his own book.

183 A pseudonym.

184 According to Rempel's *At the Devil's Table*, this proposal was formally made to almost 100 gathered cartel figures and roundly rejected by them at one of

Pacho Herrera's farms a short time after Pablo Escobar's death in December 1993.

185 As detailed in *At the Devil's Table*, a similar incident did occur in real life when Herrera brutally murdered a farmer who had made the mistake of hosting a group of Medellín Cartel *sicarios* at his farm. It was used as a staging post before their coordinated assault on a soccer match being played at Herrera's Los Cocos property outside Cali. The attack left 19 people dead. A vengeful Herrera made the farmer's capture and torture a personal crusade. Herrera surrendered to the Colombian Government in 1996. He was killed in jail in 1998.

186 Luis says the rumour is Lorena poisoned her husband but that it is not true. He believes Urdinola died of a heart attack.

187 The main character in the television series *Breaking Bad*, played by Bryan Cranston.

188 The main islands of San Andrés, Santa Catalina and Providencia make up the Colombian department of Archipelago of San Andrés, Providencia and Santa Catalina (in Spanish, *Archipiélago de San Andrés, Providencia y Santa Catalina*).

189 According to sources in Colombia, El Mono, who was born in Toro in the Valle del Cauca in either 1965 or 1966, died in 2020 from colon cancer.

190 Says Luis: 'After I got out they called me a few times saying they were offering their services at any time if I needed them and that they would like to come work with me.' El Diablo, real name Ariel Rodríguez, was tasered, beaten to death, dismembered and beheaded, and his body parts dumped in the jungle sometime in 2005. See *The Takedown*.

191 José Rafael Abello Silva aka 'Mono Abello' was in jail at the time, having been extradited from Colombia to the United States in 1989. He was sentenced to 30 years' jail but after cooperating was released in 2007. The following year, he survived an assassination attempt on a beach in Santa Marta by *sicarios* on board a jetski. The gunman had been aiming for Abello's head but instead shot him in the buttocks. Luis makes out as if it were the most normal thing in the world: 'They shot Mono in the ass. No big deal. It happens every day. People miss.' His brother wasn't so lucky. Api was assassinated in 1995 by *sicarios* allegedly working for Los Mellizos.

192 It is estimated that Prada Cortés's organisation sent 24,000 kilos of cocaine to the United States between 1988 and 2006. He moved a lot of weight for Medellín and Carlos Alberto Rentería Mantilla aka 'Beto Rentería' of North Valley.

193 Félix Chitiva has said that Los Mellizos were the first to successfully use submarines to transport cocaine. DeCubas later became well known in the United States through the ESPN magazine article/documentary/podcast *Pin Kings*. DeCubas sourced cocaine via Chitiva who dealt with Medellín. Luis, by contrast, says he had direct access to the cartel.

194 In 1995 Jorge Cabrera aka 'El Gordito' was photographed shaking hands with Hillary Rodham Clinton after donating $20,000 to the 1996 Bill Clinton–Al Gore presidential campaign. 'It was frickin' hysterical,' says Robert Harley. 'I remember seeing the pictures and going, "You have *got* to be shittin' me. That's American politics at its best.' The Democratic National Committee paid back the money. Cabrera was also photographed with Gore.

195 Smit (real name Wayne Dillon) began building the 30-metre, three-section, Russian-designed submarine in a warehouse in Facatativá, a city just outside Bogotá. It was designed to carry 10,000 kilos of cocaine. The facility was raided in September 2000. He wasn't there when the raid happened and managed to escape. Luis says DeCubas 'put up some initial money for the first submarine from earnings made from the airdrops they did off the Florida Keys and Los Mellizos ended up funding the rest'. Smit died inside a smaller, prototype, semi-submergible submarine off the coast of Palomino, La Guajira. 'He's still there; he's inside the fucking submarine that sank off the beach. I've been told by Alex he wanted to commit suicide; that he had no desire to continue living.' But Luis is not so sure: 'Here you have an American citizen that dies in a submarine that was going to be used for cocaine-transport purposes.'

196 It changed its name to Bureau of Alcohol, Tobacco, Firearms and Explosives in 2002.

197 United States Fish and Wildlife Service (FWS or USFWS).

198 A command-and-control centre for USCS radar in South Florida.

199 National Oceanic and Atmospheric Administration (NOAA). Harley estimates the buoy was 130 miles off the coast of Naples, Florida.

200 The Metro-Dade Police Department, formed in 1981, changed its name to Miami-Dade Police Department in 1997.

201 Says Harley: 'Most of the loads that led us to the cooperators who were able to identify Luis were incorporated into that original indictment.' The prosecutors' rap sheet listed nine smuggles using the ships *Carol*, *Lucky Star II*, *Bad Habits*, *Candy* and *Top Gun* from November 1991 through to May 1993. Of that nine, six loads were aborted and only three were successful. *Top Gun* alone ran four loads, three of which were aborted. Of a total of 4475.5 kilos, only 1475.5 kilos were delivered. It wasn't the most successful enterprise for Luis. He was contracted by the main conspirators after the failure of the first run on lobster boat *Carol*, which with 500 kilos on board had to turn back after mechanical problems upon leaving Marathon, Florida. The second load, 600 kilos on the *Lucky Star II,* was successful. It picked up the load after an airdrop 253 miles northwest of Marathon in the Gulf of Mexico, then rendezvoused with another vessel called *Shark*, near Cape Sable in the Everglades National Park.

202 Translates as 'The Lord of the Skies'.

203 Café Koba still operates in Cancún and has no association with Luis.

204 An amount of 10,000 pesos would be worth roughly $500. An amount of $10,000 would be worth roughly 200,000 pesos.

205 The law firm's name has been changed.

206 The company's name has been changed.

207 Vernon Dolivo is a pseudonym.

208 Says Harley: 'We did eventually get documents from the law firm, so we did see what companies [were created] and [what] investments were made and they were already liquidated.'

209 Sold in Mexico as Tafil.

210 Harley disagrees: 'The big indictment was 1995 but I think the first set of indictments were in '92 and early '93. That's when we started indicting the boatloads and he might have been indicted as an unnamed co-conspirator.' Nigel Brooks from USCS's Houston headquarters agrees with Harley: 'The Southern District of Florida docket shows the indictment was dated March

1995. While it's based on the 1991 case, Navia was not named in that case.' For confidentiality reasons the full details of the 1995 indictment will not be referenced in this book.

211 Luis had cards and IDs in various permutations: Luis Naviansky, Louis Naviansky, Louis Naviansky Bonavia, et al. Juliana was enrolled in school as Naviansky with a fake birth certificate.

212 *Guantes* is the Spanish word for gloves. Guantex was a name Luis came up with to denote 'glove technologies'. His partner had no knowledge of Luis's illicit activities.

213 Denisse Zavala is a pseudonym.

214 Durazo was jailed in 1986 but released in 1992. He died in 2000. Sahagún Baca was born with the matronym Vaca, but changed it to Baca. Sahagún Baca is the cousin of former first lady of Mexico Martha Sahagún Jiménez, wife of President Vicente Fox Quezada.

215 Former federal policeman Esparragoza Moreno, with ties to the Guadalajara, Juárez and Sinaloa cartels, remains one of the FBI's Most Wanted Fugitives despite unconfirmed reports of his death in 2014. He served prison time over the death of DEA special agent Kiki Camarena.

216 Perdomo, full name Sergio Hernán Perdomo Lievano, remains on the run from US justice. He is believed to be in Spain.

217 The best-known case of a narco having plastic surgery is Mexican drug lord Amado Carrillo Fuentes, who died in 1997 while undergoing a major operation. Another is Cali Cartel/North Valley Cartel figure Juan Carlos Ramírez Abadía aka 'Chupeta' (Lollipop), who was caught in Brazil in 2007.

218 Sicilia Falcón was also into Mikhail Bulgakov, Nikolai Gogol and Mikhail Zoshchenko. Sulla was the Roman general Lucius Cornelius Sulla Felix (138BC–78BC).

219 Santa Martha Acatitla is about a 30-minute drive from Centro Sante Fe shopping centre.

220 A discontinued Redken line of conditioning beauty bars.

221 Says Dennard: 'Alberto twisted his leg when he was being tortured, along with electrocuting him. He told me the whole story when I came to Lecumberri. He got the leg rebroken by doctors and reset and then started doing gymnastics to get back in shape.'

222 This is not true.

223 Ventura was a *comandante* of the PJF and later head of the Mexican division of INTERPOL. He was described by former CIA agent Pat Gregory in *The Underground Empire* as 'the most brutal man I have ever met . . . the most powerful police official in Latin America'. He killed Skipper the Great Dane during a raid on Falcón's home and later died by apparent suicide in 1988, though the circumstances – shooting himself in the head after murdering his wife and her friend in their car – were suspicious. There was only one witness and the witness's testimony was doubtful. The Medellín Cartel is believed to have ordered Ventura's assassination.

224 Luis and Mercedes subsequently contacted each other by email after an introduction by the author.

225 El Metro was another narco who underwent plastic surgery after he was named on Mexico's and the United States' Most Wanted lists. The DEA had a $2 million reward for information leading to his arrest. Next to nothing was known about him.

226 A pseudonym.

227 Not his real name. His first name is believed to be Franco and his surname cannot be disclosed. He is wanted on a case in Florida that similarly cannot be disclosed.

228 Jesús Aburto is a pseudonym.

229 Salinas Doria, a former policeman in the border town of Donna, Texas (near McAllen), was arrested in Mexico in 1998, then escaped, was rearrested in Venezuela, then sent back to Mexico in 1999. In 2007 he was extradited to the United States. In 2009 he was convicted of trafficking 200 tons of cocaine from Mexico to the US and sentenced to 27 years' jail.

230 There is no record of Salinas Doria murdering a doctor and his family.

231 Jesús wasn't killed but Luis is sure someone had to pay 'extra tax'. For the record, Luis went on to do some trips with Metro. As he puts it, a 'bond' had been created.

232 Sometimes spelled as 'Sony'.

233 Ramcharan was arrested in Montego Bay in 2004 as part of a takedown headed by the DEA's Kingston office and extradited to the United States three years later. He was sentenced to 37 years' jail (some reports say 35) in 2008.

234 The Flamingo Club was renamed the Tropigala. Jerk is a hot spice mixture from Jamaica that is rubbed on or used to marinate seafood or meat.

235 Fresh was killed at his daughter's home in San Andrés, Colombia, on 5 February 2018, reportedly aged 60 or 61, shot twice by an unknown assailant. He was dead on arrival at hospital from wounds to his skull and thorax. At the time of his death he was on a Colombian Most Wanted list. According to Luis, a member of Fresh's family got caught smuggling cocaine out of Santa Marta but never got permission from Los Rastrojos, a cartel that had emerged out of the ashes of the North Valley Cartel.

'The group was started in the interior of Colombia by North Valley's Wilber Varela, "El Jabón" ["The Soap"], when he was at war with [the now extradited and jailed] Diego León Montoya Sánchez, "Don Diego". They spread their presence to San Andrés to impose taxes on the people that were working.'

Los Rastrojos demanded Fresh pay a tax with land he owned and the balance in cash. Fresh flew from Montego Bay to San Andrés to confront the gang and told them he wouldn't pay. He was then told to insert a SIM in his phone and call the number of the gang's *oficina* in Medellín. He refused.

'If Fresh had stayed in Jamaica, he'd still be alive. He made a mistake I have never made: don't die for money. You can always make money again but you can't come back from the dead. They put a bullet in his head, easy, *done*, end of problem.'

236 Lansky died in Miami in 1983. For a time in the mid-1980s Luis had dated Lansky's step-granddaughter, Cynthia Duncan. Her grandmother was Lansky's second wife, Thelma, who died in 1997.

237 The date of the killing was 30 August 2001. The assassin was Jhon Freddy Orrego Marín, a figure associated with the North Valley Cartel. Rumour is it was a case of mistaken identity. Fernando is sometimes reported as Hernando.

238 According to a USCS PowerPoint presentation, 43 metric tons were seized in 1999. The figure was supplied by INTERPOL.

239 The dates of the seizures were 14 January (3803 kilos, M/V *Cannes*), 27 May (3880 kilos, M/V *China Breeze*), 31 May (4000 kilos, M/V *Castor*) and 23 December (2006 kilos, M/V *Pearl II*).

240 Luis says Sonny used his connections to buy the freighters *Regent Rose* and *Privilege*.

241 A Greek newspaper, *Ta Nea*, estimated it was 20 million drachmas, or about $70,000.

242 A pseudonym.

243 Located at 99 Avenue des Champs-Élysées.

244 Typically they carry a buoy and beacon in case they are released on the open sea, to allow for quick recovery.

245 Garcia denies there was a Colombian cop in one of the front seats: 'I don't remember any Colombians being there.'

246 At the time of writing this book Meletis was still an active agent and would not be interviewed without permission from the DEA. He texted me: 'As a result of being an active agent, I need to confirm with headquarters elements that the referenced investigation is completely adjudicated before I am authorised to release information pertaining to said investigation. As soon as I receive clearance I will let you know.' It never came. Joked another DEA agent: 'I think they wait forever to give you an answer and hope you give up.'

247 The FBI's intelligence gathering is officially restricted to the United States and the CIA's to overseas, though this is not always practically the case.

248 Brooks retired in 2001, Garcia in 2016.

249 At the time a senior special agent or SSA was one pay grade above special agent or SA. Says Brooks: 'SSA was used in US Customs to designate pay grade GS-13, which could only be gained through competitive announcement; you had to compete with others and be selected on merit. SA was pay grade GS-12. Usage was discontinued around 2007 when the grade for SA was raised to GS-13. DEA and FBI also had GS-13s and the advancement was without competition. Customs went to the same non-competitive advancement system as DEA and FBI and eliminated the "senior" from the special agent title. Now all federal criminal investigators have the same pay-grade structure regardless of agency: Customs (which is now Department of Homeland Security), FBI, DEA, etc. All call their criminal investigators "special agents".'

250 FBI and USCS also had their own attaché offices overseas, but according to Eric Kolbinsky, DEA was considered the lead office overseas. Garcia says that USCS 'back then had probably 50 offices. When I retired, we had 70 offices in 48 countries worldwide; more than any other agency or equal to the FBI.'

251 Both vessels were carrying tracking devices installed by HMCE.

252 The offices of Callisti Maritime were raided on 25 August 2000 and Elias Lemos was extradited from France to Greece in 2002. He was sentenced to 18 years' jail and fined €250,000 for his part in the conspiracy. Others arrested in Greece were Filippos Makris, Nikos Mavridoglou, Angelos Kanakis, Ioannis (Yiannis) Lemos, Constantine (Constantinos) Athanasios and Theodoros Fatsis. Baron Massimo Paonessa (a pseudonym) was arrested in Italy but his fate and whereabouts are unknown.

253 Nigel Brooks has a different recollection: 'The Harris equipment was analogue only and was not capable of intercepting digital; something that Harris did not manage to fix for a couple of years. Usually when you intercept a cell phone you do it by hooking into the cell-phone company. The Harris equipment is portable and has direction-finding capability too, but it is short range. Using the cell company, you don't need to be in proximity.'

254   There is some dispute about what arrest the fingerprints actually came from, and Carol Libbey could not confirm whether it was the Coconut Grove arrest in 1979 where Luis threw cocaine out of his car or the Coral Gables arrest in the mid-1980s when his friend Billy Basto assaulted the police officer. Both Luis and Harley believe the fingerprints came from the same arrest – Coral Gables – but Harley maintains on that occasion Luis was arrested for DUI, not driving without a licence.

'I think it was that but Luis gets the charge wrong. He wasn't the one who struck the officer. I think he was taken in because they charged him with drunk driving. The reason I think it's a DUI in my head is because the DUI would have been the potential felony charge. Driving without a licence is literally a traffic charge.'

Why would Luis remember the charge differently to you?

'For Luis, that is what he lived. So that's how he remembered it. That's probably true. But that charge was in Dade County because that's where we found the picture.'

Former Dade County detective Roberto Diaz (introduced later in the book) disagrees with Harley: 'DUI has never been a felony, especially for a first offence. Driving without a licence has always been a traffic offence for which the driver can be arrested. In either case, even back then, the subject would be taken to jail where a booking card would be created and a photo taken and attached to the booking card.'

255   'US Customs has jurisdiction with anything that has a nexus to the US border,' says Kolbinsky. 'If it came across the border or if it's coming across the border they have authority. Technically, once it comes into the US, then DEA handles it. But we also have legal jurisdiction to investigate overseas as well as they do. Over the years DEA was real territorial about the whole drug thing and the only agents with Customs who could work drugs were cross-designated with Title 21 authority, which is the federal statute that covers the drug laws. There used to be silly arguments all the time about that. But not so much anymore. Operation Journey was primarily a DEA operation.'

But he makes a concession: 'Unlike our people, [the British drugs liaison officers or DLOs for HMCE] readily passed [information] on to [US] law enforcement. We worked closely with the Brits. The Brits' dark side was intercepting a lot of satellite-phone traffic in those days. A lot of folks were very territorial. Partially since I had been with Customs, I wasn't that way. I saw the benefit of everyone working together. If you had the source then it was your case. Sometimes I felt I was excluded from information because my co-workers knew how I felt about sharing info.'

However in Peter Walsh's *Drug War*, the author quotes Nigel Brooks as saying that the FBI also had 'concurrent jurisdiction to investigation violations of the *Controlled Substances Act*'. This was enacted in 1982 by the US Attorney General.

Brooks disagrees with Kolbinsky's claim regarding DEA's primacy: 'Operation Journey was in fact a US–UK operation and it was developed by US Customs Office of Investigations Houston and HMCE's NIS. The operation name was given to it by HMCE and adopted by Customs and subsequently DEA.'

256   A pseudonym.

257   As Nigel Brooks remarked in his case notes: 'The source was a resident of Barranquilla, and his absence from there without just cause could have been a

cause of major suspicions on the part of the organisation. Because the security of the operation and the safety of the source were paramount, it was decided that all control and communications with the source would be handled from Houston, and that no face-to-face contact with the source would be attempted in-country. Due to the source's position of trust in the organisation, and the certainty that he and his family would be killed should his cooperation ever become known, it was decided that his identity would only be disclosed to law-enforcement agencies in Colombia having a strict "need to know".'

258 INMARSAT is an acronym for International Maritime Satellite Organisation, so 'INMARSAT numbers' refers to maritime communications by satellite. The devices used are commonly referred to as satellite phones or 'sat' phones.

259 Prisma was a special unit of the Dutch police set up to investigate cocaine trafficking.

260 A crewmember of the *Pearl II* subsequently turned informant.

261 Nigel Brooks does not share this view: 'All the time I knew him, I never was aware that Taylor used drugs.'

262 Brooks has a different story: 'Taylor came to us voluntarily following the seizure of the *China Breeze*. He reached out for us and we flew him from Colombia to Houston. We had no idea who he was or what his role was until that time.'

263 He'd also been given the name 'Leo' by Taylor in Operation Journey communications up to that point.

264 Brooks again: 'I also set up a backstop in case of an emergency or if Taylor needed to contact us or the law-enforcement folks in Colombia needed to contact him. I introduced him to HMCE DLO Hank Cole who was one of the DLOs in Colombia we dealt with directly.'

265 Jorge made it out of South America but was caught in Barcelona two years later, imprisoned in Cádiz, and became an informant, getting everyone in the conspiracy indicted in Spain. A Spanish-language report later claimed Jorge handed over 'several suitcases' of paperwork (including accounts) to Spanish judge Baltasar Garzón, documenting all of Los Mellizos' activities from 1994 to 2000. Garzón was famous for indicting Chilean dictator Augusto Pinochet. He officially indicted Luis as well as dozens of other Los Mellizos conspirators in a sealed indictment in the National Court of Madrid in February 2004. Taylor was also named in the indictment but not specifically identified as the snitch. Iván de la Vega Cabás, however, has publicly identified him. His real name will not be published in this book.

How was Taylor outed? Talk is that a loose-lipped DEA agent had revealed to his Colombian lover, a friend of the wife of Jorge García, that an investigation of Los Mellizos was well advanced.

'There was some pillow talk from one of the agents in Barranquilla that nearly caused some problems,' says Brooks. 'I never made an official complaint or report about it because I felt that it was not intentional and saw no reason for a DEA agent to be disciplined over it. One of the problems with running an investigation of this magnitude is one of control. We tried to control the various aspects, but other agencies like DEA pursued leads on their own and coordinated with other foreign law enforcement without our knowledge or consent. At the end of the case, DEA had thoroughly briefed the Spanish [authorities] and the examining magistrate [Garzón] had issued an indictment for most of the organisation and had included our informant in the indictment. This also happened with the Colombian authorities that also indicted him. So basically we had good reason to be concerned about our source [Taylor].

'In our case it was a constant effort to get funding for travel, paying expenses for the source, and getting him paid a reward. The two attorneys [out of Washington, DC] held up the payment for the case for a couple of years, claiming that if [Taylor] was to testify they didn't want the jury to be told that he had been paid for the information. Total bullshit. In fact after I retired I reached out to [Republican] Senator Chuck Grassley to ensure that the source was paid and that the US Government honoured its commitment.

'One of the other problems we had was that DEA was convinced [Taylor] was lying and convinced [the two attorneys from DC] that was the case too. The truth is that in all my dealings with [Taylor] I never detected a lie; the guy was always straightforward when we asked him questions and gave us a great deal of historical information about the organisation . . . [Taylor] was advising us daily of his communications and [our own] intercepts confirmed what he told us. We never advised him that his communications were being intercepted so it was a good way of ensuring he was not playing us.

'The [two attorneys] threatened to prosecute Taylor if he failed to testify before the grand jury in Miami. But they would not have been able to because when we debriefed him about prior acts we intentionally did not advise him of his Miranda rights; therefore nothing he said to us could have been used against him.

'Taylor even had to pay his own way to the US for himself and his family and was in default on the house he had purchased due to the fact that US Customs was reluctant to keep on paying him without approval from DOJ. The letter to Senator Grassley did the trick and he was paid for the information.'

The second informant inside Los Mellizos also now lives in the US. Both informants left Colombia immediately once Operation Journey took down the cartel in Venezuela.

266 Brooks: 'It's true that Venezuela was protective of its sovereignty over the use of US air assets, but without a doubt this case could never have been made without the complete cooperation of the *Guardia Nacional*. While DEA claimed that they were not to be trusted, the *Guardia Nacional* actually worked hand in hand with HMCE's DLOs and had the utmost integrity.'

267 El Caracol was arrested in June 1998 and extradited to the United States in August 2000. He was sentenced to 40 years' jail.

268 Brooks's account is slightly different: 'Following the seizure of the *Cannes*, I reviewed the classified message traffic about the seizure and determined that HMCE was involved, called my contact in London – HMCE's Graham Honey – and Operation Journey began shortly afterwards.'

269 In his case notes of Operation Journey Brooks characterised DEA's attitude to including HMCE in the investigation as 'openly hostile . . . DEA totally disregarded the fact that had it not been for the HMCE operation, the *Cannes* and the *Castor* would never have been intercepted.'

270 An attempt was made to contact the now-retired Soiles for this book but he did not respond. He went on to become DEA chief of global operations. In his case notes Brooks writes: 'In order to fully understand the problems between DEA, US Customs and HMCE in this investigation, I believe that it is necessary to view the relationship in the context of DEA Administrator

Thomas A. Constantine's 1998 congressional testimony. The Mejía Múneras were major targets of the DEA, but US Customs and HMCE had scooped them. DEA had no intention of playing second fiddle or equal partner with anyone. I would surmise that following the successful intercept of the *Pearl II*, and the resulting identification of Miguel and Víctor Mejía Múnera as being the leaders of the organisation, some very hard questions were probably asked of field offices in Colombia and elsewhere by DEA headquarters in Washington.' More damningly, he concludes: 'The Memorandum of Understanding between US Customs and DEA requires that in foreign investigative matters, the DEA country attachés represent Customs and service their requests for assistance. Throughout the investigation, DEA failed to comply with the requirements of the agreement.'

271 For a comprehensive account of the British role in Operation Journey and its information sharing with USCS, read the chapter 'Cocaine Armada' in Peter Walsh's excellent book *Drug War* (Milo Books, 2018).

272 Beto el Gitano was arrested in Spain in 2008 and extradited to the United States, where he was sentenced to 22 years' jail. His mugshot (along with Miguel Mejía Múnera's) appears on the DOS's website, under the heading 'Brought to Justice' in the Target Information section of the Bureau of International Narcotics and Law Enforcement Affairs' Narcotics Rewards Program. He was released early, whereupon he returned to Colombia and survived an assassination attempt in the Valle del Cauca in August 2019. An anonymous Miami-based lawyer euphemistically describes both Beto el Gitano and Miguel Mejía Múnera as 'highly respected' figures.

273 Pérez would be gunned down in 2001 while drinking coffee in an outdoor café in Panama City, a murder that has never been solved. Prior to his death, Pérez was approached by Brooks to cooperate. He declined. It was a fatal mistake.

274 Brooks quotes a price slightly less than Luis's estimate but is backed up by documentation sent between Callisti and the cartel.

275 Two of García's accomplices were later arrested and gave up the locations of stash sites. In his case notes Brooks writes: 'It is my opinion that the search and seizure of the *Privilege* was based largely on the urging of DEA.'

276 All three Albanians went to prison on long sentences but Frederik Durda escaped in 2005 when he visited his wife in a maternity hospital. He was recaptured a day later.

277 Brooks says USCS's battle of wills with the DEA all came down to the issue of 'control of the source and our refusal to allow DEA to document him or act as controllers. We were told continuously that the source was not being truthful and, while acknowledging that possibility, I had asked for any documentation which would prove that claim. It was never forthcoming.'

278 What is essentially known in law-enforcement parlance as a 'cold convoy'. Explains Brooks: 'Cold convoy is a term primarily used by US Customs to describe an investigative method that involves the tracking of a known subject or means of transportation to its ultimate destination. It is different from a "controlled delivery" in that a controlled delivery means a delivery of cocaine or some other illegal substance under the *control* of the law-enforcement agency. A cold convoy is the tracking and surveillance of a suspect or transportation means.

'So, for example, *Pearl II* is identified as the load vessel, HMCE installs a beacon to track the vessel, HMS *Marlborough* monitors the loading of the cocaine and the vessel is allowed to proceed while being tracked to its destination in the Netherlands. Law enforcement is provided enough information about the vessel so that they can make the search, seizure and arrests. The source of the information is not disclosed in order to protect the operation and continue the intelligence gathering. Whereas with a controlled delivery, law enforcement intercepts a load and the transporter agrees to cooperate and deliver the load under the supervision of law enforcement. The load is delivered and recipients arrested.'

279   Officially it was designated a joint investigation of USCS and the Organized Crime Drug Enforcement Task Force (OCDETF) in 2001, under the purview of the US Attorney General and DOJ. OCDETF utilises the resources of different law-enforcement agencies in the war on drugs, but primarily DEA.

'It was something I had no control over,' laments Brooks of the designation. 'I wanted to run the operation as a strictly intelligence op, passing info to the Europeans through HMCE for enforcement action. A guy in our headquarters was monitoring the initial operation and without our approval or consent proposed it to "Main Justice" as a "Linear" project. By Main Justice I'm referring to Washington, DC, working for DOJ headquarters in the Narcotics and Dangerous Drugs Section [NDDS]. Linear was a program promoted by our headquarters and was aimed at dismantling major organisations.

'Main Justice assigned two attorneys from DC to the operation and that really began all of our problems because they wanted "dope on the table". I had already decided to retire in 2001 so was not in it for the glory but for the case. Unfortunately, in addition to turf wars, agents can really promote their careers with big significant cases, and that's what happened with Operation Journey. OCDETF is not primarily a DEA initiative; it is a DOJ initiative and every federal agency has an opportunity to sponsor an OCDETF case. It's more of a PR initiative than anything, and the problem with making a case like Journey [an] OCDETF [designated investigation] is that there are too many fingers in the pudding. Success claims a thousand parents. Failure is an orphan.'

280   A total of 50 tons was seized from those vessels, excluding the *Cannes*. In Baltasar Garzón's Spanish indictment the following vessels were named as part of the Los Mellizos conspiracy: *Miami Express*, *Goiana*, *Stiletto I* (aka *Madeleine* or *Polux*), *Svetlana*, *Pearl II*, *Regent Rose*, *Kobe Queen*, *Scan Utrescht*, *China Breeze*, *Privilege* and *Suerte I*. Brooks told me Operation Jezebel, a major investigation that utilised the combined forces of British intelligence, military and law enforcement, was initiated from 'intelligence developed by HMCE's drugs liaison officer [DLO] in Miami, Martin Dubbey, from some information passed by FBI special agents Manny Ortega and Cesar Paz [in Miami]. They had an "in" with a business that was providing INMARSAT phones to dubious characters in Colombia. The phones were actually the prime communication method for the cartel between the ships and the organisations. The US could do nothing, but the Brits had much wider latitude. Martin tasked the UK's GCHQ [Government Communications Headquarters] with intercepting those communications and thus began Operation Jezebel.'

281   Brooks: 'HMCE, US Customs have varied responsibilities. The people involved in Operation Journey were criminal investigators. But there is also

the trade side, handling imports of merchandise, assessing duties, inspecting cargo and passengers: the side the public normally interact with at airports and seaports. While the uniformed and trade folks of HMCE were made part of HMRC, the investigative functions relating to drugs were rolled into the Serious Organised Crime Agency [SOCA], now NCA.'

282 According to former HMCE agent and Miami DLO Graham Honey: 'Branch 3 refers to the cocaine teams in the investigation division, which became the NIS of HMCE then HMRC.'

283 After being sentenced to 15 years' jail in 2002, Hanley was released in 2010 but sent down again for nearly 18 years in 2014.

284 Supergrass is a British term for snitch or informant. Regan went to jail, was released, then rejailed in 2005 after being convicted of the murders of five members of an entire London family, the Chohans, including two children.

285 An internet search of death records in New York pulls up a Nick Fisciatoris: 'NICK FISCIATORIS was born 17 June 1940, received Social Security number 071-36-6611 (indicating New York) and, Death Master File says, died 16 December 2012.' A 1940 birthdate would then be right. Notes Luis: 'He was a heavy smoker, a chainsmoker for years; he wasn't gonna last more than ten years.'

286 Zack Mann, a USCS spokesman, explained: 'The two were brought [to Miami] because the venue on conspiracy charges to import cocaine in 1998 and 1999 originated in South Florida.'

Nigel Brooks: 'The venue for the prosecution of Iván was based on my debriefing of one of the crewmembers from the *Pearl II* in the Netherlands. The informant had told us that the *Pearl II* had been used to smuggle cocaine into Fort Lauderdale in 1998. I pulled entry records and other Customs records showing that the vessel had been in Fort Lauderdale during that time. The crewmember (who had been on the vessel continuously since that Florida smuggle) verified what had happened and that the offload took place to go-fasts off the coast. He told us of three smuggling trips to Fort Lauderdale that year and I was able to verify that the vessel was in Fort Lauderdale on those occasions. That gave us the "venue" [location] for a US prosecution of Iván.'

Iván pleaded guilty, did not testify, paid restitution of $300 and was sentenced to almost 20 years' jail with supervised release when his sentence ended. But before he went away, he asked the court, in the words of *The South Florida Sun-Sentinel*, 'to be injected with anthrax, HIV, other viruses and the worst poison to prove he would survive because of his conversion to Christianity while in solitary confinement'.

On 9 October 2009 Iván was released from Loretto prison, Pennsylvania, after serving just over ten years. That December he was deported to Colombia. According to Luis, 'Iván lost his marbles to religion while inside [jail]. He is now in Colombia – never restored himself completely. He's living poor on the outskirts of Barranquilla.' He makes bizarre videos in Spanish on YouTube and claims he was kidnapped to United States in 'chains' by the DEA.

287 Michelle was deported to Panama City and not charged. Luis spoke to her one time from prison in the United States and never saw her again.

288 Wilmer Joiro is a pseudonym. He was not named in Baltasar Garzón's Spanish indictment. Luis believes Jorge was going to be assassinated by Los Mellizos: 'I think they would have killed him. He was going to get fucking whacked. He's alive because all this shit happened; because Tommy Taylor turned in the

organisation. He was too smart for his own good. I think he did a couple of trips behind [the cartel's] back. They were a little leery of Jorge. They wanted to do the *Suerte*; then they were going to call everybody in. They already knew "The Greek" was not Greek; that he was some Mexican guy. The Mejía Múnera brothers didn't know that I was the guy responsible for transport. The Mellizos didn't know who "The Greek" was either and I *knew* them. I wanted it that way because I knew that the Mellizos were so fucking hot. I knew Caracas was a hot situation. Once the *Suerte* left, they were going to call me in for a meeting, they were going to keep me, have me continue to buy ships in Greece and work with Elias. We had good plans going forward: we were going to be able to do at least eight trips a year – 50,000 kilos a year, easily – to Europe.'

Brooks has a different take: 'I think there may be some stretching of the truth here [from Luis]. To the best of my knowledge from Taylor, the Greeks just provided the transportation and were paid for that service. They didn't have the distribution organisation nor the supply organisation.'

289 A hunch that would seem to be well founded, according to an email sent by Tommy Taylor to USCS. In the email, dated 7 August 2000, before the *Suerte* raid, Taylor reveals Víctor Mejía Múnera had been tipped off by a corrupt Colombian lieutenant about a PNC (Colombian National Police) investigation into an Albanian group working inside Venezuela. A narco working for Los Mellizos called Pedro Vélez had been making phone calls to Albania, Jorge García and Luis. Víctor had had Pedro's phone records pulled and Taylor was of the view Víctor would have Pedro and Luis ('Leo') killed for the leak to the PNC: 'Of course Pedro will be killed and also Leo because [Víctor] told him that he wants to see Leo to give [him another] job.'

Says Brooks: 'By this time Víctor was so frustrated with the delays from the Greeks and the problems with communications security that [Taylor] felt he would probably have some people killed.'

290 Kolbinsky has a slightly different recollection of this exchange: 'I believe Luis had the conversation with Iván about the Mellizos before Garcia and I had him in the back of the SUV. That conversation I'm sure was a factor in his admitting he was Navia after I told him I had no choice but to return him to the Venezuelans if he insisted he was "Novoa". I distinctly recall him admitting he was Navia in the SUV. If my memory is correct, his exact words were, "Okay, you got me."'

291 Says Luis: '*Pinga* for Cubans is dick. Everything in a Cuban's life is his dick.'

292 Cuban-Americans Willy (or Willie) Falcón, full name Augusto Guillermo Falcón, along with Sal Magluta, full name Salvador Magluta, known together as Los Muchachos ('The Boys') were indicted with conspiracy to import and distribute 75 tons of cocaine between 1978 and 1991. They went to trial in 1995 but were stunningly acquitted in 1996. Later it was discovered they had bribed the jury foreman, Miguel Moya, with half a million dollars. He went to jail for 17 years in 1999. Three witnesses were also murdered.

The pair was reindicted in 1999 and Falcón took a plea deal on money-laundering charges in exchange for handing over $1 million, and dropping other charges such as obstruction of justice and jury tampering. In 2003 he was sentenced to 20 years' jail but released in 2017 and immediately went into detention awaiting deportation. After fighting extradition to his native Cuba because of fears he would be killed for his involvement in a 1990s CIA-supported plot to murder Fidel Castro, he was deported to the Dominican

Republic in 2018. Magluta, not so lucky, was sentenced to 205 years' jail in 2002, later reduced to 195, after money-laundering, bribery and witness-tampering charges all stuck. Says Luis: 'What saved Willy was that Sal's case involved a murder. When they separated their two cases Willy was able to sign a plea agreement and get 20 years.' Willy's younger brother, Gustavo, also indicted in 1991, went on the run for 26 years but was found by US Marshals in 2017, living under a false name in Kissimmee, Florida. He was sentenced to 135 months' jail in 2018.

293 Top cartel figures are today charged anywhere from $1 million to $5 million for a plea deal.

294 News reports that suggested Iván was 'CEO', 'drug kingpin', 'global drug boss' and 'the head of the snake' are utter nonsense. He was simply a gopher or go-between.

295 In Houston, Nigel Brooks was not so impressed with the historical revisionism on display. In his case notes he writes: 'A White House press release spoke of the joint investigation and the cooperation between United States and Colombian law-enforcement agencies. Nothing was further from the truth.' The press release, 'White House fact sheet: cooperation between the United States and Colombia on counter-drug programs', was issued on 30 August 2000.

296 Says DEA's Rick Bendekovic: 'It seems [the DEA] conflated several operations to make for a better story. The stats they listed were aggregated from several marine ops, including the *Transatlántico* seizure of 4600 kilos from M/V *Castor*.' Nigel Brooks agrees: 'The *Cannes* was not really Operation Journey although we included it – it was part of HMCE's Operation Jezebel. Even the *China Breeze* and *Castor* were part of Jezebel and it wasn't until we actually recruited the source that Journey came about.' For a full list of Operation Journey seizures, see Operation Journey: By the Numbers.

297 Martin Blanco chose not to be interviewed.

298 Luis disagrees: 'Andrés knew their visas were revoked and Patricia almost got arrested because of the fake passport. They saw the ugly side – she was raising two kids without their dad.'

299 A field-enforcement group of the DEA's Special Operations Division (SOD). According to a DOJ report, 959 Group is also known as the Bilateral Case Group or Bilateral Investigations Unit. Its sister group within SOD is called 960 Group or 960a Group, a Terrorism Investigations Unit.

300 Brooks believes they were the same two attorneys who caused him problems: 'In Houston we had massive problems with them because once DOJ gets involved we basically have to go through them; although investigative matters are the sole prerogative of the agency running the case. Usually, we would take a case to the judicial district that had jurisdiction and the attorneys from that district handle things. In the case of Operation Journey, DOJ took over the prosecution and have the authority to muscle in on a case being handled at the district level – that's probably what happened with Luis Navia and the Southern District of Florida (Miami). I can well understand the ire of a case agent in Miami and the Assistant US Attorney when two guys drop in from Washington, DC and try to take their case away.

'Once the case was taken down, I retired in January 2001 and US Customs was essentially pushed out of the investigation by DEA. There was one debriefing of De La Vega in Miami in which he lied about a previous smuggle using a vessel into the New York area. We knew it, and the Customs agent who debriefed him wrote a memo to that effect. [The two attorneys] had the memo suppressed because it would have totally destroyed any credibility should De La Vega have had to testify – he did not. After that Customs was no longer involved in the case.'

301 If a prisoner is housed in an FDC longer term and not in a regular prison, that usually means they are preparing to turn government witness: 'That means they are working on a Rule 35.'

302 Morrison was extradited from Jamaica in 1991, imprisoned for 22 years and deported back to Jamaica in 2013. He sued the Jamaican Government for wrongful extradition.

303 An indictment and an information are both formal charging documents under the US federal legal system, but only an indictment requires grand-jury approval before being initiated. According to Rule 7(b) of the *Federal Rules of Criminal Procedure*, 'an offense punishable by imprisonment for more than one year may be prosecuted by information if the defendant – in open court and after being advised of the nature of the charge and of the defendant's rights – waives prosecution by indictment'.

304 Brooks disagrees: 'The cases were consolidated and Luis pleaded guilty to both the 1995 indictment and the *Suerte* case.'

305 Luis submitted this statement as part of his sentencing deal: 'I have gained nothing by my criminal activity but instead lost everything, my self-esteem, my family, my liberty . . . I am guilty of the offence and express a sincere and profound sense of remorse and contrition for my actions.'

306 Now known as *Dirección de Investigación Criminal e INTERPOL* (Directorate of Criminal Investigation and INTERPOL or DICI).

307 It controlled huge swathes of Colombia: the North Bloc, the Bogotá/Llanos Bloc and the Central Bolívar Bloc in the country's south. Castaño was later murdered by one of his own brothers. The six-part documentary series *The Invisibles* includes an excellent profile and investigation of the AUC and its leadership.

308 On Colombia's Canal RCN network, an episode of a popular TV show called *Comando Élite* was devoted to the brothers. The DEA informant who gave up the location of Víctor and Miguel was murdered in 2009. His name was Juan Manuel Gaviria Vásquez aka 'Tocayo'.

309 Coleman is a Federal Correctional Complex (FCC), consisting of four prisons including Coleman-Low near Wildwood, Sumter County, central Florida.

310 Santi's name, date of birth and place of birth were all correct. Says Luis: 'It was a real one but pulled from the stack.'

311 An account set up for a prisoner so they can purchase everyday items in prison.

312 A reference to the album cover of *Dark Side of the Moon* (1973).

313 This was the case until 2017 when the United States abolished its 'wet-foot, dry-foot' policy, whereby if a Cuban citizen reached US soil without a visa, he or she could not be deported and could lawfully remain in the United States while applying for permanent residency.

314 Even though he got his passport in 2006, Luis didn't obtain a naturalisation certificate until 2009, back-dated to 1968 when he became a US citizen.

315 Luis may have a point. Even sugar kills more people than cocaine in the United States. Statistically 25,000 Americans die each year from health

complications related to sugar intake while 14,000 die of cocaine overdoses, usually mixed with an opioid.

316 Joseph P. Kennedy Sr, John F. Kennedy's father, was a major liquor importer in the 1930s, his company Somerset Importers bringing into the United States brands such as Gordon's London Dry Gin and Dewar's scotch whisky.

317 Austrian scientist Karl von Scherzer collected coca leaves on a scientific expedition to South America in the mid-1850s and gave them to Göttingen University chemistry professor Friedrich Wöhler. His assistant, Albert Niemann, successfully extracted cocaine in 1859.

318 Cocaine is not only decriminalised in Bolivia (up to 50 grams) but coca production is also legal. Selling and transporting cocaine, however, is illegal.

319 DEA slang for becoming a source, CI or asset.

320 According to a well-placed legal source in Miami.

321 A pseudonym.

322 David Donald is a pseudonym.

323 In October 1999 there was a meeting of 30 narcos and the DEA in Panama to nut out terms of their surrender. Rasguño was one of the attendees.

324 The Cirrus G2 Vision Jet.

325 Brooks is more sceptical: 'As far as the *Suerte* goes, Luis was a representative of the ship's owner. I don't believe he had anything to do with route-planning or distribution – the Greeks just handled the transport. Routes and onloads/offloads were all handled by the people in the organisation. In today's parlance I'd describe Luis as being a contractor. Luis would not have access to the onload/offload coordinates or codes used.' When I pointed out Luis had those codes in his possession when he was arrested by the *Guardia Nacional* in Maracaibo, Brooks doubled down: 'I was not aware that he also had the codes, but it would make sense as he was handling the crew replacement and would need to give them to the captain, etc. I know that Iván de la Vega had it in his possession when he was arrested . . . I still believe Luis was just a transportation guy when it came to Operation Journey. His role was to represent the owners of the *Suerte* to get the vessel where it needed to be; to make sure that the crew was changed and handle those things. Overall, Jorge García would have had the greatest knowledge of each smuggling venture from onload to offload.'

326 Mermelstein claimed under oath to have been responsible for trafficking 55 to 56 tons. He was also implicated in five murders, including Barry Seal's. Seal trafficked about 60 tons. Jung was only ever convicted for a ton of coke but, working as a transporter for the Medellín Cartel's Carlos Lehder, was responsible for a similar amount to Mermelstein and Seal.

327 The song, written by Raúl Marrero, was first released by Tommy Olivencia on his self-titled album on the Top Hits label in 1983. Ruiz was the vocalist. Marrero, Olivencia and Ruiz, all dead, were Puerto Ricans.

328 This individual, an extremely famous cartel figure, was arrested in 2001 in Colombia and extradited to the United States for drug trafficking. He was eventually deported to Colombia in 2019. For safety reasons he will not be described or named.

329 In 2000, the year Luis was arrested, the White House said in a press release: 'Each year, illegal drug abuse is linked to 52,000 American deaths and costs our society nearly $110 billion in health care, accidents, and lost productivity.'

330 This is true. Most of the top-tier Colombian narcos of the 1980s were from peasant or lower-class stock.

331 Luis is correct. The DEA used more than 18,000 sources between 2010 and 2015, according to a 2016 DOJ audit.

332 Roberto Diaz is a pseudonym. He requested one due to fear of reprisal – even years after Poli's death.

333 The opening track of John's 1970 album, *Tumbleweed Connection*.

334 Vicente Blanco died in 2017, two days after the death of Luis's mother. Their funerals took place the same day.

Index

Index